William S. Rosecrans and
the Union Victory

William S. Rosecrans and the Union Victory

A Civil War Biography

DAVID G. MOORE

McFarland & Company, Inc., Publishers
Jefferson, North Carolina

LIBRARY OF CONGRESS CATALOGUING-IN-PUBLICATION DATA

Moore, David G., 1953–
  William S. Rosecrans and the Union victory : a Civil War biography / David G. Moore.
      p.   cm.
  Includes bibliographical references and index.

  ISBN 978-0-7864-7624-4 (softcover : acid free paper) ∞
  ISBN 978-1-4766-1306-2 (ebook)

  1. Rosecrans, William S. (William Starke), 1819–1898. 2. Generals—United States—Biography. 3. United States—History—Civil War, 1861–1865—Biography. 4. United States—History—Civil War, 1861–1865—Campaigns. 5. United States. Army of the Cumberland—Biography. 6. United States. Army—Biography. I. Title.
E467.1.R7M66 2014
973.7'41092—dc23
[B]   2014001989

BRITISH LIBRARY CATALOGUING DATA ARE AVAILABLE

© 2014 David G. Moore. All rights reserved

No part of this book may be reproduced or transmitted in any form or by any means, electronic or mechanical, including photocopying or recording, or by any information storage and retrieval system, without permission in writing from the publisher.

On the cover: Portrait of General William Starke Rosecrans by Samuel W. Price, 1868. Oil on canvas, 29$^{15}/_{16}$" × 25$^{3}/_{16}$". (National Portrait Gallery, Smithsonian Institution/Art Resource NY)

Manufactured in the United States of America

McFarland & Company, Inc., Publishers
  Box 611, Jefferson, North Carolina 28640
    www.mcfarlandpub.com

To the late Cornelius (Con) F. Sheehan,
with whom the voyage began many years ago so unexpectedly.
I only wish he were here to see where the road led.
His presence is on every page of this book.

To my family, Matthew, Thomas, Cecilia and Maggie,
who willingly made libraries, battlefields and
cemeteries a part of our family vacations.
Thank you. We made it.

And to the boyhood friend
without whose friendship the name Rosecrans
would have had no meaning for me.

Table of Contents

Acknowledgments   ix
Introduction   1

1. Before the War   5
2. West Virginia   10
3. Iuka   23
4. Corinth   38
5. In Command   52
6. Stones River   61
7. Creating a New Army   72
8. Tullahoma   85
9. Opposition from Many Sides   91
10. Chickamauga   100
11. After Chickamauga   121
12. Grant in Control   137
13. Missouri   151
14. A Spy in the Army   163
15. Washburne   170
16. After the War   188
17. A Final Note   199

Appendix A   201
Appendix B   205
Chapter Notes   211
Bibliography   221
Index   235

Acknowledgments

It would have been impossible for this book to have ever been written without the great network of libraries, public and academic, throughout the United States. Furthermore without the accessibility policy of almost every library I visited this book would not have been possible. It is a credit to this country that a person like myself, interested but uncredentialed, can have access and utilize the collections of great university and municipal libraries. Additionally the help I received from dedicated library workers in retrieving information was essential to the creation of this work. Libraries are truly one of the greatest resources of this country. Over the years as I shared the William S. Rosecrans story with friends and associates, I noticed their interest and their encouragement that I tell his story. This support was particularly important in contrast to the predominant historic view that Rosecrans' obscurity was deserved. To all of you who have helped this endeavor with your words, I thank you. Your support has played a big part in its creation. If you think I may be referring to you, I am. I hope the result was worth the wait.

I want to thank Philip Mobley for the maps he formatted and created for me. I wish to acknowledge Hal Jespersen's public domain maps, some of which have been adapted for this work. Access to good maps has never been easier because of the Internet and I encourage the reader to use them while reading this book.

The battle descriptions have been cobbled together from various sources. I have striven for accuracy in the details, but mistakes have no doubt crept in. The larger point of this work is not so much how these battles were fought but the important consequences of these battles which are largely unknown to the American people.

As far as sources, I have cited editions of books that can be most easily accessed by the reader. This means older editions of works that are available online are preferred to newer editions of the same works that may be difficult to obtain and consult. The purpose of this is so that the accuracy of what is written here, much of it rarely or never before cited, can be checked. If I ask for a margin of error for battle details, I invite close scrutiny of the opinions and conclusions made by the people who lived the events of 1861 to 1865.

Introduction

In 1905 a group of Civil War veterans gathered in Chattanooga, Tennessee—a city they had captured and occupied forty-two years earlier in one of the key moments of the American Civil War. They were in Chattanooga for the Thirty-Third Annual Meeting of the Society of the Army of the Cumberland. That army had fought and marched across Middle Tennessee in 1863, climbing mountains and traversing rivers before fighting the Confederate Army of Tennessee at West Chickamauga Creek in the greatest battle of the western theater of the war. In the minds of these veterans, Chickamauga was not a Union defeat but rather the battle for the capture and permanent possession of the city where they were meeting, which eventually led to the capture of Atlanta and Union victory in the war.

At the third session of the meeting, an unexpected topic came up: a statue for the man who had led the Army of the Cumberland during the period of its most important battles and campaigns, Major General William S. Rosecrans.

The men began to express themselves: "I worship the memory of General William S. Rosecrans. I hold for him a reverence in my heart never to be effaced," said one veteran.

"He was certainly second to nobody in the army of the United States. There was no one superior to Rosecrans," said another.

A third voice added, "I want to say that I think in strategy Rosecrans was not surpassed by anyone in [the Civil] war or any previous one. He secured this city in the face of a strong and powerful enemy, overcoming almost insurmountable difficulties, but he had the nerve to undertake it, and I think the success of General Grant was due to Rosecrans' matchless strategy."

A fourth veteran opined, "Anyone who studies the campaigns from Murfreesboro to this city, gained by his splendid strategy, cannot fail to accord to him the place of one of the greatest leaders of his age. And this statue should have a place in Washington where it will stand as long as this republic endures."

Who was this man, largely unknown to the American people today, who evoked such strong emotions and comments? To the extent William Rosecrans is known at all, it is as the defeated general of Chickamauga whose army was rescued by General Grant, who is in most accounts the "general who won the Civil War."

I knew little about William S. Rosecrans until an unlikely string of events sparked my curiosity about him. More than twenty years ago a search for the grave of Lincoln assassination conspirator Mary Surratt in Washington D.C.'s Mt. Olivet Cemetery led to the unexpected discovery of a gravestone which read, "Ann Eliza Rosecrans, Wife of Gen. W.S. Rosecrans." I remarked to my co-explorer that Rosecrans "wasn't a very good general." We wondered where General Rosecrans was entombed, and learned that it was across the Potomac in Arlington National Cemetery. That fact led to our curiosity as to why the two were buried in essentially the same city but in different cemeteries.

A short biography of Rosecrans in a guidebook to Arlington stated that Abraham Lincoln had offered the vice presidency to Rosecrans in 1864 and Rosecrans' acceptance telegram had been intercepted by Secretary of War Edwin Stanton. Without that intervention Rosecrans would presumably have become president upon Lincoln's assassination.

Now our interest spiked. The fact that Rosecrans was a Roman Catholic made the story even more astounding. We discovered that a biography of Rosecrans, *The Edge of Glory*, by William M. Lamers had been published in 1961. We read it looking for the "fun trivia" of the vice presidential offer but found far more compelling information about unknown, to us, battles like Rich Mountain, Iuka and Corinth, Murfreesboro, Tullahoma and Pilot Knob. Even Chickamauga became a more complex story than what we had always heard about it.

There were also the superlatives: outgeneraling Robert E. Lee, winning the battles that made the capture of Vicksburg possible, achieving the victory without which Lincoln felt "the nation could scarcely have lived over," and conducting the most brilliant campaign of the war.

Lamers' book led us to the then relatively few in-print books on Rosecrans and his military career. Those books led us to the many forgotten books and papers in the Library of Congress and other libraries. After many years of study we reached a conclusion that at one time would have seemed preposterous to us: William Starke Rosecrans was the man most responsible for the Union military victory in the Civil War. We looked for others who had come to the same conclusion, and although we found many who agreed on Rosecrans' singular importance in specific battles and campaigns, no one linked all of those successes into a complete portrait of the man and his achievement.

Over the years each of us would discuss Rosecrans with those curious enough to listen, and we wrote a couple of newspaper articles. As no one stepped forward to tell the story, a sense of obligation fell to us, rank amateurs, to tell the story.

My co-discoverer and explorer, Cornelius "Con" F. Sheehan, died several years ago. The burden fell to me to tell the story, and slowly in the free time left over from the duties and responsibilities of life, I began to write down and develop what Con and I had discovered. The result is this book. It is the belief of this writer that William S. Rosecrans is the man who comes closest to claiming the title of "the general who won the Civil War." I know few who begin this book will believe that. I know I wouldn't and didn't believe it before accidentally stumbling upon his story. All I ask is that the reader approach the Rosecrans story with an open mind and then decide whether the statements made in Chattanooga in 1905 by the men he commanded are true.

The reader will also discover a unique personality, a man who not only won battles by his personal bravery and strategy but who advanced innovations in cartography, sanitation, and engineering, a man who was interested in both science and theology. The reader will also learn whether Lincoln did in fact offer Rosecrans the vice presidency in 1864 and whether the statue in Washington was ever built.

The book is also an attempt to answer the question, Why is Rosecrans so little known today and his achievements almost unknown? The answer to that question, as best as I could answer it, was also unexpected.

To walk the Rosecrans road was a solitary journey. The preponderance of accepted wisdom was against him. However there were the voices from the nineteenth century: Donn Piatt, Henry Van Ness Boynton, and most importantly the men who knew him best, those who fought with him. Luckily many of their words were preserved in the libraries within a few days' drive from my home in Washington, D.C. Rosecrans' papers were the farthest away, at the UCLA library, making it impossible to consult them as often as I would have liked.

I also discovered twentieth-century historians who appreciated Rosecrans and questioned the predominant Grant-Sherman orthodoxy. I had the pleasure of meeting one of them, Albert Castel, at a Civil War round-table talk on his book *Decision in the West*. If he were younger he would no doubt write the modern definitive Rosecrans biography. I only hope this book approaches his high standards.

The Civil War is unique among topics in American history in that the public has a fascination and input at least equal to the professional historians in academia. Obviously the standards of popular history are not as rigorous as in academia, but because of technology it has never been easier for anyone with an informed opinion to express, discuss and dispute interpretations of the war. I have striven to hold myself to strict accountability and would ask those who question my conclusions to check the sources before dismissing them.

Late in 2010 I came, via the Internet, upon a group of "citizen historians" in Rosecrans' birth county of Delaware, Ohio. Led by the resolute Polly Horn they aspired to the honorable, and unprecedented, goal of erecting a statue to Rosecrans in Sunbury, Ohio. They have already gotten a school named for him. Ms. Horn also has created a website with an abundance of wonderful information—pictures, maps, citations, and genealogy—about Rosecrans. That site, truly a labor of love and scholarship, can be accessed at http://Big WalnutHistory.org.

The William S. Rosecrans story is an amazing story, particularly because it is unknown and largely untold. I invite the reader to discover that story, a story that changed my understanding of the Civil War and American History.

1. Before the War

William Starke Rosecrans was born on September 6, 1819, in Kingston Township, Delaware County, Ohio. His first American Rosecrans ancestor, Harmon Henrick Rosenkrantz, had come to America from Holland via Norway in 1651 and settled in the Hudson Valley near present-day Kingston, New York. This line of the family made its way west to the Wyoming Valley of northeastern Pennsylvania and eventually to Ohio over the course of several generations and name spelling changes.

William's father Crandall Rosecrans was born in Wilkes-Barre, Pennsylvania, in 1794 and arrived with his family in Ohio at the age of fourteen. He served under General William Henry Harrison in the War of 1812 and earned a commission as a captain. He married Jemima Hopkins in 1816. She was said to be a descendent of Stephen Hopkins of Rhode Island, a signer of the Declaration of Independence. It appears the preferred pronunciation of the family name was "Rosa krontz."

Their first child, a boy Chauncey, was born in 1816 and died the next year. Two years later William was born. Three more sons, Charles Wesley, Henry Crandall and Sylvester Horton, were born over the next eight years. William later as a young officer would write, "I have a mother who loves me well. A father whose fortune is his father's blessing, his own hands and my good mother. Father is strong-willed, self reliant man who is popular and well respected in spite of his 'iron will' and hot temper. Mother was gentle, deeply religious and insisted on everyone speaking the truth."[1]

Crandall moved his family to Homer, Ohio, in neighboring Licking County where he acquired a farm and opened a store, tavern and potash factory. William helped out at the family business. Despite little formal education, William became a good reader, memorizing the Declaration of Independence by the age of six. A favorite book of his youth was *Thaddeus of Warsaw*, which he read while convalescing from an illness. When he discovered the final pages of the book were missing, he worked three months in order to save up and buy his own copy. He also became good at arithmetic, which proved helpful in the family businesses.

As he grew, the young Rosecrans worked in various stores in the area, impressing those he worked for with his industriousness and intelligence. A fellow clerk remembered him as a "thin, awkward looking, but remarkably thoughtful and industrious boy" whom he "never doubted for a moment would distinguish himself."[2]

At sixteen he took a trip down the Ohio and the Mississippi rivers to Vicksburg where he became ill and returned to Ohio. He drove T.W. Barkley, a lawyer and future Ohio Supreme Court justice, to Columbus who was so impressed by William that he told him, "Your conversation has been so intelligent that I strongly urge you to get more education." However the Rosecrans family had little money for college. That made an appointment to West Point appealing. Rosecrans traveled fifty miles to seek an appointment from Congressman Alexander Harper. When that appointment didn't materialize he applied directly to Secretary of War Joel R. Poinsett who gave him a nomination to the Academy.[3]

William however had had only four quarters of formal education and only three months to prepare for the entrance exams, so he enrolled at Kenyon College to better prepare himself. In 1838 he traveled to New York to be admitted to West Point. In his class of 1842 were future luminaries Don Carlos Buell, Earl Van Dorn, John Pope and James Longstreet who would be Rosecrans' roommate. At the Academy were upperclassmen George H. Thomas, Abner Doubleday, and William T. Sherman. It was at West Point where he received the nicknames "Rosy" and "Old Rosy."

In the fall of 1841 he enrolled in engineering courses under Dennis Hart Mahan. He graduated fifth in the class of 1842, which allowed him to enter the prestigious Engineering Corps, the first westerner ever so commissioned. West Point was primarily an engineering school in that pre–Civil War period, and military science took a secondary position. Mahan started a "Napoleon Club" which studied the campaigns and grand strategy of Bonaparte to supplement the regular military curriculum. Rosecrans was a member of that select group. He earned from his fellow cadets the nickname the "brilliant Rosy Rosecrans."

During the summer of his last year, Rosecrans had his first encounter with a fellow Ohioan, Hiram Ulysses Grant, whose name was changed at the Academy quite by accident to Ulysses S. Grant. Rosecrans was serving as officer of the day and found Grant in the yard. "I'm guarding the pump," the naive Grant explained. "I have orders to stand here until the next call." "You go to bed at tattoo and douse the lights at taps," Rosecrans told him. "But how do I know that you are not playing a trick on me too?" asked Grant.

Rosecrans replied, "See my chevrons. I'm officer of the day."[4]

Two things happened while Rosecrans was at the Academy that would have the greatest impact on his personal life. First he met at his graduation

Miss Ann Elizabeth Hegeman, daughter of a prominent New York jurist. After an evening that included a walk to the Crow's Nest, a local scenic meeting place, William had fallen in love. They would marry in St. Paul's Episcopal Chapel, New York City, in 1843.

The second thing that consumed young Rosecrans was a search for a spiritual home. Although he had been baptized and raised in a pious home, he still searched for answers to the great spiritual questions.

This search started at West Point and had intellectual as well as emotional elements. He decided that there was a God and that God had communicated his will and desires to mankind. Rosecrans began to read, purely as

General Rosecrans, painted by George P.A. Healey in Wheeling, West Virginia, in 1862 (UCLA Library Special Collections, Charles E. Young Research Library).

an intellectual experiment, the various books that claimed to be revelations of God. He then began to pray even though, "When I knelt down, I felt ashamed, and thought quite likely I was a damned fool, but then I remembered it was one of the experiments and so I prayed on, though it seemed to me no more than talking to a stick or stump." His religious inquiries, which went on for four years, led him to accept the Bible and the Christian religion. As to which denomination of Christianity, he wanted one that claimed an "authorized supernatural teacher." Perhaps influenced by reading the book *The End of a Religious Controversy* by John Milner, an English Catholic bishop, he chose Roman Catholicism. Eventually his brother Sylvester would join the Church, become a priest and be made the first bishop of Columbus, Ohio. One of Rosecrans' sons would become a priest, and two daughters would enter the religious life. His ardent Catholicism would be one of the salient features of his personality.[5]

After graduation Rosecrans was assigned to Fortress Monroe, Virginia, where he worked on protecting the fort from the encroaching sea. After about a year he applied for a professorship at West Point, which he received along with a promotion to first lieutenant, his only promotion prior to the Civil War. After his August marriage to Ann he taught engineering and served as post commissary and quartermaster.

As an engineer he stayed home during the Mexican War. In 1847 he began a five-year period at Newport, Rhode Island, where his duties included building a military wharf and redesigning a system of permanent barracks. He developed dredging machinery which proved eight times more efficient than the former diving-bell process. He also worked on St. Mary's Catholic Church in Newport, which a century later would be the site of the wedding of Jacqueline Bouvier and John F. Kennedy.

In 1852 he worked on the harbor of New Bedford and a year later was assigned to the Washington Navy Yard as civil and constructing engineer. He constructed a marine railway, built a large sawmill, and remodeled and improved the Dahlgren ordnance buildings, which were found to be in poor condition. He also made plans for an immense machine shop, a block of buildings 450 by 288 feet. These were to be so constructed that one engine would drive the machinery of the establishment. Plans were also submitted for the blacksmith shop, it being so arranged that the smoke from the forges would pass off from one stack.[6]

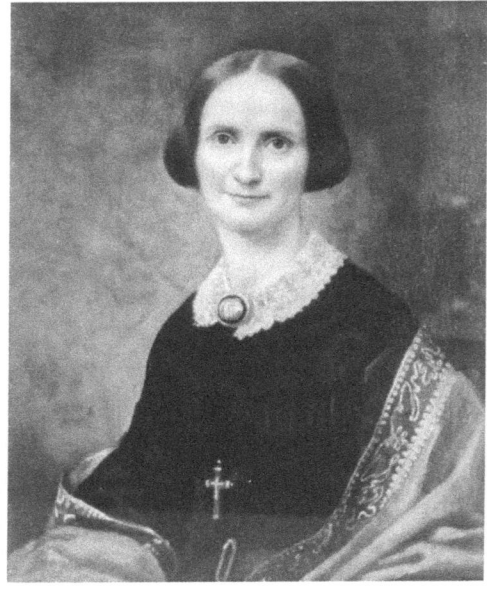

Ann Elizabeth Hegeman Rosecrans, painted by George P.A. Healey in Wheeling, West Virginia, in 1862 (UCLA Library Special Collections, Charles E. Young Research Library).

While in Washington his widowed mother-in-law lived with his family. Rosecrans also served as superintendent of a Negro Sunday school for 600 children. Overall his time in Washington was a happy time for his family.

Despite Rosecrans' achievements, a military career was poorly compensated and advancement was slow. He applied for a professorship at the Virginia Military Institute in 1851, an appointment that went to the then obscure Thomas J. Jackson, later to become the famous Stonewall.

His health began to deteriorate and he requested a leave from the army. When it was refused he resigned, but Secretary of War Jefferson Davis gave him a three-month leave of absence, confident "that before it expires you will probably change your mind." Still Rosecrans tendered his resignation to take effect in 1854. His military career behind him, he would now try and make his way in the civilian world of engineering and business.[7]

The first work he did after separating from the army was as an architect and engineer. He then worked in a similar capacity for a British-American company with extensive landholdings in the mountains of Kanawha County, Virginia. He determined that the seemingly exhausted mines could still be productive, and as a result the state of Virginia authorized and became a majority investor in a canal to transport the coal out of the mountains. Rosecrans became president of the New Coal River–Slack Water Navigation Company. He led the company into the coal-oil business, which was however not successful. Later Rosecrans himself went into business with partners and built a refinery in his now home city of Cincinnati. The objective was to produce a good oil for illumination. While experimenting one day, a lamp exploded, burning him severely on the face. His beard covered most of the scars, but it left him with a permanent mark which many perceived as a smirk.

Rosecrans claimed to be "the first to obtain a good, odorless oil from petroleum" and developed a "cheap and sure process" of manufacturing a soap with chlorine properties. He obtained patents for several inventions including a lamp wick raiser and an improved scale.

During the period after his graduation and marriage, seven children were born, four of whom survived infancy.[8]

The great national political issue during that period was the extension of slavery into the new territories acquired as a result of the Mexican War. In the pivotal election of 1860, Rosecrans, like Grant and most in the army officers corps, voted for northern Democrat Stephen A. Douglas. Few could imagine that the new year of 1861 would forever change the nation and William S. Rosecrans.

2. West Virginia

April 12, 1861, the day of the firing on Fort Sumter, found William Starke Rosecrans in private business life in Cincinnati. One week later he was in the Ohio capital of Columbus to offer his services to Governor William Dennison. Dennison appointed Captain George B. McClellan major general for Ohio troops and asked Rosecrans, still a civilian, to help McClellan select a campsite for the Ohio militia. A site thirteen miles north of Cincinnati was chosen and Rosecrans was assigned the task of laying out the camp, which he named Camp Dennison.

After three weeks, Dennison sent Rosecrans east to Philadelphia to buy supplies for Ohio troops. From there Rosecrans went to Washington where he applied to the War Department for a commission as brigadier general of volunteers. Meanwhile Dennison offered the newly created office of chief engineer of the state of Ohio to Rosecrans who accepted the commission which conferred the rank of colonel. The day after he was appointed colonel of the Ohio volunteers, Rosecrans received a commission of brigadier general in the U.S. regulars to date from May 16, 1861. On May 20 he was ordered to Camp Jackson and then to the new Camp Chase, named after Attorney General Salmon P. Chase, which Rosecrans helped lay out.

The first significant campaign of the war was in western Virginia. There had long been antagonism between the eastern half of the Old Dominion with its slave-labor plantation economy and the mountainous free-labor western half. After Virginia adopted the Ordinance of Secession on April 17, 1861, a convention of anti-secession "loyalists" was called to meet in Wheeling on May 13.

Western Virginia had great strategic importance. It bordered, and at the northern panhandle divided, Ohio and Pennsylvania. The Baltimore and Ohio Railroad, which traversed the area, was the major link between Washington and the west. Roads through the area led to the Great Valley of Virginia which in turn led to eastern Tennessee with its large Unionist population. The area was also rich in important minerals such as salt, lead, coal, iron and saltpeter.

Robert E. Lee, who after resigning his commission in the old army had been appointed head of Virginia forces, ordered Colonel George Porterfield to go to Grafton and defend the Baltimore and Ohio. McClellan in Ohio had concentrated troops at points along the Ohio River opposite Wheeling and Parkersburg. On the night of May 24, Confederates burned two railroad bridges. Two days later McClellan ordered troops in Wheeling to cross the Ohio and march toward Grafton. Porterfield withdrew to Philippi. On June 3 the Northerners surprised and routed the Confederates who retreated chaotically to Beverly. This skirmish became known as the "Philippi Races."

On June 15 Robert Garnett was appointed commander of Confederate troops in northwestern Virginia. He made his headquarters at Beverly at the eastern base of Rich and Laurel mountains. Realizing the importance of the passes through the mountains, he decided to fortify them. The Staunton and Parkersburg Turnpike, linking the Shenandoah Valley and the Ohio River, divided at Beverly, with one route going north to Wheeling and the other crossing Rich Mountain and continuing to Parkersburg. He fortified the pass

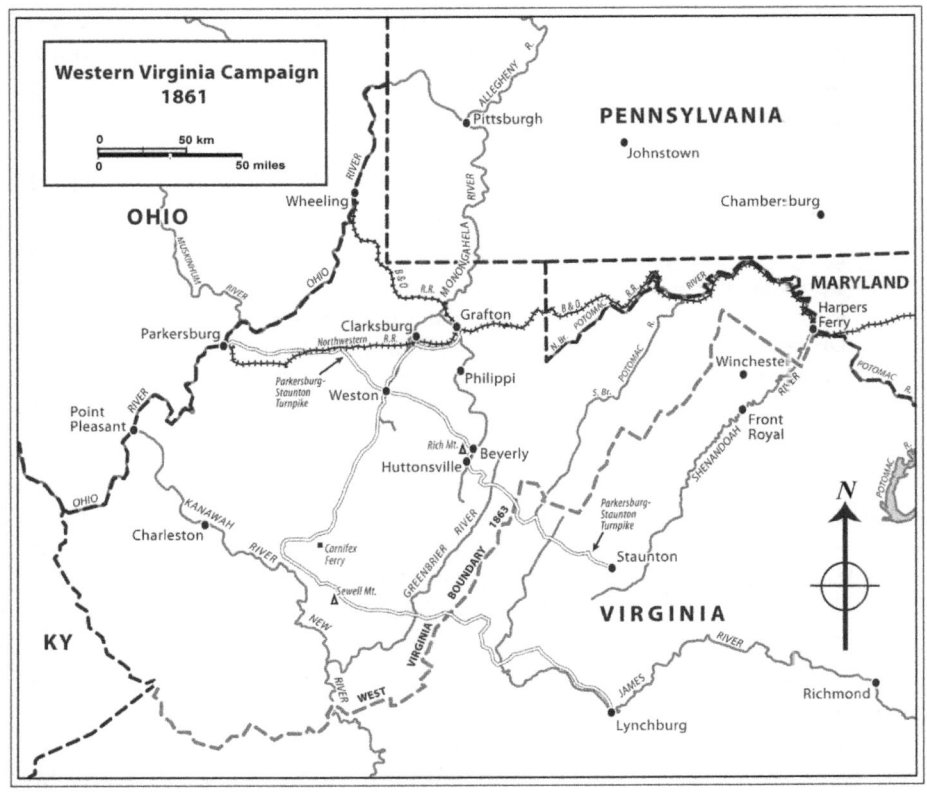

Western Virginia Campaign 1861. (Map by Phil Mobley).

at Rich Mountain with 1,300 men and four cannon under Colonel John Pegram. Garnett guarded the pass at Laurel Hill, which he considered a more likely target for a Yankee attack.

On June 22 McClellan himself entered western Virginia, proceeded through Grafton, and on July 9 made camp at Roaring Creek, about two miles from Pegram's position. Among his three brigades was that of Rosecrans.

McClellan's plan was to make a frontal assault on Pegram. However, late in the evening of July 10, David Hart, a local youth, came into the Federal camp. A sentry brought him to Rosecrans who questioned him about the local terrain. Hart told of a trail that led to his family's farm that could be used to get to the summit of Rich Mountain and the rear of the Confederate position. Rosecrans took Hart to McClellan. Rosecrans suggested that the attack be made in two parts. He, led by Hart, would take troops up the trail and attack Pegram in the rear. Upon hearing the sound of battle, McClellan would then engage Pegram in the front. After some discussion McClellan agreed to Rosecrans' plan. The march was to start at daybreak, but by mistake reveille was sounded at midnight, thus alerting Pegram, who felt that the attack would come from his right, between his position and that of Garnett. Pegram did send Captain Julius A. De Lagnel, a New Jersey native, with 350 men and one piece of artillery to guard the Hart farm.

Rosecrans set out at dawn with 1,917 men; the narrow trail precluded taking any artillery. One participant described the trek as

> a very tedious march, following a path which led us through thickets so dense and woods so filled with undergrowth that it was impossible to see fifty feet on either side, now following the bed of a mountain stream for our path and then using the compass for our only guide, we climbed and scrambled to the top of the mountain in their rear. Just as we reached the summit of the mountain we were overtaken by a terrific storm, which raged with great fury, making it seem as if our duty led us to encounter nature, the elements, and man.[1]

At about twelve o'clock Rosecrans' brigade reached the top of Rich Mountain. Hart was too scared to continue and fled. It was discovered that there was still another valley to cross, another hill to climb, and another descent before the Staunton–Parkersburg road could be reached. At about three o'clock the head of the column reached the Hart farm and was fired on by Confederate pickets.

Rosecrans ordered his troops to advance, fire and then throw themselves on the ground for cover. The Rebel artillery continued firing at the rate of four rounds a minute. It appeared to the Rebels that the Federals were retreating and they gave out a loud shout, a shout that was heard and interpreted by McClellan as a sign that Rosecrans had failed. But Rosecrans, who was experiencing combat for the first time in his military career, was not failing and was not retreating. He placed himself at the head of Jeremiah Sullivan's 13th Indiana and led the attack. The Nineteenth Ohio fired a volley at the same time Rosecrans was attacking. The entire Union brigade charged the enemy breastworks. De Lagnel tried but failed to rally his Southern troops before falling with a side wound. The Rebels dispersed.

Rosecrans learned from a prisoner that Camp Garnet was defended by the 44th Virginia Infantry and decided to bivouac for the night. At six the next morning Rosecrans entered Camp Garnett and found it abandoned. Pegram, who had visited the Hart farm to check on the battle, realized that the loss of the Hart farm made Camp Garnett's position untenable. At a war council held at eleven at night, the Confederates decided to evacuate. Thus ended the first major land battle of the Civil War.

What of McClellan? He was to have attacked Camp Garnett when he heard the sounds of battle. John Beatty, who was with McClellan, wrote in his diary:

> Between two and three o'clock we heard shots in the rear of the fortifications; then volleys of musketry, and the roar of artillery. Every man sprang to his feet, assured that the moment for making the attack had arrived. General McClellan and staff came galloping up, and a thousand faces turned to hear the order to advance; but no order was given. The general halted a few paces from our line and sat on his horse listening to the guns, apparently in doubt as to what to do; and as he sat there with indecision stamped on every line of his countenance the battle drew fiercer in the enemy's rear. Every volley could be heard distinctly. There would occasionally be a lull for a moment, and then the uproar would break out again with increased violence. If the enemy is too strong for us to attack, what must be the fate of Rosecrans' four regiments, cut off from us and struggling against such odds? Hours passed; and as the last straggling shots and final silence told us the battle had ended, gloom settled down on every soldier's heart, and the belief grew strong that Rosecrans had been defeated and his brigade cut to pieces or captured. This belief grew to certain conviction soon after, when we heard shout after shout go up from the fortifications in our front.[2]

Of course Rosecrans had not been destroyed. Not only had Pegram abandoned Rich Mountain, but Garnett, realizing that his position on Laurel Hill was now untenable, also evacuated. Pegram would surrender at Beverly, and Garnett would be killed at Corrick's Ford while leading his troops in retreat. Garnett, designer of the state seal of California while stationed at the Presidio in San Francisco in 1849, became the first general officer of either side killed in the war, and this Southern general was buried in Green Wood Cemetery in Brooklyn, New York. Once McClellan learned of Rosecrans' victory, he proceeded to Beverly where he received Pegram's surrender.

The importance of Rich Mountain was great. And if the battle is not well known, its importance is to those who have studied it. Allan Nevins called it "the most important battle of the campaign by which McClellan virtually freed the Trans-Allegheny counties of organized bodies of Confederates." Of course McClellan's actual role was minimal.

The political consequences of the battle were perhaps even greater than the military ones. Three weeks after Rich Mountain, the Wheeling Convention met and the first steps were taken that would lead to the formation of the separate state of West Virginia. Douglas Southall Freeman concluded that it was the Confederate loss of military control of western Virginia that made possible the formation of a new state. In the words of historian Festus Summers, Rich Mountain "settled summarily the political destiny of northwest Virginia."

On July 21, 1861, the Battle of Bull Run or Manassas was fought. This battle, fought ten days after Rich Mountain, was a great Union disaster, and fear and panic gripped Washington. On the night of the battle, General Winfield Scott telegraphed McClellan, "Circumstances make your presence necessary here. Charge Rosecrans or some other general with your department and come hither without delay." On July 23, McClellan put Rosecrans in command and headed to Washington. It was on the basis of the victory at Rich Mountain, a battle in which he took no active part, that George B. McClellan was placed in command of the Army of the Potomac.[3]

Northwestern Virginia was not the only scene of military activity in western Virginia in July of 1861. The Kanawha River valley was a natural invasion route that led from the Ohio River to Charleston and into central Virginia. The Rebels could use the same route to threaten the state of Ohio. Because of this, General McClellan ordered Brigadier General Jacob D. Cox to move up the Kanawha, and on July 11, the same day as the fight at Rich Mountain, Cox's Kanawha Brigade started out.

The Confederate forces opposing Cox were led by General Henry A. Wise. Wise, who was governor of Virginia at the time of John Brown's raid at Harper's Ferry, had no military experience. Cox's movement up the Kanawha proceeded almost effortlessly until July 17 when he faced the Rebels at Scary Creek. Wise, outnumbered and fearing a threat to his rear from McClellan's forces to the north, decided to retreat to White Sulphur Springs. Cox entered Charleston unopposed on July 25; four days later he reached the town of Gauley Bridge, where the Gauley and New rivers combine to form the Kanawha. Rosecrans assumed command of the Department of the Ohio, embracing western Virginia, on July 23. Although Union forces had been successful in pushing the Confederates back, they were not destroyed and in fact were emboldened after the Southern victory at Manassas.

Rosecrans fortified the mountain passes at Red House, Elkwater, and Cheat Mountain. He issued orders regarding the conduct of his troops against civilians and their property. He stated in a letter to the "Loyal Citizens of West Virginia,"

The old constitution and laws are only in force in Western Virginia. These laws you must maintain. Let every citizen, without reference to past political opinions, unite with his neighbors to keep these laws in operation, and thus prevent the country from being desolated by plunder and violence, whether committed in the name of secessionist or Unionism.... Let each town and district choose five reliable and energetic citizens as a committee of public safety, to act in concert with the civic and military authorities and be responsible for the preservation of peace and good order.[4]

After Rich Mountain, Robert E. Lee, who was "commander of the military and naval forces of Virginia," sent General W.W. Loring to Monterey, Virginia, to take command of the forces there. On August 1, Loring ordered General John B. Floyd to join Wise at White Sulphur Springs. Floyd, like Wise, had been governor of Virginia. He also had no military experience even though he had been secretary of war in James Buchanan's administration. General Henry Heth would later say of Floyd, "I had conceived an idea that a man who had been Secretary of War knew everything pertaining to military matters. I soon discovered that my chief was as incapacitated for the work he had undertaken as I would have been to lead an Italian opera." The recipe for failure was being written. Failure however was in the future. At the time all that could be determined was that the Confederates were concentrating to take the offensive against Rosecrans' forces in western Virginia (henceforth West Virginia). Lee decided to go to the front himself, leaving Richmond on July 28.[5]

Floyd met Wise at White Sulphur Springs on August 6. Floyd, who outranked Wise, derided Wise's Kanawha Valley retreat and proposed to go on the offensive. He would attack and defeat Cox, strike Ohio and break up the Wheeling Convention. He was told that Carnifex Ferry, twenty miles northeast of Gauley Bridge, was "the principle point at which the Gauley might be crossed by a considerable force." On the night of August 21, Floyd crossed the Gauley at Carnifex Ferry and set up Camp Gauley high on a horseshoe-shaped bluff overlooking the river. Wise however did not link his forces with Floyd's, keeping his troops on the south side of the Gauley. Floyd's position was now between the armies of Rosecrans and Cox.

A series of skirmishes between Cox and Wise and Floyd, who did not work together, took place over the next few days. The most famous being the rout, by Floyd, of the 7th Ohio at Cross Keys on August 26. This victory convinced Floyd of his invincibility. Rather than recross the Gauley to combine with Wise, he decided to entrench at Camp Gauley.

Rosecrans surmised that the Confederates were planning to attack Cox and decided to join up with him. He set out from Clarksburg with 4,500 troops formed into three brigades.

The 1st Brigade was headed by General Henry W. Benham. Rosecrans considered the regiments in the First Brigade to be his finest, especially the 10th Ohio. The commander of the "Bloody Tenth" was Cincinnati lawyer, soldier, politician and poet William H. Lytle. Also part of the First Brigade were the 12th and 13th Ohio regiments and two companies of Cavalry.

The 2nd Brigade consisted of the 9th, 28th and 47th Ohio regiments and was headed by Colonel Robert L. McCook, one of the "fighting McCook's" of Ohio. The 9th Ohio consisted largely of German-speaking soldiers from Cincinnati.

The 3rd Brigade under Colonel Eliakim P. Scammon was composed of the 23rd and 30th Ohio plus Battery I of the 4th U.S. artillery. Among the soldiers of the 23rd Ohio were future presidents Major Rutherford B. Hayes and Private William McKinley. Another soldier, Lieutenant Colonel Stanley Matthews, would become a Supreme Court justice.

Rosecrans and his "monstrously green" troops reached Sutton on September 6. A *New York Times* correspondent reported that Rosecrans "mapped all Western Virginia, highways, byways, mountain passes, ravines, blind paths, bridal paths, cow paths."[6]

On September 9, after meeting skirmishers and climbing and descending the 2,142-foot Powell Mountain, his army reached Muddelty Creek where it bivouacked for the night. The next morning the 1st Brigade started out between 4:00 and 4:15; by five Rosecrans' entire column was on the road to Summersville about eight miles south.

Rosecrans reached Kessler's Cross Roads at 2 p.m. his advance guard, the 10th Ohio, "chased a strong detachment of the rebels [and pursued] them in the woods." This was the abandoned camp of the 50th Virginia. Rosecrans ordered Benham, in command of the 1st Column, "to move forward cautiously into the woods for the purpose of reconnoitering."[7]

When Benham entered the deserted camp he felt certain that he had the enemy on the run. He advanced through a wooded area without deploying skirmishers. When his troops emerged from the woods they came upon and were fired on by Floyd's entire force. Benham had blundered into battle. Realizing his dire situation, he sent word to Rosecrans for reinforcements. Rosecrans ordered his two other brigades forward and went to the front himself.

Rosecrans had no real knowledge of the size of Floyd's force. He ordered McCook to attack the Confederate right. At about seven o'clock as dusk became a factor, Rosecrans decided to call off the attack and withdraw. The battle had begun at about 3:30 p.m. and the soldiers had been up since 3:30 a.m. The exhausted soldiers slept on their arms ready to resume the battle early the next morning. Rosecrans "retired to an oat loft" to sleep at 2 a.m.

There would be no battle the next morning. After meeting with his staff, Floyd, who had been slightly wounded in the fight, decided to make a night withdrawal. Rosecrans learned at 4 a.m. from a runaway slave of Floyd's retreat across the Gauley. Rosecrans had suffered 134 casualties including 27 killed. The Confederates lost about 32 with none killed. Yet it was the Yankees who had gained the field of battle and maintained the offensive.

Floyd, his force now united with that of Wise, agreed to retreat to Big Sewell Mountain on the James River and Kanawha Turnpike. On September 15, Rosecrans and Cox met at Cross Keys where it was decided that Cox should move toward the enemy. The West Virginia campaign would now center on the Sewell Mountain area, and the Confederates would have a new commander: Robert E. Lee.

The detente between Floyd and Wise was short-lived. After first agreeing to consolidate with Wise at Sewell Mountain, Floyd decided to retreat farther east to Meadow Bluff. Wise, upset at not being consulted about the change, decided to stay put and named his position at Sewell Mountain "Camp Defiance." This increasingly poisonous situation between Confederate generals would have to be resolved.

Since arriving in West Virginia in late July, Lee had not played a very assertive role. His actual powers were vague, and he seemed reluctant to urge General Loring to action. Finally in September he decided to try and dislodge the Yankees from their position at Cheat Mountain. These positions, under the immediate command of General Joseph J. Reynolds, had been well fortified since their capture after the fight at Rich Mountain in July. Whatever small chance of success might have existed was negated by Lee's overly complex battle plan. Lee's first campaign ended "ingloriously."

On the Union side things went more smoothly. Because of poor roads it was decided to shift the army's supply base to Gallipolis, Ohio, and make the Kanawha River the main transportation route. Cox was ordered to follow Floyd's retreat, and Rosecrans sent McCook's brigade to Cox. Because the ferry boats across the Gauley had been destroyed, Rosecrans was delayed in his pursuit. He joined Cox on September 26, and the two armies united two days later.

Lee arrived at Meadow Bluff on September 21 still facing the question of which of his two subordinates to support: Floyd at Meadow Bluff or Wise at Camp Defiance on Sewell Mountain. Lee inspected both camps and eventually decided that Wise's position was the best from which to meet the massing Yankees to the west.

Lee's feuding generals problem was resolved when orders came from Richmond instructing Wise to "turn over all the troops heretofore immediately under your command to General Floyd, and report yourself in person to the Adjutant-General in this city with the least delay." With this problem taken care of and with reinforcements arriving with General Loring, Lee began to strengthen his defenses at Sewell Mountain in anticipation of a Federal attack. By the end of September the two armies were on parallel ridges of Sewell Mountain separated by about a mile.[8]

Then the rains began. It was one of the worst storms in West Virginia's history. At Charleston, to Rosecrans' rear, the Kanawha rose forty-five to fifty feet. Rosecrans wrote that "telegraphic communications between me and all parts of West Virginia were interrupted." Eighteen horses in Rosecrans' army died in one night. Sickness followed the rain. The countryside was barren of forage. Not surprisingly Rosecrans decided to withdraw to a position closer to his supply bases.[9]

The withdrawal began on the night of October 5. General Cox remembered that

> hardly less than the commanding general's own authority and energy could have got the column forward in the mud and darkness. The troops had marched but a mile or two when they overtook part of the wagon train toiling slowly over the steep and slippery hills. Here and there a team would be stalled in the mud, and it looked as if daylight would overtake us before even a tolerably defensive position would be reached. Rosecrans now gave his personal supervision to the moving of the wagons and artillery, wagon-master's work, it may be said, but it was work which had to be done if the little army was not to be found in the morning strung out and exposed to the blows of the enemy if he should prove enterprising.

The sounds of the retreat were heard in the Confederate camp but were interpreted as preparations for a Federal attack. When morning revealed the true situation, Lee ordered a pursuit, but the poor conditions forced it to be called off. One Confederate remembered, "General Rosecrans had evacuated Big Sewell, and only left a few broken down horses and wagons, and a few tents pitched to make it appear that he still occupied his position. This was considered a very ingenious piece of strategy, as General Lee was much disappointed when he found that General Rosecrans had so quietly and adroitly eluded him on the previous night."

Indeed General Lee was disappointed as he wrote his wife, "I wish he had attacked us, as I believe he would have been repulsed with great loss."[10]

Rosecrans' new position was near Gauley Bridge; he deployed his brigades along the James River and Kanawha Turnpike. Schenk was closest to Sewell Mountain ten miles from Gauley Bridge; McCook was eight miles away; Benham six; Cox was at Gauley Bridge. Rosecrans made his headquarters at the farm of Confederate colonel Christopher Q. Tompkins. Tompkins' wife, Ellen, requested a pass from Rosecrans to travel to Richmond for winter clothes and supplies. An exchange of letters between General Rosecrans and Colonel Tompkins gives an interesting insight into the two men. On October 14 Rosecrans sent the following letter:

My Dear Colonel,

Your noble wife and fair daughter take this to you.

The only condition I impose on the visit is that while giving pleasure to you the visit shall have to me and the Government of the United States no painful consequences.

It is unnecessary to suggest to you, whose nice sense of honor I know so well and highly appreciate, that conversation on the number, condition, or position of military forces, or their equipment, discipline, supplies, or movements should be avoided. But I mention it that those of your friends and others who will probably converse with Mrs. T and Miss Ellen may be cautioned against embarrassing them conversing on these subjects.

I send you my warm regards. Anything I can do to contribute to your comfort or happiness I shall be happy to do.

Your Sincere Friend
W.S. Rosecrans

Tompkins responded six days later with the following:

My dear Sir:

Dropping the etiquette of official and more formal correspondence, I beg to thank you for your letter of the 14th instant and especially for your manifestations of kindness to my family at Gauley farm. You will do me the justice to believe that I feel most deeply the kindness which you have bestowed upon those so dear to me, and you find your reward in the consciousness of having exercised those Christian virtues which go so far to elevate ourselves in the estimation of all respecting people.

Aside from truce considerations, I shall continue in all sincerity to refer briefly to the unfortunate condition of our divided country. It has been a source of great and momentous concern to myself and whilst I have no idea that either of us will live to see the end of the evils that now exist, I do cherish the hope that we in our respective spheres accomplish much to mitigate their atrocities. I wish I could talk to you and many of my old friends on your side of the question. I believe we could manage affairs better than the politicians or at least honestly differ in our respective views. But this may never be. Once more I repeat my obligations to yourself and other officers of your Army for your kindness to my family. I only ask that they may be permitted to leave the place and return within our lines, and I need hardly add that I shall be bound by every sentiment of honor to observe the strictest regard for the observance of such silence as you will require in reference to your official affairs.

With much respect and regard I remain, dear Sir

Very Truly
C.Q. Tompkins[11]

Little could these men know that the next four years of war would result in over 625,000 deaths, 2 percent of the total American population.

After settling near the confluence of the New and Gauley rivers, Rosecrans took care of two important concerns of the troops: clothing and payment. He then prepared for an expected Confederate offensive movement. In fact Lee was planning one last attempt to drive the Yankees from the Kanawha Valley. He ordered Floyd toward Gauley Bridge along the south side of the New River. Lee himself planned to march along the north side and link up with Floyd. But that was never to happen. Bad roads, troops depleted by sickness, lack of forage and supplies and a new threat by General J.J. Reynolds to Confederate positions in Lee's rear caused him to decide not to unite with Floyd. Not only did he decide to send Loring and his troops to reinforce General H.R. Jackson at Greenbrier but he also returned to Richmond himself. On October 21 Lee left Sewell Mountain never to return; his role in the Kanawha Valley campaign was over.

Floyd continued on, passing through Fayetteville and stopping at Cotton Hill across the New River from Rosecrans' headquarters. From atop Cotton Hill he shelled Rosecrans' supply depots and ferry on November 1. After the initial surprise faded, Rosecrans realized that Floyd's position was a vulnerable one and devised a plan to encircle and capture Floyd's army.

The complex plan began November 10 with parts of Cox's brigade driving the Rebels from the front of Cotton Hill. However General Benham's delay in cutting off the Confederate's retreat allowed Floyd to escape. Floyd retreated out of the Kanawha Valley all the way back to Virginia.

Rosecrans was furious at Benham, writing in his official report, "It has been with great regret that I found it necessary to censure a general officer for failure to capture the rebel forces that were justly ours." He ordered Benham's arrest and requested his court-martial, an action that was not upheld in Washington.

Although Rosecrans was disappointed by his failure to capture a Rebel army, he had accomplished much, and in the words of Southern historian E.A. Pollard, Rosecrans "was esteemed at the South as one of the best generals the North had in the field; he was declared by military critics, who could not be accused of partiality, to have clearly outgeneraled Lee in western Virginia, who made it the entire object of his command to 'surround the Dutch general' and his popular manners and amiable deportment towards our prisoners, on more than one occasion, procured him the respect of his enemy." Even worse for Virginia and the Confederacy, a referendum on October 24 resulted in a majority vote for the formation of a new state. In late November Rosecrans' army went into winter quarters, with his own headquarters at Wheeling.[12]

As the focus of the war shifted to the Potomac in the east and the Tennessee in the west, Rosecrans' department ebbed in importance. Consequently a total of twelve regiments were shifted to Don Carlos Buell in the west. As fall ended, Rosecrans decided to go to Washington to try and sell his idea for a winter campaign.

When he arrived in the capital, McClellan was ill with typhoid fever and unable to meet with him. Rosecrans did meet with General Fitz-John Porter and explained to him his plan to unify the scattered forces in western Virginia and seize Winchester with 25,000 men, thus outflanking the Confederates at Manassas. While in Washington he was summoned to testify before the Committee on the Conduct of the War. In early February he returned to Wheeling to learn that McClellan had transferred 20,000 of Rosecrans' troops to guard the Baltimore and Ohio Railroad, leaving him with a force of 1,700. While in Wheeling he devised a four-wheel ambulance which became known as the Rosecrans ambulance. His wife Annie joined him, and the two sat for portraits by the noted artist G.P.A. Healey.

March brought a seismic change in Rosecrans' fortunes. He was replaced by John C. Fremont, the first presidential candidate of the Republican Party in 1856 and a darling of the Radicals. While in Missouri, Fremont had issued an emancipation proclamation which was quickly overturned. Although he had won no battles, his removal made him a martyr to the Radicals who wanted a new post for him. Lincoln created the Mountain Department, which included West Virginia, and named Fremont its head. Rosecrans, the most successful Union general to that point in time, was sacrificed for political expediency.

On March 18, Rosecrans turned over his command to Fremont and a few days later went to Washington. He met with the new secretary of war Edwin Stanton still trying to sell his idea of the unification of the armies in the mountain west. The secretary received Rosecrans cordially but told him he was unable to give him a command. He did however give him an undefined assignment to go back to General Fremont and await orders. He was also to meet and confer with Major General Nathaniel Banks in Winchester. He met with Banks on April 14 and discussed his proposal to unite the armies of Banks, McDowell, and Fremont creating a force of about 75,000 to face the 11,000 to 13,000 Confederates under Ewell and Jackson. This force would protect Washington and threaten Richmond from the west as McClellan was threatening the Confederate capital from the east. The day after the meeting, Banks telegraphed to Stanton, "Had full interview [with Rosecrans]. Opinions concurring."

Back in Washington, Secretary Stanton was not supportive of Rosecrans' plan to combine and coordinate Union forces: "The president will not sanction the plan you propose until it is more fully matured, and after full conferences and agreements by all who are to participate in it. You will return immediately to Washington and await orders."[13]

Major Lucas Hartsuff, an assistant to Stanton, wrote in a private letter to Rosecrans that "Stanton has taken a strong dislike to you." Rosecrans had made an enemy of a powerful figure. Of course the subsequent rout of Union forces by Stonewall Jackson in the Shenandoah Valley in 1862 proved Rosecrans correct. Historian Margaret Leech observed, "Divine interposition could scarcely have scattered the Federal forces more perfectly than those two amateurs of war, Mr. Stanton and Mr. Lincoln."[14]

Rosecrans' fortunes changed for the better when he received orders to join General Henry Halleck in northeastern Mississippi. He would now become a "western general."

William S. Rosecrans' exploits in West Virginia are not well known to even the advanced Civil War student. But to those who have studied them their importance is understood. No one denies the far-reaching consequences of the battles of Rich Mountain and Carnifex Ferry. No one disputes that it was Rosecrans and not McClellan who was the principle architect of that success. Everyone agrees on the importance of the Baltimore and Ohio Railroad to the North. Everyone agrees that the formation of a new state was due to the success of the Federal forces in 1861. Everyone agrees that William S. Rosecrans outgeneraled Robert E. Lee in the Kanawha Valley. None of this is denied; it is just forgotten or ignored. As one historian concluded, "Rosecrans, not McClellan, was the hero of Rich Mountain, which battle was decisive of the campaign in West Virginia in 1861; which defeated and discredited Lee, and cleared the field for the restoration of Civil government in Virginia."[15]

If he had accomplished nothing else, Rosecrans would be an important if minor figure. However, his role in and importance to the Civil War was just beginning.

3. Iuka

The battle of Shiloh, or Pittsburg Landing, had been fought in April 1862. That battle, the largest of the war to that point, was fought for the railroad crossroads of Corinth, Mississippi, twenty-five miles south and resulted in a Confederate retreat to Corinth. Grant, the Union commander at Shiloh, was superseded by General Henry Halleck who resolved to unite the Union forces in the west and crush the Southerners at Corinth. He assembled Grant's Army of the Tennessee with Don Carlos Buell's Army of the Ohio and John Pope's Army of the Mississippi.

Halleck commanded the largest army ever to be assembled in the western theater, 170,000 men with 108,000 ready for duty. Rosecrans reported to Halleck in May and was assigned to Pope who commanded the left. He in turn was to command Pope's right. For Rosecrans, who had commanded a department in West Virginia, this was a demotion. Journalist Whitelaw Reid wrote,

> For a General who has commanded a department and planned his own campaigns, to be reduced not merely to the position of a subordinate, but to that of a subordinate's subordinate, as General Rosecrans now was by his assignment to the command of some divisions in General Pope's column, constituting the left wing of Halleck's army, is never a grateful change; but the General bore it handsomely; was alert enough to be among the very first in discovering the evacuation of Corinth and getting off troops in pursuit; kept his place in the advance till the enemy were found in new positions; held this front till ordered back to assume command of the Army of Mississippi on the departure of General Pope for the East.[1]

Entrenched at Corinth was General P.G.T. Beauregard with a force of 60,000 consisting of Braxton Bragg's Army of the Mississippi and Earl Van Dorn's Army of the West. It took Halleck nearly a month to traverse the twenty miles from Pittsburg Landing to a point just outside of the Rebel position at Corinth. On the evening of May 29 there seemed to be "remarkable activity" in the Rebel camp. Halleck warned Pope of the apparent massing of Confederate troops and an assault on the Union left. At 4:00 a.m. a series of explosions began inside the Rebel fortification, dense columns of smoke arose and Rosecrans suspected a Confederate evacuation.

Four brigades were sent toward Corinth; when they arrived they found the town deserted. Beauregard had retreated south. Halleck ordered Rosecrans to lead the pursuit. At Twenty Mile Creek the combined forces of Rosecrans, Pope and Buell prepared for what might have been the greatest battle in the western theater. But it never happened. Beauregard retreated farther south to Tupelo, fifty-five miles from Corinth, and after eight days at Twenty Mile Creek the Federals returned to Corinth on June 11.

In the next weeks, changes in command took place that would have momentous consequences not just for the western theater or the Union army but for the entire war effort on both sides. When Beauregard went on temporary sick leave, Jefferson Davis used the opportunity to replace Beauregard with one of his favorites, Braxton Bragg. On June 15, Pope was called east to head a new Army of Virginia that unified four scattered commands of the eastern theater. It should be remembered that Rosecrans had earlier proposed a unification of the eastern armies. Rosecrans succeeded Pope as commander of the Army of the Mississippi. On July 15, Halleck was called to Washington to become general in chief. Grant assumed Halleck's place as commander in the west.

Ironically Grant himself might have been gone if not for the intervention of William T. Sherman. Grant, sick and despondent over his fallen reputation after Shiloh, had repeatedly asked Halleck to relive him. Sherman found Grant at his camp and persuaded him to stay. Grant agreed to stay but moved his headquarters from Corinth to Memphis.

In addition to these changes in command there were changes in the forces themselves. Halleck's gigantic command was broken up. Buell was sent east toward Chattanooga. Sherman went west to Memphis. On the Southern side, Bragg left Mississippi to try and beat Buell to Chattanooga. He left his remaining force to Generals Sterling Price and Earl Van Dorn. Halleck, Sherman, Bragg and especially Grant and the city of Chattanooga would play large roles in the life of William S. Rosecrans in 1863.

Once again in command of an army, Rosecrans proceeded with his customary industriousness. Noting that about 35 percent of his army was sick, he moved it to Camp Clear Creek southwest of Corinth where he established a hospital and instituted changes in diet that resulted in the number of sick soldiers falling to 13 percent. One observer noted,

> The Army of the Mississippi is evidently in a much more efficient condition than it was before the evacuation of Corinth. Though there is still a great deal of sickness among those regiments which came into the field this spring the health of the Army is, on the whole, I think much improved. This is, to a great extent the result of increased attention to sanitary measures as well as to a diminishing of the fatigue and extra duty of which there was so much during our slow approaches to the rebel stronghold. General Rosecrans is a strict disciplinarian and stringently enforces

3. Iuka

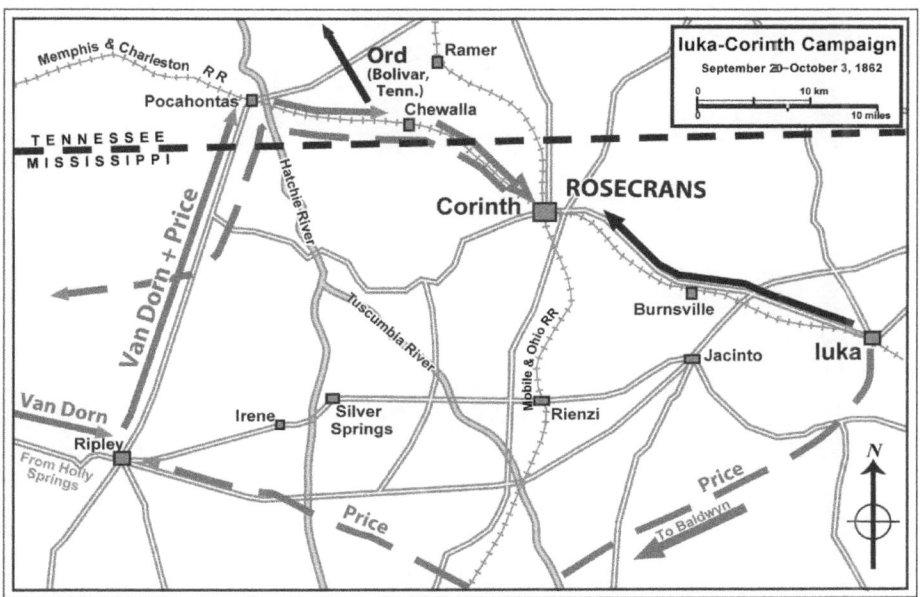

Iuka-Corinth 1862 (Map by Hal Jesperson, www.cwmaps.com).

the regulations requiring cleanliness in and about the camps and the persons of the soldiers. The strict yet kind and gentlemanly course the general has pursued since taking command of the corps has won the respect and confidence of both officers and men, and, under his command the army of the Mississippi are ready and willing to go wherever our imperiled country may call. Such a general as Rosecrans with such an army as he now commands will not be likely to let the laurels won by his skill and gallantry among the mountains of Western Virginia wither on any other field.[2]

He instituted a new method of map making. He ordered his staff engineers to make skeleton maps on which more topographical information could be drawn. Photographic copies were made of the map and distributed to division leaders who then made additions to them. These enhanced maps were returned to headquarters for the production of a detailed general issue map.

Rosecrans had a creative and effective solution to the problems caused by runaway slaves or "contrabands" that came into the Union lines. Sherman had ordered,

> The well-settled policy of the whole army now is to have nothing to do with the negro. "Exclude them from camp" is General Halleck's reiterated order. We cannot have our trains encumbered by them, nor can we afford to feed them, and it is deceiving the poor fellow to allow him to start and have him forcibly driven away

Rosecrans fostered innovations in many fields including cartography.

afterward. For these and many good reasons the general now especially directs the colonels of regiments, captains of companies, and regimental quartermasters to give their personal attention to this matter, to remove all such now in camp, and to prevent any more from following our camp or columns of march.

Grant amended this policy to allow black labor to perform "such menial service as should not be put upon soldiers." Rosecrans, however, created a battalion of black engineer troops, the first employed in the army. These troops played an important role in October when Van Dorn's Confederates attacked Corinth.[3]

Grant was now Rosecrans' superior, and relations between the two were friendly. After the Union occupation of Corinth, Halleck had begun work on an inner line of defenses one and a half miles from the center of town. Work continued on this line under Grant throughout the summer. Rosecrans judged these defenses to be too difficult to man. He suggested to Grant that a new inner line of breastworks be built on five low hills. Grant agreed with Rosecrans' suggestions and ordered the construction of five open batteries: Robinett, Williams, Phillips, Tannrath and Lothrop. This inner line of defense would prove to be the decisive factor in October's battle.

The autumn of 1862 was the real high-water mark of the Confederacy. That was the last time that the South would attack the Northern armies along the three major fronts of the war. In late August, Pope, recently arrived from the west, was defeated by Lee at Second Bull Run. Buoyed by this victory Lee set out to invade the North crossing the Potomac in September. McClellan replaced Pope and pursued Lee's Army of Northern Virginia into Maryland. The culmination of this campaign was the deadliest day in American history, September 17, 1862, the date of the battle of Antietam.

To the west, Bragg, who had left Mississippi in June, had beaten Buell to Chattanooga. In late August he headed north into Kentucky hoping to unite with a Confederate force under Edmund Kirby Smith. Buell requested troops from Grant in Mississippi and pursued Bragg into Kentucky. Recalled Rosecrans, "The suspense lest McClellan should not be in time to head off Lee— lest Buell should not arrive in time to prevent Bragg from taking Louisville or assaulting Cincinnati was fearful." This second Confederate offensive in the autumn of 1862 would result in the battle of Perryville.[4]

These events in Kentucky affected the armies in Mississippi. Bragg feared that Rosecrans or other parts of Grant's army would be sent to reinforce Buell. Indeed two divisions were detached from Rosecrans and sent to Buell. Bragg ordered Sterling Price to watch Rosecrans' army and prevent its juncture with Buell.

On the Northern side Grant was unsure of what the Confederates were up to. One possibility was that Price might move north to join Bragg. Another was that Price and Van Dorn might unite and attack Grant's scattered forces. In July Grant had at his disposal about 63,000 troops, one-third of which was the Army of the Mississippi under Rosecrans. Rosecrans' five divisions were spread out along a fifty-mile front from Tuscumbia, Alabama, to Rienzi, Mississippi, guarding the Memphis and Charleston Railroad. After the detachment of the two brigades sent to Buell, Rosecrans' line became even thinner.

On the Confederate side a lack of cooperation hindered the effort. Price had asked Van Dorn to join him in an attack along the eastern flank of Grant's line—that is, Rosecrans' front. Van Dorn in turn wanted Price to unite with him at Ripley and attack or maneuver against the Union west flank. There was also confusion over which of the two Confederate generals outranked the other. After an appeal to Richmond it was decided that Van Dorn would be the higher-ranking officer during combined but not independent operations.

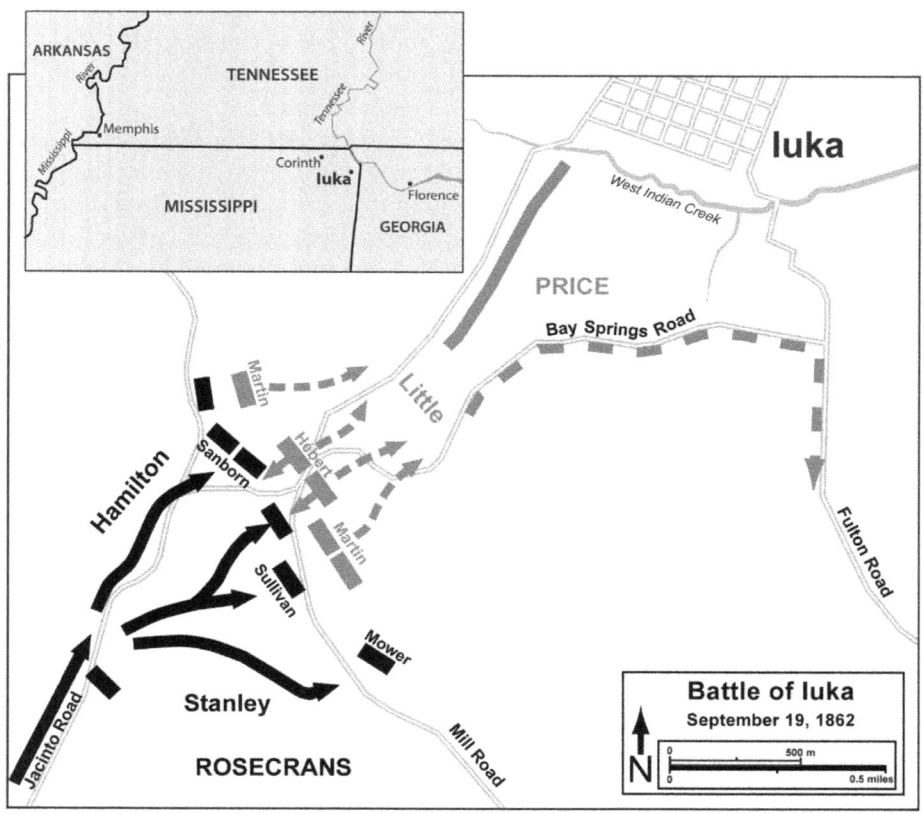

Battle of Iuka (Map by Hal Jesperson, www.cwmaps.com).

On August 29 Price received the following: "Buell's whole force in full retreat upon Nashville, destroying their stores. Watch Rosecrans and prevent a junction; or if he escapes you follow him closely."[5]

Frustrated in his failure to get Van Dorn to cooperate, Price decided to march against Rosecrans alone. On September 11 he set out for Iuka, Mississippi, where he surmised Rosecrans was. Grant, meanwhile, had decided that Price would likely attack Corinth. Iuka was ordered evacuated, but because a hospital and a large store of supplies were there it took until September 11 for the Union to vacate it. Only Colonel Robert Murphy's brigade was left to defend the town. On September 13 the Southerners began to attack Iuka. Colonel Murphy, unable to communicate with his superiors because of downed telegraph wires, decided to vacate Iuka, leaving behind a considerable number of stores. At seven o'clock the morning of September 14, Price's army of 17,000 marched into an abandoned Iuka.

Although Price occupied Iuka, he was in a precarious situation. He was about a four-day march from Van Dorn, Grant's larger force was to his west, and the Tennessee River was to his north and east. Rosecrans realized this and proposed to Grant a plan to attack Price from the northwest and the south, thus effectively trapping Price. In Grant's own words, Rosecrans "had a most excellent map prepared showing all the roads and streams in the surrounding country. He was also personally familiar with the ground, so that I deferred very much to him in my plans for the approach."[6]

The plan called for Grant and General Edward Ord to advance with 8,000 men from Burnsville, seven miles northwest of Iuka. Rosecrans would march south with David Stanley's division to Jacinto, combine there with Charles Hamilton's four brigades and then move east to Barnett's crossroads four miles southwest of Iuka. His force of 9,000 would then divide and march up the Jacinto and Fulton roads. Grant's force at Burnsville would initiate the attack at daybreak on September 19, with Rosecrans sealing Price's escape route to the south.

A pincers movement is a tricky thing, as Rosecrans had learned at Rich Mountain, and the attack on Iuka would be no exception. Stanley's division was led down the wrong path behind Ross of Ord's command. This caused a delay of four to five hours. When Rosecrans learned of the delay he telegraphed to Grant the night of September 18: "Stanley's division arrived after dark having been detained by falling in the rear of Ross through fault of guide....We shall move as early as practicable, say 4½ a.m. .... Shall not therefore be in [Iuka] before 1 or 2 o'clock [PM], but when we come in will endeavor to do it strongly."[7]

Up to this point the story of the battle is neither disputed nor contentious. However what did or did not happen over the next forty-eight hours was crucial not only to the battle of Iuka but to the future Grant-Rosecrans relationship. It is at this point that the story takes turns subject to different interpretations.

In his *Memoirs*, Grant wrote that upon learning of the delay, "I immediately sent Ord a copy of Rosecrans' dispatch and ordered him to be in readiness to attack the moment he heard the sound of guns to the south or south-east." No such dispatch is in the Official Records. Ord in his official report wrote that on the morning of September 19 at about ten o'clock he received the following:

SEPTEMBER 19, 1862.

GENERAL: I send you dispatch received from Rosecrans late in the night. You will see that he is behind where we expected him. Do not be too rapid with your advance this morning, unless it should be found that the enemy are evacuating.

By order of Major-General Grant.[8]

Two important things to note: First, Grant says he immediately sent a dispatch to Ord after learning of Rosecrans' delay. That would have been on the night of September 18. However Ord says he received the note the next morning. Ord was with Grant so a dispatch sent immediately should not have taken ten hours to reach him. More importantly, the note Ord received says nothing about Ord attacking "the moment he heard the sound of guns to the south or south-east." Instead it says to "not be too rapid with your advance this morning."

The story took a curious turn when the following telegram arrived at Grant's headquarters on the evening or night of September 18:

The reports from Washington this evening contain intelligence of general engagement on 16th near Sharpsburg, between rebel army under General Lee and Union forces....Longstreet and his entire division prisoners. General Hill killed. Entire rebel army of Virginia destroyed, Burnside having reoccupied Harper's Ferry and cut off retreat.

General Hooker slightly wounded. Action very sanguinary. Requisitions for surgeons and hospital supplies larger than ever before.

Later advices say entire rebel army must be captured or killed, as Potomac is rising and our forces pressing the enemy continually.

J.C. VAN DUZER

Grant, perhaps feeling that this battle of Antietam had ended the war, sent a truce party to General Price with the news of Lee's supposed annihilation. He was hoping that Price would surrender rather than suffer more bloodshed in a now lost war. Price rejected this "insolent" demand and retorted,

If the facts were as described ... they would only move him and his soldiers to greater exertions in behalf of their country, and that neither he nor they will ever lay down their arms... until the independence of the Confederate States shall have been acknowledged by the United States."[9]

An important consequence of this strange sequence of events is that it immobilized Grant from carrying out his part of the battle plan until he heard from Price, which was around ten o'clock on the morning of September 19. Rosecrans received the erroneous news from Grant at 1:30 a.m. on the morning of September 19. The letter read, "The following message just rcvd. McClellan has driven the rebels out of Maryland with Tremendous slaughter. Genl Lee taken prisoner."[10] Rosecrans claimed this was the last communication he received from Grant's headquarters for over thirty hours.

At 5:00 a.m. September 19, Rosecrans set out for Iuka unaware that Grant was waiting for a reply from Price. At six o'clock he telegraphed Grant:

> Troops are all on the way, in fine spirits by reason of news [Lee's supposed defeat] .... eighteen miles to Iuka, but I think I shall make it by the time mentioned, 2:00 o'clock P.M. If Price is there he will have become well engaged by the time we come up, and, if so twenty regiments and thirty pieces cannon will finish him.[11]

The phrase "will have been well engaged" indicates that Rosecrans was expecting that Grant would initiate the fight, not Rosecrans as Grant later claimed in his *Memoirs*. There was no reply from Grant. Surely such a critical misunderstanding should have brought out a clarification from the commanding general.

At noon Rosecrans reached Barnetts, eight miles from Iuka. The original plan had called for Hamilton's division to approach Iuka via the Fulton road and Stanley's division to use the Jacinto road. The distance between the two roads was five miles. Rosecrans now made a crucial decision; he decided to have both divisions march up the Jacinto road. He reasoned that if he divided his army by sending it up two roads, he was vulnerable and could be defeated in detail. There was a road, the Mill Springs road, that connected the two closer to Iuka. Rosecrans reasoned he could utilize this road later.

He telegraphed this information to Grant. This "failure" to block Price's escape route from Iuka is often used against Rosecrans. This decision will be examined later.

At about noon two members of Grant's staff, Colonels C.B. Lagow and Theophilus Dickey, arrived at Barnetts. They asked Rosecrans, "General do you think the enemy is in force at Iuka?"

"Yes," said Rosecrans.

"Are you going to pitch into him?"

"Yes, of course, that is the understanding of my movement and we are only five or six miles from the enemy. We ought to hear Grant's opening guns on the railroad by this time."

"Maybe he is waiting for you to begin."

"Not so. The main attack should begin on the Railroad to attract the enemy's attention and enable me to surprise his left flank and get the roads in his rear."[12]

They left for Grant's headquarters at 4:30. Meanwhile a battle was about to begin.

Rosecrans' forces, with the 3rd Michigan Cavalry leading the way, had made initial contact with Confederate pickets a half mile west of Barnetts. Intermittent skirmishing occurred between the Yankees and Colonel Armstrong's Confederate cavalry under Lieutenant E.B. Trezevant until they were within three miles of Iuka around 4 p.m. Price was northwest of Iuka on the Burnsville Road. His army consisted of two divisions headed by Generals Henry Little and Dabney Maury. About 2:30 a courier ran up to Price with word that a large Federal force was approaching Iuka from the south. Price had assumed that the attack would come from Burnsville where Grant's headquarters were and where skirmishing had occurred earlier. Upon hearing this alarming news Price ordered General Louis Hebert's brigade of Little's division to meet the threat from the south.

Hebert's brigade was closest to Iuka and therefore was able to get south of town on the Jacinto road before Rosecrans' army could enter Iuka. Later Colonel John D. Martin's brigade was dispatched south. For the Yankees, Brigadier General Charles Hamilton's brigade led with Colonel John Sanborn's division at the front. The opposing forces each halted on opposite hills separated by a ravine. To counter an attack from Confederate artillery, the 11th Ohio Battery was sent to the front alongside the 5th Iowa, 48th Indiana and 4th Minnesota.

The Confederates took the initiative. Hebert's brigade charged down their knoll through the ravine and up the knoll where the Yankees were, the screech of the Rebel yell accompanying the charge. Infantry from the 3rd Texas Dismounted Cavalry charged into artillery fire from the 11th Ohio. Next came assaults from the 3rd Louisiana and 1st Texas.

These attacks resulted in the retreat of the 48th Indiana, leaving the left flank of the 11th Ohio exposed. The 5th Iowa was also decimated, leaving the 11th Ohio's right flank endangered. Eventually the 11th Ohio's guns were captured. Price endeavored to outflank the Union position, sending Alabama and Mississippi troops from Martin's brigade to the left and right. Troops from General Sullivan's brigade replaced Sanborn's beleaguered division at the Union front.

At the height of the battle Generals Price and Little convened east of the Jacinto road. Price had just ordered Little to bring up two more brigades when a minié ball passed under Price's arm and struck Little in the head killing him instantaneously.

As dusk approached Rosecrans sent troops from Stanley's division to the front, but before they could see action, night brought an end to the fighting. During the night, noises from the Southern side were heard, but the meaning of these noises was not clear. Rosecrans, assuming the battle would resume in the morning and having no assurance that Grant would participate, repositioned his troops, replacing Hamilton's battle-weary soldiers with fresh ones from Stanley's division. A.W. Gilbert "found Rosecrans busy posting our forces massing the artillery in the rear on an eminence from whence the shot could be thrown over our heads into the enemies lines. During the night we brought up and distributed rations for our men their supply being exhausted so that they would not go into the fight next day on empty stomachs."[13]

At 10:30 p.m. Rosecrans sent a telegram to Grant: "We met the enemy in force. Firing was very heavy. You must attack in the morning and in force." He had not heard from Grant since 1:30 that morning more than twenty-one hours. Rosecrans gave orders for his army to march at dawn. Grant in his official report says he received Rosecrans' telegram at 8:35 a.m. and immediately sent orders to Ord to "Get your troops up and attack as soon as possible. Rosecrans had two hours fighting last night and now this morning again, and unless you can create a diversion in his favor he may find his hands full. Hurry your troops all possible." However Grant also wrote an order to Ord at 3:30 a.m. earlier that morning: "Dispatch just received from Rosecrans. He is two miles south of Iuka where he met the enemy in force last evening.... You must engage the enemy as early in the morning as possible bringing your forces as well together as possible." Interestingly the 3:30 telegram is not in the Official Records but is in the National Archives. The 8:35 telegram evidently is only in the official report. Assuming Grant did receive Rosecrans' telegram at 3:30 a.m. (Grant scholar John Y. Simon believed that to be the case), it raises the question why Grant took no actions. Why didn't Grant himself go to join Ord upon receiving word of the battle? Why does he mention the 8:35 telegram but not the 3:30 one?[14]

The Federal army moved into Iuka in the early morning of September 20 to discover that Price had slipped out using the unblocked Fulton Road. When Rosecrans entered the town he still had heard nothing from Grant since 10:30 the night of September 18. He ordered a pursuit of the retreating Confederates led by Stanley's division.

That morning he sent three more dispatches to Grant. At about 10 a.m. Ord's forces approached "with drums beating and banners flying." Rosecrans asked him, "Why did you not come to me in accordance with our mutual understanding? Why did you leave me in the lurch?" Ord pulled out a piece of paper and handed it to Rosecrans. It was Grant's order to postpone the attack. Grant himself arrived about noon. This was the first communication between the two since Rosecrans received Grant's erroneous report about Antietam.[15]

The Battle of Iuka is also important because it resulted in the first rift between Grant and Rosecrans. Since it is Grant who is generally considered to be the "general who won the Civil War" and not Rosecrans, it is important to examine the causes and nature of this rift.

The case against Grant is that he played at best a distracted role during the battle. There is no record of Grant trying to contact Rosecrans for a period of more than thirty hours. The main decision he made during the period leading up to the battle was to ask Price to surrender and to halt his own movement on Iuka until he received a reply from Price. This episode is not mentioned by Grant in his *Memoirs*. Meanwhile Rosecrans continued on to Iuka and fought a battle alone.

In his *Memoirs* Grant claimed that he sent a note to Ord telling him to attack the moment he heard the sounds of guns from Rosecrans' direction. There is no copy of this order in the Official Records. There is a copy of an order directing Ord to "not be too rapid with your advance." It should be noted that Grant's *Memoirs* were published in 1885 before the volumes of the Official Records on Iuka were published in 1887.

Grant's lax attitude toward the battle is further illustrated by the fact that he sent Ord on a movement toward Corinth, away from Iuka, until 3:00 p.m. the day of the battle. This hardly seems to be the action of a man about to fight a battle at Iuka.

As to why he did not attack during the battle Grant later claimed that a "wind inversion" carried the sound of battle away from his army. In other words he didn't know that a battle was being fought.

This claim remains controversial among those historians who choose not to accept Grant's claim at face value. There are participants who claim to have heard the sounds of an engagement, among them Colonels Dubois and McArthur. John Wilson of the 56th Illinois wrote in his diary on September 19, "We hear our division doubles toward Iuka. Rebel pickets were drove in as we pass Jacinto.... We hear cannonading this evening. Our troops are ready for a fight."[16]

Thomas Christie of the 1st Minnesota Battery wrote the following in a letter to his sister two days after the battle:

> "Action front," is the command, and we come round into position like the crack of a whip, the guns are unlimbered, and brought to bear on the road ahead and the limbers and caissons take position in the rear. Axes are brought into requisition, and every tree and limb that would impede the sighting of the pieces is leveled to the ground. The cannoniers take their posts and we wait. Old Gen. Ord rides by and looks with grim satisfaction at our bronze bulldogs. A half hour passes and no

enemy, not even a shot in front. Presently an orderly dashes up, "Limber to the front," and we pass ahead followed by our Right Section which has come up. Another quarter mile, another hill, and again we take position. Here we stay untill [sic] evening, hearing brick cannonading to the right where Rosencrans is pushing them in. Is there nothing for us to do?[17]

Even if the "wind inversion" explanation is accepted, questions arise from the non-audible signs of battle. At 4:00 p.m. right as the battle was beginning, General L.F. Ross, who was at the head of Ord's position, telegraphed the following to Ord: "For the last twenty minutes there has been a dense smoke arising from the direction of Iuka. I conclude that the enemy are evacuating and destroying the stores."[18]

Ord received this dispatch at 6:00 p.m. If Grant's army was either awaiting the sounds of battle or advancing cautiously to the planned battle site, surely "dense smoke" would signal that something important was happening. Surely the commanding general should make a decision upon receiving this information. However not only did the commanding general's wing of the army not attack, but he claimed not to have known about the battle until the day after it was fought. The question now becomes, where was Grant? This is a question that was asked back in 1862. One explanation is drunkenness in high places.

William S. Stewart of the 11th Missouri wrote in a letter to his parents dated September 23,

> At the fight the other day, General Grant had a force of 8,000 men on the road west of Iuka and was to come upon the enemy while we should attack them from the South, and thus capture the whole Army of Price, and if Grant had come up the whole rebel Army would have been captured or killed. But Gen. Grant was dead drunk and couldn't bring up his Army. This is true. I was so mad when I first learned the facts, that I would have shot Grant.

Stewart elaborated in an article he wrote under the name W.S.S. for the *Cincinnati Commercial* which was published on September 29:

> Great victory against Confederates, and appeared that they were beaten and surrounded. Union forces waited for morning to complete the job, but by that time the enemy had run off in the night. The question among our troops then arose: how did the enemy get away? Why did not our forces on the Burnside [sic] Road engage them in the rear during the battle, and thus entirely capture them? You may slightly, but not fully, imagine the bitter curses that went up from our subordinate officers and men when they learned Hellish Whiskey was the whole cause. And yet, when we contemplated that "drunkenness in high places" prevented us from capturing General Price with his twenty-three thousand men, which could have been easily done, the enthusiasm of victory was cooled very much indeed.[19]

This article appears to be the source of much of the speculation that Grant was drunk during the battle of Iuka. There is no conclusive proof as to whether Grant was incapacitated by drink before the battle or not. It is possible that upon receipt of the telegram proclaiming Lee's destruction and the end of the war that a celebration, which may have included alcohol, took place among top officers and Grant may have participated. Neither Mrs. Grant nor Major John A. Rawlins, both of whom were "good influences," were with Grant at the time.

More important than the disputable rumors of drunkenness in high places is the indisputable fact of Grant's inactivity: his failure to communicate with Rosecrans and his failure to attack when clouds of smoke, if not the sounds of battle, indicated the fight had commenced. Furthermore his failure to go to Ord when he heard about the battle at 3:35 on the morning of September 20 but instead waited several hours shows at best a lack of a sense of urgency about the battle.

Reverend J.B. Rogers, the chaplain of the 14th Wisconsin, wrote in 1863, "Had Gen. Grant co-operated with Rosecrans, as was expected, the rebel army may have been 'bagged.'... Some of these things so inexplicable will doubtless be explained hereafter, and censures will then rest where they belong."[20]

The case against Rosecrans, the charge that it was he who was lax and negligent at Iuka, is based almost exclusively on what Grant wrote in his *Memoirs*. It is enlightening to compare what Grant wrote in 1885 with what he wrote in his reports in 1862. In his *Memoirs* Grant wrote, "Rosecrans ... had put no troops upon the Fulton road, and the enemy had taken advantage of this neglect and retreated by that road during the night."

Rosecrans did leave the Fulton road open. He believed it would be unsafe to divide his army by sending it up both the Fulton and Jacinto roads. Surely after the battle, still having heard nothing from Grant, it would have been risky for Rosecrans to divide his army by sending troops to the Fulton road. Grant, in his official report of October 22, 1862, concurred, writing, "A partial examination of the country afterward convinced me that troops moving in separate columns by the routes suggested could not support each other until they arrived near Iuka." The Grant of 1885 found "neglect" where the Grant of 1862 found prudence.[21]

Grant alleges that "the enemy was not being pursued even by the cavalry. I ordered pursuit by the whole of Rosecrans' command and went on with him a few miles in person." This is not accurate. In fact Rosecrans had ordered pursuit that morning before Grant had arrived at Iuka. In his own report of October 22, 1862, Grant wrote, "I immediately proceeded to Iuka, found that the enemy had left during the night. Generals Stanley and Hamilton were in pursuit." Historian Stephen Z. Starr wrote that Grant's "dislike and hostility to Rosecrans is obvious throughout his account of the fight at Iuka" and concluded that "Grant's statement of Rosecrans' unhelpful role in the pursuit appears to be erroneous" and raised the question as to "whether it is so intentionally or otherwise."[22]

Grant wrote two reports on the battle of Iuka. In his first report of September 20 he wrote, "I cannot speak too highly of the energy and skill displayed by General Rosecrans in the attack, and of the endurance of the troops under him." In his second report of October 22, Grant writes, "Our only defeat was in not capturing the entire army or destroying it as I had hoped to do. It was a part of General Hamilton's command that did the fighting, directed entirely by that cool and deserving officer." Rosecrans is not mentioned.

In his *Memoirs* Grant asserted that Rosecrans "had his advance badly beaten and driven back upon the main road. In this short engagement his loss was considerable for the number engaged and from battery taken from him."[23]

Perhaps the best reply to the allegation of Rosecrans being "badly beaten and driven back" was made by Colonel John Sanborn whose brigade bore the worst of the fight,

> I certainly would make no comments if it did not seem to reflect upon the officers and soldiers of the brigade that stood up and held that field against twice or three times their number, as well as against those who sacrificed their lives and limbs to maintain the Federal power and supremacy over the Confederacy... and to say that an army is beaten, that holds the fields, buries the enemy's dead, gathers in quartermasters' wagons thousands of its small arms, is a great injustice to the memory of those fallen in battle, to the maimed and wounded living and dead.[24]

In *The Edge of Glory*, William Lamers lists ten discrepancies between what Grant wrote in his reports and *Memoirs* and the generally accepted record. Iuka is a little-known battle and is the smallest part of the theater of war that includes Shiloh and Corinth. Despite this, its casualty rate was among the highest of any battle of the war. The Union losses were 782, and the Confederates suffered 700 casualties. Special attention should be paid to the 11th Ohio Battery which suffered a 60 percent casualty rate, the largest of any light artillery unit in any single action of the war.[25]

Had the pincers closed at Iuka, had Grant shown up, Price's army would almost surely have been destroyed. The fruits of this would have been very great. Van Dorn alone would have been no match for Grant's army. After disposing of Van Dorn, the Federal army in Mississippi could have moved in concert with Buell against Bragg. The war in the west may have been over in 1862. This is speculation; the fact is that Price did escape to fight another day.

4. Corinth

After retreating from Iuka, Price joined Van Dorn at Ripley, Mississippi, on September 28. Their combined force numbered about 22,000. Van Dorn informed Price of his plan to attack Corinth. He hoped to gain control of the two railroads that intersected there and then march into Tennessee, Kentucky and eventually the Ohio River. Price, who had just tangled with Rosecrans at Iuka, preferred to wait for the arrival of 12,000 to 15,000 exchanged Confederate prisoners who had been captured at Fort Donelson in February. These prisoners were being rearmed in Jackson, Mississippi. However Van Dorn, who believed he outnumbered Rosecrans' forces at Corinth by a 3–2 ratio, as the senior officer prevailed.

On September 29 part of Van Dorn's force headed north to Pocahontas, Tennessee, which they reached after a three-day march. In doing this he hoped to confuse Grant as to whether the attack would be at Bolivar, Tennessee, or Corinth. Van Dorn turned east toward Chewalla, Tennessee, ten miles northwest of Corinth and along the Memphis and Charleston Railroad. There he camped until October 3.

After Iuka, Grant went to St. Louis, ostensibly to consult with General Curtis but more likely because he wanted to visit his wife. At any rate, facing a threat posed by the concentration of the enemy, Grant elected to take a sojourn to St. Louis. Before leaving he divided his army of 60,000 into four geographical divisions. Sherman was at Memphis, Stephen Hurlbut at Bolivar, and Rosecrans at Corinth. Grant made his headquarters at Jackson, Tennessee.

Rosecrans arrived in Corinth on September 26. He immediately ordered the defensive works that had been constructed in the summer (Batteries Robinett, Williams, Phillips, Tanrath and Lothrop) to be connected by breastworks. To facilitate this he employed "colored engineer troops organized into squads of twenty-five each, headed by a man detailed from the line or the quartermaster's department, and commanded by Captain William B. Gaw, a competent engineer."[1]

He also ordered this line extended to cover the north front of town; Battery Powell was finished just before the attack commenced. Still the line front

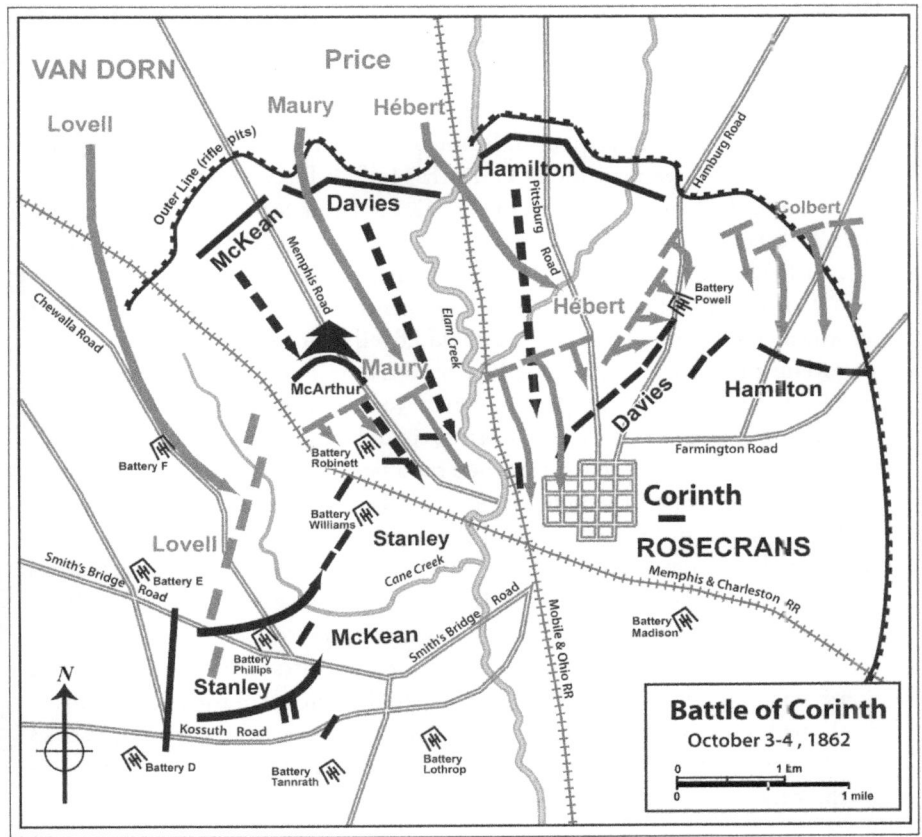

Battle of Corinth (Map by Hal Jesperson, www.cwmaps.com).

between Battery Robinett and the Mobile and Ohio railroad was "mostly open and without rifle pits."

Rosecrans had 15,000 troops—the divisions of Thomas J. McKean and Thomas A. Davies—garrisoned in Corinth itself and another 8,000 in the vicinity. Van Dorn knew he would need to attack before Rosecrans could concentrate all his men or receive reinforcements from Grant. Rosecrans in turn realized the necessity of having all his men at Corinth and on September 30 called in David Stanley's and Charles Hamilton's divisions.

The next day he sent Colonel John Oliver with three regiments out the Chewalla road to try and determine whether Corinth was to be Van Dorn's objective. On October 2, Oliver skirmished with Van Dorn's advance. Also on October 1 Grant telegraphed Halleck: "It is now clear that Corinth is to be the point.... Price, Van Dorn, Villepigue, and Rust are together." If Grant believed this to be true he did little to act on it. He stayed at Jackson and sent no reinforcements to Rosecrans until October 3. For a third time Rosecrans would fight a battle alone.[2]

At 1:30 a.m. on October 3, Rosecrans called a meeting of his division leaders at the Curlee mansion in Corinth. Half his force would move out two and a half miles from Corinth to the old Confederate fortifications. Hamilton with 3,700 men would hold the right; Davies with 3,204 the center; and McKean with 5,315 the left. Stanley's would be held in reserve.

Van Dorn's army marched out to Corinth at dawn on October 3. As it approached the outer defenses, Mansfield Lovell formed the right (west), Dabney Maury the center and Louis Hebert the left. The outer defenses, which had been dug under Beauregard in April, were in turn protected by a belt of fallen timber or abatis. The Confederates marched in formation despite fierce Union fire, however when they reached the abatis their lines broke down. Running over and around the fallen trees they astonished the Yankees with their audacity. When the Rebels reached the outer fortifications they climbed up the steep dirt embankments in groups of three or four. The northern defenders retreated hastily back a half mile to the second line of defenses toward Corinth; by noon the Confederates held the outer defenses.

Rosecrans, unsure from which direction the attack on Corinth would come, had only committed half of his force to the defense of the outer defenses. He hoped to retard the assault long enough to discover where a counterstrike would be most effective. The Rebels pursued until conditions—temperatures in the nineties, a lack of water and sheer fatigue—caused them to halt and regroup. After an hour the Rebels resumed the attack. This time the northerners' defense was more tenacious.

As daylight gave way to dusk and the Confederates failed to break through the innermost defenses, Van Dorn decided to postpone the final assault until dawn the next day. For his part Rosecrans had tried to launch an attack on the enemy's left flank, but miscommunication and confusion prevented Hamilton from delivering a crushing blow. Years after the battle, both sides claimed that one more hour of daylight would have resulted in victory for its own side.

That night Rosecrans was confident enough to telegraph Grant, if they "fight us tomorrow I think we shall whip them." He repositioned his force to meet the expected Rebel attack. He had his chief engineer round up 1,500 "contrabands" and hired them to work on the unfinished Battery Powell. Sergeant John Lomax of the 18th Missouri wrote, "I attribute much of our success at Corinth to the labors of the Black men. Our army had been driven back all day Friday and from the heat and efforts of the day's fight.... And while [the soldiers] lay and rested from the fatigues of the day about 1300 Blacks were working all night throwing breast works and at 3 o'clock next morning we had cannon mounted sufficient to repel the attack and save Corinth and our army."

Chaplain J.B. Rogers of the 14th Wisconsin recalled that "Gen. Rosecrans seemed everywhere present during the night. The positions of regiments were changed, as found necessary from time to time to meet changes in the disposition of the enemy's force."[3]

Utilizing the innermost defenses Rosecrans had ordered constructed during the summer, he placed McKean on the left, Stanley to McKean's right, Davies in the center and Hamilton on the right flank. He lay down for sleep at 3 a.m. only to be awakened by Confederate cannonading an hour later.

Van Dorn's plan called for simultaneous attacks on three fronts beginning at daybreak. Hebert, commanding the rebel left, failed to begin at the appointed time. Eventually at seven o'clock Hebert reported himself sick and unable to fight. His command was assumed by General Martin Green.

In one of the most valiant charges of the Civil War, Price's corps of Arkansans, Texans and Missourians marched shoulder to shoulder like a "prodigious mass, with gleaming bayonets, ... dark and threatening" against the Union center. Despite terrible Union fire they marched on, "their faces averted like men striving to protect themselves against a driving storm of hail." The Union center under Davies broke, and Confederate infantry poured into the streets of Corinth. Victory seemed won. But this had been an uncoordinated attack lacking support. The Yankee forces on the right and left were able to counterattack and reinforce Davies. Captain Edward H. Cummins remembered, "We scarcely got in when we met and were overwhelmed by the enemy's massive reserves. Our lines melted under their fire like snow in thaw." They were forced to surrender or retreat in panic.[4]

Rosecrans' presence at the center of the fight proved an inspiration to the soldiers. William Holden of the 2nd Iowa wrote, "Major Gen. Rosecrans was riding down the lines cheering on the men. ...General Rosecrans rode along and showed us where to form." A Wisconsin soldier said, "General Rosecrans was ubiquitous—he saw everything himself." David Henderson of the 12th Iowa and later Speaker of the U.S. House of Representatives remembered that Rosecrans

> was one of the most fearless officers that I ever saw in battle. He seemed to be unconscious of danger. On the fourth of October, 1862, when the armies of Price and Van Dorn were pressing our lines and symptoms of our falling back were manifest, he suddenly dashed between the Federal and Confederate lines like the very spirit of war. He passed but a few steps in front of where I was. I can feel his presence yet. His hat had blown off. His firmly set face seemed as though he was made for a god of battle. Swinging his sword he called out to us: "Stand by your flag and

country, my men!" How he escaped. God only knows. It seemed as though the very air was full of lead, and death was holding high carnival along his pathway, and yet fearless he rode into the very teeth of death, rallying successfully his men for the mighty struggle before them. That splendid, fearless, heroic dash was the death knell to the armies of Price and Van Dorn.

Chaplain Rogers wrote,

> No western battle had, previous to this, been so well managed on our side. Gen. Rosecrans, besides, had the entire confidence of his men. he was greeted all day long, on Saturday, wherever he went, with shouts and cheers, and a shower of hats and caps in the air. The army saw that he was awake and knew what the enemy were doing, and that they would not surround us and take us by surprise while we had Rosecrans to lead us.[5]

This attack had occurred on the Union right to the east of the Mobile and Ohio Railroad. The Confederates had also attacked the center left of the Union position. Moore's brigade of Alabamians, Arkansans, Mississippians and Texans charged toward Battery Robinett. Leading them was Colonel William P. Rogers of the 2nd Texas bearing the regimental flag. When his horse was shot from under him he continued on foot still carrying the colors. Marching first in perfect formation then yelling and running as they neared the redoubt, the Rebels climbed over the parapet driving the Yankees from their position.

Again a Rebel victory appeared achieved. But once again the Federals had strong reserves and were able to drive the Confederates back. Rogers was killed, the fifth flag bearer to fall during the charge. The Southerners began to retreat in a rout; at 2 p.m. Van Dorn ordered a withdrawal. The battle of Corinth was over. The Confederate losses totaled 4,838 with 505 dead. Union casualties numbered 2,359 with 355 dead. The Southerners had lost nearly a fourth of their troops.

Rosecrans made a decision not to pursue the enemy immediately but instead to rest and be ready early the next morning for the pursuit.

At Battery Robinett, Rosecrans had the more than 200 Southern dead buried in a single trench. Colonel Rogers was buried in a separate grave with military honors. Colonel John Fuller, who commanded Stanley's First Brigade, remembered Rosecrans saying, "I take off my hat in the presence of men as brave as these. No man near enough to hear them will ever forget them."[6]

That night he visited his own troops. Cyrus Boyd wrote, "Gen'l Rosecrans, our commanding General came around this evening and was almost taken from his horse by the soldiers. The wildest enthusiasm prevailed and every man seems ready to pursue the enemy. We have had but few battles so well managed as old 'Rosa' has managed this one. ... We are tired and hungry tonight and the excitement and fatigue of the two days battle and its glorious termination entitles us to a rest."[7]

Grant had ordered reinforcements to Rosecrans on October 3. McPherson arrived in Corinth with five regiments on October 4, two hours after the conclusion of the battle. His force camped that night in Corinth; Rosecrans ordered it to be prepared to move the next morning at 3 a.m. and lead the pursuit.

Van Dorn's army spent the night of October 4 at Chewalla. He was planning a new attack on Corinth, this time from the south. His generals were incredulous when they got the orders, and they went to Van Dorn to tell him that the army was in no condition to fight again. Van Dorn eventually countermanded the orders and decided to move farther south to Ripley, Mississippi.

The next morning the Confederates were approaching Davis Bridge on the Hatchie River when they learned of a force of 5,000 under Major General Stephen Hurlbut also nearing Davis Bridge from the opposite direction. This force was part of the reinforcements sent by Grant to Rosecrans two days earlier. A fight at the Forks of the Hatchie bought enough time for Van Dorn to find an alternative crossing at Crum's Mill, thus evading the main part of Hurlbut's force.

Rosecrans' pursuit on October 5 started slowly and in a disorganized manner. Stanley took the wrong road and ran into Hamilton's force. McKean became lost, which resulted in a great tangle created by his army and the armies of Stanley, Davies, and Hamilton. Rosecrans had stayed in Corinth to manage the movements and communicate with Grant who was the overall commanding general.

At 9 p.m. on October 5 he telegraphed of his departure from Corinth "out to Chewalla with a carload of water." He arrived at the camp of the Union pursuit early the next morning.

Rosecrans was now in personal command of the pursuit as it set out after the retreating Rebels. The nature of that retreat was apparent. Colonel John Bryner of the 47th Illinois remembered,

> October 5th was the Lord's Day, and he was with Rosecrans. The retreating army was hard pressed; their entire train was abandoned, wagons, mules, horses, ammunition, quartermaster's and commissary's stores were strewn for miles and became the spoil of the Union troops. Prisoners were taken and passed to the rear. For over forty miles the chase continued. Two hundred Confederates under a flag of truce came in to aid in burying their dead.[8]

Cyrus Boyd wrote in his diary on October 6,

> We found General Price's buggy with a fine robe in it. But the owner was gone on. All along the roadside under the bushes and in the hollows and behind logs the

panting fugitives were found glad to surrender. Glad to do anything to save all they had left and that was their lives. They all agreed in saying that no such terrible calamity had overtaken them in the West as the battle of the 4th.[9]

A letter from Confederate Sergeant Edwin Fay to his wife written on October 7 confirms the dire situation of Van Dorn's army:

> Our retreat was conducted with the greatest confusion.... We lost half of Price's army killed and straggling. Such demoralization was never seen in the army before. I think the cause of the Confederacy is lost in the West. ... I hope we can get back as far as Vicksburg. I mean our cavalry. I tell you the times look much darker than I ever expected to see them.[10]

Rosecrans sensed that the moment to destroy Van Dorn's army was at hand. He sent the following dispatch to Grant:

> I have ordered rations sent to [Hurlbut] and have begged him not to return to Bolivar until I can communicate with Sherman: I want him to appear to threaten the enemy. I think Sherman should go to Holly Springs by all means, and that the roads should be opened to take supplies to him.... I repeat, it is of the utmost importance to give the enemy no rest day or night, to push him to Mobile or Jackson. Beg the authorities North to send us more troops. Ship everything you can: our time is now: we must not give the enemy time to reinforce or recruit. Every nerve must be strained. Everything will be sent to see our troops lack nothing of the necessities to keep them going.

It was Rosecrans, the subordinate, who was at the front, making suggestions, exhorting the commanding general Grant to action.

Grant did take action. He ordered Rosecrans to stop the pursuit and return to Corinth. When Rosecrans received Grant's order he was shocked. He decided to try and convince Grant how great an advantage the Union possessed:

> GENERAL: Yours 8.30 p.m. received. Our troops occupy Ripley. I most deeply dissent from your views as to the manner of pursuing. We have defeated, routed, and demoralized the army which holds the Lower Mississippi Valley. We have the two railroads leading down toward the Gulf through the most productive parts of the State, into which we can now pursue them with safety. The effect of our return to old position will be to pen them up in the only corn country they have west of Alabama, including the Tuscumbia Valley, and to permit them to recruit their forces, advance and occupy their old ground, reducing us to the occupation of a defensive position, barren and worthless, with a long front, over which they can harass us until bad weather prevents an effectual advance except on the railroads, when time, fortifications, and rolling stock will again render them superior to us. Our force, including what you have with Hurlbut, will garrison Corinth and Jackson and enable us to push them. Our advance will cover even Holly Springs, which would be ours when we want it. All that is needful is to continue pursuing and whip them. We have whipped, and should now push to the wall and capture all the rolling

stock of their railroads. Bragg's army alone west of Alabama River and occupying Mobile could repair the damage we have it in our power to do them. If, after considering these matters, you still consider the order for my return to Corinth expedient I will obey it and abandon the chief fruits of a victory, but I beseech you bend everything to push them while they are broken and hungry, weary and ill-supplied. Draw everything possible from Memphis to help move on Holly Springs and let us concentrate. Appeal to the Governors of the States to rush down some twenty or thirty new regiments to hold our rear and we can make a triumph of our start.[11]

Grant decided to ask General in Chief Halleck for advice:

Before telegraphing you this morning for re-enforcements to follow up our victories I ordered General Rosecrans to return. He showed such reluctance that I consented to allow him to remain until you could be heard from if further re-enforcements could be had. On reflection I deem it idle to pursue farther without more preparation, and have for the third time ordered his return.

Halleck replied, "Why order a return of our troops? Why not re-enforce Rosecrans and pursue the enemy into Mississippi, supporting your army on the country?"

To this Grant replied,

An army cannot subsist itself on the country except in forage. They did not start out to follow for more than a few days, and are much worn out, and I have information not only that the enemy have reserves that are on their way to join their retreating columns, but they have fortifications to return to in case of need. The Mobile road is also open to the enemy to near Rienzi, and Corinth would be exposed by the advance. Although partial success might result from farther pursuit disaster would follow in the end. If you say so, however, it is not too late yet to go on, and I will join the moving column and go to the farthest extent possible. Rosecrans has been re-enforced with everything at hand, even at the risk of this road against raids.[12]

Rosecrans remained hopeful that Grant would relent and let the pursuit continue. He strung telegraph wire and positioned his troops for an attack the next day. But Grant would not change his mind. Rosecrans was ordered to return to Corinth. Rosecrans replied,

The dispatch of the major-general commanding, dated the 8th instant, directing our return to Corinth, is just received. I shall take the most prompt and efficient measures to carry the orders into execution with as little prejudice as practicable to the interest of the service.[13]

W.A. Lyman was an eyewitness to Rosecrans' reaction to the recall: Rosecrans was "tramping back and forth in his office, cursing like the proverbial trooper that he should thus be prevented from proceeding any further."[14]

Could Vicksburg have been taken in the fall of 1862? Rosecrans surely thought so:

This was early in October. The weather was cool, and the roads in prime order. The country along the Mississippi Central to Grenada, and especially below that place, was corn country—and the corn was ripe. If Grant had not stopped us, we could have gone to Vicksburg. My judgment was to go on, and with the help suggested we could have done so. Under the pressure of a victorious force the enemy were experiencing all the weakening effects of a retreating army, whose means of supplies and munitions are always difficult to keep in order. We had Sherman at Memphis with two divisions, Hurlbut at Bolivar with one division, and John A. Logan at Jackson, Tennessee with six regiments. With these there was nothing to save Mississippi from our grasp. We were about six days march from Vicksburg and Grant could have put his force through to it with my column as the center of the pursuit, Confederate officers told me afterward that they were never more scared in their lives as they were after the defeat before Corinth.[15]

How strongly defended was Vicksburg at that time? The commander of Vicksburg, General M.L. Smith, confessed to Van Dorn,

I am seriously apprehensive that the safety of this important place may be, and actually is, overlooked. My conviction is that this command is today at the mercy of the [Union] army at Helena.... Their unaccountable inertness has saved Vicksburg from succumbing, for since the departure of General Breckinridge's division, there has never been a day on which a successful land attack might not have been made by the force at Helena.

Many years after the battle, an Ohio veteran remembered:

The Confederate Army which held the Mississippi Valley had been routed and demoralized. The Union forces had two railroads leading down through the most productive part of the state, where corn was ripe, supplying plenty of forage so that the enemy could have been pursued with safety. The weather was cool and the roads were getting in prime condition. We should have gone to Vicksburg then, but General Halleck ordered otherwise.[16]

Of course it was not Halleck who called off the pursuit but Ulysses Grant.

Even without Vicksburg, Corinth was seen by both sides as an important Union victory. Sherman wrote, "The effect... was very great. It was, indeed, a decisive blow to the Confederate cause in our quarter, and changed the whole aspect of affairs in West Tennessee. From the timid offensive we were at once enabled to assume the bold offensive. In Memphis... the citizens openly admitted that their cause had sustained a death-blow."

In Richmond, Jefferson Davis was said by a visitor to be "very much depressed at the news from Corinth, and said we had been out-generaled."[17]

The Rebel defeat in northeastern Mississippi also had a great impact in the third arena of the Southern offensive of 1862—Kentucky. Not only was Van Dorn prevented from joining Bragg in Kentucky, but his defeat at Corinth caused Bragg to withdraw completely from Kentucky after the battle of Perryville.

Despite the importance of Corinth it remains little known to this day. Incredibly some of the few who are familiar with the battle attribute the victory to Grant and censure Rosecrans for not beginning the pursuit immediately after the fighting. The basis for this position is, not surprisingly, Grant's *Memoirs*.

However there are a number of discrepancies between what is in the memoirs and what is in the Official Records. Grant claims he "had given specific orders in advance of the battle to pursue the moment the enemy was repelled. He did not do so, and I repeated the order after the battle." There is no record of any such orders in the Official Records.

In regard to his calling off the pursuit, Grant writes, "Had he gone much farther he would have met a greater force than Van Dorn had at Corinth and behind entrenchments or on chosen ground, and the probabilities are he would have lost his army." Grant doesn't identify or locate this "greater force," but the Official Records show that Grant received the following from Hurlbut on October 8: "I have just heard from Holly Springs. There are no forces there; all left on Sunday. There is but one company of Cavalry at Davis Bridge. Everything in shape of force above Wolf River has moved south. I am of the opinion that the rout of Van Dorn's army is complete, and that Pillow's force late of Holly Springs has caught the panic."[18]

Another important consequence of the events in northeastern Mississippi in 1862 was the rift that developed between Grant and Rosecrans. Because the claims and positions of the two men are diametrically opposite it is impossible to say both Rosecrans and Grant were right. One can either agree with Grant or Rosecrans, but not both. Since it was Grant who ended up the great military hero of the Union and later served as president, it is his claims that have been generally accepted. However it is interesting to listen to the opinions of those who were present when these events took place. They make a different point.

David Stanley wrote,

> General Grant, Rosecrans's superior, severely censured him at the time for not following Van Dorn's retreat on the 4th, and for his tardiness on the 5th. There may be some justice in this, but it is easy to criticize after the fact. The test is, put yourself in his place. Rosecrans's troops had marched for two and three days, had fought two days, had scarcely a supply of even drinking water, the heat was excessive, and the men were worn out. They had narrowly escaped a most terrible defeat, and no one was anxious to crowd their late antagonists.[19]

It should be pointed out that Stanley was in the heat of the fight and Grant was absent.

Private S.M.H. Byers of the Fifth Iowa on the pursuit and recall:

> Our regiment pursued the flying rebels with great vigor. The quantities of broken batteries, wagons, tents, knapsacks, guns etc. strewn along the road behind them were immense.... The pursuit of the enemy was being pushed with vigor when the army was ordered to desist and return to camp. It was an astounding order, as it was in our power to destroy the defeated and flying columns. That order was one of the mistakes of Grant's earlier days as a commander. Indeed, we in the rank and file had little confidence in Grant in those days. We reflected that at Shiloh he was miles away from the battlefield at the critical moment... at Iuka Grant, though commander, did not even know the battle was going on, at Corinth he was forty miles away, and now, when we had the enemy almost within our grasp, he suddenly called us back.

Byers wrote in his diary, "Our commander of the district is General U.S. Grant, who took Donelson; but aside from that one hour's fighting, and a little fighting at Shiloh, the troops know little about him. Rosecrans is at present the hero of this army, and, with him leading it, the boys would storm Hades."[20]

Arthur Ducat, chief of staff of the Army of the Mississippi, wrote to Rosecrans in 1885:

> If Grant had supported you ... the Vicksburg campaign would never have been necessary....More men were lost from sickness and fever and exposure, digging ditches ...about Vicksburg before the place fell. I regard the calling back of you at Corinth as an unexplained military crime, and shall so regard it while I live unless your superiors will admit they were insane or jackasses.
>
> But miserable gloryfilchers like to dwell upon it as something attaching to you. It is a burning shame that every honest man who knows about it should not come forward and deny it, and attack some monstrous outrages upon history.[21]

The return of Rosecrans' army did not stop the bad feeling between him and Grant. Over the next few weeks there were disputes about Rosecrans' handling of paroled prisoners, newspaper accounts of the battles of Iuka and Corinth, rifle shipments and alleged tensions between Rosecrans and Ord. It was now evident that the two men could not work together. Rawlins, McPherson and Hurlbut went to Julia Grant to try and have her husband dismiss Rosecrans. Rosecrans wrote to Halleck in Washington asking to be transferred:

> I am very sorry to say that ever since the battle of Iuka there has been at work the spirit of mischief among the mousing politicians on Grant's staff to get up in his mind a feeling of jealousy. They have at last so far succeeded that General Grant last evening telegraphed me that he thought certain leaky members of my staff and newspaper correspondents justified his insinuating that he thought I was getting up a spirit of division and trying to make my army appear independent of him. I dispatched, declaring that he had not had a truer friend or more loyal subordinate than myself; that no such sentiment existed or had been countenanced at these

headquarters as the one he alluded to; that no headquarters in these United States were less responsible for the sayings of newspaper writers and correspondents than mine, and that I wished it to be distinctly understood that this remark was especially applicable to what had been said about the affairs of Iuka and Corinth. After these declarations I said, "If you do not meet me with the frank avowal that you are satisfied, I shall consider that my ability to be useful in this department has ended." That now is my opinion.

I am bending everything to complete the new defenses of Corinth so that we may hold it by a division against a very superior force. As soon as I finish this work and my report of the late battle and pursuit I shall hope for something that will settle this matter. I am sure those politicians will manage matters with the sole view of preventing Grant from being in the background of military operations. This will make him sour and reticent. I shall become uncommunicative, and that, added to a conviction that he lacks administrative ability, will complete the reasons why I should be relieved from duty here, if I can be assigned to any other suitable duty where such obstacles do not operate.[22]

A resolution to the conflict arrived on October 23 when Halleck ordered Rosecrans to Cincinnati to receive orders. He would replace Buell as head of the Army of the Cumberland.

In his *Memoirs* Grant wrote, "I was delighted at the promotion of General Rosecrans to a separate command, because I still believed that when independent of an immediate superior the qualities which I, at that time, credited him with possessing, would show themselves. As a subordinate I found that I could not make him do as I wished, and had determined to relieve him from duty that very day."[23]

The idea that Rosecrans, who in reality had won two battles for Grant, presented a problem for him is dubious at best and ludicrous at worst. A more likely possibility is that Grant felt threatened by his successful subordinate. Certain actions by Grant support this conclusion. In his official report Grant relegates the actual battle of Corinth to one clause. Most of the report concerns Hurlbut and Ord's pursuit after the battle.

Grant also wrote a new report on the battle at Iuka. In his first report, written just after the fight, Grant couldn't "speak too highly of the energy and skill displayed by General Rosecrans" in his second report dated October 25, Hamilton alone is singled out for praise.

Grant's concern about newspaper coverage of the battle was expressed in a letter to his chief political supporter in Washington, Congressman Elihu Washburne: "I do not see my report of the battle of Iuka in print. As the papers in General Rosecrans' interest have so much misrepresented that affair, I would like to see it in print."[24]

Whatever Grant's true motivation in calling back Rosecrans, less than a month later on November 2, he was writing Halleck: "With small re-enforcements at Memphis I think I would be able to move down the Mississippi Central road and cause the evacuation of Vicksburg and to be able to capture or destroy all the boats in the Yazoo River."[25]

It appears that Grant now considered the taking of Vicksburg a relatively simple task. On November 2, less than a week after Rosecrans' departure, Grant began his first Vicksburg campaign. With his force concentrated at Grand Junction, Tennessee, Grant headed south. Van Dorn abandoned Holly Springs which was later occupied by the Federals and built up into their largest supply depot for the campaign.

Grant planned to move his force of 40,000 due south along the Mississippi Central Railroad; in addition Sherman with 32,000 would move by the Yazoo River against Chickasaw Bluffs just north of Vicksburg. Grant's overland march was halted by 3,500 cavalrymen under Van Dorn who, venturing behind Grant's line, attacked and destroyed the Holly Springs Depot on December 20. An eyewitness remembered:

> A million dollars' worth of our army supplies had been burned up in a night. The pretty town, too, was in ashes, and Van Dorn's bold cavalry swung their sabers in the air and rode away laughing. General Grant's father and mother, in the town at the time on their way to visit their illustrious son with the advance of the army, were captured, but politely paroled and left among the ruins. The loss of the town was a disgrace to the North. ...With the loss of Holly Springs and the destruction of our base of supplies there was nothing for that whole army of Grant's to do but to trudge its weary way back to Corinth and Memphis, through the mud and the wind and the rain.[26]

Sherman, who outnumbered the Confederate defenders by more than two to one, foundered in the swampy terrain and murderous Confederate fire and was forced to retreat after suffering 1,776 casualties compared to 207 for the Rebel defenders. On January 2, the same day Rosecrans was fighting at Stones River, Sherman met and turned over his command to McClernand. Thus ended the first of five unsuccessful attempts to take Vicksburg before the successful campaign and siege of March–July 1863.

As the careers of Rosecrans and Grant diverged in the fall and winter of 1862, it was Rosecrans whose star was ascendant among the soldiery, citizenry and even the enemy. Dabney Maury, whose troops had suffered terrible losses in the assault on Corinth, wrote,

> It has always seemed inexplicable that General Grant retained the confidence of his Government after the failures of this campaign. His mistakes were palpable and their consequences disastrous. At Iuka Grant's combined movement concerted with Rosencrantz [sic], failed through Grant's delay.... [Grant] actually remained all night two miles from the battlefield, with no enemy in his immediate front....

This unexplained slowness enabled Price to... escape what would have been certain capture, had Grant been as prompt as Rosencrantz.

Again, two weeks later, after the defeat of Van Dorn at Corinth, Grant failed to press his beaten enemy, but permitted him to lie unmolested at Holly Springs for one month, and until his (our) army was refitted, reinforced and reorganized.

...Van Dorn seized the opportunity which Grant's crowning blunder afforded, swooped down upon his unguarded depots, and terminated his campaign in North Mississippi. What was the mysterious influence of this man over his government that he was treated with unabated confidence after such flagrant *lachesse* and incapacity?[27]

The idea that something other than military success was at work in the rise and fall of Union generals is reflected in a letter from Joseph Medill, editor of the *Chicago Tribune*, to Congressman Elihu Washburne, Grant's patron in Washington:

> When do you think the Union is going to be saved out west? I write to you because it is through your influence mainly that he [Grant] holds the trust which he thus betrays. No man's military career in the army is more open to destructive criticism than Grant's. We have kept off of him on your account. We could have made him stink in the nostrils of the public like an old fish had we properly criticicised his military blunders. Look at that miserable and costly campaign into northern Miss. when he sent crazy Sherman to Vicksburg and agreed to meet him there by land. Was there ever a more weak and imbecile campaign. But we forbore exposing him to the examination of the people.[28]

As the fall of 1862 gave way to winter and the North suffered reverses in the east and along the Mississippi, the hopes of the Union centered on Tennessee and the new commander of the army, William Starke Rosecrans.

5. In Command

The army that Rosecrans took command of had had several names and commanders. It was organized in the spring of 1861 as the Department of Kentucky under Brigadier General Robert Anderson, the hero of Fort Sumter. In August this department was merged into the newly created Department of the Cumberland. Anderson's most consequential decision was to bring Generals Thomas and Sherman from the east.

In October Anderson became ill and was replaced as commander by William T. Sherman. Derided by some in the press as crazy, Sherman apparently suffered a nervous breakdown and asked to be replaced. Don Carlos Buell became the new head, and the name of the army was changed to the Army of the Ohio.[1]

It was under Buell that the Army of the Ohio participated in its most famous battles: Shiloh and Perryville. Indeed it was the arrival of Buell's army on the night of the first day of Shiloh that proved to be one of the key factors in that battle. After Shiloh and the replacement of Grant by Halleck, Buell was sent east to seize Chattanooga. Bragg got to Chattanooga before Buell and proceeded to invade Kentucky. Buell followed Bragg into Kentucky, reaching Louisville before any Confederates in late September. On October 1 Buell marched south with 60,000 troops to attack Bragg. The result of this campaign was the battle of Perryville on October 8. Perryville was the last act of the three-part Confederate autumn offensive that included Antietam and Corinth.

Although Bragg was repulsed at Perryville and retreated back into Tennessee, Buell was criticized for not achieving a greater victory. On October 24, Halleck, now general in chief in Washington, sent this order to Buell:

> The President directs that on the presentation of this order you will turn over your command to Maj. Gen. W.S. Rosecrans, and repair to Indianapolis, Ind., reporting from that place to the Adjutant General of the Army for further orders.

At the same time the Department of the Cumberland was created and defined as "the State of Tennessee east of the Tennessee River and such parts of Northern Alabama and Georgia as may be taken possession of." Rosecrans was made head of this department and the 14th Army Corps, which would later be known as the Army of the Cumberland.

5. In Command

On October 30, Rosecrans wrote the following letter to Buell:

> I know the bearer of unwelcome news has a "losing office," but feel assured you are too high a gentleman and too true a soldier to permit this to produce any feelings of personal unkindness between us. I, like yourself, am neither an intriguer nor newspaper soldier. I go where I am ordered; but propriety will permit me to say that I have often felt indignant at the petty attacks on you by a portion of the press during the past summer, and that you had my high respect for ability as a soldier, for your firm adherence to truth and justice in the government and discipline of your command. I beg you, by our common profession and the love we bear our suffering country, to give me all the aid you can for the performance of duties of which no one better than yourself knows the difficulties.[2]

Rosecrans took rein of his army at Bowling Green, Kentucky, on November 1. His left wing was commanded by Kentucky native Major General Thomas L. Crittenden. Crittenden was the son of a U.S. senator and brother of Confederate general George Crittenden. The right was led by Ohioan Alexander McCook, one of fourteen "Fighting McCooks" who fought for the Union. The center was headed by George Henry Thomas.

Thomas, a Virginian who remained loyal to the Union, is, like Rosecrans, one of the undeservedly neglected figures of the Civil War. Thomas, an 1840 graduate of West Point, saw action at Monterrey and Buena Vista in Mexico. After the outbreak of the Civil War he served in the Shenandoah Valley and then was called west to Kentucky by Robert Anderson. He was victorious at Mill Springs in January 1862, one of the first Union victories in the war. He was promoted to major general dating from April 25. This would present a problem when Rosecrans was made his superior in October 1862.

Thomas, a career soldier, outranked Rosecrans. When Thomas learned that a general less senior than himself would replace Buell he wrote Halleck that he was "deeply mortified and aggrieved." But Lincoln had antedated Rosecrans' commission to March 21, 1862, in recognition of his service in West Virginia. This made him senior to Thomas, and Halleck informed Thomas of this fact. When Thomas and Rosecrans met at Bowling Green, Rosecrans offered Thomas his choice of second in command of the entire army or independent command. Thomas chose the latter and took the center.

Rosecrans also brought in his own people: Arthur Ducat became his chief of staff; David Stanley head of cavalry; and Captain James St. Clair Morton chief of engineers and pioneers. He set up a pioneer brigade, provided detailed instructions for the couriers, and strengthened the surgical corps.

On paper the 14th Army Corps (the official name of what would be renamed the Army of the Cumberland) had over 90,000 troops, but in reality it could count on barely half that number. Desertion and inadequate cavalry were two particular problems. It fell to Rosecrans to remedy this situation.

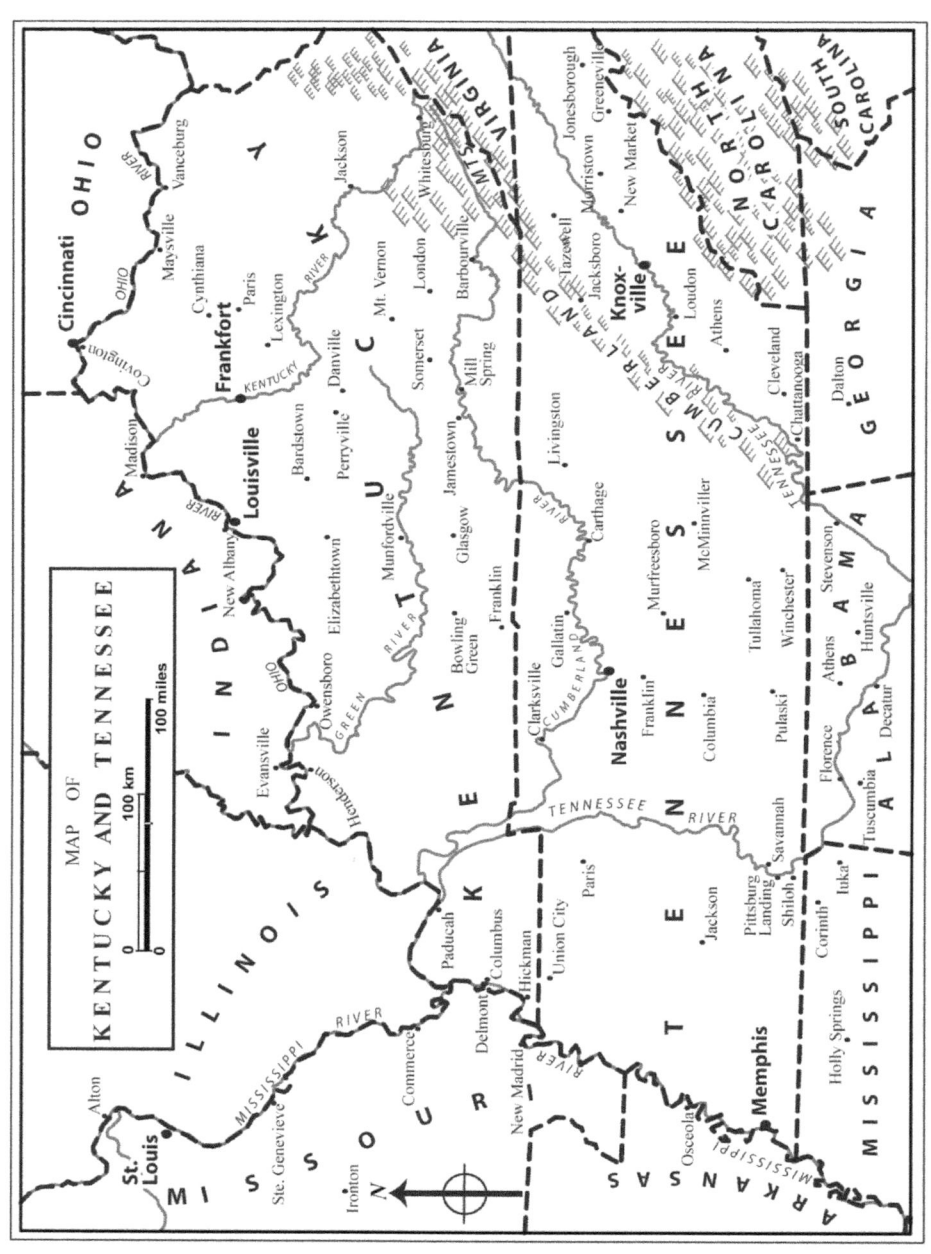

Kentucky and Tennessee (Map by Phil Mobley).

The troops noticed a change as Rosecrans set out to improve his army. James Haynie recalled,

> We were already beginning to like Rosecrans, and we are proud to have served with him, as we did for nearly a whole year. Few commanders of his time possessed such military knowledge and fertility in the hour of trial, seems to be the summing up of military critics of Major General Rosecrans. To us he was always a soldier, brave, accomplished, and devoutly religious. "Old Rosey," as we soon came to call him, was, however, a man of fiery nature, the hot spirit sending a flush into his face. His temper subsided as quickly as it rose, and his troops adored him.

Colonel Hans Heg of the Fifteenth Wisconsin, the Scandinavian Regiment, wrote "how pleased everybody is of the change of Buell for him." Stephen F. Flaherty of the 102nd Illinois after a grand review observed,

> He has a pleasant countenance, and the soldiers are of the opinion that in becoming a general, he has not forgotten that he is a man. The review was an imposing spectacle, and one that will be long remembered by those who witnessed it. The rays of the setting sun gleamed from many thousand polished bayonets, and that long line of loyal hearts, was animated by a common feeling—confidence in their united strength, the justness of their cause, and the ability of their new general.

John A. Martin of the 8th Kansas Infantry remembered, "On the whole, the army rejoiced to learn that Rosecrans had been assigned to command. To those who served under him in Mississippi, his presence was peculiarly gratifying, and the enthusiasm with which they hailed his coming was unbounded."[3]

At the time he informed Rosecrans that he would replace Buell, Halleck also told him:

> The great objects to be kept in view in your operations in the field are: First, to drive the enemy from Kentucky and Middle Tennessee; second, to take and hold East Tennessee, cutting the line of railroad at Chattanooga, Cleveland, or Athens, so as to destroy the connection of the valley of Virginia with Georgia and the other Southern States. It is hoped that by prompt and rapid movements a considerable part of this may be accomplished before the roads become impassable from the winter rains....You will fully appreciate the importance of moving light and rapidly, and also the necessity of procuring as many of your supplies as possible in the country passed over. Where you cannot obtain enough by purchase of loyal men or requisitions upon the disloyal you will make forced requisitions upon the country, paying or receipting, as the case may be, for the supplies taken. The time has now come when we must apply the sterner rules of war, whenever such application becomes necessary, to enable us to support our armies and to move them rapidly upon the enemy. You will not hesitate to do this in all cases where the exigencies of the war require it.[4]

This ambitious plan came from someone who had taken twenty days to travel the twenty-five miles from Pittsburg Landing to Corinth.

Halleck underestimated the difficult terrain that lay between Kentucky and Chattanooga: mountains, hills, plateau, creeks and the Tennessee River. In addition there was the logistical problem of marching deep into enemy territory dependent on an increasingly exposed supply line.

And there was also the matter of the opposing army.

After Perryville, Bragg's army retreated to Knoxville. He had sent Breckinridge to Murfreesboro with 6,000 men to prepare "for the defense of Middle Tennessee or an attack on Nashville." In late November the rest of Bragg's army arrived in Murfreesboro.

The Army of Tennessee was created by the joining of the Army of Kentucky and Bragg's Army of Mississippi. Headed by Bragg, a strict martinet unpopular with his own staff and the rank and file, the army was divided into two corps.

Georgian William J. Hardee, former commandant of cadets at West Point and author of the standard text *Rifle and Light Infantry Tactics*, headed one of the corps. The other corps was led by West Point graduate turned Episcopal bishop Leonidas Polk. Bragg's army was particularly strong in cavalry, with Nathan Bedford Forrest, John H. Morgan and Joseph Wheeler having commands. Over the next eleven months these two generals and their armies would fight two of the bloodiest battles of the war, battles which to a great extent determined the outcome of the war.

Nashville had been in Union hands since February of 1862, when it was surrendered to Buell, a by-product of the Forts Henry and Donelson victories. On November 4, Rosecrans gave orders to advance to Nashville; on the 7th McCook arrived in the Tennessee capital, and on the 10th Rosecrans and his staff arrived. During the month of November Rosecrans went about building up his army.

When Chief of Staff Arthur Ducat became ill, Rosecrans requested Colonel Julius P. Garesche to come from Washington and replace him. Garesche was born in Cuba to an American diplomat of French ancestry and raised in Delaware. He enrolled in Georgetown College and there underwent a religious transformation. A downturn in his family's financial situation caused him to withdraw from Georgetown and apply to West Point where he graduated in 1841. While at the Academy he became friends with William Rosecrans.

Garesche's beliefs extended beyond good works to mysticism. He read daily from Thomas a Kempis' *Imitation of Christ*. He had premonitions of an early death, and his brother, a priest, told him that he would die in his first battle. Garesche, who served in the adjutant general's office, was nowhere near a battlefield until his old friend Rosecrans called him west to be his chief of staff.[5]

As November gave way to December, pressure of a different nature threatened Rosecrans—this threat came from Washington. Despite the repulse of the three Confederate attacks in the fall of 1862, the overall military situation for the North had deteriorated.

Republicans had suffered losses in the elections of 1862. On December 4, Halleck wrote Rosecrans,

> The president is very impatient at your long stay in Nashville.... Twice I have been asked to designate someone else to command your army. If you remain one more week at Nashville, I cannot prevent your removal. As I wrote you when you took the command, the Government demands action, and if you cannot respond to that demand someone else will be tried.

To this threat Rosecrans replied,

> Your dispatch received. I reply in few but earnest words. I have lost no time. Everything I have done was necessary, absolutely so; and has been done as rapidly as possible. Any attempt to advance sooner would have increased our difficulty both in front and rear. In front, because of greater obstacles, enemies in greater force, and fighting with better chances of escaping pursuit, if overthrown in battle. In rear, because of insufficiency and uncertainty of supplies, both of subsistence and ammunition, and no security of any kind to fall back upon in case of disaster.... Many of our soldiers are to this day barefoot, without blankets, without tents, without good arms, and cavalry without horses.... If the Government which ordered me here confides in my judgment, it may rely on my continuing to do what I have been trying to—that is, my whole duty. If my superiors have lost confidence in me, they had better at once put someone in my place and let the future test the propriety of the change. I have but one word to add, which is, that I need no other stimulus to make me do my duty than the knowledge of what it is. To threats of removal or the like I must be permitted to say that I am insensible.

The next day Halleck responded:

> Your telegram of last evening, in explanation of your delay at Nashville, is just received. My telegram was not a threat, but merely a statement of facts. The President is greatly dissatisfied with your delay, and has sent for me several times to account for it. He has repeated to me time and again that there were imperative reasons why the enemy should be driven across the Tennessee River at the earliest possible moment. He has never told me what those reasons were, but I imagine them to be diplomatic, and of the most serious character. *You can hardly conceive his great anxiety about it. I will tell you what I guess it is, although it is only a guess on my part. It has been feared that on the meeting of the British Parliament, in January next, the political pressure of the starving operatives may force the Government to join France in an intervention.* If the enemy be left in possession of Middle Tennessee, which we held last July, it will be said that they have gained on us. We have recovered all they gained on us in Kentucky, Virginia, Missouri, Arkansas, and Mississippi, and in North Carolina, South Carolina, Florida, Louisiana, and Texas we have gained on them. Tennessee is the only State which can be used as an argument in favor of intervention by England. You will thus perceive that your movements have an importance beyond mere military success. The whole Cabinet are anxious,

inquiring almost daily. "Why don't he move?" "Can't you make him move?" "There must be no delay." "Delay there will be more fatal to us than anywhere else." *You will thus perceive that there is a pressure for you to advance much greater than you can possibly have imagined. It may be, and perhaps is, the very turning-point in our foreign relations. It was hoped and believed when you took the command that you would recover all lost ground by, at furthest, the middle of December, so that it would be known in London soon after the meeting of Parliament.* It is not surprising that our Government should be impatient and dissatisfied under the circumstances of the case. A victory or the retreat of the enemy before the 10th of this month would have been of more value to us than ten times that success at a later date. [Emphasis added][6]

Halleck's reference to the British Parliament was probably in reaction to a speech made on October 7, 1862, by British cabinet member William Gladstone in which he said,

We may have our own opinions about slavery; we may be for or against the South; but there is no doubt that Jefferson Davis and other leaders of the South have made an army; they are making, it appears, a navy; and they have made,—what is more than either,—they have made a nation. We may anticipate with certainty the success of the Southern States, so far as their separation from the North is concerned.[7]

The Union's political and diplomatic worries were compounded with military woes when eight days after Halleck's letter Ambrose Burnside and the Army of the Potomac suffered a disastrous defeat with over 12,000 casualties at Fredericksburg on December 13. On the 20th, Grant's supply depot at Holly Springs, Mississippi, was destroyed in a raid by Van Dorn, causing Grant to halt his march to Vicksburg. On the 29th, Sherman was repulsed at Chickasaw Bayou. The first attempt to take Vicksburg would end in failure. This was the bleak situation that the North faced as the second year of the war drew to a close.

The Confederates also had problems. The three offensive strikes of the autumn of 1862 resulted in Southern retreats. Morale and dissension issues particularly affected the Army of Tennessee. After Perryville and his retreat to Knoxville Bragg was ordered to Richmond to confer with Confederate President Davis. Later, in December, Davis traveled to Tennessee to meet with Bragg and his army. Joseph Johnston had been appointed commander of the Department of the West, a position that would lead to conflict with both Davis and Bragg.

The Confederate victory at Fredericksburg brought a change in the mood of the South. At Murfreesboro where Bragg's army camped, the Christmas season was made even more festive by the marriage of cavalry general John H. Morgan, a thirty-six-year-old widower, and seventeen-year-old Murfreesboro belle Mattie Ready. The nuptials took place on December 14 and were performed by bishop turned general Leonidas Polk. A week later Morgan was off on the third of his four famous raids. Absent from the Yuletide wedding was Nathan Bedford Forrest, who was off with 2,500 men on his second raid. Morgan's and Forrest's departures combined with the earlier transfer of Carter Stevenson's 7,500-man division to reinforce Pemberton at Vicksburg presented Rosecrans and the Army of the Cumberland with an opportunity.

By late December the Louisville and Nashville railroad was reopened for Union use. Enough rations for a month's campaigning were ready. When word of the detachments from Bragg's army filtered into Rosecrans' camp, the Ohioan was ready to move and confront his enemy.

On December 26 the Army of the Cumberland marched southeast from Nashville. The three corps of the army each took a different route. McCook with three divisions advanced on the Nolensville pike to Triune. Thomas with two divisions marched to McCook's right along the Franklin and Wilson pikes. Thomas' division then turned left along the Old Liberty road to support McCook at Nolensville. Crittenden pushed south along the Murfreesboro pike to Lavergne. Rosecrans suspected that the major fighting would take place at Triune near Stewart's Creek fifteen miles west of Murfreesboro, but Hardee's division had pulled back toward Stones River.

The next day, slowed by fog, sleet and rain, McCook arrived at Triune only to discover that Hardee had retreated east. Crittenden reached Stewart's Creek where James Negley's division of Thomas' corps joined him. On Sunday, December 28, Rosecrans, as was his preference on Sundays, ordered a day of rest for his army. On Monday all parts of the army moved to converge at Murfreesboro. About 3 p.m. John Palmer sent word to Rosecrans that the enemy was running, and the commanding general in turn ordered Crittenden to send a division to occupy Murfreesboro. The enemy, however, was not retreating. Crittenden wrote headquarters,

> The order was given as you directed, the troops were advancing, but just at this point General Palmer and General Wood have ridden up and protest against it as very hazardous to move troops in the night, unacquainted with the ground, against troops in position. A good citizen, who is just now here, says if we were not opposed by the enemy, the crossing of Stone's River is so difficult we should have trouble in crossing. Under these circumstances, believing, if you were here, you would not order an advance, and as it will not get any darker, and I can communicate with you in an hour, I have concluded to suspend your order until I can again hear from you. If ordered to move, I will instantly execute it, but consider it impossible to take the artillery, and suggest that it should be left.

Crittenden ordered a one-hour suspension of the order; during that time Rosecrans arrived at the front and approved the decision to postpone the order, saying, "The order to occupy Murfreesborougho was based on information received from General Palmer that the enemy was running. You did right not to attempt its execution."[8]

It is important to note here that Rosecrans gave an order based on faulty information but was pleased when the order was not carried out. It is equally important to note that it was General Thomas Wood who successfully protested the order. A similar situation with different results would occur later at Chickamauga.

On the night of the 29th, Joseph Wheeler's cavalry set out on a ride and raid around Rosecrans' army that resulted in the capture of a thousand soldiers and the destruction of all or part of four wagon trains. The superiority of Confederate cavalry even without Forrest and Morgan was painfully demonstrated to the Northerners.

On the 30th, Rosecrans finalized the placement of his 44,000-man army. Crittenden's divisions of Palmer and Wood were on the left along Stones River. Negley's division of Thomas' wing held the center to Wilkinson Pike. McCook's wing with three divisions of Philip Sheridan, Jefferson C. Davis and Richard Johnson extended the right to the Franklin road. Lovell Rousseau's division was held in reserve.

Opposing the Army of the Cumberland were the 37,000 troops of the Army of Tennessee. Two divisions of Hardee's corps, those of John P. McCown and Patrick Cleburne, were placed on the Confederate left. Polk's corps of two divisions, Jones P. Withers and Benjamin Cheatham, anchored the Southern center. John C. Breckinridge's division of Hardee's Corps was on the right separated by Stones River from the rest of the army.

Rosecrans' plan was to have Crittenden, on the left, cross Stones River and attack Bragg's right. By coincidence Bragg's plan was nearly identical; he would have his left, led by Hardee, strike Rosecrans' right. Rosecrans used a ruse to make his right seem larger than it was. He had unattended campfires lit beyond his right flank. However, this trick may have had the unintended consequence of Bragg putting more troops into the attack against Rosecrans' right.

As night fell on that cold rainy penultimate night of 1862, the two armies, separated by a few hundred yards, struggled to sleep. The military bands of the two sides began to play: *Yankee Doodle, Dixie, Bonnie Blue Flag,* and *Hail Columbia.* Then a Yankee band struck up *Home Sweet Home.* A Southern soldier remembered, "Immediately a Confederate band caught up the strain, then one after another until all the bands of each army were playing Home Sweet Home. And after our bands had ceased playing, we could hear the sweet refrain as it died away on the cool frosty air on the Federal side." It would be the last refrain ever heard for many of those camped along Stones River.[9]

6. Stones River

In the pre-dawn hours of December 31, Rosecrans along with chief of staff Julius P. Garesche and a few officers heard Roman Catholic Mass in a small tent. Afterward Thomas Crittenden, whose corps was to begin the Union attack, joined Rosecrans, and they watched Horatio Van Cleve's division splash across the river to engage Breckinridge's troops. Wood's division was to follow. Rumblings from the right were heard and were assumed to be McCook demonstrating in front of the Confederate left. The two returned to headquarters where they heard more sounds and learned of activity on the right. A report came from McCook saying, "The right wing is heavily pressed and needs assistance." This understated in the extreme what was unfolding.

That morning shortly after six o'clock, 11,000 Confederates from John McCown's and Patrick Cleburne's divisions marching silently in double line then running and yelling swept down upon the Union right. Bragg had struck first and was reaping the benefits of surprise. The brigades of Edward Kirk and August Willich of Richard Johnson's division bore the brunt of the initial attack. Some of Kirk's troops were watering their horses and some of Willich's men were getting breakfast when the Rebels attacked. The Yankees quickly tried to repulse the attack but with little success. Within a few minutes both brigades were routed; Kirk was mortally wounded in the thigh, and Willich was captured and would spend four months in Libby Prison. In addition John Wharton's cavalry threatened the outnumbered Union cavalry under Lewis Zahn in the Union right rear.

The fighting blazed like a wildfire moving northwest along the Union line. Troops from John Loomis, Alfred Vaughan, George Maney and Arthur Manigault of Benjamin Cheatham's and Jones Withers' divisions engaged the brigades of William P. Carlin and William Woodruff of Davis' and Joshua Sill of Sheridan's divisions. Despite heroic efforts on their part, the Northern troops were eventually outflanked on the right and compelled to withdraw behind the Wilkinson Pike. Colonel George Roberts, on Sheridan's left, led a gallant charge to try and stop the Rebel onslaught, but his brigade was eventually forced to retreat. However this sacrifice had purchased precious time for the Union army. Two-thirds of the right had been forced to retreat. If the

Confederates could reach the Nashville Pike, three miles distant, they would cut the Army of the Cumberland from its base and retreat route. The battle had come to this: could Rosecrans somehow regroup and rebuild his line before Bragg's army reached the pike and railroad?

As Rosecrans realized the severity of the situation he made several decisions that would determine whether or not his army would survive. First he ordered Crittenden to recross the river leaving just one brigade, Samuel Price's, to guard against an attack from Breckinridge on the Rebel right. This was crucial because an attack on the Union left while Rosecrans was trying to rebuild the right would almost certainly be fatal. Rosecrans had the following exchange with Price:

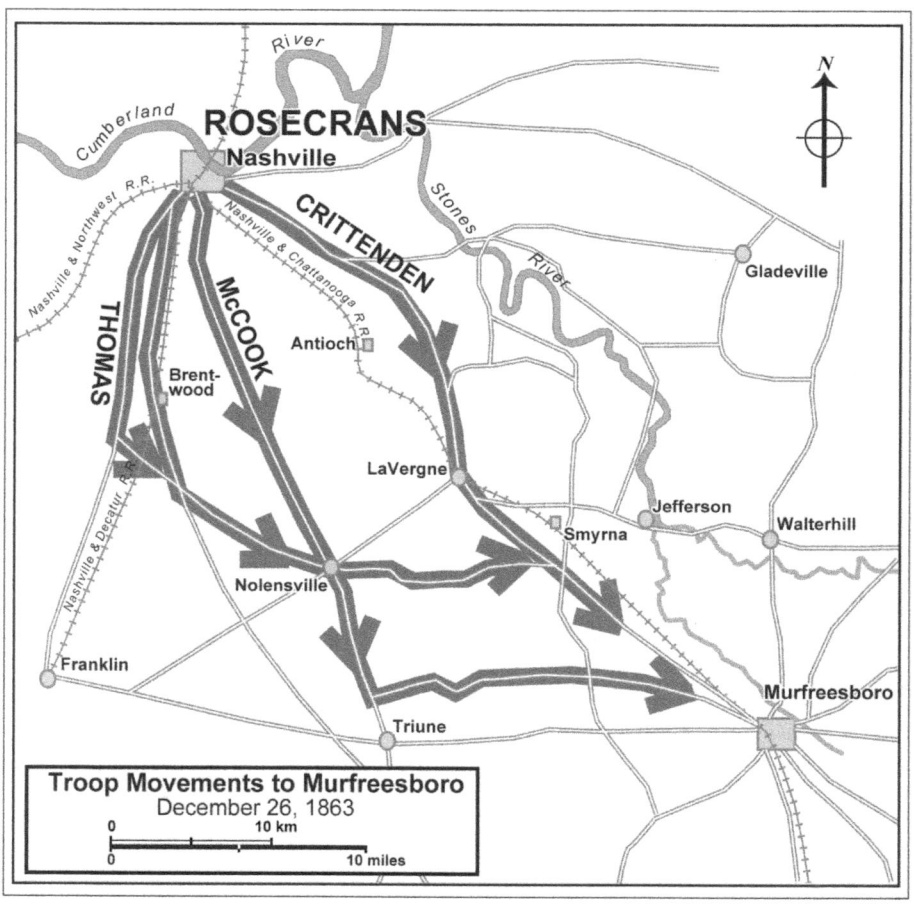

Movements from Nashville to Murfreesboro (NPS).

"Will you hold this ford?"
"I will try, sir."
"Will you hold this ford?"
"I will die right here."
"Will you hold this ford?"
"Yes, sir."
"That will do."[1]

After the war Price became an artist and painted a portrait of Rosecrans which is today in the collection of the National Portrait Gallery in Washington, D.C. Rosecrans ordered Thomas to send Rousseau, who had been held in reserve, into the cedar breaks to support Sheridan's right. He sent Sam Beatty's and James Fyffe's brigades of Van Cleve's division to the right of Rousseau. Charles Harker and Milo Hascall of Wood's division were ordered to form a new position farther down the turnpike to the right of Van Cleve. However, Hascall was unable to get into position because his path was clogged by retreating troops.

Along the turnpike itself Rosecrans personally placed several units and massed troops, particularly the Pioneer Brigade and the Chicago Board of Trade Battery. Now the question became, could the Union center buy enough time to enable the right to be rebuilt?

As well as things had gone for Bragg's army, things had not gone perfectly. McCown's and Cleburne's divisions became separated during their pursuit of the retreating Northerners. McCown's units drifted west rather than wheeling east as had been planned. This put Cleburne's division unexpectedly in the front lines of the attack. Units intermingled, and a lack of cohesion slowed the advance.

On the Confederate center right, where General Polk's division was attacking, a lack of coordination between the brigades of Cheatham, Loomis, Maney and Manigault allowed Sheridan enough time to offer stiff resistance. The Southern advance had been paid with a casualty rate of over 30 percent. Hardee sent a request to Bragg for reinforcements. The only available infantry troops were Breckinridge's on the right across Stones River. Bragg ordered two brigades to be sent to Hardee, but Breckinridge believed he was about to be attacked. Bragg countermanded the order and instead told Breckinridge to attack the Union troops supposedly at his front. As he did this Breckinridge discovered that there were no enemy troops east of the river. Van Cleve had been recalled earlier by Rosecrans and redeployed, but his crossing that morning fooled Breckinridge and kept him inactive for a crucial period. About 10 a.m. the center of the Union line had formed into an angle with the brigades of Oliver Shepherd, Benjamin Scribner and John Beatty of Rousseau's division on the right and Sill, Frederick Schaefer and Roberts of Sheridan's division connecting on the left with the divisions of Negley and Palmer. John Beatty

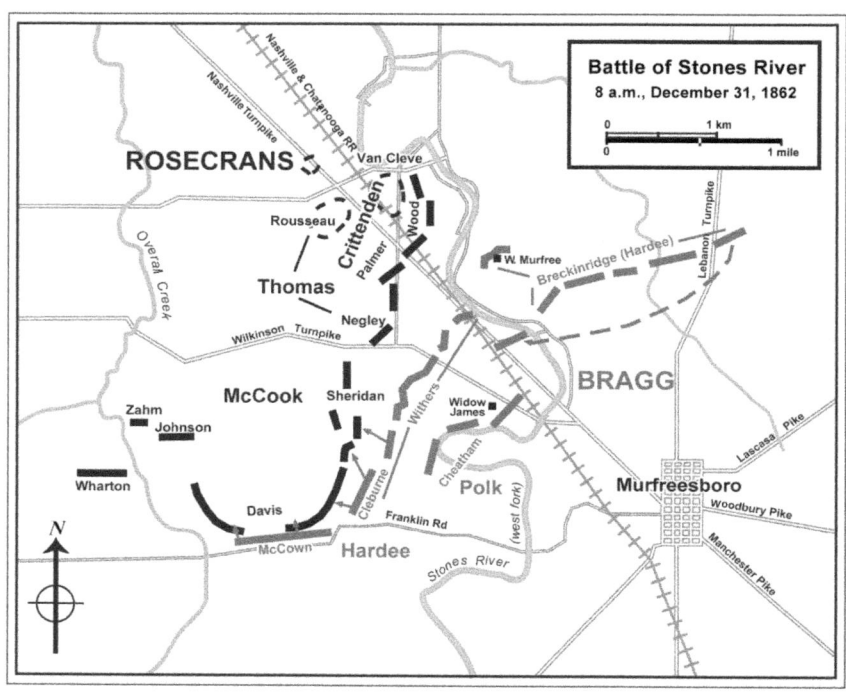

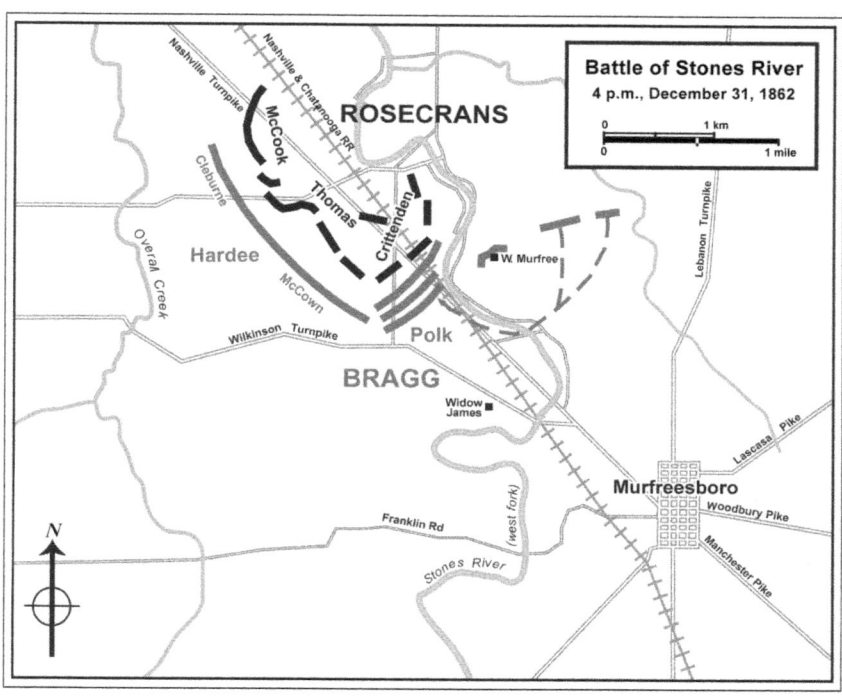

was ordered by Rousseau to hold his position "until hell freezes over." McCown's re-formed troops assaulted the right of this salient while the brigades of Stewart and Anderson did the same to Sheridan and Negley on the left. Eventually all this proved too much for the Northerners and they had to retreat back to the Nashville Pike. The flight of Sheridan, who had run out of ammunition, and Negley on his left and Shepherd on his right led John Beatty to conclude that "the contingency has arisen to which General Rousseau referred—that is to say, that hell has frozen over." Sheridan had lost three brigadier commanders—Sill, Roberts and Schaefer—but he had fought one of the great fighting retreats of the entire war.

As the Northern troops made their way back to the Nashville Pike, they re-formed into a new defensive line. The brigades of Harker, Fyffe and Sam Beatty anchored the right. To their rear the Pioneer Brigade and a massed artillery group defended the all-important Nashville Pike. Rosecrans had personally directed the rebuilding of the right. His personal presence infused the troops with confidence.

The withdrawal of Rousseau created an opportunity for the Confederates to attack and seize the Nashville Pike. Matthew Ector's Texans and James Raines' Arkansans charged through a cotton field to their objective, the pike. But Rosecrans had massed together a formidable defense, especially the Pioneer Brigade and Stoke's Chicago Board of Trade Battery. The commanding general had told Stokes that "if he could hold that place for one hour, we would save the day." As the Rebel attack stalled the Yankees counterattacked. The brigades of Sam Beatty and Fyffe pursued the Confederates for 300 yards supported by the massed artillery to their rear. This Southern assault had failed. However a new threat to the Yankee line appeared on the extreme right.[2]

A gap had opened on the Union right and Cleburne's troops intended to exploit it. Harker, on the extreme right, found himself separated from Fyffe on his left. If St. John Liddell's and Bushrod Johnson's brigades could get past Harker, the Nashville Pike and the Union rear would be in Confederate hands. Again Rosecrans sprang into action; he ordered the 21st and 51st Illinois regiments of Roberts' brigade, which had fought so valiantly earlier in the "slaughter pen," to confront the enemy. When the brigades were almost out of ammunition they were ordered to fix bayonets and charge. The Confederates were unable to understand how they were repulsed with so few shots being fired. Some attributed the repulse to simple exhaustion on the part of the Rebels. This action, occurring around 3 p.m., ended the major threat to the Union right, but the day's fighting was not over. Bragg still had Breckinridge's brigades to throw into the fray. He decided to use them against the salient at

Opposite: Battle of Stones River (Maps by Hal Jesperson, www.cwmaps.com).

the Union "center-left" in the Round Forest. The fighting there would give the area the name "Hell's Half Acre."

About 4 p.m. the brigades of Daniel Adams and John Jackson had crossed Stones River and were poised to strike at the Union position of William Hazen and George Wagner. The Union position was strong and backed by fifty cannon on a hill to the rear. The Confederates were repulsed with great loss. Bragg had two more brigades, Joseph Palmer's and Gideon Pillow's, to throw against the Yankees, but the result was the same.

Throughout the day Rosecrans and his entourage had raced from point to point giving orders, moving and placing troops and emboldening the soldiery with their presence.

Franklin Moyer of the 3rd Ohio Cavalry wrote home,

> Where the fight raged hardest, where the men fell fastest, there was Rosencranz, encouraging and directing. I tell a fact that I saw myself, when the Rebels were pressing our division the hardest Gen. Rosencranz rode along the front line, where the men were falling by scores—the men stopped firing and swung their hats cheering them as he passed along. ...I tell you Rosencranz is the man.

Sergeant Henry Briedenthal of the 3rd Ohio recalled that

> the opportune arrival of Gen. Rosecrans and part of his staff saved us from total rout....In his everlasting old black conical wool hat, which looked as if it, like us, could not withstand the outside pressure and had caved in; his old blue overcoat hanging somehow on his shoulders; his face all scratched up by the brushes; with a stump cigar about two inches long, unlighted, between his fingers, and himself generally as cool as a cucumber.

Hans Heg wrote in a letter a week after the battle,

> Rosecrans was himself on the field. I saw him while riding to and fro at furious rates, the sweat pouring down his face, and his clothes spattered over with blood, and I could not help expressing my gratitude to Providence for having at last given us a man that was equal to the occasion. A general in fact as well as in name.

Surgeon Eban Swift in his official report wrote,

> About 9 o'clock the commanding general, with his staff, dashed boldly forward to the front of the left wing, and in person directed the movements of troops and placed batteries in position. His daring presence so near the enemy's line brought down upon him an angry and spiteful fire of musketry, round shot and shell, almost at point-blank range. But utterly disregarding this metallic storm, our brave commander moved calmly on from left to right, cheering and inspiring our faltering troops. And throughout the day wherever the tide of battle most fiercely raged, General Rosecrans bore his charmed life and ubiquitous presence.

But one of his entourage was not so charmed. A shell struck Garesche in the face, leaving only his lower jaw. The headless body stayed on its horse for twenty paces until it at last fell off. The premonition had come true: Julius P. Garesche was killed in his first battle.

General John Palmer remembered:

> General Rosecrans exhibited the greatest personal bravery. Colonel Garesche was killed by a cannon shot at his side, and his blood and brains were scattered over Rosecrans. He never blanched, and kept his position. I made up my mind then, that if I was about to fight a battle for the dominion of the universe, I would give Rosecrans the command of as many men as he could see and who could see him.[3]

As night approached the guns fell silent and the fighting ceased. The Army of the Cumberland had suffered 7,000 casualties. Twenty-eight pieces of artillery were lost to the Rebels. A meeting was held at headquarters; the preeminent question: should the Army retreat to Nashville?

There are several versions of what was said at the meeting. Rosecrans' own account says that after polling his commanders on the question, "Shall we fight it out here, or withdraw to an advantageous position covering our depots at Nashville?" he went for a ride with General Stanley "to inspect the ground in our immediate rear over which our first movements in retreat would have to be made." After two hours Rosecrans returned and said, "Well, gentleman, we shall not retreat, but fight it out here and to the front."

John Fitch wrote in 1864 that General Rosecrans said, "Gentlemen, we have come to fight and win this battle, and we shall do it. Our supplies may run short, but we will have our trains out again tomorrow. We will keep right on, and eat corn for a week, but we will win this battle. We can and will do it."

In the mid–1880s John Yaryan recalled,

> Rosecrans slowly turned toward his commanders with the air of having come to the cross roads, not certain which one to take, and said, beginning with the left of the row: "General McCook, have you any suggestions for to-morrow?" "No, only I would like for Bragg to pay me for my two horses lost to-day." So from man to man he went round the room, the answer of each, in substance, the same as the first. Thomas was held for the last. I watched him closely to see if I could discover any proposition to be stated, already showing in his face, but he never changed a muscle; his eye never left the bed of red coals that were now aglow on the old hearth; he did not appear to hear any of the replies; the same set, determined look I saw when I came in, was there. Rosecrans hesitated a little when he came to him, slight as it was it was understood, and said: "General Thomas, what have you to say?" Without a word of reply he slowly rose to his feet, buttoned his great coat from bottom to top, faced his comrades and stood there a statue of courage chiseled out of the black marble of midnight, by the firelight, and said: "Gentlemen, I know of no better place to die than right here," and walked out of the room into the dripping night. The council was over. No one else moved for a moment, when Rosecrans, quick as a flash, and with the dash that was a part of him, said: "If you

are not attacked by 6 o'clock this morning, you will open the fight promptly, posted as you are and move on to Murfreesboro. Clear the field yet tonight of all wounded and see to it that your ammunition is well up; we will whip this fight to-morrow." And we did.

Also in the 1880s, Crittenden recalled that

after the fight on the night of the 31st a number of general officers were assembled by Rosecrans's order, including McCook, Thomas, Stanley, and myself. There was some talk of falling back. I do not remember who started the subject, but I do remember that I expressed the opinion that my men would be very discouraged to have to abandon the field after their good fight of the day, during which they had uniformly held their position.... Rosecrans called McCook to accompany him on a ride, directing us to remain until their return. McCook has since told me that the purpose of this ride was to find a position beyond Overall's Creek to which the array might retire. Upon approaching the creek Rosecrans, perceiving mounted men moving up and down with torches, said to McCook: "They have got entirely in our rear and are forming a line of battle by torchlight." They returned then to where we were, and Rosecrans told us to go to our commands and prepare to fight or die.

In 1907 Colonel Gilbert Kniffen said,

Headquarters were located in a double log house, which then stood on the east side of the turnpike about opposite the lower ford of Stones River. In a room on the left hand, General Thomas sat before a fire, asleep; the officers of his staff, stretched upon the floor, with their feet to the fire, were also asleep. Ready at a moment's warning to obey any order that might be given him, the old soldier was snatching a brief respite from care, in the friendly arms of Morpheus. To a question of General Rosecrans, earlier in the evening, he had made the characteristic reply: "The question of retiring from the battle-field is one of such delicacy that I am quite willing to leave it to the judgment of the commanding general." On the right of the passageway a far different scene was presented. General Crittenden paced the floor with quick, impatient stride. "Communication is cut off," said one. "We must fall back," said another, and the words were deliberately uttered by a brave man. "My corps is not whipped," shouted Crittenden, "and we must not fall back." At this moment General Rosecrans entered the room and caught the expression as it fell from the lips of his heroic commander. "Gentlemen, we fight or die right here," said the chief as he passed them and took a seat by the fire.[4]

There may be questions about what was said on that New Year's Eve night, but there is no doubt about what was decided. The Army of the Cumberland did not retreat.

As for the Confederates, Bragg telegraphed President Davis, "God has granted us a Happy New Year." Confident Rosecrans would pull back, he made little adjustments in his position and went to sleep. Rosecrans did not sleep. He pulled in his troops from the Round Forest, making his defensive position even tighter. Most importantly at 3 a.m. he sent Sam Beatty, in command for the wounded Van Cleve, to cross Stones River and hold a hill overlooking McFadden's Ford. Two brigades of reinforcements arrived from Nashville.

In Washington, Abraham Lincoln was having the reoccurring dream which he associated with portentous events during the war. He had more on his mind than usual because the next day he would sign the Emancipation Proclamation.[5]

January 1, 1863, was a cold, rainy and sleety day. Polk's corps moved into the now abandoned Round Forest so hotly fought for the day before. Despite expectations on both sides of a return to fighting, the only hostility was from sporadic artillery fire.

The second day of the New Year also started cold and with little activity. However when Bragg realized that Rosecrans' left was now in command of the heights east of the river and threatened his right, he decided to attack and dislodge the Yankees from their position. He summoned Breckinridge and ordered him to attack the Union left at 4 p.m. so that the soon-to-arrive darkness would impede any Union plans to counterattack. Breckinridge, who was better informed than Bragg about the strength of the Union position, objected vehemently to the attack. Bragg's plan called for 4,500 troops from the brigades of Roger Hanson, William Preston and Pillow to march and attack the Yankee brigades of William Grose, Fyffe and Price.

Breckinridge was dismayed at the order and is said to have told General Preston, "This attack is made against my judgment and by the special orders of General Bragg. Of course we all must try to do our duty and fight the best we can. But if it should result in disaster and I be among the slain, I want you to do justice to my memory and tell the people that I believed this attack to be very unwise and tried to prevent it." Nonetheless, being a good soldier he gave orders to attack.[6]

The Rebels marched in double-quick time toward their opponents 1,000 yards distant. Enjoying a two-to-one numerical advantage, the hard-charging Southerners were surprisingly successful in driving the Yankees from their position. But the success was short-lived. Rosecrans and his staff had not been passive while the Confederates plotted their attack. Reinforcements had been sent to the left, and, critically important, Major John Mendenhall, Crittenden's artillery chief, began to mass guns, eventually totaling fifty-eight, on a hill overlooking the area of conflict. As the Rebels pursued the retreating Federals they came into sight of Medenhall's guns. As one author put it, it was "as if the Rebs had opened the door of hell, and the devil himself was there to greet them." L.D. Young wrote, "The great jaws of the trap on the bluff from the opposite side of the river were sprung and bursting shells that completely drowned the voice of man were plunging and tearing through our columns."[7]

The Rebels began to fall back. General Hanson was killed. Union Colonel John F. Miller ordered his brigade to pursue the Rebels. By 5 p.m. the Rebel assault had become a rout. One account recounted,

> "Here," says an officer, "we were joined by Gen. Breckinridge, who had come around from the right front, where he had gone to direct in person some movement near the old mill on that flank. I never, at any time, saw him more visibly moved. He was raging like a wounded lion, as he passed the different commands from right to left; but tears broke from his eyes when he beheld the little remnant of his own old brigade—his personal friends and fellow-countrymen; and a sorrowful exclamation escaped his lips, to find, as he said, his 'poor Orphan Brigade torn to pieces.'"[8]

More Union reinforcements arrived that day from Nashville. Rosecrans used a ruse to make Bragg think an attack would be made on his right. Soldiers were moved to the Union east flank to shout and make noises, light fires and simulate a massing of troops. Bragg held a war council at 10 p.m. to determine future moves. After midnight Bragg was awakened with reports that Rosecrans was threatening the Confederate right. Rosecrans' deception had paid off.

The rains of the last three days had caused Stones River to rise, threatening to separate Bragg's scattered divisions. Still Bragg was determined to "maintain our position at every hazard." His subordinates were less optimistic about their prospects. The next morning, after meeting with Hardee and Polk, it was agreed retreat was the best option. The Army of Tennessee headed southeast from Murfreesboro to Tullahoma. The battle of Stones River was over. With nearly 25,000 casualties, about the same if not more than the more famous Shiloh, it is one of the ten biggest battles of the war. Although not as well known as other battles, the consequences were great, especially in light of what could have happened had the Confederates driven the Army of the Cumberland from the field. One historian of the Battle summed them up:

> Confederate victory,—at one time so near,—would have been followed by the weightiest and most far-reaching consequences. Had Bragg been able to drive his infantry across the Nashville pike on the last day of 1862, or had he been able to crush the Union left on the second of January, 1863, the capture or destruction,—whole or partial,—of his enemy would have been one of the least of these consequences. For the way to the Ohio would then have been open, and Cincinnati and other opulent Northern cities would have been at the mercy of Confederate arms. Vicksburg would not have been an historic name, for over-whelming forces could have been turned against Grant to crush him, or drive him from Mississippi. Tennessee,—second State in population below Mason and Dixon's line, and first in such food as armies consume, would have been held to furnish the vital recruits and supplies to the Confederacy. East Tennessee,—would have waited in vain for the relieving Northern forces. Kentucky and Missouri might have been wrested from Union control, and Arkansas freed from the presence of the invader. Finally,

Europe's recognition, with the manifold complexities for the North that must have ensued therefrom, could have been no longer logically denied to the Richmond government.

Confederate Albert Marks, who lost a leg at Stones River and later became governor of Tennessee, believed,

> Events had made Murfreesboro the hinge upon which the fortunes of the Confederacy must turn. That battle won by the Confederates, the paper blockade would be torn to tatters and the independence of the Confederacy assured.... On that field the genius of Rosecrans turned the paper blockade into one of adamant....On that field his genius destroyed the Confederacy and reestablished the Union.[9]

Rosecrans, who was described as "one of the few men in the war who enters upon all his duties with a deeply devout religious feeling, and looks to God as the disposer of the victory," closed his official report with the following Latin prayer:

> Non nobis, non nobis Domine, Sed nomini tuo da gloriam.
> Not to us, not to us O Lord, But to thy name give glory.[10]

7. Creating a New Army

On Monday, January 5, Rosecrans' army entered Murfreesboro. The commanding general, recuperating from "lung fever," made his headquarters in the Keeble home. The news of the outcome at Stones River, coming soon after the Union disaster at Fredericksburg and Sherman's repulse at Chickasaw Bayou, electrified the North. Abraham Lincoln telegraphed Rosecrans, "God bless you and all with you. Please tender to all, and accept for yourself, the nation's gratitude for your and their skill, endurance, and dauntless courage." Secretary of War Stanton wrote, "The country is filled with admiration of the gallantry and heroic achievement of yourself and the officers and troops under your command." Halleck continued the praise: "The victory was well earned and one of the most brilliant of the war. You and your brave men have won the gratitude and the admiration of the world. The field of Murfreesborough is made historical, and future generations will point out the places where so many heroes fell, gloriously, in defense of the Constitution and the Union."[1]

In Washington, a city gloomy from weeks of bad news, reporter Noah Brooks noted that "in January the effect of good news from the front was clearly discernible on the faces of returning legislators." It was easy to see that they were far more cheerful than when they adjourned for the holiday recess. Senator Joseph Wright of Indiana gave a forceful speech in the Senate. Brooks wrote that the senator

> said he was glad to know that there was at least one general who was not fighting for the Presidency; and had been heard of at the head, not the rear, of his army, and had had two of his staff shot down by his very side. This was an allusion to Rosecrans, who was then the favorite of the hour, and the applause that followed was so deafening and indecorous that Senator Powell, of Kentucky, white with wrath and shaking his fist at the galleries, demanded that those seats be cleared.[2]

Congress passed a formal resolution of thanks as did the legislatures of Indiana and Ohio.

Stones River remained an important event for Abraham Lincoln. In August of 1863, eight months after the battle, he wrote, "It is hard to say that anything has been more bravely and well done, than at Antietam, Murfreesboro, Gettysburg, and on many fields of lesser note." And to Rosecrans himself

Lincoln wrote, "I can never forget, whilst I remember anything, that about the end of last year, and beginning of this, you gave us a hard earned victory which, had there been a defeat instead, the nation could scarcely have lived over."[3]

Despite this positive turn, Rosecrans and his army still faced major obstacles. The Army of the Cumberland was deep in hostile territory over 200 miles from its main supply base in Louisville. In order to advance, his army would necessarily have to stretch its line. This would require more troops to protect the line and give the enemy more opportunities to attack it.

The winter rainy season began shortly after Murfreesboro was occupied, making the roads nearly impassable. The railroad, normally the surest route, was particularly vulnerable and subject to Confederate attacks. Bragg's cavalry, which included such stellar names as Forrest, Wheeler and Morgan, greatly outnumbered Rosecrans' cavalry.

Bragg on the other hand had an advantage in being but sixty miles from his base at Chattanooga in friendly territory and protected by mountains and rivers. Bragg's Army of Tennessee had, as the Confederate central army, the possibility of being reinforced from either Lee in the east or Johnston in the west. Eventually he would get troops from both sources.

A widespread belief is that Rosecrans did nothing for six months after Stones River. In fact he made decisions and took actions that bolstered his army and prepared it for the campaigns that would follow. A look at these actions will dispel the notion that the Army of the Cumberland "sat idle" after Stones River.

One of the first things Rosecrans did was to ask Washington to designate the wings of the Army of the Cumberland as corps as was the case in the Army of the Potomac. Thomas,' McCook's and Crittenden's wings became the XIV, XX, and XXI corps. Rosecrans enlarged his staff and created several innovative and unique positions, among them a mustering and disbursing officer, a staff commissary separate from the chief quartermaster to feed the army, an inspector general separate from the senior aide de camp, and a chief paymaster. Separate chief signal officer, telegraph officer and railroad superintendent departments were also created.

Rosecrans issued an order: "To establish a method of pointing out to this army and the nation those officers and soldiers of this command who shall distinguish themselves by bravery in battle, by courage, enterprise, and soldierly conduct, and also to promote the efficiency of the service, it is ordered that in every company in this army—infantry, artillery, and cavalry included—there shall be kept a roll of honor." This roll of honor idea was rejected by the War Department.

Particular attention was paid to engineering. Rosecrans had two distinct engineering staff departments: the chief engineer and topographical engineer.

Prior to the battle of Stones River he had created a Pioneer Brigade whose mission was to go before the army and clear a path for its advance. This was in addition to the Michigan Engineers and Mechanics.

He expanded the use of blacks to work on engineering projects, and he pressed that they be paid as employees of the engineering department. This view was expressed in a message to Washington: "The general commanding this department has expressed his wish that the negroes employed upon the fortifications at Nashville be paid wages, and so enabled to support their families. Their case being at present a very hard one." Rosecrans added the following endorsement: "The necessity for paying them is, that from want, say, nine-tenths have deserted, and I think justly." Rosecrans issued orders to hire and pay blacks as cooks, teamsters, nurses, hospital attendants, and laborers.

The Topographical Department created the most detailed, up-to-date and accurate maps of any army in the war, utilizing cameras, draftsmen, and lithographic presses. William C. Margadent, an officer in the Topographical Department, in a post-war letter to Rosecrans wrote,

> The Topographical Department of the Army of the Cumberland was the best organized and best equipped and most effective Topographical Department in the field. Considering the circumstances, time and urgent want of such a department, it may be safely said that it was a perfect one. We had representative engineer and surveyors with brigades, divisions and army corps and even with regiments and outposts. No scouting or reconnoitering party went out without its engineer; additions and corrections to our information maps had to be sent daily to our office at headquarters; We corrected, enlarged and combined our maps in accordance with such reports, and such information as we procured ourselves at the headquarters, through information of prisoners, scouts and our own personal reconnoitering. The revised information maps were then printed at night or in a special printing wagon, in the time of the march, and distributed by special messengers or through the usual channels of the army. Engineers and commanders of troops were thus constantly kept advised and ordered to make additions or corrections at once and report the same to headquarters. We often employed as high as thirty draftsmen; we had a large and full equipment of photographic apparatuses, among them solar cameras to enlarge views of Rebel fortifications. We had two lithographic presses, and no doubt, you remember well our black field maps, printing and multiplying quickly the maps on the wagon in time of the march. We furnished every commander with the black maps and a bottle of potassium, which should be used same as ink, producing white lines. (You remember General, that this process was an invention of my own and that the so called "blueprint" of drawings and maps now so largely used, has sprung from them.)
>
> You well remember the maps which we printed on the reversed side of neckties and handkerchiefs, yes, even on the reversed side of shirt-bossoms [sic] and sleeves, for the use of scouts and spies.

Most certainly, there was no department more serviceable and which had done more service than the Topographical Engineer Department of the Army of the Cumberland. The organization of a Topographical Dept. was not specified in the Army regulations. It was a creation of our own, brought to life by your orders and directions, and inspired by your personal influence. I said above, that there was no material change in the department when you left; we kept onward following the spirit of the founder.

Always interested in health and sanitation issues, Rosecrans fostered the development of hospital trains and railroad cars for the wounded which in the view of one historian "was the beginning of our modern approach to triage and evacuation of the wounded. The concept came to its realization under the military leadership of Generals William Rosecrans and George Thomas through the medical directors of the Army of the Cumberland." Another historian has noted that "Rosecrans was greatly interested in the health, welfare and medical needs of his soldiers. This pro-medical attitude ranged from his intolerance for poor sanitation to his insistence on evaluating each of the Army's physicians for medical competency. Empirical evidence of Rosecrans' attitude may be found in the disease rates for the Army. The rate of disease per 1000 soldiers in 1863 under Rosecrans fell 9.8 percent from the rate reported in 1862 under Major General Buell."[4]

To combat the vices of war Rosecrans had a chief of police William Truesdale.

The difficult terrain that Rosecrans' army needed to traverse fostered the development of a new type of light, easily portable and sturdy pontoon bridge: the "Cumberland pontoon."

Rosecrans authorized the creation of a brigade of "mounted infantry," infantry on horseback who would be more mobile than regular infantry but more of a fighting force than cavalry.

The supply lifeline of the Cumberland Army was the railroad from Louisville to Nashville and southeast toward Chattanooga. To protect the line, blockhouses were built along the line to defend it from Confederate attacks.

Fortress Rosecrans, the largest enclosed earthen fort built in the war, encompassing 200 acres, was constructed by 7,000 men working twenty-four hours a day seven days a week. It provided space for rifle pits and artillery. Additionally there were four steam-powered sawmills to supply wood for warehouses and blockhouses. The fortress was designed and stocked to provide refuge for 50,000 troops for up to ninety days.

The leading student of the engineering innovations of the Army of the Cumberland under Rosecrans concluded,

> The value of Rosecrans's engineer reforms should not be measured solely by their contributions to the campaign of 1863 but also by their impact on subsequent

operations. The institutions created by Rosecrans remained in place long after his departure from the army, and they achieved their full potential the following year.... The Army of the Cumberland boasted the most efficient engineer and topographical engineer departments of any among ...Sherman's three field armies—indeed, of any Federal army—and they rendered crucial service to Sherman during the campaign that captured Atlanta in 1864.

Additionally Rosecrans bombarded Washington with requests for horses, shoes, rifles, gunboats for the rivers and other materiel of war. Eventually he was told, "Everything has been done and is now being done for you that is possible.... Your complaints are without reason. You cannot expect to have all the best arms."[5]

Rosecrans and Military Governor Andrew Johnson came into conflict over the role of the military versus civilian authority in Middle Tennessee. The general's concerns were expressed in a letter to Halleck:

> No one appreciates the sacrifice and the delicate and trying position of Governor Johnson more than I do. I have done, and will do, all in my power to give him aid and comfort; but Nashville is an inclosed garrison, and my grand depot. It is full of traitors and spies, and to it go all the rascals and speculators that follow an army. I am, therefore, obliged to have it commanded by an able and experienced officer, and to exercise a most rigid military policy.

An interesting incident occurred when Johnson's son Robert had been reported drinking to excess. Rosecrans wrote to the young man's father, "Robert has been drinking so as to become a subject of remark everywhere. I sent for him told him I wanted him to stop and he promised me he would. If he keeps his word I will do all I can for him, but he is Junior to several other Colonels. It depends upon himself for he can distinguish himself if he will." The governor thanked the general for "the gentle admonition you gave my son and the kind manner in which it was done." As Rosecrans drove deeper into Tennessee the conflict over spheres of authority faded in importance.[6]

William Starke Rosecrans was a man of strong convictions. He also at times had a sharp tongue and wasn't reluctant to use it to verbally redress those he felt had fallen short of his expectations. A striking example of this involved Colonel John Beatty, one of two brigade commanders in the Army of the Cumberland with that surname. When an order to move his brigade arrived late at night, Beatty disregarded it feeling it, had been sent to him in error. The next day he remembered

> that General Rosecrans shook hands with me cordially, and seemed pleased to see me; but I had no sooner announced my business, and informed him that the order had been delivered to me not ten minutes before, than he flew into a violent passion, and asked if a battery and regiment had not reported to me the night before. I replied yes, and was proceeding to give my reasons for supposing that the officers

reporting them were in error, when he shouted: "Why, in hell and damnation, did you not mount your horse and come to head-quarters to inquire what it meant?" I undertook again to tell him ... but he would not listen to me. His face was inflamed with anger, his rage uncontrollable, his language most ungentlemanly, abusive, and insulting. ...For an instant I was tempted to strike him; but my better sense checked me. I turned on my heel and left the room. Death would have had few terrors for me just then. I had never felt such bitter mortification before, and it seemed to me that I was utterly and irreparably disgraced.

Beatty carried this "millstone on my heart" for several days before sending Rosecrans a letter in which he said, "I demand from you an apology for the insulting language addressed to me." A response arrived shortly and Rosecrans requested a meeting which Beatty described:

> I obeyed the order to report promptly. He took me into his private office, where we talked over the whole affair together. He expressed regret that he had not known all the circumstances before, and said, in conclusion: "I am your friend. Some men I like to scold, for I don't like them; but I have always entertained he best of feeling for you." Taking me, at the close of our interview, from his private office into the public room, where General Garfield and others were, he turned and asked if it was all right—if I was satisfied. I expressed my thanks, shook hands with him, and left, feeling a thousand times more attached to him, and more respect for him than I had ever felt before. He had the power to crush me, for at this time he is almost omnipotent in this department, and by a simple word he might have driven me from the army, disgraced in the estimation of both soldiers and citizens. His magnanimity and kindness, however, lifted a great load from my spirits, and made me feel like a new man; and I am very sure that he felt better and happier also, for no man does a generous act to one below him in rank or station, without being recompensed therefore by a feeling of the liveliest satisfaction. I may have been too sensitive, and may not, probably did not, realize fully the necessity for prompt action, and the weight of responsibility which rested upon the General.[7]

On January 25, 1863, James A. Garfield, a man who would play a pivotal role in the Rosecrans story, arrived at headquarters. Garfield, best remembered today as the second president to be assassinated, had been an educator, college president, lay preacher in the Disciples of Christ Church, lawyer, Ohio state senator and soldier. Commissioned as a lieutenant colonel in 1861 and rising to brigadier general in January 1862, he led troops at Middle Creek and Pound Gap in eastern Kentucky. He was with Buell's army at Shiloh but arrived too late to take part in the main action.

Garfield came down with camp fever (severe dysentery) and convalesced for two months at his home in Hiram, Ohio. Called to Washington after a two-month convalescence, he became friends with Salmon Chase and served on the Fitz-John Porter court-martial trial.

Garfield had been nominated and in November was elected to the U.S.

House of Representatives for a seat from Ohio. However the Congress to which he was elected would not meet until December 1863. Garfield desired to return to the war front in the interim. In January he was ordered to report to the newly reorganized Army of the Cumberland. His first impression of Rosecrans is revealed in a letter to his wife:

> I am however greatly pleased with some features of Gen. Rosecrans' character. He has that fine quality of having his mind made up on all the great questions which concern his work....Gen. R. thinks rapidly and strikes forward into action with the utmost confidence in his own judgment. In this he is perfectly unlike McClellan, who rarely has a clear-cut decisive opinion, and dare not trust it when he has. The officers whom I have met since I came here seem to have the most unbound confidence in Rosy, and are enthusiastic in his praise.

Perhaps attracted by Garfield's background in philosophy and religion, Rosecrans took an instant liking to the new arrival. He engaged Garfield in conversation "till his darkey came and took him by the shoulder and led him away to bed." Later Rosecrans insisted Garfield sleep in his room while they discussed religion, sometimes until three in the morning. He offered Garfield the possibility of command of a division, something he much desired. He also offered him the position of chief of staff, Julius Garesche's old role. Garfield agonized over what to do; he preferred a combat position but accepted the staff position hoping perhaps he would have the chance to influence strategy. Garfield, who was at heart a politician, confided to a friend, "By taking that position I should make a large investment in Gen. Rosecrans, and will it be wise to risk so much stock in that market?"[8]

Rosecrans' ardent and intellectual Catholicism produced different reactions in those who experienced it. Most of the soldiery saw it as

General James A. Garfield. He said he "loved every bone in Rosecrans' body" yet their friendship ended under suspicions of disloyalty.

7. Creating a New Army

a general Christian religiosity and saw no denominational distinctions. Some, like newspaperman Albert D. Richardson, found that Rosecrans "believes in some of the most staggering claims of his Church; sends requests to have certain sisters pray for him; thinks Gareschi (his old chief of staff) helped to buy the Stone River victory by a religious sacrifice of himself, *per contract* with the Almighty, etc. Of course I learn these things from men about Rosecrans not from himself, but fanatic or no fanatic, it is wonderful how enthusiastically everybody believes in him.... And he impresses me as a pure, earnest, strong man."

A starkly different perception came from Milo Hascall:

> My recollections of him were not such as to inspire me with confidence in him as the proper person to be placed in command of an army. At that time he seemed to be a great enthusiast in regard to the Catholic Church; seemed to want to think of nothing else, talk of nothing else, and in fact do nothing else, except to proselyte for it and attend upon its ministrations. No night was ever so dark and tempestuous, that he would not brave the boisterous seas of Newport Harbor to attend mass, and no occasion, however inappropriate, was ever lost sight of to advocate its cause; in fact, he was what would nowadays be called most emphatically a crank on that subject, and might not inappropriately be considered a one-ideaed man lacking in the breadth and poise, so necessary to success in the commander of an army in the field.
>
> Having by this time surrounded himself, in addition to the usual staff and appliances ordinarily to be found at the headquarters of an army in the field, with a numerous coterie of newspaper correspondents, and Catholic priests, who seemed in his estimation to be vastly more important than anyone else about him, and laid in a good supply of crucifixes, holy water, *spiritus frumenti*, Chinese gongs, flambeaux, jobbing presses, printers' devils, javelins, white elephants, and other cabalistic emblems and evidences that a holy crusade was about to be entered upon.... As this magnificent and resplendent cavalcade of Holy, Oriental, and gorgeous splendor moved about from camp to camp during the weeks that we lay at Nashville making these gigantic and awe-inspiring preparations for the advance, every knee was bowed, and every tongue confessed, that Allah was great, and thrice illustriously great was this Savior that had been sent to us.

Newspaperman William Bickham wrote

> The temper of conversation, of course, depended altogether upon the direction given it in the beginning. If religious, it was apt to absorb the hours until they run almost into daylight. The Chief took the argument and carried it, often into the realms of Mother Church, where the vehemence of his intellect and his zealous temper developed themselves thoroughly. He had the Fathers of the Church at his tongue's end, and exhibited a familiarity with controversial theology that made him a formidable antagonist to the best read, even of the clerical profession. He would admit no fallibility whatever in any department of his own church, but he did not permit his strong reliance in the Church of Rome to warp his judgment

in material things, especially in military matters. It has been recklessly said that he required the attendance of the Roman Catholics of his staff, escort, and attendants, at mass every Wednesday and Sunday. It is a gross calumny. He never interferes with the spiritual affairs of any subordinate, regarding those as sacred personal matters, to be governed by the convictions of each individual. Moreover, General Stanley and Garesche' were the only Romanists on his staff.

Colonel John S. McCalmont, a classmate at West Point, remembered,

In [later] life I learned that he was of the Roman Catholic persuasion, and that his brother was a bishop in that church, but though I frequently conversed with him at Washington, on the most friendly terms, I do not recollect that he ever mentioned the sect to which he belonged. He was, I have no doubt, a very sincere and faithful communicant of that church. He did no discredit to it. His walk and conversation were consistent with his profession. He was a courteous Christian gentleman. I allude to this because Rosecrans' religious, as well as political, opinions were used, exaggeratedly, by his enemies to his disadvantage. That they did not succeed in crushing him, or in materially lowering him in the estimation of his army, or the country, is the best proof of his eminent merits.

Perhaps Garfield, a veteran of many a late-night discussion, had the best insight into Rosecrans' deep religious convictions and how it affected people. He called Rosecrans "the intensest religionist I ever saw." However, after listening to his theological reasonings and observing his piety, Garfield in a letter to his mother wrote, "I have no doubt the Catholics have been greatly slandered."[9]

As Spring arrived and the Army of the Cumberland remained in camp, Garfield began to grow impatient and urged the army to move forward. The government in Washington wanted a victory. Of the three major armies only the Army of the Cumberland had made progress since the first of the year. As a possible goad for a victory, Halleck sent the following to his generals:

"There is a vacant major generalcy in the Regular Army and I am authorized to say that it will be given to the general in the field who first wins an important and decisive victory."

Rosecrans, never one to mask his feelings, replied,

As an officer and a citizen I feel degraded to see such an auctioneering of honor. Have we a general who would fight for his own personal benefit, when he would not for honor and the country? He would come by his commission basely in that case, and deserve to be despised by men of honor. But are all the brave and honorable generals on an equality as to chances? If not, it is unjust to those who probably deserve most.[10]

There were several reasons why Halleck and the administration wanted a decisive victory, not the least of which were political reasons. In the spring of 1863 it became obvious that victory would not be soon coming, and many in the North were doubtful that Lincoln was the man who could lead the Union to victory. Among those doubters was Horace Greeley, perhaps the most influential newspaper editor of the day. Greeley had harbored doubts about Lincoln's leadership capabilities since Bull Run when he sent Lincoln a secret letter telling him that he was "not a great man" and advising Lincoln to consider resigning. Subsequent battles had done little to change Greeley's mind. He began to search for a new candidate for 1864; one of those he considered was William S. Rosecrans.

To determine if Rosecrans was a suitable and willing candidate and most importantly "good on the goose," that is strong for emancipation, he sent the writer James R. Gilmore to Tennessee. Gilmore arrived at army headquarters in May, where, "in a rosewood armchair sadly out at the elbows, a cigar in his mouth, and a paper-cutter in his hand, with which he was rapidly dissecting a large pile of unopened letters that lay before him—sat the man whom the Republican leaders had selected as their next candidate for the presidency."

Gilmore asked Rosecrans, "What should be done with the Negro?" to which Rosecrans replied, "Give him the Bible and a spelling-book, freedom, and a chance for something more than six feet of God's earth—and let him alone." This response indicated Rosecrans was for emancipation and not colonization of the emancipated slaves out of the country. He was "good on the goose."

Gilmore spent two weeks with Rosecrans and his army and concluded he was "a man of remarkable executive ability, extensive culture, broad, comprehensive views, and, moreover, a true Christian gentleman, who would do honor to any station within the gift of the American people."

Eventually the time came for Gilmore to reveal the purpose of his visit: to inform Rosecrans that Greeley and other important Republicans wanted him to run for the presidency in 1864. Gilmore recalled Rosecrans' response:

> The good opinion of those gentlemen is exceedingly gratifying to me, and so is yours, and I assure you that I have not had the remotest suspicion that you were here for any such purpose. I have supposed you were merely gathering literary material; but, my good friend, it cannot be. My place is here. The country gave me my education, and so has a right to my military services; and it educated me for precisely this emergency. So this, and not the presidency, is my post of duty and I cannot, without violating my conscience, leave it. But let me tell you, and I wish you would tell your friends who are moving in this matter, that they are mistaken about Mr. Lincoln. He is in the right place. I am in a position to know, and if you live you will see that I am right about him.[11]

Rosecrans showed himself to be politically unambitious, unlike several other generals.

The six-month period between the battle of Stones River and the beginning of the Tullahoma campaign was not without military activity. On February 3 an attack against Fort Donelson, at Dover, Tennessee, by 2,500 under Wheeler and Forest was repulsed with a loss of 700 Confederates to 126 Union casualties. On March 4, Van Dorn encountered and captured several Union regiments at Spring Hill Thompson's Station Tennessee. A week later troops under Sheridan and Minty were sent to attack Van Dorn who was forced to evacuate Spring Hill and retreat temporarily across the Duck River.

On the 20th of March at Milton, Tennessee, the Confederates were defeated with minimal Union losses. Various raids and expeditions continued through April, most famously Abel Streight's raid into Northern Alabama, made in part on mule back. This incursion, supported and planned chiefly by Garfield, failed and resulted in Forrest capturing Streight and his troops in May.

On March 25, Ambrose Burnside, still in a command position despite his failures at Antietam and Fredericksburg, replaced Horatio Wright in the Department of the Ohio. He was told, "The movements of your own troops will depend in no small degree upon those of the army under General Rosecrans. You will, therefore, frequently consult with him in regard to his intended operations." Burnside would become another important figure in the Rosecrans story.

In May, General Lucas Hartsuff, second in command to Burnside, visited Rosecrans to plan joint actions of the armies. Burnside would move against General Simon Bolivar Buckner in East Tennessee, and Rosecrans would attack Bragg. Thus Burnside would cover Rosecrans' left while Rosecrans moved against Bragg. It was also decided that Bragg should not be forced back too quickly lest he reinforce Joe Johnston's army and move against Grant. Rosecrans wrote to Stanton, "What we want is to deal with their armies piece for piece, which is good when we have the odds." Rosecrans believed that Bragg, by keeping Rosecrans from moving, was himself held in check because he was unable to move against Grant or send troops to Lee. He told Hartsuff, "Bragg is holding us by his nose which he has inserted between our teeth for that purpose. We shall keep our teeth closed on his nose by our attitude until we are assured that Vicksburg is within three weeks of its fall."[12]

Over the next few weeks of April and May, 1863 the war began to heat up. Grant crossed the Mississippi River below Vicksburg and began his campaign toward Jackson, Mississippi. Johnston had left Tennessee and was on his way to Jackson to assume command of the Confederate forces in Mississippi. In the east Hooker had crossed the Rappahannock beginning the Chancellorsville campaign.

By the end of May, Hooker had been defeated and thrown back across the Rappahannock. Grant, after victories at Jackson and Champion Hill, continued on to Vicksburg but was repulsed by the stronger-than-expected Confederate defenses. Rather than fight a battle to take the city he decided to lay siege to Vicksburg. Rosecrans was now willing to advance. He wrote Burnside, "How soon will your troops reach their destination? The time appears ripe for a movement here, and much depends on the position of your forces." When he didn't hear from Burnside, he wrote, "I wish to make a forward movement in the next four days.... I inquired about your transportation and supplies because we may be able to unite our forces and move straight on to Chattanooga."

On June 2, Rosecrans began to move, but Halleck had ordered Burnside to hurry reinforcements to Grant. Burnside protested, "Rosecrans is now relying upon my advance into Tennessee and I am all ready." But Halleck's final order was, "You will immediately dispatch 8,000 men to General Grant, at Vicksburg." Burnside declared his plans all "deranged." Thus after a long and controversial delay Rosecrans' plans were upset by Halleck in Washington. He decided to reassess his military situation.[13]

On June 8, Rosecrans presented a confidential note to his three corps, thirteen division and cavalry commanders, asking each to answer three questions:

1. From the fullest information in your possession do you think that the enemy in front of us has been so materially weakened by detachments to Johnston or elsewhere that this army could advance on him at this time with strong reasonable chances of fighting a great and successful battle?

2. Do you think an advance of our army at present likely to prevent additional re-enforcements being sent against General Grant by the enemy in our front?

3. Do you think an immediate or early advance of our army advisable?

The results were strong against an advance including negatives from all three corps commanders. Thirteen of the seventeen generals did not believe Bragg had been significantly weakened. All seventeen generals were unanimous in answering no to the advisability of an immediate or early advance

There was one general who did not have a vote but had a contrary opinion—Garfield. He presented nine reasons for an immediate advance, among them his belief that Bragg was weaker than at any time since Stones River, that no matter the outcome at Vicksburg, Bragg would be reinforced after it and that the government and War Department believed that the army ought to move upon the enemy.

On June 11, Rosecrans relayed the results of his survey to Halleck adding that by waiting they would observe "a great military maxim not to risk two great and decisive battles at the same time." Halleck in his response pointed out that that maxim did not apply to two armies fighting independently of each other. He also cited another maxim of war: "councils of war never fight."

Actually Bragg had been weakened. Breckinridge and most of his division, McCown's division, and two brigades of cavalry had all departed in May. Rosecrans was never ordered to move. Halleck, on June 12, wrote him, "If you say that you are not prepared to fight Bragg I shall not order you to do so, for the responsibility of fighting or refusing to fight at a particular time and place must rest upon the general in immediate command."[14]

On June 23, Rosecrans and the Army of the Cumberland, after a delay of 169 days, began to move. The resulting action would be one of the most spectacular, but least known, successes of the war.

8. Tullahoma

After the retreat of the Army of Tennessee to Tullahoma, a simmering dissatisfaction with Bragg among his subordinates boiled over the top. Bragg decided to confront the situation. On January 11, he wrote his commanders asking them to uphold his contention that the decision to withdraw from Murfreesboro had been supported and even urged by them. He also requested that they "consult your subordinate commanders and be candid with me.... I shall retire without regret if I find I have lost the good opinion of my generals."[1]

The result was Bragg being exculpated of any blame for the retreat. However Hardee, Cleburne, and Breckinridge all expressed a lack of confidence in his leadership. Polk, who had been away on family matters, upon his return felt unable to confront Bragg directly and instead wrote to President Davis suggesting Joseph Johnston as a replacement: "He will cure all discontent and inspire the army with new life and confidence."[2]

In January, Johnston, on official business in Mobile, was ordered by Davis to Tennessee to investigate the situation in the Army of Tennessee. He spent three weeks with the army and in a letter to Davis on February 12 wrote that he should not be considered as Bragg's replacement.[3]

Johnston, feeling his mission in Tennessee accomplished, returned to Mobile. However on March 9 he received instructions from Davis to go to Tullahoma, order Bragg to Richmond, and assume control of the army. Because Bragg's wife was gravely ill, Johnston was reluctant to give Bragg the order to surrender his command. He assumed temporary control while Bragg went away to care for his wife. When Bragg returned in April, Johnston was so ill that he couldn't resume command. Thus Bragg, through an unlikely series of events and not aware of the real situation, retained command of the Army of Tennessee.

It was this internally divided army that now faced Rosecrans' strengthened, enlarged and confident army. Despite these internal problems, the Army of Tennessee remained a formidable force of 46,665—30,449 infantry, 13,962 cavalry, and 2,254 artillery—defending a terrain that favored the defender against the attacker.

Eleven miles from Murfreesboro was a range of hills known as the Highland Rim, which was cut by a series of gaps or passes. From westernmost to easternmost they were Guy's Gap, Bell Buckle Gap, Liberty Gap and Hoover's Gap.

The Manchester Pike passed through Hoover's Gap. Liberty Gap was to the west of Hoover's Gap. The Nashville and Chattanooga Railroad passed through Bell Buckle Gap directly to Tullahoma. The direct route to Shelbyville traversed Guy's Gap. Bragg's army was also protected by breastworks and hundreds of yards of abbatis at Shelbyville and Tullahoma.

The area to the west of Bragg's position was less hilly and more developed in roads than the area to the east. Recognizing this, Bragg expected Rosecrans to strike west and accordingly strengthened his left. He placed his largest corps, Polk's, on the left near Shelbyville facing Guy's Gap. Hardee was positioned near Wartrace eight miles east of Shelbyville near Liberty Gap. Most of Forrest's cavalry was to the far west, beyond the hills, to protect against a move by Rosecrans from that direction. Wheeler's horsemen anchored Bragg's extreme right near McMinnville.

Rosecrans had an effective force of 50,017: 40,146 infantry, 6,806 cavalry, and 3,065 artillery. Held in reserve was a corps of 12,575. His plan was to feint to the west, hoping Bragg would think that he was attacking from that direction. Instead the main attack would come from the east to Bragg's right. The objective was to turn Bragg's right, get to his rear, cut the railroad bridges to the south of Tullahoma, and force Bragg out of his defenses and make him fight a battle in the open. In order to do this, Rosecrans would have to somehow move most of his troops through the rugged and difficult terrain to the east.

On June 23 the campaign began when elements of the cavalry moved out toward Eagleville and Rover northwest of Shelbyville. The next day the movement continued to Middleton and Christiana. All of this activity on the right was intended to convince Bragg that the attack would take place to the west on Bragg's left. On the 23rd, Rosecrans met with his corps commanders and revealed his plan. Thomas was to take the most direct route to Manchester through Hoover's Gap. McCook was to move south toward Christiana then turn southeast through Liberty Gap to Bell Buckle. From there he could assist Thomas if necessary. Brannan's division of Crittenden's Corps accompanied McCook's Corps to Christiana but continued through Guy's Gap to Shelbyville rather than heading to Liberty Gap.

On June 24th, Rosecrans' army moved out at 4 a.m. One thing that hadn't been planned for was rain. For the next seventeen days what one soldier called "no Presbyterian rain ... but a genuine Baptist downpour" would present the greatest obstacle to the Union advance.[4]

McCook's corps attacked at Liberty Gap. Over the next two days spirited fighting, especially by Willich's brigade against Cleburne's Confederates at

Liberty Gap, resulted in a Southern withdrawal. The most important battle of this campaign was at Hoover's Gap. Technology, as well as courage, played a decisive role. The task of clearing and taking the Gap fell to Thomas' corps. Starting at 4 a.m. Wilder's brigade of mounted infantry led the advance. Six miles behind them was the rest of Reynold's division followed by Rousseau and Negley.

At ten o'clock, Wilder entered Hoover's Gap. There they encountered cavalry resistance which was quickly swept away. Exceeding orders, the mounted infantry continued forward into the gap, seizing and fortifying the hills at the southern end of the gap. Facing a counter-offensive from A.P. Stewart's division, a three-hour fight ensued in which a new type of weapon would prove decisive.

Wilder's brigade was armed with the new Spencer repeating rifle. It was Wilder, with Rosecrans' approval, who had arranged for a private bank loan to purchase the guns for his men, the loan to be repaid with deductions from the soldiers' pay. This was done without the approval or perhaps even knowledge of the War Department in Washington, which had been unexcited by the Spencers.

It was a contest of numbers against technology, and the result wasn't in doubt for long. Wilder wrote, "The effect of our terrible fire was overwhelming to our opponents, who bravely tried to withstand its effects. No human being could successfully face such an avalanche of destruction as our continuous fire swept through their lines. This was the first battle where the Spencer repeating rifles had ever been used."

During the battle Wilder was ordered by an aide to General Reynolds to retreat several miles and rejoin the rest of the division. Wilder refused the order, confident that he could hold his position, and willing to take responsibility. Later Generals Rosecrans and Thomas arrived. When informed of the situation Rosecrans said, "You took the responsibility to disobey orders, did you? Thank God for your decision. It would have cost us two thousand lives to have taken this position if you had given it up." When Reynolds arrived, Rosecrans told him, "Wilder has done right. Promote him, promote him." Reynolds concurred, telling Wilder, "You did right, and should be promoted and not censured."[5]

As well as things were going for the Union at Liberty and Hoover gaps, to the east things literally bogged down. Crittenden's corps, which Rosecrans hoped would be the first to get to the Confederate rear, had been all but halted by the tough terrain of the Barrens. The continuing rains made a bad situation only worse. Crittenden's corps was only able to move twenty-one miles in four days. Thus the action at Hoover's Gap became the unintended crucial action of the campaign.

On June 26th, Thomas' corps passed through Hoover's Gap on its way to Manchester, which was reached the next day. Later two of McCook's divisions were shifted to the east and followed Thomas through Hoover's Gap to Manchester.

Bragg now realized that his right had been turned. He called off a planned attack by Polk on McCook's flank at Liberty Gap and decided to withdraw back to his base at Tullahoma. Cleburne was ordered to withdraw from Liberty Gap and retreat to Tullahoma. Granger's reserve corps and Stanley's cavalry pushed through Guy's Gap and drove the Rebels out of Shelbyville and across the Duck River. Shelbyville was the site of one of the greatest saber charges of the war. Confederate cavalry soldier John A. Wyeth, who served with Morgan and Forrest, and after the war became a surgeon and author, called it "the most brilliant cavalry maneuver he ever witnessed." In taking Shelbyville, Pauline Cushman, "the spy of the Cumberland," was rescued and saved from the gallows.[6]

By June 27th Rosecrans was at Manchester with two of his corps and a third, Crittenden's, twenty miles away. On the 28th Wilder was ordered to move southeast and destroy the railway bridge on the Elk River. If successful Bragg would be completely cut off from his main base at Chattanooga. Luckily for the Confederate commander, Wilder was not able to destroy the bridge but did inflict some damage on the railroad at Decherd. Bragg, back in Tullahoma on the 29th, realized his precarious situation and decided to hold a council of war. Bragg wanted to fight; Polk advised retreat; Hardee wasn't sure. The next day the Army of the Cumberland was united at Manchester and marched to Tullahoma. Bragg's army retreated across the Elk River near Decherd and Winchester.

On July 1 three Union divisions entered Tullahoma. Hot in pursuit Sheridan crossed the Elk utilizing a cable to help some soldiers across the swollen waters. Bragg retreated once again to Cowan at the base of the Cumberland Mountains. He now had to decide whether to fight or retreat southward. Bragg, who had retreated after Perryville and Stones River, decided once again to retreat, this time to Chattanooga. He is reported to have said, "I am utterly broken down.... This is a great disaster."

Eventually Thomas' and Crittenden's corps also crossed the Elk, only to discover that Bragg had retreated. After eleven days of marching and fighting during one of the heaviest rainfalls in the recorded history of Middle Tennessee, the Tullahoma campaign ended. In the span from June 23 to July 3 Rosecrans had driven Bragg and his army out of Middle Tennessee at a cost of only 550 casualties, 84 of which were fatalities. During the same time that Bragg was fleeing across the mountains to Chattanooga, Lee was being repulsed at Gettysburg, and Vicksburg was surrendered to Grant. Because the Tullahoma campaign is almost unknown compared to the battle in Pennsylvania and siege in Mississippi, its importance is overlooked.

On July 7, Stanton telegraphed Rosecrans, "We have just received official information that Vicksburg surrendered to General Grant on the 4th of July. Lee's army overthrown; Grant victorious. You and your noble army now have a chance to give the finishing blow to the rebellion. Will you neglect the chance?"

Rightly or wrongly, Rosecrans perceived a snub in this message. He replied, "Just received your cheering telegram announcing the fall of Vicksburg and confirming the defeat of Lee. You do not appear to observe the fact that this noble army has driven the rebels from Middle Tennessee.... I beg in behalf of this army that the War Department may not overlook so great an event because it is not written in letters of blood."[7]

Because Tullahoma is largely unknown, it is valuable to listen to the words of those who were alive in 1863 as well as those who have studied the campaign. David Stanley, who led the cavalry in the campaign, wrote, "If any student of the military art desires to make a study of a model campaign, let him take his maps and General Rosecrans' orders for the daily movements in this campaign. No better example of successful strategy was carried out during the war than in the Tullahoma Campaign."

August Willich, who had been captured at Stones River and then paroled in May, had returned to the Cumberland Army to lead a brigade. In his Official report he concluded, "It must be to every thinking mind evident that the tide of the rebellion is turned, its hours are measured; that the evil spirits of the Commonwealth have lost their pride and confidence; that they are doomed to their just fate."

Abraham Lincoln is said to have called the flanking of Bragg out of Middle Tennessee "the most splendid piece of strategy he knew of."[8]

The relatively few historians who have looked in the depth at the Tullahoma Campaign are likewise laudatory. Andrew N. Morris concluded,

> Major General William S. Rosecrans deserves to be given major credit for the plan and its execution. His plan met every criteria for success. It combined a clear understanding of the mission, a deep knowledge of the strengths and weaknesses of the enemy, troops that were well trained and imbued with confidence in their leaders and their own abilities, and a sharp eye for the ground.

Richard J. Brewer wrote,

> It was a campaign of brilliant operational planning and maneuver by Rosecrans. Despite its relative obscurity, the Tullahoma Campaign had far reaching effects on the course of the war in Middle Tennessee. Rosecrans' victory coincided with the two great Union victories at Vicksburg and Gettysburg and as a result is often overlooked. Yet, this little known or studied campaign resulted in the opening of the path to Chattanooga, and ultimately, the capture of Chattanooga and Atlanta.

Julian D. Alford compared Tullahoma with Gettysburg and Vicksburg:

> Compared to Tullahoma and Vicksburg, Gettysburg was a tactical stalemate. Lee lost a third of his army and Meade lost more than a quarter of his. For the south, the raid north was not going to end the struggle, take Washington or save the Mississippi Valley; therefore it had no strategic value. For the north, Gettysburg was a desperate blocking movement and when it was over, they had not gained a strategic advantage either, except for a boost in morale.

Alford continues his analysis:

> For the south, losing Vicksburg was a huge strategic blow, largely because of its effect on the morale of the southern people. Strategically, Vicksburg was comparable to Tullahoma; however in the greater scheme of the war, the loss of Middle Tennessee was a much more severe blow than was the loss of the Mississippi Valley. This was due to the fact that Middle Tennessee was the head of the great body of supplies in the Deep South and territory west of the Mississippi was not.

Michael Bradley observed that Tullahoma was not only a classic of planning and execution but "also a classic of improvisation. Rosecrans, intended his far left, under Crittenden, to strike, the main blow. When this column literally bogged down, Rosecrans was flexible enough to juggle his plans and improvise a scheme by which Thomas and McCook could trap Bragg."

In comparing Tullahoma with Vicksburg and Gettysburg, Bradley notes that

> Grant did achieve a victory which had important psychological and public relations dimensions, and since the usual goal of grand strategy at that time was the destruction of the opposing army, Grant fulfilled that goal. But the Confederacy, arguably, could have survived the fall of Vicksburg and still won the war. It did survive for two more years.
> ...Meade won a defensive victory at Gettysburg. This boosted moral, especially for the Army of the Potomac, which had never known such a clear cut win, but defensive victories would not win the war.... Lee won defensive victories almost every week during 1864 and still wound up at Appomattox.

He asks, if there had never been a successful Tullahoma campaign, "if the [Atlanta] Campaign of 1864 had begun in the vicinity of Murfreesboro ... would Atlanta have been taken before the November elections? Would Lincoln have received a second term?"

Gettysburg, Vicksburg, and Tullahoma, when recognized, are generally considered to be the turning points of the American Civil War. But the fact is that nearly two more years of deadly fighting remained. In early July 1863, it was still not certain that the Union would prevail. What would happen over the next five months would definitively resolve that question.[9]

9. Opposition from Many Sides

The distance from the Army of the Cumberland's new headquarters at Winchester to Chattanooga was sixty-nine miles by rail—more than the distance from the Rappahannock to Richmond in Virginia. Those sixty-nine miles encompassed the most difficult terrain faced by any army in the entire war.

In front of Rosecrans' army stood the 2,200-foot Cumberland Plateau. Beyond it lay the Sequatchie Valley, nearly four miles wide and sixty miles long. The eastern border of the valley was Walden's Ridge, 1,300 feet high. Further to the east was the Tennessee River, 400 to 600 feet wide north of Chattanooga.

Chattanooga was on the southern side of a bend in the river. West of the city was Lookout Mountain, eighty-five miles long and 1,000 feet high. West of the mountain was Lookout Creek, which emptied into the Tennessee. Sand and Raccoon mountains were west of Lookout Creek. The Tennessee, curving west and south of Chattanooga and at points up to 900 feet wide, presented the final barrier to Rosecrans' army as he devised a plan to take the city.

These natural barriers were not the only problems Rosecrans faced. Every mile he moved southeast took him further away from his base at Louisville and depots at Murfreesboro and Nashville. His army's lifeline was the Nashville and Chattanooga Railroad, still vulnerable to attacks by the numerically superior Confederate cavalry. The railroad crossings of the Tennessee had been destroyed and needed to be repaired. The roads across the various mountains were primitive at best. The Tennessee River was not navigable past Muscle Shoals, Alabama; there could be no naval support for Rosecrans as Grant received at Vicksburg.

There was the problem of forage for the animals of the army in a land that had been stripped bare by Bragg's retreating army. Finally there was the unresolved question of where Rosecrans would make his main attack, north or south of Chattanooga.

Rosecrans listed six tasks his army faced before it could move:

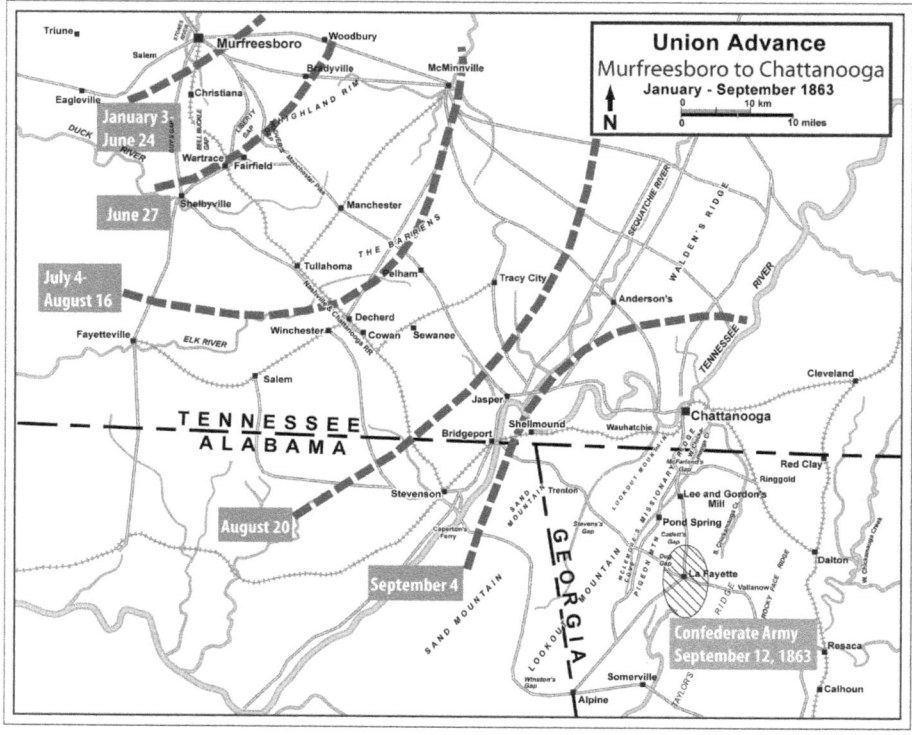

Union Advance Murfreesboro to Chattanooga (NPS).

1. To convince Bragg that Rosecrans would cross above Chattanooga.
2. Repair the railroad, "without attracting ... attention" to Bridgeport on the Tennessee.
3. To accumulate twenty days' rations, "without allowing ... the faintest intimation of our intentions and doings."
4. To construct a pontoon bridge at Stevenson, Alabama, on the Tennessee.
5. To delay the movement until a new crop was fit for horse feed.
6. To threaten Bragg's rail communications to force him to evacuate Chattanooga and allow Rosecrans' army to concentrate between Bragg and Chattanooga.[1]

In July Rosecrans sent General Lovell Rousseau and Colonel J.P. Sanderson to Washington with a plan approved by Governors Andrew Curtin of Pennsylvania, John Andrew of Massachusetts and Richard Yates of Illinois to reenlist 10,000 two-year veterans who would go to the Army of the Cumberland as mounted infantry. Rousseau bore a letter for Stanton explaining how these troops would guard Rosecrans' long extended supply line. According to Rosecrans, "every such mounted man... would give us three infantry men at the front." Stanton's reply to Rousseau was, "I would rather you would come to ask the command of the Army of the Cumberland yourself, than to ask reinforcements for General Rosecrans. He shall not have another damned man."[2]

President Lincoln did later meet with Sanderson who recorded in a letter to his wife, "Halleck is violent against granting our wishes, and Stanton but little better. But the president is decidedly favorable. The prospects are that he will take the matter in his hands, and act accordingly, giving us a triumph of the bull-headed general-in-chief and the bearish and unmannerly Secretary of War." Stanton later was supportive of the plan, then changed his mind again and suggested the troops be mounted on mules and finally promised nothing. Sanderson concluded that Rosecrans' doom was "inevitable."[3]

On July 24 an exchange of letters began between Rosecrans and Halleck. Halleck wrote:

> You must not wait for Johnston to join Bragg, but must move forward immediately against the latter. Take with you hard bread, sugar, coffee, and salt, and push forward rapidly, supplying yourself with forage, bacon, beef, and mutton in the country. Organize supply parties under you quartermaster and commissaries, and live as much as possible on the country. Reduce your trains to the lowest point possible, and move rapidly. There is great disappointment felt here at the slowness of your advance. Unless you can move more rapidly, your whole campaign will prove a failure, and you will have both Bragg and Johnston against you.

General Rosecrans' reply is not in the Official Records, but its contents can be surmised by Halleck's reply to it:

> GENERAL: The tone of some of your replies to my dispatches lately would indicate that you thought I was unnecessarily urging you forward. On the contrary, I have deemed it absolutely necessary, not only for the country but also for your own reputation, that your army should remain no longer inactive. *The patience of the authorities here has been completely exhausted, and if I had not repeatedly promised to urge you forward, and begged for delay, you would have been removed from the command.* It has been said that you are as inactive as was General Buell and the pressure for your removal has been almost as strong as it has been in his case. I am well aware that people at a distance do not appreciate the obstacles and difficulties which they would see if nearer by; but, whether well founded or without any foundation at all, the dissatisfaction really exists, and I deem it my duty, as a friend, to represent it to you truly and fairly; and I think I ought to do so, if for no other reason, because it was at my earnest solicitations that you were given the command. [Emphasis added][4]

On July 25 Rosecrans wrote Halleck,

> Your dispatch received. All is very good. Your views accord with my own. All your suggestions about baggage and rations have been anticipated and carried out from the energy of which we are capable. We never think of moving with any but the minimum baggage, nor of taking anything but essential parts of rations; but to move our troops beyond our means of supply would but break down and disable both men and horses without results. This, I am sure, you do not desire. Any disappointment that may be left at the apparent slowness of our movements would be readily removed by a knowledge of the obstacles and a true military appreciation of the advantages of not moving prematurely. I confess I should like to avoid such remarks and letters as I am receiving lately from Washington, if I could do so without injury to the public service. You will, I think, find the officers of this army as anxious for success, and as willing to exert themselves to secure it, as any member of the Government can be. As to subsistence being drawn from the country over which we are to travel to Chattanooga, it was always barren—with but few fertile spots. Those spots have been gleaned and scraped by rebels with a powerful cavalry force ever since last winter. We shall get some hay and cattle in the region of Fayetteville, Huntsville, and south of there—none south or east of us. We shall move promptly, and endeavor not to go back. *What movements of General Grant will affect us?* [Emphasis added]

To this Halleck replied:

> GENERAL: I perceive from the tone of your dispatch to-day that you are displeased at my urging you to move forward your army against Bragg. In other words, general, while I am blamed here for not urging you forward more rapidly, you are displeased at my doing so. Whatever I have written or telegraphed to you on this subject has been from motives of kindness and friendship. It was my only desire to impress upon you the wishes and expectations of the Government, in order that you might be fully acquainted with those wishes. Having now explained to you frankly that you can have no possible grounds for your tone of displeasure toward me, I shall not again refer to this matter.[5]

Two important things should be noted in these letters. If Halleck is to be believed, the pressure for Rosecrans to move immediately and the accompanying threat to relieve him if he did not move came from a source more powerful than Halleck.

Second is the lack of a similar pressure on Grant to either move or assist the Army of the Cumberland. Rosecrans asked this question of Halleck. His response and the actions of Grant and his army after Vicksburg will be discussed later.

On August 1, Rosecrans spelled out in detail the reasons for the decisions he had taken and the situation of his army and even suggested the government replace him:

> I thank you for your notes of the 24th and 25th instant [ultimo], and for your support and confidence hitherto. These letters relieve my mind from a growing apprehension that the injustice which I have experienced from the War Department was extending to you. *But as my ambition is something like your own—to discharge my*

duty to God and our country—I say to you frankly that whenever the Government can replace me by a commander in whom they have more confidence, they ought to do so, and take the responsibility of the result. [Emphasis added] Meanwhile let me call your attention to the conditions of the problem before this army:

    1st. Our base at Louisville is 264 miles distant from our present position

    2nd. We are 83 miles from our principal depot—Nashville.

    3rd. We must transport all our subsistence, our clothing, camp and garrison equipage, wagons, animals, ammunition, and most of our forage over these distances by rail.

    4th. We have before us 60 or 70 miles of barren mountain country, destitute of forage and subsistence, traversed by a few difficult roads, over which to advance.

    5th. We have to cross the difficult defile of the Tennessee, a river from 600 to 1,000 yards wide, in the face of powerful enemy, and maneuver or fight him from an entrenched position, in a mountainous country with several lines of retreat; the nearest points of this position being from 26 to 45 miles from our railroad, over mountains.

    6th. To advance in the face of these obstacles is not the only nor even the most important point in the problem. We must so advance as never to recede. The citizens say, and not without justice, "Whip our armies, and then, when we no longer fear their return to power, we will show you that we are satisfied to be in the Union; but until you do that, we are not safe from proscription."

    7th. Not only so, but this must be done in view of the possibility of Joe Johnston joining Bragg.

These are the conditions of the first problem. The preliminaries to its successful solution are, first, to open the railroad, establish and provide for guarding depots at the nearest accessible points, and, secondly, to provide means of crossing the river and maintain communication over it. To these ends every effort is now being bent. Rest assured these things would have to be done by any commander, and I think we are doing them as rapidly as our means will admit.[6]

However on August 4 Halleck sent the following to Rosecrans:

Your forces must move forward without further dearly. You will daily report the movement of each corps till you cross the Tennessee River.

Rosecrans asked for a clarification in a letter sent the same day:

Your dispatch, ordering me to move forward without further delay, reporting the movement of each corps until I cross the Tennessee, is received. As I have been determined to cross the river as soon as practicable, and have been making all preparations, and getting such information as may enable me to do so without being driven back, like Hooker, I wish to know if your order is intended to take away my discretion as to the time and manner of moving my troops?

The next day Halleck bluntly telegraphed Rosecrans:

The orders for the advance of your army, and that its movements be reported daily, are peremptory.

He also sent the following order to Burnside in Cincinnati:

> You will immediately move with a column of 12,000 men by the most practicable roads on East Tennessee, making Knoxville or its vicinity your objective point. ... As soon as you reach East Tennessee, you will endeavor to connect with the forces of General Rosecrans, who has peremptory orders to move forward. The Secretary of War repeats his orders that you move your headquarters from Cincinnati to the field, and take command of the troops in person.[7]

On August 6, Rosecrans sent the following to Halleck asking to be relieved if he could not modify his plans:

> My arrangements for beginning a continuous movement will be completed and the execution begun by Monday next. We have information to show that crossing the Tennessee, between Bridgeport and Chattanooga is impracticable, but not enough to show whether we had better cross above Chattanooga and strike Cleveland, or below Bridgeport, and strike their rear. The preliminary movements of troops for the two cases are very different. It is necessary to have our means of crossing the river completed, and our supplies provided to cross 60 miles of mountain, and sustain ourselves during the operations of crossing and fighting, before we move. *To obey your order literally would be to push our troops at once into the mountains on narrow and difficult roads, destitute of pasture and forage, and short of water, where they would not be able to maneuver as exigencies may demand, and would certainly cause ultimate delay and probably disaster. If, therefore, the movement which I propose cannot be regarded as obedience to your order, I respectfully request a modification of it, or to be relieved from the command.* [Emphasis added][8]

Rosecrans also corresponded directly with Lincoln and raised the same points he had with Halleck, closing his long message with, "We must learn the country, which appears very differently in reality from what is shown on map." Lincoln responded,

> Since Grant has been entirely relieved by the fall of Vicksburg, by which Johnston is also relieved, it has seemed to me that your chance for a stroke has been considerably diminished... but I can see and appreciate the difficulties you mention. The question occurs ... does preparation advance at all? Do you not consume supplies as fast as you get them forward?
>
> ...And now be assured once more that I think of you with all kindness and confidence, and that I am not watching you with an evil eye.

Rosecrans replied and raised the question of Grant's army:

> Permit me to assure you that I am not and have not been touched with any of that official pride which desires to have its own way.... You think Johnston was freed by the fall of Vicksburg. Was not Bragg set free by the evacuation of Middle Tennessee? You think we ought to have prevented Bragg from reinforcing Johnston. *Why cannot Grant keep Johnston from reinforcing Bragg? Has he not a nearer base of supplies and a more favorable country; a better railroad and more rolling-stock than we have here?* [Emphasis added]

He concluded the missive to Lincoln, "Thanking you for your kindness, may I ask, when impulsive men suppose me querulous, to believe I am only straightforward and in earnest, and that you may always rely upon my using my utmost efforts to do what is best for our country and the lives and honor of the soldiers of my command."[9]

Halleck did not accept his resignation, and on August 16 the campaign for Chattanooga began. Another aspect to this debate of when the Army of the Cumberland should move was a letter Garfield wrote to Treasury Secretary Salmon Chase. In it Garfield wrote,

> I have since then urged, with all the earnestness I possess, a rapid advance, while Bragg's army was shattered and under cover, and before Johnston and he could effect a junction. Thus far the General has been singularly disinclined to grasp the situation with a strong hand, and make the advantage his own.
>
> I write this with more sorrow than I can tell you, for I love every bone in his body, and next to my desire to see the Rebellion blasted is my anxiety to see him blessed. But even the breadth of my love is not sufficient to cover this almost fatal delay. My personal relations with General Rosecrans are all that I could desire. Officially I share his counsels and responsibilities, even more than I desire; but I beg you to know that this delay is against my judgment and my every wish.
>
> Pleasant as are my relations here, I would rather command a battalion that would follow and follow, and strike and strike, than to hang back while such golden moments are passing. But the General and myself believe that I can do more service in my present place than in command of a division, though I am aware that it is a position that promises better in the way of promotion or popular credit. But if this inaction continues long, I shall ask to be relieved, and sent somewhere where I can be part of a working army. But I do hope that you will soon hear that this splendid army is at least trying to do its part in the great work. If the War Department has not always been just, it has certainly been very indulgent to this army. But I feel that the time has now come when it should allow no plea to keep this army back from the most vigorous activity.[10]

After the war this letter would be a source of much public and personal controversy.

The Army of Tennessee was in Chattanooga, and the question before it was whether to attack, defend or retreat. One possibility was for Bragg to move his army west and join Johnston in an attack on Grant. Johnston's reply to this offer was simply, "It was too late. Such a combination might have been advantageous before or during the siege of Vicksburg, but not after its disastrous termination."

Another option was for a reinforced Bragg to assume the offensive and attack Rosecrans. After considering the situation, particularly the geography of the theater of war, Bragg concluded, "The defensive seems to be our only alternative, and that is a sad one." Bragg decided to adopt a defensive posture.

Although Bragg was on the defensive, his army was not passive, and changes were made that strengthened and enlarged it.[11]

William Hardee left the army to go to Johnston's army in Mississippi. His replacement as head of his corps was not someone from within the Army of Tennessee but an outsider, D.H. Hill from the Army of Northern Virginia. Hill's corps, consisting of Cleburne's and Stewart's divisions, was posted at Tyner's Station on the Knoxville railroad northeast of Chattanooga. Polk's corps, made up of Hindman's and Cheatham's divisions, was positioned in and around Chattanooga, with one brigade at Bridgeport, Alabama, on the Tennessee River.

In late July troops under General Simon Bolivar Buckner at Knoxville were placed under Bragg, although Buckner retained responsibility for the administration of the department of East Tennessee.

In August, General James Longstreet, understanding the importance of the center theater of the war, proposed to Confederate Secretary of War James Seddon a plan to send troops from Lee's Army to Bragg. Eventually Lee, after consulting with Davis in Richmond, agreed to the plan. The movement via a circuitous route through Wilmington, North Carolina, and Augusta, Georgia, didn't begin until September 9. Bragg asked for and got help from a somewhat reluctant Joseph Johnston who agreed in late August to send W.H.T. Walker's and Breckinridge's divisions to Bragg. Thus on the eve of the campaign for Chattanooga, the Confederate army was in the process of significantly strengthening itself. What about its Union foe?

Since Stones River, Rosecrans had badgered Washington for more troops, especially cavalry. Rousseau and Sanderson were sent to Washington with a plan to raise troops specifically for the Army of the Cumberland. Troops from Burnside, whom Rosecrans deemed protection for his left, had been detached and sent to Grant. The surrender of Vicksburg, however, created new possibilities for strengthening the Army of the Cumberland.

John A. Rawlins. Without him Grant may not have been able to survive his own worst actions.

9. Opposition from Many Sides

After the fall of Vicksburg, Grant and Sherman had a combined force of 80,000 men against Johnston's 23,000. Sherman marched to Jackson and after Johnston retreated thirty-five miles east to Morton, Mississippi, burned the city, giving it the nickname "Chimneyville" for the sole structure that remained from many destroyed buildings. Sherman, feeling his army unable to pursue in the hot weather, returned to his camp while Johnston continued on to Mobile.

Now what to do with the giant Grant-Sherman force? Grant wanted to attack Mobile. He was instead ordered to send troops to Banks and Schofield in Arkansas and Texas. Rosecrans asked several times about Grant moving on Johnston, whom he considered a threat to his right, and was brusquely told by Halleck, "Grant's movements at present have no connection with you."[12]

So as the Confederate forces were beginning a concentration from Virginia and Mississippi at Chattanooga, Union forces remained separate. No troops were sent from the Army of the Potomac, no troops from Mississippi. Grant actually left his army at Vicksburg and went to New Orleans where he fell off a horse, possibly drunk. Several generals reported him drinking, and if General Rawlins is to be believed, Grant indulged in "intoxicating liquors." Sherman remained encamped and idle in Mississippi. Once again, as at Rich Mountain, Iuka and Corinth, Rosecrans was about to fight a battle alone.[13]

10. Chickamauga

On August 16 the Army of the Cumberland began the Chattanooga Campaign. Rosecrans had three alternatives before him. All required crossing the Tennessee River. This could be done either above, below or in front of Chattanooga. To cross in front of Chattanooga was the least desirable option as it would have the army approach the city through a narrow gorge vulnerable to attacks from the surrounding heights.

To attack Chattanooga from the north offered a better chance of success, especially if the army could unite with Burnside who was on march to Knoxville, but it would dangerously separate Rosecrans from his base at Stevenson, Alabama, and the lifeline of the Nashville and Chattanooga Railroad. To attack from the south necessitated traversing two imposing mountains: Sand and Lookout. Although closer to the railroad base, it would require Rosecrans to divide his army as it moved across the few passes over the mountains. Rosecrans elected to take the southern approach and hopefully cut Bragg's army's lifeline to Atlanta. In order for this plan to succeed Rosecrans would need to deceive Bragg once again. Therefore Rosecrans, as during the Tullahoma campaign, would feint an attack from one direction while actually making his main thrust from another. His plan was to trick Bragg into believing the main blow would come north of Chattanooga.

The left wing of the army under Crittenden began the campaign. Palmer's and Wood's divisions crossed the Cumberland Plateau and occupied the Sequatchie Valley from Jasper to Pikesville. Hazen's and Wagner's brigades crossed Walden's Ridge into the Tennessee Valley where it joined with Minty's cavalry and Wilder's lightning brigade.

Once again deception was used to confuse the Confederates. Hazen recalled, "We had performed a good deal of 'dumb but noisy show' in stationing the bands and field-music, divided into many detachments, in different parts of the valley, and causing them to play as for parades, tattoo and reveille, as if there were at least one army corps present with more troops constantly arriving." In a similar vein Wilder wrote, "Details were made nearly every night to build fires indicating large camps, and by throwing boards upon others and hammering on barrels and sawing up boards and throwing the pieces in streams that would float them into the river, we made them believe we were preparing to cross with boats."

These four brigades totaling 7,000 men took possession of all the fords of the Tennessee from William's Island to Kingston, a distance of seventy-five miles. On August 21, a day which had been set aside by the Confederate government for fasting and prayer, Wilder reached Stringers Ridge across from Chattanooga and shelled the city for seven hours. In response to all this activity, Bragg moved troops from his left (southwest) to his right (northeast) to meet what he perceived to be the main thrust of Rosecrans' attack.

Thomas' corps ranged from Crittenden's right to Stevenson, Alabama, and McCook's XX Corps stretched from Bridgeport to Stevenson. Meanwhile Rosecrans had accumulated supplies including pontoon bridges at Stevenson. He contracted for the rebuilding of the bridges at Bridgeport and Running Water. He commissioned the immediate construction of five stern-wheel steamers to use for service between Bridgeport and Chattanooga. Pontoon bridges were built at Caperton's Ferry and Shellmound.

The crossing of the Tennessee began on August 29. Most of McCook's corps crossed the Tennessee at Caperton's Ferry (near Stevenson) and Bridgeport. The first to cross was Colonel Hans C. Heg's brigade, which rowed across in pontoons and drove away the Rebel cavalry to secure the opposite side of the river while the Pioneer Brigade laid a 1,254-foot pontoon bridge in four and a half hours. Sheridan crossed at Bridgeport, where the Pioneers and Michigan Engineers built a part trestle, part pontoon bridge that spanned 2,700 feet over two channels of the river, between August 28 and September 3. Thomas' corps crossed at four places: Caperton's, Bridgeport, Shellmound and the mouth of Battle Creek where Brannan's division crossed on rafts. Most of Crittenden's XXI Corps crossed at Shellmound. By September 4 all but parts of the Reserve Corps were across the Tennessee.

Once across, McCook was to climb Sand Mountain and move to Valley Head, Alabama, and seize Winston's Gap on Lookout Mountain where Sheridan, traveling via Trenton, Georgia, was to rejoin him. Thomas, after crossing Sand Mountain, was to concentrate his corps at Trenton.

Meanwhile Crittenden, leaving Wagner's brigade north of the river under the command of Hazen, concentrated his remaining troops, moved down the Sequatchie Valley and crossed the river at three points. Part of his command went on Murphy's Hollow Road to Wauhatche. The rest went along the railroad toward Chattanooga. Thus by September 6 the Army of the Cumberland lay along the western base of Lookout Mountain from Wauhatche, Tennessee, to Valley Head, Alabama, a distance of thirty-six miles. Earlier on September 6, Ambrose Burnside's army had marched into Knoxville unopposed as Buckner had been called toward Chattanooga by Bragg.

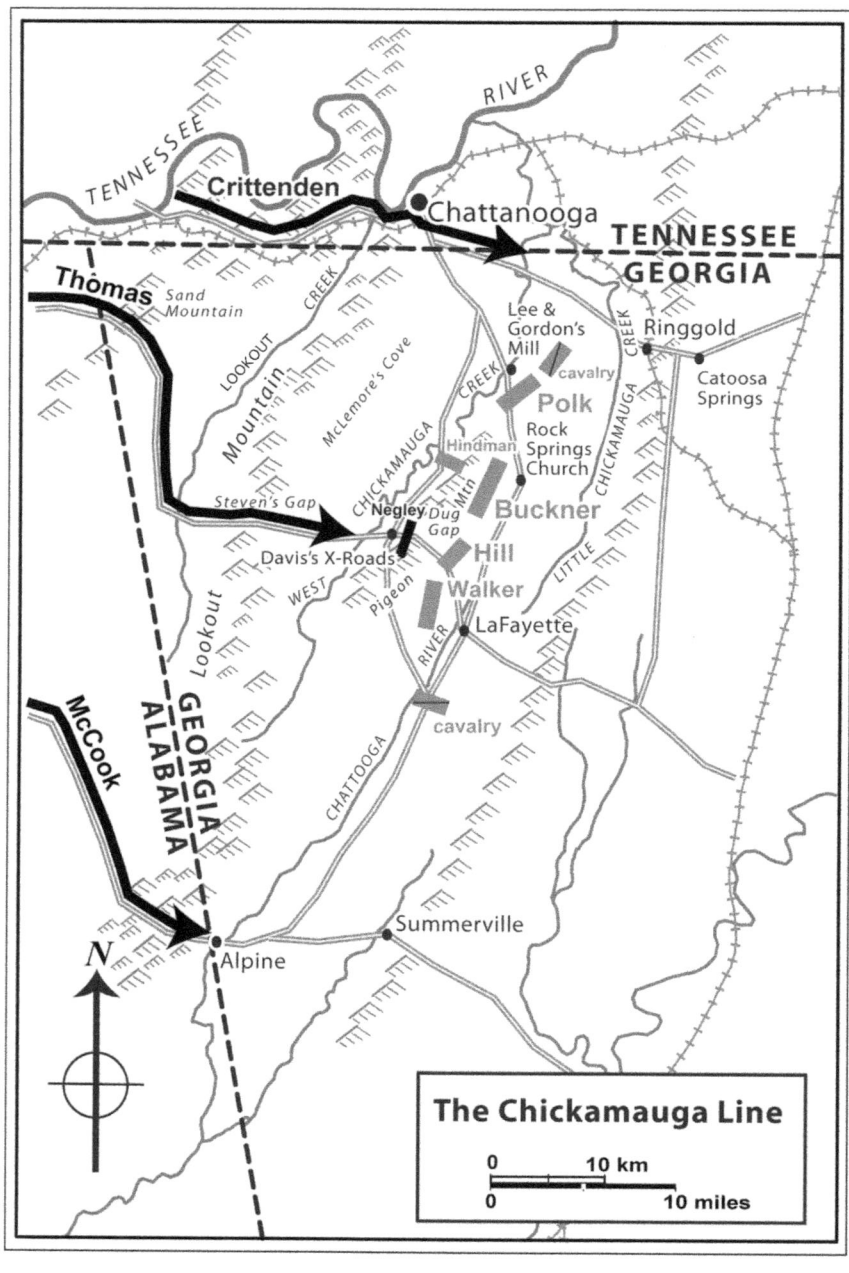

Movement to Chickamauga (Map by Phil Mobley based on one by Donald S. Frazier).

An interesting episode was a dispute between Thomas Wood and Crittenden over a reconnaissance movement which Wood judged too dangerous and retreated from without the approval of Crittenden. When two officers asked Wood about the incident he reacted with strong language. Wood wrote, "I cannot believe General Rosecrans desires such a blind adherence to the mere letter of his order for the general disposition of his forces as naturally jeopardizes the safety of the most salient portions of it, and certainly cripples the force and vigor and accuracy of its reconnaissances." Eventually a successful movement was carried out, but future events would make this otherwise unremarkable incident noteworthy.[1]

Up to this point Braxton Bragg remained convinced that Rosecrans' plan was to effect a junction with Burnside and attack Chattanooga from the north. As word of Union troops crossing south of Chattanooga reached him, he realized that the threat now was to his rear and the railroad link to Atlanta. In fact Bragg was thoroughly confused about Rosecrans' army: its location, size, and intention. On the night of September 7, Bragg decided to abandon Chattanooga, join with Buckner and eventually engage Rosecrans in battle. He moved his army to a point near LaFayette, Georgia, about thirty miles south of Chattanooga.

Rumors of Bragg's abandonment of Chattanooga began to come into Rosecrans' headquarters. On September 8, fifty mounted infantry climbed the northern tip of Lookout Mountain to see if the rumors were true. They discovered that the city was guarded by just a small Rebel force and returned with this information. Orders were issued for the 92nd Illinois to lead a force into the city. The next day that regiment's banner flew above Bragg's former headquarters, the Crutchfield House hotel.

Although Chattanooga had been abandoned, Bragg's army was very much alive. In fact it was growing thanks to reinforcements arriving from Mississippi and later from Virginia. Events began to move quickly. Rosecrans, believing now was his chance to destroy Bragg's army, ordered McCook to proceed to Alpine and Summerville in Georgia. Crittenden was ordered to leave a single brigade in Chattanooga and pursue the retreating Rebels. Thomas was ordered to proceed through McLemore's Cove to Lafayette, Georgia.

The decision to pursue Bragg's army and not to consolidate his forces in Chattanooga has been the source of much of the criticism of Rosecrans. The usual negative comment is that Rosecrans became too certain that Bragg was in full flight toward Atlanta and threw caution to the wind as he wildly sought to capture Bragg. Like so many things regarding Rosecrans, the accepted story becomes less clear cut when examined more closely. A review and timeline of the events of early September may lead to a better understanding of why Rosecrans made the decisions he did.

First it should be remembered that the orders to pursue Bragg were, in Halleck's words, "peremptory"; that is, there should be no further delay in carrying them out. Bragg evacuated Chattanooga because he felt his route to Atlanta was threatened, which it was. In order to threaten Bragg's southern flank, Rosecrans had to cross Lookout Mountain, which was only crossable at a few widely separated points. Therefore, to cause Bragg to leave Chattanooga, Rosecrans had to separate his army. On September 9, the day a part of one of Rosecrans' corps entered Chattanooga, most of his army was atop Lookout Mountain with plans to enter into the valleys east of the mountain. Rosecrans came to the conclusion that Bragg's army was in full flight in part because of misinformation supplied by "deserters" from Bragg's army. In fact it was Bragg who sent these "deserters" into Union lines. Washington proved no help in providing valid information. A dispatch on September 11 from Halleck told Rosecrans, "After holding the mountain passes on the west and Dalton, or some other point on the railroad, to prevent the return of Bragg's army, it will be decided whether your army shall move farther south into Georgia and Alabama. It is reported here by deserters that a part of Bragg's army is re-enforcing Lee. It is important that the truth of this should be ascertained as early as possible."[2]

In addition to the wildly erroneous suggestion that Bragg was reinforcing Lee, it should be noted that Halleck assumed that Rosecrans would take Dalton, which is more than thirty miles southwest of Chattanooga. To compound the inaccurate and dangerous information from Washington was the fact that the capital was apparently ignorant that Lee was reinforcing Bragg. This despite the fact that in the *New York Herald* of September 9 was the following: "It appears that some of Lee's best regiments, horse, foot, and artillery have been sent southward, but whether to Charleston or Chattanooga, we have yet to learn."

General John Foster, commander of Fort Monroe on the Virginia Peninsula, learned about the transfer before the authorities in Washington. He consequently informed Halleck that "trains of cars had been heard running all the time, day and night, for the last thirty-six hours, on the Petersburg and Richmond road, evidently indicating a movement of troops in some direction. Rosecrans had written Halleck on September 4, "Burnside's cavalry should close down and cover our left flank. Is it not possible the Lee's movements are intended to cover the temporary detaching of troops to Bragg?" Surely the military authorities in Washington played a large role in influencing the decisions that Rosecrans made.[3]

Another criticism of Rosecrans is that he ignored the advice of George Thomas at a meeting on September 9 to consolidate the Army of the Cumberland in Chattanooga instead of pursuing Bragg's army. There is no contemporary evidence of any meeting and nothing in the Official Records. The source usually cited is Thomas van Horne's biography of Thomas published in 1882. Such a recommendation is not mentioned in an earlier book by Van Horne, *The Army of the Cumberland*, published in 1875.

Rosecrans believed that with McCook being fifty and Thomas twenty-five miles away from Chattanooga, to withdraw in sight of the enemy would leave Crittenden's corps vulnerable to an attack from Bragg's total force. Therefore he deemed descending the eastern slope of Lookout Mountain and moving to the left to join Crittenden the only practical way to consolidate his army.

Late on September 9, Bragg received, among much conflicting information, word that Thomas was advancing toward McLemore's Cove. Bragg devised a plan to trap that part of Thomas' corps, commanded by James Negley, that was moving through the cove. Thomas Hindman would lead a force through Worthen's Gap on Pigeon Mountain into the northern end of McLemore's Cove. Patrick Cleburne of Hill's division would enter through Dug Gap and meet Hindman at Davis' Crossroads. There the combined force under Hindman would strike at the Union forces. This attack never came off. Several reasons and excuses have been given: confusion between written and verbal orders, illness of Cleburne, caution bordering on cowardice on the part of Hindman, and lack of confidence in Bragg by his subordinates. Moreover, Bragg could not be certain that Rosecrans' army was in fact so widely dispersed. Having been deceived about his enemy's position during the Tullahoma campaign and the recent campaign at Chattanooga, he could not be sure that the force in McLemore's Cove was not also part of a ruse. Bragg was still not sure of the exact disposition of Rosecrans' forces. When at 6 p.m. on September 11 the Confederates finally entered the cove, Negley was gone.

Bragg sensed a second chance to attack and defeat Rosecrans in detail, this time against Crittenden's divided corps to the north. After taking possession of Chattanooga Crittenden left one infantry and one cavalry brigade in the city and as ordered sent two divisions southeast toward Ringgold and one south along Chickamauga Creek toward Lee and Gordon's Mills. Bragg ordered the Corps of Polk and William H.T. Walker to strike first at the single division at Lee and Gordon's and then drive north and cut the road to Ringgold at Crittenden's rear. Again uncertainty led to delay and allowed Crittenden enough time to unite his three divisions. No attack was made.

Rosecrans now realized the perilous situation of his army. Not only was his enemy not in flight; it was being reinforced. From the offensive Rosecrans now needed to go on the defensive. His first requirement would be to reunite the separated corps of his army. McCook was ordered to close up on Thomas, and then the Thomas and McCook corps were to link up with Crittenden at Lee and Gordon's Mills. What should have taken one day using the shortest route instead became a three-and-a-half-day ordeal as McCook marched west via Lookout Valley, crossing and then recrossing Lookout Mountain rather than taking a road along Lookout Mountain to reach Thomas. Confusion about orders, which would be a hallmark of the ensuing battle, was the cause of McCook's delay. Nevertheless, by September 17 Rosecrans' army was united, with Crittenden's corps anchoring the left, Thomas in the center and McCook on the right at Steven's Gap.

Rosecrans had also ordered part of his reserve corps forward to Rossville. This force, made up of Steedman's division and Daniel McCook's brigade, was under Major General Gordon Granger. Rosecrans again asked Washington to send at least part of Burnside's troops to cover his left.

Bragg, who had twice failed within a three-day period to destroy or even attack Rosecrans' scattered forces, did not give up the initiative. His new plan called for Bushrod Johnson's corps to cross the Chickamauga at Reed's bridge and then turn left (south). Walker's corps was to cross farther upstream, that is closer to Crittenden, at Alexander's Bridge, unite with Johnson's corps and then attack the Union flank. Forrest's cavalry was to screen these movements. If this plan was carried out successfully, Bragg's army would be between Rosecrans and Chattanooga.

Bragg's plan may have succeeded but for the fierce resistance put up by Minty at Reed's bridge and Wilder's mounted infantry at Alexander's Bridge. Three infantry regiments, a battalion of cavalry and part of the Chicago Board of Trade artillery were able to hold off Johnson's corps and Forrest's cavalry for over eight hours. Finally driven across Reed's Bridge and outflanked on his left, Minty retired, and Johnson with 3,600 troops crossed the bridge at 4:30 p.m.

Further upstream (south), Wilder, with only part of one brigade and just four artillery pieces, was able to hold off Forrest and Walker's corps for almost five hours. As at Hoover's Gap, the Spencer repeating rifle proved to be the difference. Eventually Wilder withdrew and Walker crossed West Chickamauga Creek at Alexander's Bridge at 5:30 p.m.

This action on September 18 alerted Rosecrans to Bragg's intentions and caused him to make one of the most important decisions of the campaign. Realizing that his left was the key to his position, Rosecrans decided to send Thomas' corps to the left. In a movement that began at 4 p.m. and continued through the night, Thomas moved from McLemore's Cove, passed to the rear of Crittenden at Lee and Gordon's Mills, and began to take up positions on the Union left. By dawn on September 19, two of Thomas' divisions, Baird's and Brannan's on the extreme left, were in position while the rest continued their march north.

While this maneuvering occurred between the two armies, events far away were taking place that would ultimately determine the outcome of the battle. Three brigades of Longstreet's troops had already arrived on the morning of September 18. Six more brigades plus artillery were due to arrive over the next two days.

Washington had at last awakened to Rosecrans' precarious situation, in large part because of messages from General John Foster, commander of Fort Monroe on the Virginia Peninsula, to Halleck regarding the transfer of some of Lee's troops to Bragg. On September 13 orders to Grant, Sherman, Burnside and even John Pope in Minnesota were issued to rush troops to the Army of the Cumberland. None of these troops would arrive in time to help Rosecrans. Indeed the orders to Grant were "misplaced" and not received until after the battle of Chickamauga had been fought. As at Rich Mountain, Iuka, and Corinth, Rosecrans would fight a battle alone.

In addition to these purely military moves, another strange element was added to the picture. In mid-September, Charles A. Dana, officially assistant secretary of war, but in actuality a spy for Edwin Stanton, arrived at Rosecrans' headquarters. He had been in Mississippi where he had observed Grant and his army and reported to Stanton. Now he would do the same with Rosecrans. Dana would become perhaps the key figure in determining the fate of William S. Rosecrans.

The Battle of Chickamauga, the second greatest battle of the American Civil War, began unexpectedly on Saturday, September 19, at 7:30 a.m. Like so much of this battle it began in part because of incorrect information. General Thomas, now on the left, received word from Colonel Dan McCook, brother of corps commander Alexander McCook, that one isolated brigade of Bragg's army was west of the Chickamauga. Thomas decided to send Brannan's division to attack and destroy the presumed lone Rebel brigade. In fact all of W.H.T. Walker's and most of Bushrod Johnson's divisions, about twelve in total, were across the Chickamauga ready to move south and attack what the Rebels presumed was Rosecrans' left flank.

At about 8 a.m., Croxton's brigade of Brannan's division encountered Forrest's cavalry, which was in an area just west of Jay's Mill, and the battle was on. After driving the famed Rebel horseman's troops back, Croxton's forces themselves were hit hard and driven back by two divisions of Walker's corps. In response Thomas sent the remainder of Brannan's troops and three brigades of Absalom Baird's division into the fray. To counter this, Walker sent his other division commanded by St. John Liddell into Baird's right, driving it back almost two miles.

Already the pattern for the battle appeared. This was not to be a battle of troops marching in clear formations according to distinct plans. This would be more a brawl, with troops assembled randomly and thrown into wherever

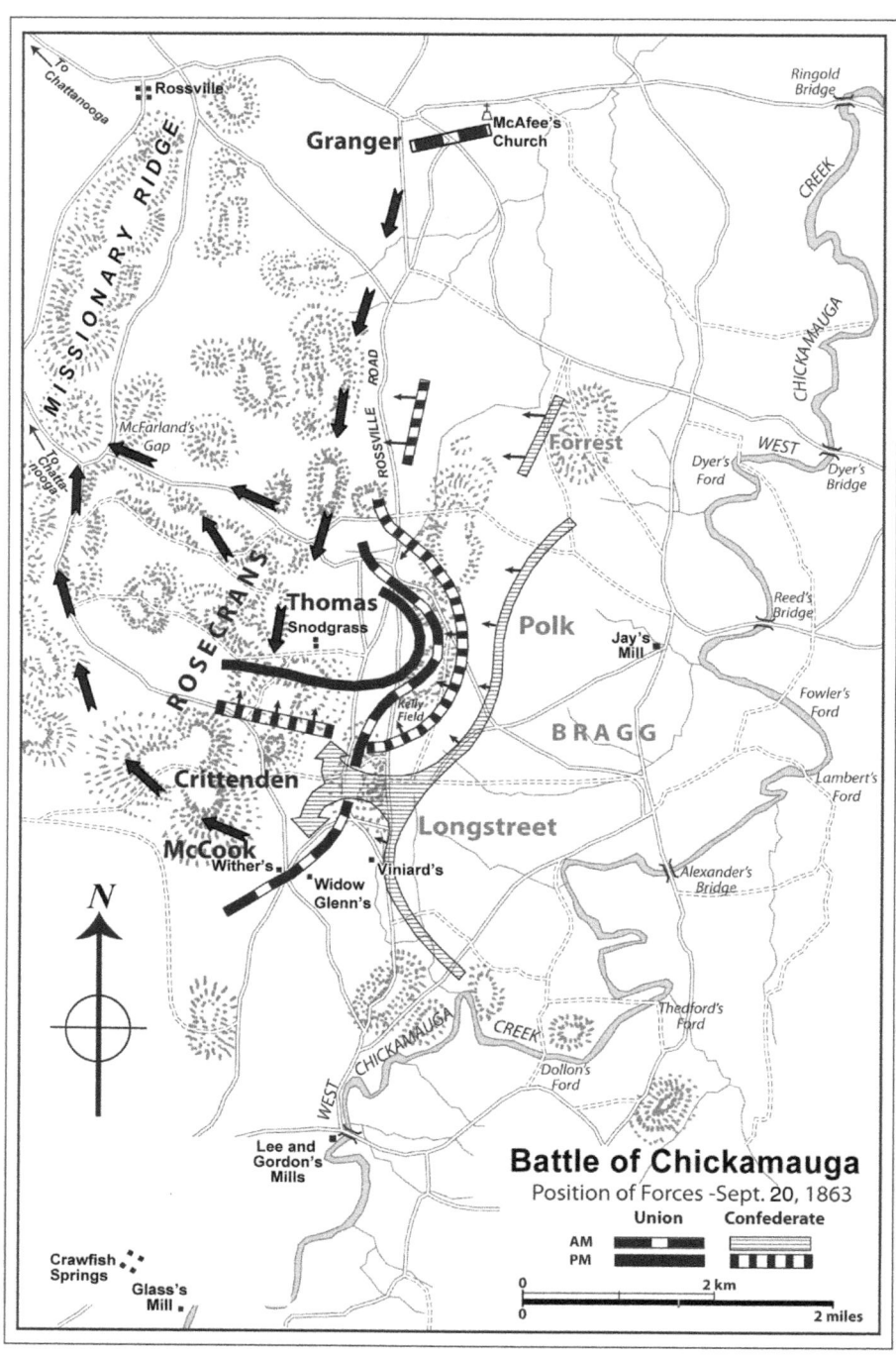

Battle of Chickamauga (NPS).

the fighting was hottest at a particular moment. Two important things had already happened. First, Bragg was wrong in his belief that his army outflanked Rosecrans. Because of the Union's nighttime maneuverings, the opposite was true. Second, somewhat inadvertently the Union army had taken the offensive away from Bragg. It was now the Rebels who were reacting to Union actions.

Thomas, after sending Brannan and Baird into the fight, was now out of his own troops as Negley and Reynolds were still marching behind Crittenden and had not yet reached him. Thomas asked for help from Rosecrans, still at Crawfish Springs near Lee and Gordon's Mills, who sent him Richard Johnson's division of McCook's corps. Marching up the Lafayette road and then turning east to the Reed House, these new troops slammed into Liddell's and halted the Rebel drive—temporarily.

The Confederate counterstroke came in the form of Cheatham's division of five brigades. Meeting this Rebel force were Richard Johnson's troops and Palmer's division of Crittenden's corps and Reynold's of Thomas' corps, which succeeded in driving Cheatham back. The tide of battle, on the north end of the battlefield at least, seemed to be tipping in the Union's favor. However, to the south the Rebels would launch attacks that would, if successful, sever the Union line.

At 2:00 p.m. Bragg, continuing to concentrate his efforts on the fighting on his right, next ordered Stewart to march downstream (north) and go to the aid of Cheatham. Stewart initially obeyed the non-specific order, but sensing that the battle line area just south of the fighting was quiet, he decided to attack it. The results proved spectacular. The Union forces he met, Van Cleve's division, were unprepared for battle and were swept back across the Lafayette road, the main artery connecting Thomas with Crittenden. The Union line was pierced as Stewart's men rushed forward. Rosecrans' headquarters at the Widow Glen cabin and the Dry Valley road, one of the two roads that connected the battlefield with Chattanooga, were within sight and reach of the Rebels. As fortune would have it the divisions of Negley and Reynolds, on the march to Thomas, were passing just as the Rebels were making their deepest penetration. Reynolds unleashed the power of twenty cannon against the Rebels, blunting their drive. Joining Negley and Reynolds was Brannan's division, dispatched by Thomas from the left. The Rebels were repulsed back across the Lafayette road, and this immediate threat to the Union center was over. However a new danger was about to arise.

To the left of Stewart was Hood's corps, recently arrived from its long journey from Virginia. Hood had not received any orders from Bragg all day. Hearing the noise from Stewart's encounter with Van Cleve and impatient to get into the fight, Hood, without orders, marched his two divisions into battle at 4 p.m. The six brigades of Evander Laws and Bushrod Johnson plunged into the three brigades of Jefferson C. Davis. The brigade of Hans C. Heg was almost demolished; Heg himself was killed. Again the Union line was breeched; again Rosecrans' headquarters was within the Rebels' grasp. However troops under Thomas Wood, Phil Sheridan, and Wilder's ubiquitous lightning brigade repulsed Hood's charge and saved the Union position. Wilder remembered the carnage as being so terrible that it seemed "at this point a pity to kill men so. They fell in heaps, and I had it in my heart to order the firing to cease, to end the awful sight."[4]

The fighting of September 19 was still not over. Cleburne's division, as of mid-afternoon still not engaged in the fight, was ordered by Bragg to attack the Union left. Had these troops been used to support either Stewart or Hood, a Confederate victory on September 19 was very possible. Instead Cleburne's men forded the icy-cold, shoulder-high Chickamauga at twilight and descended on Thomas. Thomas however had sensed the possibility of a late attack and had five brigades ready to meet any Confederate assault. Despite initial successes, the Rebel attack by Cleburne and Cheatham ended with the Yanks in control of the vital Lafayette road. The fighting of the first day of Chickamauga was over.

That night 130,000 men lay on the battleground fighting the cold and the lack of water. Thirst was a particular agony for the Union soldiers as they had no access to Chickamauga Creek and their only sources for water were the occasional spring and a pond that became known as the Bloody Pool. Although the Confederates were nearer to the creek that gave its name to the battle, some still needed to walk or crawl a mile to reach it.

Between the two armies lay the wounded and dying. Alva Griest of the 72nd Indiana wrote in his journal, "It is now 9 p.m. The thunder of battle has ceased for the first time since 8 a.m. but oh, a worse more heartrending sound breaks upon the night air. The groans from thousands of wounded in our front crying in anguish and pain, some for death to relieve them, others for water. Oh, if I could only drown this terrible sound, and yet I may also lie thus ere tomorrow's sun crosses the heavens, who can tell? I must sleep in spite of it all."[5]

Each commander planned for the next day. Rosecrans called a council of war at 11 p.m. at his headquarters at the Widow Glen house. He sensed that he was outnumbered, so to take the offensive was out of the question. He also sensed that Bragg would continue to strike at his left, hoping to get between his army and Chattanooga. Thomas, who according to Charles A. Dana's account written more than thirty years after the event deservedly napped after his night march and nearly continuous day of fighting, when asked for his opinion, replied, "I would strengthen the left." The question was, where would the troops to strengthen the left come from? Finally it was decided that

Thomas would essentially hold his position paralleling the Lafayette road. McCook would move the divisions of Sheridan and Davis to close up on Thomas' right. Van Cleve and Wood were moved behind Thomas' right. Granger in reserve was to move to a position where he could support either Thomas or McCook. Thomas was ordered to "defend your position with the utmost stubbornness. In case our army should be overwhelmed it will retire on Rossville and Chattanooga. Send your trains back to the latter place."[6]

Some may read an expectation of defeat in those words while others may see a plan for survival in case the worst transpired. The chief prize was control of Chattanooga, not Chickamauga Creek.

On the Confederate side, Bragg, knowing that Longstreet's arrival was imminent, decided to restructure his army. His three corps were reduced to two, one headed by Polk, the other by Longstreet. The merits of such a change in the middle of a battle are open to questioning. Surely the change didn't improve what had been a problem for Bragg during the whole Chickamauga Campaign—communication. Longstreet himself did not arrive until late on the night of the 19th, and then only after a circuitous trip from Catoosa Station that almost saw him captured by Union pickets.

Bragg's battle plan was the same as before: to attack the Union left, cut it off from Chattanooga and destroy Rosecrans' army in the mountains of north Georgia. Polk's corps would begin the attack followed by Longstreet. In a way this was to be a battle of might against might, the force of Bragg's army against the strongest part of Rosecrans' army. And for one of the very few times in the Civil War, the Confederates had the mightier force. When Thomas returned to his position after the war council, he learned from Baird that his division could not reach Reed's Bridge road, the direct route to Rossville and Chattanooga, without being dangerously weakened. More troops would be needed. Thomas asked Rosecrans for Negley's division which had been the last to arrive from Crawfish Springs and had been little involved in the fighting of the 19th.

Rosecrans personally inspected the lines of his entire army that night and early into the next morning. He discovered that Negley had not begun to move. He personally ordered Negley to move immediately to Thomas and for McCook to move more to the left to compensate for Negley's move. Then Rosecrans went himself to inspect the left. He, like Thomas, was convinced that Bragg would continue to hammer away at the left. Consequently Thomas would have six of the ten divisions of the army at his command.

The commanding general returned to the center only to discover that Negley still had not moved. Fearing that the fight would resume before the shifting troops were in place, he told Crittenden to have Wood's division replace Negley's place in the line rather than wait on McCook to arrive. Rosecrans went to McCook on the right, inspected the right line, and then returned to the center only to find that Negley was moving very slowly and Wood had not yet arrived and taken Negley's place in the center line. He personally started John Beatty's brigade of Negley's division toward Thomas and then searched out Wood. According to one source, when Rosecrans found Wood, whom he seemed at that moment to blame for Negley's slow departure, "he expressed himself very forcibly" and set in motion a succession of events that would affect the outcome of the battle. The fact is that the source for the alleged dressing down of Wood by Rosecrans, Henry M. Cist, was not at Chickamauga and therefore was not an eyewitness. Wood himself wrote that he did not feel he had been censured by Rosecrans, and the commanding general did not mention it in his official report. One of the most famous incidents of the battle of Chickamauga is based on one source written by someone who wasn't there.[7]

On the Confederate side of the battle line an old demon bedeviled the Army of Tennessee—delay in attacking. Polk's delay of nearly four hours bought the Army of the Cumberland valuable time. Much of that time was used in the felling of trees and the construction of fortifications by the soldiers of the Union left.

When the Rebel attack came it, as expected, hit the Union left. Breckinridge's division of three brigades initiated the fighting. Two brigades, those of Adams and Stovall, overlapped the Union left and found success against Baird. Help for Baird came, however, with the arrival of Beatty's brigade of Negley's division, which it should be recalled had been personally dispatched by Rosecrans after his trip to inspect the center. Soon more help came with the arrival of another of Negley's brigades, that of Stanley.

The tide turned slowly for the Union; in fact Adams was wounded and captured. Breckinridge had a third brigade, the "Orphan Brigade," commanded by Benjamin Hardin Helm. Helm was a brother-in-law of Abraham Lincoln married to Mary Todd Lincoln's half sister Emilie. Had Helm's brigade been sent in to support Adams and Stovall, Bragg's goal of rolling up Rosecrans' left may have been achieved. Instead Helm was sent against the part of the Union left that was protected by fortifications. Offensive bravery would be no match for a well-protected defensive line. The Orphans got caught in an enfilading fire and retreated. Helm was killed. After the battle, when Lincoln learned of his brother-in-law's death, he said, "I feel as David of old when he was told of the death of Absalom." After her husband's death, his widow, Emilie Todd Helm, stayed at the White House periodically at Lincoln's invitation.[8]

Cleburne's division was the next to go into action. Lucius Polk's division marched to the front. However the thrust came apart in the confusion of underbrush, smoke and a non-existent command structure and crashed and stalled at the breastworks of the Union line. When the divisions of Cheatham and Walker were thrown into the fight, they too met a similar fate against the strong Yankee defense.

In summary, for over two hours the Union left, which guarded the routes to Chattanooga, successfully repulsed repeated Confederate attacks. But the Union army was outnumbered. Thomas felt more troops were needed on the left, and Rosecrans agreed. From the Union perspective the battle was all about holding the left. Troops for the left would have to come from the center and right, but the center and right must still be maintained. This caused a need to shift troops in the midst of a battle. At 10:10 the following order was sent to McCook:

> General Thomas is being heavily pressed on the left. The general commanding directs to make immediate disposition to withdraw the right, so as to spare as much force as possible to re-enforce Thomas. The left must be held at all hazards—even if the right is drawn wholly back to the present left. Select a good position back this way, and be ready to start re-enforcements to Thomas at a moment's warning.

Twenty minutes later another order was sent to McCook:

> The general commanding directs you to send two brigades, General Sheridan's division, at once and with all dispatch to support General Thomas, and send the third brigade as soon as the line can be drawn up sufficiently. March them as rapidly as you can without exhausting the men. Report to these headquarters as soon as your orders are given in regard to Sheridan's movement.[9]

Here was the singular focus of the Army of the Cumberland on September 20, 1863: "The left must be held at all hazards even if the right is drawn wholly back to the present left." Things were about to become still more complicated and confused. At the same time the first order was sent to McCook, a sequence of events that would affect the outcome of the battle began. Around 10:15 Thomas sent Captain Sanford Kellogg to call for Brannan's division as had been agreed to the previous night at the Widow Glen meeting. Brannan's brigade was sandwiched between Reynolds to the left and Wood to the right. Since Brannan knew his departure would leave Reynolds' right "in the air" (that is a gap would exist), Brannan decided to consult with him. Reynolds believed he could hold his position and recommended that Brannan carry out Thomas' order. Kellogg, Wood and Reynolds also conferred about Reynolds' right being "in the air" after Brannan's departure. It was determined that Kellogg should go to Rosecrans and inform him of the situation that would arise as a result of Brannan's departure and to ask for replacement help on his right.

When Kellogg reached Rosecrans at his new headquarters in the Dyer Field, he told him of the gap that was about to be created. Rosecrans then turned to Frank Bond (rather than Garfield who was busy writing other orders), who wrote the following:

The general commanding directs that you close up on Reynolds as fast as possible, and support him.

Respectfully, etc.

Frank S. Bond, Major and Aide-de-Camp

The order was given to Lieutenant Colonel Lyne Starling who later testified under oath,

> General Rosecrans ordered me, in the presence of General Crittenden, to go to General Wood and order him to close to the left on Reynolds and support him. There was no firing, and no evident need of support for any one, and I hesitated, not understanding the object of the order, when General Garfield, General Rosecrans' chief of staff, called out to me that the object of the order was that General Wood should occupy the vacancy made by the removal of Brannan's division, Brannan having been ordered to General Thomas' left. I gave the orders to General Wood, told him the object of it, and he stated General Brannan was in position, and that there was no vacancy between him and Reynolds. I told him then there is no order, for that was the object of it.

Wood said he discussed the order with Alexander McCook who counseled that the order should be obeyed, as Rosecrans probably had a better understanding of the situation. A famous story is that Wood, still smarting from his supposed reprimand by Rosecrans earlier that morning, decided to carry out the order regardless of its practicality. The story has Wood saying, "Gentlemen, I hold the fatal order of the day in my hand and would not part with it for five thousand dollars." It seems incredible that Wood would risk the fate of the army, not to mention his own life, by doing something he considered "fatal." Again the eyewitness documentation of this is very slim. However, Wood apparently had been told by Stirling that the situation as it now existed meant "there was no order." If Starling's sworn testimony given to a court-martial jury is true, it raises questions about Wood's decision to carry out the order, especially in light of Wood's objection to carrying out an order he considered dangerous back on September 6.[10]

No matter what he may or may not have said, what he did is beyond dispute. He pulled out his two brigades and created a gap. By itself, a temporary gap isn't necessarily fatal, but just across the Lafayette road, General James Longstreet, veteran of Pickett's Charge, was about to strike at the Union center.

"Old Pete" Longstreet, present at Chickamauga for less than twenty-four hours, had already scouted out the ground in front of his position utilizing information from the Brotherton brothers who lived on the ground currently inhabited by the Union center. He amassed a column made up of three divisions divided into five lines. Longstreet's charge would be massive and deep as opposed to the piecemeal attacks of Bragg and Polk. Unlike the famous Pickett-Pettigrew-Trimble charge at Gettysburg, which covered an area over

General Thomas J. Wood his decision created the "fatal gap." Whether it was intentional or not is still disputed.

a mile wide, this charge would concentrate on an area just one-half mile wide. Counting Thomas Hindman's division just to the south of the main column over 12,000 Confederates would take part in the attack.

Under any scenario this massive column, led by one of the ablest generals of the Confederacy, would have had a good chance of success. But it encountered not just a weakened Union center but an open gap caused by Wood's division's departure. At ten past eleven on Sunday, September 20, 1863, the signal was given for the charge to begin. Bushrod Johnson's division was in the center, with Thomas Hindman's on his left and John Bell Hood's on the right. As the force marched, it found next to no resistance. Within minutes Johnson had reached the Dry Valley road. The Union line was cut in two, Davis and Sheridan on the right separated from Reynolds to the left. Additionally there is evidence in the records of three commanders on the right, Sheridan, Davis and Wood, that the initial penetration came through the right flank of the Union line. Wood maintained in a letter to the *New York Times* written in 1882 that

> the all-important fact to be here noted is this: That through the gap thus made in the line, to the right and rear of Gen. Davis's position, the Confederates not only could have passed, but did actually pass and gain the rear of the national line, entirely irrespective of the opening made in the line by the withdrawal of my division. This statement is fully sustained by the fact, first, that Laibold's brigade, which was further to the right and rear than was Gen. Davis's division, was struck by the Confederates before Gen. Davis's division; and, second, by the fact that Gen. Davis's division was not simply struck by the Confederates—it was almost wholly enveloped by them.

Davis wrote in his Official report of Laibold "deploying his troops to form line on my right, but before the movement was fully completed his brigade received a heavy attack from that part of the enemy's line which had passed thus far unopposed around my right flank."

Sheridan in his Report said,

> I had just abandoned my position, and was moving at a double-quick when the enemy made a furious assault with overwhelming numbers on Davis' front, and, coming up through the unoccupied space between Davis and myself, even covering the front of the position I had just abandoned the enemy made a furious assault with overwhelming numbers on Davis' front, and even covering the front of the position I had just abandoned, Davis was driven from his lines.[11]

It's possible that Longstreet would have broken the Union right whether there had been a "fatal gap" or not.

When Longstreet's breakthrough happened, Rosecrans was behind Davis' division. Initially he, along with his aides, underestimated the extent of destruction to his right wing. As he had at Stones River he personally tried to rally the fleeing troops. William Sumner Dodge wrote, "Here General Rosecrans threw himself into the very thickest of the fight. He rallied the disorganized masses from the Dry Valley Road, and with General Sheridan repulsed the enemy."

Austin Stebbins of the 89th Illinois remembered,

> Rosecrans came riding up the ridge from the south, and cried "Form a new line! Don't fall back! Make a stand here. Hold this ridge for General Sheridan's sake." He rode on north along the ridge, and we began and had formed nearly our whole regiment in line when Sheridan came up on his black horse from the south, the same as General Rosecrans had, and said: "Fall back, boys! Fall back!" His keen eyes had seen off to the left, north of us, what general Rosecrans could not have seen 15 minutes before, because they were not there then, in an open field not more than a quarter of a mile away—15,000 or 20,000 rebel troops marching to cut us off. It was a grand sight, a score of battle-flags floating triumphantly on the breeze. This was Longstreet's Corps, flushed with victory. They were marching rapidly to the west.

Dean R. Chester wrote a letter to his brother, who in turn sent it to Abraham Lincoln:

> The last we saw of him on that eventful Sunday (Sept. 20) was when he was attempting to rally his troops in a perfect hailstorm of shot, shell and minie balls and if you could have heard the remarks of the men after they had fallen back and the whole army was supposed to be in retreat you would have learned something of the reliance we placed in him as our commander.... I saw him myself in the very thickest of the fight he was not in the least excited, as a man under the influence of liquor would certainly have been at such a time (for it was when things looked darkest on the right) but rode along with perfect calmness saying what he did in an ordinary tone: As he passed us he stopped and said; Now boys, *rally* and make one charge *for me*.

Thomas J. Ford of the 24th Wisconsin recalled that

> Rosecrans said, "The rebels are defeated and are retreating at another part of the line, and if you could have held them here five minutes longer the battle would be ours." Some stood and listened, and three times as many went on. The general took off his hat and said, "Boys, form a line here; there are enough of us to whip those rebels. We have them on the run in another part of the field. If you won't do it for my sake, do it for God's sake and for your country's sake."[12]

Rosecrans, a devoutly religious man, also did something any religious person would do at a moment of crisis—pray. He wrote his brother Bishop Rosecrans after the battle, "I could hear the roar of the battle and knew the swarming rebel host were surging against our brave men. But in the midst of it all I prostrated myself in spirit at the feet of our Crucified Lord and implored His most Sacred Heart to pity us and I repeated to our Holy Lady the prayer of the church very often Monstra te esse Matra ['Show Yourself to be a Mother' from the Latin prayer 'Ave Stella Maris']." In a moment of supreme need, Rosecrans was calling for divine intervention.[13]

The Confederate tide pushed Rosecrans back along the Dry Valley road, a road that passed through McFarland's Gap, then to Rossville and Chattanooga. With him were Davis, McCook, and Sheridan. Also on the road was chief of staff Garfield. Now was the moment for a crucial decision. If the fight for Chickamauga Creek was lost, there still remained the main prize of Chattanooga to protect. If part of the army, under Thomas, still survived, to what extent should it be reinforced? In other words, who should go to Chattanooga and who to Thomas? Rosecrans or Garfield?

There are, not surprisingly, two versions of how that question was resolved. The Rosecrans version is that the commanding general told Garfield to go to Chattanooga and he would go to Thomas. He listed six orders that Garfield should make upon reaching Chattanooga.

"General Garfield, can you not give these orders?" I asked. Garfield answered:

"General, there are so many of them, I fear I might make some mistake; but I can go to General Thomas for you, see how things are, tell him what you will do, and report to you."

"Very well. I will take Major Bond and give the orders myself. I will be in Chattanooga as soon as possible. The telegraph line reaches Rossville, and we have an office there. Go by Sheridan and Davis and tell them what I wish, then go to Thomas and telegraph me the situation."

Garfield's version, as told to General Jacob Cox, was that Rosecrans, "rode silently along, abstracted, as if he neither saw nor heard." Garfield went to him and suggested that he be allowed to try to make his way by Rossville to Thomas. Garfield had to beg Rosecrans to let him go. Rosecrans "assented listlessly and mechanically."[14]

Although one-third of the Army of the Cumberland had been driven off the field, that still left two-thirds still on the field. The left wing under Thomas had so far survived the morning attacks against it. Not all of the right wing of the army was driven away. Before Longstreet's assault, parts of the divisions of Brannan, Wood and Van Cleve had been sent to the left. These troops eventually reached Thomas near the Snodgrass farm and formed a line south and perpendicular to troops already there. This new line formed along an outcropping of stone that came to be known as Horseshoe Ridge. Thus the remnant of the Army of the Cumberland formed into a reverse-shaped L along hilly terrain known as Snodgrass Hill.

The Army of Tennessee had scored a great triumph in destroying its opponent's right. But it had not achieved its ultimate goal of cutting the Army of the Cumberland from Chattanooga and driving it south into the mountains of north Georgia and destruction. Ironically, in routing the Cumberland Army's left, it drove that army north toward Chattanooga. If the Tennessee Army was to achieve its ultimate goal, it would have to launch new attacks against the opponent on Snodgrass Hill and capture the roads that led to Chattanooga.

Over the next few hours a series of attacks, Longstreet said twenty-five, were made against the Yankees at Snodgrass Hill. The Northerners were outnumbered, and a gap of about a quarter mile existed between the right and left wings of the army. This gap was never discovered by the Rebels and thus was never exploited. As gallant as the stand of the army's left wing had been and was continuing to be, gallantry alone would not be enough to win. Luckily the Cumberlanders had one last card to play: the reserve corps under Gordon Granger.

Rosecrans had telegraphed Granger the night of the 19th, "You must help us in the fight tomorrow by supporting Thomas." This order was vague as to a specific time, but it did give Granger the authority to make a move on his own. That is exactly what he did. First hearing the sounds of battle at about 10:30 a.m., he concluded, "We are needed over there and if we don't hurry up it will be too late." He marched to Thomas with the two brigades of James Steedman. The timely arrival of these 7,500 troops and ammunition made the difference in driving the Confederates from Horseshoe Ridge.[15]

Rosecrans arrived at Chattanooga between 3:30 and 4:00 p.m. He was close to exhaustion and had to be helped from his horse. He was overheard to say, "I am nearly worn out and I want someone with me to take command, if necessary to assist me."[16]

However, he was able to carry out the tasks he had wanted Garfield to do. He sent the following to Thomas:

> Assume command of all the forces, and with Crittenden and McCook take a strong position and assume a threatening attitude at Rossville. Send all the unorganized force to this place for re-organization. I will examine the ground here and make such dispositions for defense as the case may require and join you. Have sent out ammunition and rations.

And to Garfield:

> See General McCook and other general officers. Ascertain extent of disaster as nearly as you can and report. Tell General Granger to contest the enemy's advance stubbornly, making them advance with caution. Should General Thomas be retiring in order, tell him to resist the enemy's advance, retiring on Rossville to-night.

He even tried to contact the wandering Burnside:

> We have met with a severe disaster. The extent of it is not yet known. If you are near enough to join us, do so at once. If you are still too far away to form a junction, let me know your exact position, and I will advise you what you had better do.[17]

And to Halleck:

> We have met with a serious disaster; extent not yet ascertained. Enemy overwhelmed us, drove our right, pierced our center, and scattered troops there.

Thomas, who had seven divisions, remained intact at last news. Granger, with two brigades, had gone to support Thomas on the left. Every available reserve was used when the men stampeded. Burnside will be notified of the state of things at once, and you will be informed. Troops from Charleston, Florida, Virginia, and all along the seaboard are found among the prisoners. It seems that every available man was thrown against us.[18]

But Halleck already knew because Charles A. Dana had telegraphed on his own initiative the following: "My report to-day is of deplorable importance. Chickamauga is as fatal a name in our history as Bull Run."[19]

Just before 4 p.m. Garfield reached Thomas. He sent a message to Rosecrans which ended,

The hardest fighting I have seen to-day is now going on here. I hope General Thomas will be able to hold on here till night, and will not need to fall back farther than Rossville; perhaps not any. All fighting men should be stopped there, and the Dry Valley and Lookout roads held by them. I think we may in the main retrieve our morning disaster. I never saw better fighting than our men are now doing. The rebel ammunition must be nearly exhausted. Ours is fast failing. If we can hold out an hour more it will be all right. Granger thinks we can defeat them badly to-morrow if all our forces come in. I think you had better come to Rossville to-night and bring ammunition.

Another dispatch was sent by Garfield at 8:40 and concluded,

General Thomas has fought magnificently. From the time I reached the battle-field (3.45 p.m.) till sunset the fighting was by far the fiercest I have ever seen. Our men not only held their ground, but at many points drove the enemy splendidly.... The rebels have, however, done their best to-day, and I believe we can whip them to-morrow. I believe we can now crown the whole battle with victory. Granger regards them as thoroughly whipped to-night, and thinks they would not renew the fight were we to remain on the field.... The troops are now moving back, and will be here in good shape and strong position before morning. I hope you will not budge an inch from this place, but come up early in the morning, and if the rebs try it on, accommodate them.

To which Rosecrans replied,

You may stay all night. If the enemy are drifting toward our left (Rossville position), have men ordered up. I like your suggestions.[20]

Thomas began withdrawing his troops from the battlefield at twilight. Nearly as heroic as the stand at Snodgrass was the removal of troops in the darkness through McFarland's Gap to Rossville where they rested until morning. "Like magic," Longstreet wrote, "the Union army had melted away in our presence." The second-greatest battle of the Civil War was over.[21]

11. After Chickamauga

When Rosecrans arrived in Chattanooga on September 20, he telegraphed the following to Washington:

> We have met with a serious disaster; extent not yet ascertained. Enemy overwhelmed us, drove our right, pierced our center, and scattered troops there. Thomas, who had seven divisions, remained intact at last news. Granger, with two brigades, had gone to support Thomas on the left. Every available reserve was used when the men stampeded. Burnside will be notified of the state of things at once, and you will be informed. Troops from Charleston, Florida, Virginia, and all along the seaboard are found among the prisoners. It seems that every available man was thrown against us.[1]

However Washington had already learned about the fight of the 20th from Charles A. Dana, officially assistant secretary of war but considered by many a spy for Stanton. His dispatch began, "My report to-day is of deplorable importance. Chickamauga is as fatal name in our history as Bull Run" and concluded "Rosecrans escaped by Rossville road. Enemy not yet arrived before Chattanooga. Preparations making to resist his entrance for a time."[2]

Dana is one of the key figures in the William Rosecrans story. His role is second to no one's in the perception of Rosecrans as a "dazed and mazy commander" incapable of leading his army in the aftermath of Chickamauga. Not only were his dispatches instrumental in determining Rosecrans' fate in 1863, but they are still regarded today as being authoritative by historians. However Dana was not an impartial and disinterested observer, and his own conduct on September 20 was not only less than courageous but detrimental to the Union cause. Nevertheless in the hours and days immediately after Chickamauga, when the need for honesty and frankness was paramount, his dispatches to Washington are not an unbridled catalog of pessimism. His second dispatch to Washington illustrates this point:

> CHATTANOOGA, September 20, 1863—8 p.m.
>
> I am happy to report that my dispatch of 4 p.m. to-day proves to have given too dark a view of our disaster. Having been myself swept bodily off the battle-field by the panic-struck rabble into which the divisions of Davis and Sheridan were temporarily converted, my own impressions were naturally colored by the aspect of

that part of the field. It appears, however, that only those two divisions were actually routed, and that Thomas, with the remainder of the army, still holds his part of the field ... strengthened by the addition of that portion of the reserve lately stationed at Rossville under Granger."

Dana concluded, "Some gentlemen of Rosecrans' staff say Chickamauga is not very much worse than was Murfreesborough. *I can testify to the conspicuous and steady gallantry of Rosecrans on the field. He made all possible efforts to rally the broken columns; nor do I see that there was any fault in the disposition of his forces.*" [Emphasis added][3]

What Dana leaves out is his own dubious actions at the time of Longstreet's breakthrough. John Wilder with his mounted infantry planned to fight his way to Thomas on the left. In his official report written less than two months after the battle, he wrote, "General Dana, Assistant Secretary of War, came up and said that 'our troops had fled in utter panic'; that it was a worse rout than Bull Run; that General Rosecrans was probably killed or captured; and strongly advised me to fall back and occupy the passes over Lookout Mountain to prevent the rebel occupancy of it."[4]

In his *Reminiscences*, written in 1898, Dana claimed to have come upon Wilder who asked, "Will you give me any orders?" Dana said he had no authority to give orders, "but if I were in your situation, I should go to the left, where Thomas is." He then headed for Chattanooga.[5]

In 1908 Wilder told a story more critical of Dana:

> He then said I must take him at once to Chattanooga to enable him to telegraph the situation to Washington. I told him he had been going in the opposite direction of Chattanooga and would have been in Bragg's lines before he had gone much farther.... With a scared look, he insisted that it was the enemy pursuing and killing Thomas' men, and again asserting that he was the Assistant Secretary of War, directed me to move with my command, escorting him to Chattanooga, that he might communicate with Washington at once. I told him I had scouts who knew the country to Chattanooga, and that they could guide him there in as little time as it would take me to get up my lead horses and mount my men. He agreed to go with the scouts and again directed me to fall back to Chattanooga as quickly as possible and place my command on Lookout Mountain and hold it at all hazards, and to send my transportation across the Tennessee River, and then left us in the direction of Chattanooga with the scouts.[6]

Whose story is true? There is an account from a third person who witnessed the exchange between Wilder and Dana: Smith D. Atkins who in 1875 wrote,

> Dana ...positively ordered Wilder to withdraw to Chattanooga. Wilder was daring and desperate; Dana a coward and an imbecile; and but for Dana's order Wilder would have undertaken that desperate charge, and would have succeeded in joining Thomas with a portion of his gallant brigade.

Wilder firmly believed the charge would have resulted in the route of Longstreet's corps and the defeat of Bragg's army: "I would have struck them in flank and rear with five lines of Spencer rifles, in the hands of the steadiest body of men I ever saw, and am satisfied we would have gone through them like an avalanche. I have gone over Chickamauga field with a great many ex-rebels who all admit that if I had been allowed to attack as I wished, it would have been fatal to Bragg's army."[7]

The preceding shows that at the very least what Dana wrote should be subject to scrutiny.

On the 21st, Thomas was at Rossville between Missionary Ridge and Chattanooga. It became apparent to him as well as others that the army was not safe at Rossville. Thomas wrote in his report:

> From information received from citizens, I was convinced that the position was untenable in the face of the odds we had opposed to us, as the enemy could easily concentrate upon our right flank, which, if driven, would expose our center and left to be entirely cut off from our communications. I therefore advised the commanding general to concentrate the troops at Chattanooga.

The movement from Rossville began at 9 a.m. Thomas wrote,

> The troops were withdrawn in a quiet, orderly manner, without the loss of a single man, and by 7 a.m. on the 22d were in their positions in front of Chattanooga, which had been assigned to them previous to their arrival, and which they now occupy, covered by strong entrenchments thrown up on the day of our arrival, and strengthened from day to day until they were considered sufficiently strong for all defensive purposes.[8]

As for Bragg, he has been criticized for not immediately attacking Rosecrans after Chickamauga. Again the real situation he faced is not so simple. Bragg's army on the night of the 20th was a very badly hurt army. It may have been victorious in the sense that it had driven the Cumberland Army from the field of fighting, but it had not destroyed the Northern army. In fact Bragg was not sure if he had even won. Doubt about whether a victory had been won also affected Polk and Longstreet. In addition to the loss of men, Bragg's army faced problems of a lack of food, wagons, pontoons and other essentials needed for an offensive. On September 21, Nathan Forrest sent the following to General Polk:

> We are in a mile of Rossville. Have been on the point of Missionary Ridge can see Chattanooga and everything around. The Enemy's trains are leaving going around the Point of Lookout Mountain.
>
> The prisoners captured report two pontoons thrown across for the purpose of retreating. I think they are evacuating as hard as they can go. They are cutting timber down to obstruct our passage. I think we ought to push forward as rapidly as possible.

Forrest assumed that what he was seeing was Rosecrans retreating from Chattanooga when in fact it was Thomas moving his troops from Rossville to Chattanooga. The claim that Bragg could have beaten Rosecrans on the 21st of September ignores all of the factors mentioned above; plus it assumes that Rosecrans was evacuating Chattanooga in full flight. In reality Rosecrans, since his hasty arrival at Chattanooga on the 20th, had prepared the defenses of the city to protect against just such an attack. For the next few days the Army of the Cumberland waited for the expected Confederate assault, but none came. Bragg realized that Chattanooga had become impregnable. He wrote to Jefferson Davis, "It would be murderous to assault the enemy's superior forces in his intrenchments. Our efforts will be devoted to drawing him out." He decided to lay siege to Chattanooga.[9]

It is instructive to read the dispatches of Charles A. Dana to Washington in the immediate days after Chickamauga, a time when an honest assessment was most needed. Four messages sent on September 22–23 are especially interesting.

CHATTANOOGA, September 22—6 p.m.

Rosecrans is considering question of retreat from here. I judge that he thinks that unless he can have assurance of ample re-enforcements within one week, the attempt to hold this place will be much more disastrous than retreat. That part of the army which was routed on Sunday is much demoralized. If you have any advice to give, it should come to-night.

CHATTANOOGA, September 22, 1863—9.30 p.m.

Rosecrans has determined to fight it out here at all hazards. The official returns show the army to consist of 35,000 effectives. There are here ten days' full rations, sufficient for twenty days in case of need. Besides it will be difficult for enemy to interfere with our hauling from Bridgeport via Jasper. Of ammunition there is enough here for two days' hard fighting in field, and this will last much longer behind rifle-pits.

The enemy will most probably attack in morning.

CHATTANOOGA, September 23, 1863—10 a.m.

All quiet yet. Enemy is in front along our whole line. The troops rested well last night, and are greatly refreshed. Everything ready.

CHATTANOOGA, September 23, 1863—11.30 a.m.

The net result of the campaign thus far is that we hold Chattanooga and the line of Tennessee River. It is true this result has been attended by a great battle with heavy losses, but it is certain that the enemy has suffered quite as severely as we have. The first great object of the campaign, the possession of Chattanooga and the Tennessee line, still remains in our hands, and can be held by this army for from fifteen to twenty days against all efforts of the enemy, unless he should receive re-enforcements of overwhelming strength. But to render our hold here perfectly safe no time should be lost in pushing 20,000 to 25,000 efficient troops to Bridgeport. If such re-enforcements can be got there in season, everything is safe, and this place—indispensable alike to the defense of Tennessee and as the base of future operations in Georgia—will remain ours.[10]

Here in a nutshell was the Army of the Cumberland's situation. It held Chattanooga, its morale had improved, but it needed what had for so long been denied it—reinforcements. At last Washington would do something about that.

Upon receiving this telegram from Dana, Stanton immediately went to work to reinforce Rosecrans' army. That evening he had Lincoln, Halleck and Chase awakened for a middle-of-the-night meeting where he proposed the transfer of 30,000 troops from the Army of the Potomac to the Cumberland Army. The 11th and 12th corps under Hooker were sent west and arrived at Bridgeport within twelve days. This transfer has been justly praised as one of the great logistical triumphs of the war, but it was not perfect. Hooker was not allowed to take his best horses and mules with him.

Instead of these seasoned animals, he was supplied with inferior ones at Nashville. As William G. Le Duc remembered,

> General Grant says [in his *Memoirs*], "Hooker had brought with him from the east a full supply of land transportation. His animals had not been subjected to hard work on bad roads without forage but were in good condition...." This should have been the fact but unfortunately was not. Hooker's command when ordered west had land transportation of the most efficient description, more than 6000 mules and horses seasoned to army work in marches made through

Secretary of War Edwin Stanton. Perhaps the most powerful man in Washington.

> Virginia clay and quicksand from Fredericksburg to Gettysburg and back to the Rappahannock; but against protest they were ordered to be turned in to the corrals at Alexandria and Washington. Hooker's troops were supplied from the corral at Nashville with all sorts of animals, young and old, broken and unbroken. These choice and efficient trains [animals], that could be relied on to do effective work day and night, were thus broken up and the want of them was soon after most seriously felt on the Tennessee.... Many died on the roads before reaching Bridgeport.[11]

The discrepancy between an eyewitness, Le Duc, and Grant's *Memoirs* should be noted.

On September 15, Halleck had ordered Grant to reinforce Rosecrans, but Grant didn't receive the order until September 18. On the 22nd, Grant ordered one division sent to Rosecrans. The following telegram sent to Rosecrans on September 21 illustrates the woeful ignorance of the authorities in Washington:

> Nothing heard from General Burnside since the 19th. He was then sending to your aid all his available force. It is hoped that you will hold out till he can re-enforce you. He was directed to connect with you ten days ago, and the order has been repeated several times since. I can get no reply from Hurlbut or Sherman.

Despite all the urgings, including the terse order from Lincoln to "Go to Rosecrans with your force without a moment's delay," Burnside never would arrive.[12]

By September 24 reinforcements from two armies were on their way to Rosecrans. The defenses of Chattanooga were strong enough that Dana wrote Stanton, "With our present defenses it is desirable they [the enemy] should attack us." The confidence and morale of the army had been restored. About Chattanooga, Dana had

> no further doubt about this place; it will hold out. Indeed, it has now been made so strong that it can only be taken by regular siege. The labors of this army for last forty-eight hours have been herculean. As soon as Hooker arrives and Sherman and Hurlbut make their appearance in Tuscumbia Valley, it will be able to resume the offensive irresistibly.[13]

Yet beginning with a dispatch on September 27, the tone and content of Dana's missives to Washington take a negative turn. It began,

CHATTANOOGA, September 27, 1863.

> A very serious fermentation reigns in the Twentieth and Twenty-first Army Corps, and, indeed, throughout this whole army, growing out of events connected with the battle on Sunday last.

Later Dana touched on Rosecrans:

> The defects of his character complicate the difficulty. He abounds in friendliness and approbativeness, and is greatly lacking in firmness and steadiness of will. He

is a temporizing man; dreads so heavy an alternative as is now presented, and hates to break with McCook and Crittenden. Besides, there is a more serious obstacle to his acting decisively in the fact that if Crittenden and McCook fled to Chattanooga, with the sound of artillery in their ears, from that glorious field where Thomas and Granger were saving their army and their country's honor, he fled also; and although it may be said in his excuse that, under the circumstances, it was proper for the commanding general to go to his base of operations, while the corps commanders ought to remain with their troops, still he feels that that excuse cannot entirely clear him either in his own eyes or in those of the army. In fact, it is perfectly plain that while the subordinate commanders will not resign if he is retained in the chief command, as I believe they certainly will if McCook and Crittenden are not relieved, their respect for him as a general has received an irreparable blow. And that not from his abandonment of the army alone but from his faulty management on the field, especially in leaving a gap of a whole brigade distance between the divisions of Wood and Davis, and not providing for it till after the battle had become furious, when he attempted to fill it with Van Cleve's forces as I have explained in former reports. But for this gap General Davis thinks the enemy could not have broken his lines and routed the right wing. Thus you will see that here in the face of the enemy this army is in a dangerous condition. The officers who have taken this grave resolution are among the bravest and most discreet in our service. In my judgment the removal of Crittenden and McCook is imperatively required, not merely as a matter of discipline, but to preserve the efficacy, not to say the organization, of this army. *If it be decided to change the chief commander also, I would take the liberty of suggesting that some Western general of high rank and great prestige, like Grant, for instance, would be preferable as his successor to anyone who has hitherto commanded in East alone.* [Emphasis added]¹⁴

So now Dana, who just three days earlier was optimistic about the army's situation, not only becomes pessimistic but he suggests the removal of Rosecrans and even recommends a successor—Grant.

Interestingly another visitor, Quartermaster General Montgomery C. Meigs, arrived at Chattanooga on September 27 and sent a letter to Washington:

CHATTANOOGA, September 27, 1863. [Received 450 a.m., 28th.]
Honorable E. M. STANTON,
Secretary of War:

I have with General Rosecrans visited the lines of defense of this place. I have seen the men vigorous, hearty, cheerful, and confident. The position is very strong already, and rapidly approaching a perfect security against assault. Nothing but a regular siege could, I think, reduce it. That would take time. The difficulties of transportation of supplies are immense. The roads are rocky and mountainous, yet trains get through without much destruction of wagons. When the river rises the bridges will go, but the river will become navigable. One steam-boat and a few flats are ready for service. Another steam-boat is nearing completion. For another the machinery is at Bridgeport. The water is too low at present for the Paint Rock, the captured steam-boat, to navigate the river, and the rebels command the channel. When the troops understood to be on their way here arrive, General Rosecrans expects to recover command of the river to Bridgeport. Supplies can then be accumulated by water. A month's hard service has much injured the wagon-trains; animals still in very fair condition, so far as I have seen them. Plenty of them here and at Nashville. *I have spent the time thus far with the commander and the chief officers of this army. It is difficult for the leaders to abstain from claiming a complete victory. They believe they could have remained upon the battle-field, and that in that case the enemy would have retired. The crushing of the right and center, or of a portion thereof, led to the movement by which the army fell back upon and occupied Chattanooga. Chattanooga is fast becoming a fortress and depot which will serve as a base of future operations. As I now see this field it appears to me that the great effort of the rebels by which, concentrating in Georgia, they hoped to crush this army and recover possession of Tennessee and Kentucky, has failed. If so, the fruits of victory are with General Rosecrans, though the trophies, the battle-field, and part of the wounded have fallen into the hands of the enemy.* Still, the rebels have not yet abandoned their purpose. Their camp-fires covered the hills last night. Their pickets are within rifle shot, and are visible from the intrenchments. The men await them with confidence. I doubt their attempting an assault. If they are wise I think they will not. ...*Things look much better here than I expected to find them when I left Nashville; still success will demand efforts from the army and from the country. Of the rugged nature of this region, I had no conception when I left Washington. I never traveled on such roads before.*

M.C. MEIGS, [Emphasis added][15]

Thus we have two starkly contrasting assessments made on the same day. It is in these conflicting views that the story of William S. Rosecrans turns. It is essential to now examine his actions and his state of mind in the days after Chickamauga.

Rosecrans said he went to Chattanooga because Garfield felt incapable of doing all the things required there. The first order of business was to do those things. Next was to prepare the city for the eventual arrival of Thomas and the rest of the Army of the Cumberland and to strengthen the defenses for an expected Confederate attack. That attack never came, in part because of the strong Union position. With more troops finally on the way, two issues were now paramount: the morale of the army and the need to resupply it. Rosecrans visited the troops in the days after the retreat into Chattanooga. General William Carlin remembered,

> Rosecrans rode around our line, and addressed a few words to each regiment. When he reached my brigade he seemed almost overcome with emotion, and leaned forward from his horse as if intending to embrace me....But in this tour around the line, though the marks of care and grief were plainly visible on his face, he spoke cheerily to the troops, and endeavored to infuse into them his own cheerful spirits.[16]

James H. Montgomery wrote in his diary:

Tuesday September 22: We are much reduced in numbers—but not in spirits.

Wednesday September 23: We were visited this afternoon by Maj. Genl. Rosecrans—he spoke in glowing terms of the bravery and endurance of this brigade. I was glad to see him.... We moved to the front in rifle pits and worked on fortifications to night.... Old Rosa says he will stay here for here was where we started to come.[17]

Lyman Bennett of the 36th Illinois recalled,

General Rosecrans passed along from left to right, encouraging the men and receiving hearty cheers wherever he went. "We started for Chattanooga"; said he, "we are in Chattanooga, and we will stay in Chattanooga."

On September 27, Harvey Reid wrote his parents of

the deep satisfaction and pride that one army has gained (if they, have not *whipped* the enemy) a great *moral* victory. In spite of the concentration before him of largely superior numbers gathered with the resolution of annihilating his army entirely, the iron-hearted Rosecrans has held firmly all the ground he won by his matchless strategy and now we can say with positive assurance that Tennessee is redeemed.

Colonel Oscar Harmon of the 125th Illinois wrote to his family on September 29:

The enemy were in great force, probably two to our one. We held our ground both days, but fell back at night to a stronger position. We were not whipped, but repulsed. Chattanooga is now held by us, and will be held forever. It is a very strong place and is now hemmed in by at least three ditches dug by General Rosecrans. Am sorry he was not re-enforced, so that we could have routed the enemy.[18]

These are just a few quotes from an army of over 35,000 men, but the overwhelming evidence shows a defiant and confident army. With Chattanooga strengthened against attack, morale restored and more troops on the way, the one remaining task was to resupply the army. Rosecrans, who was nothing if not a meticulous planner, had, before Chickamauga, already taken measures for the next phase of the campaign. He had contracted with two companies to repair the railroad bridge crossings at Bridgeport and Running Water in late August before his army began its move across Lookout Mountain. He also ordered the construction at Bridgeport of five flat-bottom stern-wheel steamboats to be used between there and Chattanooga. After Chickamauga and the retreat to Chattanooga, Rosecrans ordered the construction of two pontoon bridges so that communication and transportation north across the Tennessee could be made. A sawmill, necessary for the building of the bridges, was also ordered built.

Although the soldiers of the Army of the Cumberland suffered because of reduced rations, it should be noted that the soldiers of the Army of Tennessee suffered as well. One soldier wrote in his diary, "Bragg is as badly off for provisions as Rosecrans." The result of the deprivations was an increase in desertions. Bragg wrote Johnston, "The deserters are an incumbrance to me and must be shot or they run off again."[19]

Rosecrans made the decision to remove troops from Lookout Mountain. Many critics have considered this a major blunder. The truth is more complicated. The Federal troops on Lookout Mountain commanded by General James G. Spears were given orders to contest the enemy for the mountain "inch by inch foot by foot." On September 22 the Union force was attacked and driven back by four regiments of Confederate infantry and artillery. The next day Rosecrans ordered all but one regiment into Chattanooga; one regiment was to remain at the mountain's point as a picket. Before that order was received, "a considerable force of the enemy" appeared and demanded a surrender of the Union troops.

On September 24 the following was sent to General McCook: "The general commanding directs that you take immediate measures to hold the foot of Lookout Mountain as an outpost, and take every means to annoy the enemy and thwart him in his attempts to gain possession of it."[20]

However reports from McCook and Sheridan of being in the line of fire from Confederate sharpshooters on the mountain persuaded Rosecrans that it would be impossible to hold the mountain. In 1865 in sworn testimony before the Joint Committee on the War he justified his decision:

> General Halleck in his annual report says I abandoned the passes of Lookout Mountain, leaving the public to imagine that these passes were within the possible control of my army, and their abandonment not justified as a military measure. I call the attention... to the fact that one of these passes was 42 miles south of Chattanooga, and the next nearest 26 miles south of Chattanooga, and the nearest at the extremity of Lookout Mountain in front of our lines.... I was satisfied that I could not even hold this pass [the closest] and Chattanooga at the same time if the enemy did his duty, and therefore withdrew my troops from it.

Rosecrans did not simply give up Lookout Mountain to the Confederates but said he "established batteries on the other side of the river, which rendered it practically of little, if any, use to them."[21]

This placement of artillery at Moccasin Point, now called Moccasin Bend, opposite the point of Lookout Mountain, has been ignored by historians. This battery largely prevented Bragg from entering and occupying Lookout Valley with a sizable force. One of the very few historians to study the topic found that "the Federal batteries at Moccasin Bend played a critical role in the military operations around Chattanooga. From the very beginning, Longstreet would be unable to maintain an effective presence in Lookout Valley, largely because the 'Moccasin Battery' prevented him from easily moving troops across

Lookout Mountain or into Lookout Valley, and made it all but impossible to supply any troops that did make it into Lookout Valley." He concluded, "Rosecrans's decision to place artillery on Moccasin Bend on September 22 was easily his most important action in establishing a successful defense of Chattanooga. The efficient Union gunners contributed much more than their full share to the defense and relief of Chattanooga. In fact, the defense and relief of Chattanooga was due, in great part, to their nearly forgotten service at isolated Moccasin Bend during two months in the cold, wet Fall of 1863."[22]

The next task was the building of pontoons. On September 23, Rosecrans called for Colonel P.V. Fox, head of the first Michigan engineers, telling him, "I want a pontoon bridge across the river east of Cameron Hill as soon as possible. You have carte blanche to take anything you can find for it." A problem was the lack of timber sufficient to build the pontoon bridge. Fox came up with a design for a different-shaped boat that would require less wood. When Captain Fox went to army headquarters with his new design, it was ridiculed by General Morton, chief engineer of the Army of the Cumberland, who said it would not work. Rosecrans, however, said he thought it might work and told Fox to carry out his plans. When a few boats were completed Rosecrans and some other officers went down to the river where they got into one of the boats to test its buoyancy. Satisfied that the boats would work, he said, "The boats are all right, go on with your work." By October 7 the bridge was complete and put in use. It was about this time that a rift occurred between Rosecrans and Morton. Rosecrans felt that Morton was trying to have his prediction that Fox's boats were worthless come true. He reprimanded Morton and turned over the operation of the sawmills to Fox, telling him, "I want you to take charge of both sawmills; get out another bridge as soon as possible. Use your own ideas about the form of boats. You can have all the details you can use; the entire Pioneer Brigade, Morton's, if you want them." By October 23, fifty boats were ready for a new bridge.[23]

Rosecrans' next and biggest problem was supply, not just food rations but ammunition and forage for the animals. Although the Confederates did not have a strong presence in Lookout Valley west of Lookout Mountain, they did maintain a picket line along the south bank of the Tennessee River preventing Union use of the direct supply route along the river. Denied use of the railroad on the south side and Haley Trace on the north, Rosecrans improvised a route up the Sequatchie Valley and over Walden's Ridge via the Anderson road. This route had the benefit of being out of range of Confederate fire but was an arduous forty miles over twisting and in some places almost nonexistent roads from the Union base at Bridgeport.

On September 30 Bragg sent Wheeler on a raid against the Union supply lines. Wheeler crossed the river at Washington, Tennessee, forty-five miles northeast of Chattanooga, traversed Walden's Ridge and entered Sequatchie Valley. Wheeler sent John Wharton's division to take the supply depot at McMinnville. Upon hearing of Wheeler's crossing of the river, Rosecrans ordered Colonel Edward McCook and General George Crook to pursue the Rebel cavalry to the "utmost."

While in the Sequatchie Valley, Wheeler attacked a train of supply wagons nearly five miles long that was crossing Walden's Ridge. Although between 350 and 500 wagons were destroyed, Wheeler was counter-attacked in the valley by cavalry troops of Colonel Edward McCook who boasted of whipping the rebels badly and inflicting "nearly every wound ... with the saber."[24]

The real objective of Wheeler's raid was Murfreesboro and the Nashville and Chattanooga Railroad. Crook beat the Confederates to Murfreesboro and then united with McCook at Shelbyville. This combined force then began to pursue Wheeler, and on October 7 at Farmington, Tennessee, Crook defeated Wheeler who retreated southwest into Alabama.

Bragg intended Wheeler's raid to be part of a larger attack involving troops of Philip Roddy and Stephen Lee. A consequence of this attack was Rosecrans' decision to use the newly arriving XI and XII Corps from the Army of the Potomac to guard the railroad and supply line from Murfreesboro to Bridgeport. This delayed their use in the plan to reopen the supply route to Chattanooga.

Another unanticipated factor was rain. As long as the weather stayed dry, the long trip over Walden's Ridge was difficult but doable. At the beginning of October a soaking rain began that would render the roads nearly impassable. Rations were cut back; animals began to drop dead for lack of fodder; the morale of the troops began to resemble the weather. It became imperative to open a supply line. Most histories tell a story of a dazed and confused commander, "stunned like a duck hit on the head," incapable of saving his army. The truth is more complicated.

Before the battle of Chickamauga, Rosecrans had contracted with companies in Cleveland and Chicago for construction of a railroad bridge at Bridgeport, Alabama. After Chickamauga the immediate concern was to strengthen the defenses of Chattanooga. On September 24, Rosecrans was informed by Halleck that reinforcements from the Potomac Army were on their way to him:

> The corps of fourteen or fifteen thousand men to be sent from here has the usual amount of artillery, but no cavalry. If the artillery is not deemed necessary, the railroad transportation will be greatly diminished. Please answer.

Rosecrans replied:

> Please send the infantry by brigades as fast as possible. Let the artillery follow at leisure. The great point is to have troops at Stevenson and Bridgeport, to secure

those points and the railroad. We can hold this point if we can keep up communication and supplies.[25]

On September 30 the first of Hooker's troops arrived at Bridgeport. Lieutenant Henry Hodges, quartermaster at Nashville, inquired, "Will you please give me an idea as to where the troops now coming in [Hooker's] will be for the present?" Rosecrans responded, "The troops coming in will operate on the Lookout Valley line unless called northward." On October 1, Hooker was ordered to "put down a pontoon bridge and make immediate preparation for crossing your command at that point." Rosecrans' plan was for Hooker to advance to Wauhatchee in Lookout Valley.[26]

However, September 30 was also the day Wheeler set out on his raid against the Union supply lines. Rosecrans was forced to deploy the XI and XII Corps to protect the railroad, thus postponing their move into Lookout Valley. While this was taking place, work continued in Chattanooga on a pontoon bridge that Rosecrans had ordered built. Dana telegraphed Stanton, "[Rosecrans] is about to lay a bridge across Tennessee at mouth of Lookout Creek, so that he can operate from here in that valley without crossing the mountain." Thus the outline of a plan to reopen the water route from Bridgeport to Chattanooga can be discerned. Hooker would enter Lookout Valley, and the Tennessee River would be bridged at Lookout Valley.[27]

On October 4, Hooker received the following: "The general commanding hopes the enemy's cavalry will soon be destroyed, and that he may be able to bring your whole command forward to this side of the river. I have just sent you a set of maps I hope soon to supply your officers."[28]

By October 12, after the repulse of Wheeler at Farmington, Rosecrans was ready to try again to have Hooker enter Lookout Valley. He sent the following to Hooker: "Can you ready a column of one division to move up to Shellmound and push an advance brigade to Whitesides to start by daylight in the morning? They can take ten days' rations in haversack and knapsack."

Hooker, however, felt himself not ready, as shown in his reply: "I can do it, but only with infantry. I should prefer to have a battery to accompany the column, but as the horses have just arrived I doubt if they will be in readiness that early."

Rosecrans deferred to Hooker's judgment, telling him, "I will delay the order until your batteries are ready. Hasten their preparation and report when ready. The object is to get possession of the line of the river up to this place." He also told Hooker to "hasten on the steam boat. The preparation of that is of primary importance for your movements and mine."[29]

Rosecrans' plans are revealed in an October 16 missive from Dana to Stanton:

> I have just had a full conversation with General Rosecrans upon the situation. He says the possession of the river as far up as the head of Williams' Island, at least is a sine qua non to the holding of Chattanooga, but that it is impossible for him to make any movement toward gaining such possession until General Hooker's troops are concentrated and his transportation gets up. Hooker's troops are now scattered along the line of the railroad, and cannot be got together before next Wednesday [October 21].
>
> The wagons must all have arrived by that time, and if the enemy does not interfere sooner the movement upon Raccoon Mountain and Lookout Valley may then be attempted.[30]

By the middle of October many steps had been taken to solve the army's supply problem: steamboats were under construction in Chattanooga and Bridgeport, pontoon bridges were being built in both places, and troops were gathering in Bridgeport for an imminent move into Lookout Valley by Hooker. One last detail remained: where to place the pontoon bridge that would link up with Hooker's force.

On October 19, Rosecrans, W.F. "Baldy" Smith, J.J. Reynolds, and Frank Bond rode across the pontoon bridge crossing the Tennessee at Chattanooga. The group separated as Rosecrans and Bond visited a hospital and then went to a spot called Brown's Ferry, which had been selected as the site for the laying of the pontoon bridge that would meet up with Hooker. Baldy Smith also separately visited Brown's Ferry that day. Meanwhile at headquarters a telegram from Washington arrived. When Rosecrans and his party returned to Chattanooga, he read the following:

> Washington, October 16, 1863.
>
> I. By direction of the President of the United States the Departments of the Ohio, of the Cumberland, and of the Tennessee will constitute the Military Division of the Mississippi.
>
> II. Major General U.S. Grant, U.S. Army, is placed in command of the Military Division of the Mississippi, headquarters in the field.
>
> III. Major General W.S. Rosecrans, U.S. Volunteers, is relieved from the command of the Department and Army of the Cumberland. Major General G.H. Thomas is hereby assigned to that command.
>
> By order of the Secretary of War:
>
> E.D. TOWNSEND,
> Assistant Adjutant-General.[31]

Rosecrans decided to leave the next morning at five o'clock. "I can't bear to meet my troops. I want to leave before the announcement is made." He summoned Thomas who at first objected to taking Rosecrans' position, but Rosecrans insisted,

George ... we are in the face of the enemy. No one but you can safely take my place now; and for our country's sake now you must do it.... Don't fear, no cloud of doubt will ever come into my mind as to your fidelity to friendship and honor.... I can't bear to meet my troops. I want to leave before the announcement is made, and I will start out early in the morning.

He then went over with Thomas the plans for relieving Chattanooga Thomas, asking, "General I want you to be kind enough to explain the exact plan for the taking of Lookout Valley as you proposed it."[32]

Finally William S. Rosecrans wrote the following to be read to his troops after his departure:

CHATTANOOGA, TENNESSEE, Oct. 19, 1863.

The General Commanding announces to the officers and soldiers of the Army of the Cumberland that he leaves them under orders from the President. Major-General George H. Thomas, in compliance with orders, will assume the command of this army and department. The chiefs of all the staff departments will report to him. In taking leave of you, his brothers in arms, officers and soldiers, he congratulates you that your new commander comes not to you, as he did, a stranger. General Thomas has been identified with this army from its first organization. He has led you often in battle. To his known prudence, dauntless courage, and true patriotism you may look with confidence that under God he will lead you to victory.

The General Commanding doubts not you will be as true to yourselves and your country in the future as you have been in the past. To the division and brigade commanders he tenders his cordial thanks for their valuable and hearty co-operation in all that he has undertaken. To the chiefs of the staff departments and their subordinates, whom he leaves behind, he owes a debt of gratitude for their fidelity and untiring devotion to duty.

Companions in arms, officers and soldiers, farewell, and may God bless you.

W.S. ROSECRANS, Major General[33]

Harvey Reid who was at Fort Rosecrans near Murfreesboro as the railroad car carrying Rosecrans passed through noted that "the grim old Chieftain ... was seated entirely alone on the side of the car.... He had on an old blue overcoat, and wore a common white wool hat drawn down over his eyes, and looked so much like a private soldier.... He was either tired with riding all night, or he had something on his mind for he appeared almost *sad* as he looked vacantly out the window without seeming to see anything that he was passing." Reid mistakenly believed Rosecrans was on his way to take command of the Army of the Potomac.[34]

In most histories this is where the Rosecrans story ends; his trip from Chattanooga is a trip to historical obscurity. But the Rosecrans story should not and does not end with his removal from command. He still had a role to play in the war. That role will be discussed later. But before leaving Chattanooga it is important to look at the story surrounding Rosecrans' removal.

Indeed historian Allan Nevins has written, "His removal, like that of other high officers, was long to be a theme of controversy. The precise circumstances surrounding it have never been clarified." So before moving on it is important to examine those unclarified circumstances.[35]

12. Grant in Control

After Vicksburg, Grant and his army had been largely absent from any military activity. During this interval Grant had proposed to Halleck a movement against Mobile. Halleck instead wanted troops sent west to Texas to face any threat on the border from French-occupied Mexico. Rosecrans, who was crossing the mountains and rivers around Chattanooga at this time, was not on either's priority list. Grant went to New Orleans, arriving September 2, to confer with General Banks. While attending a gala in the Crescent City, Grant suffered the mishap on horseback that practically rendered him an invalid. Rumors of alcohol abuse also resurfaced.[1]

This reverie was ruptured suddenly by Halleck's telegram of September 15 ordering Grant to send troops to Rosecrans. Because of delays, Grant didn't receive this order until September 27 while he was now back at Vicksburg. A dispatch dated October 3 directed Grant to go to Cairo, Illinois.

When he reached Cairo on October 16, he received a new order directing him to Louisville where he would receive further instructions from a figure from the War Department. The trip to Louisville took Grant to Indianapolis where the train, as it was departing, was stopped so an important passenger could get on. That passenger was Edwin Stanton. Stanton carried two orders, both putting Grant in command of the combined armies of the Ohio, Cumberland and Tennessee. One kept Rosecrans as head of the Cumberland Army; the other replaced him with Thomas. Grant chose the latter.

In his *Memoirs*, Grant implies that he made this decision based on the fear that Rosecrans was about to retreat from Chattanooga:

> On the receipt of Mr. Dana's dispatch Mr. Stanton sent for me. Finding that I was out he became nervous and excited, inquiring of every person he met, including guests of the house, whether they knew where I was, and bidding them find me and send me to him at once. About eleven o'clock I returned to the hotel, and on my way, when near the house, every person met was a messenger from the Secretary, apparently partaking of his impatience to see me. I hastened to the room of the Secretary and found him pacing the floor rapidly in his dressing-gown. Saying that the retreat must be prevented, he showed me the dispatch. I immediately wrote an order assuming command of the Military Division of the Mississippi, and telegraphed it to General Rosecrans. I then telegraphed to him the order from

Washington assigning Thomas to the command of the Army of the Cumberland; and to Thomas that he must hold Chattanooga at all hazards, informing him at the same time that I would be at the front as soon as possible. A prompt reply was received from Thomas, saying, "We will hold the town till we starve."

Thomas' response is usually taken as a last-gasp sign of desperation. His full reply was,

> Two hundred and four thousand four hundred and sixty-two rations in storehouses; ninety thousand to arrive tomorrow, and all the trains were loaded which had arrived at Bridgeport up to the 16th—probably three hundred wagons. I will hold the town till we starve.

Rosecrans later wrote, "I well remember the receipt of that telegram, and the surprise and indignation with which Thomas and I viewed it. We regarded it as an aspersion on the Army of the Cumberland and its commander, founded either in ignorance or malice. We had as little idea of abandoning Chattanooga as anybody in the world.[2]

The problem with Grant's story of the order relieving Rosecrans is that it was sent and received during the day of October 19; the order to Thomas was sent at 11:30 that night. The order to relieve Rosecrans was sent before and not after Grant says he saw Dana's telegram. In fact, as will be seen, Grant never had any intention of retaining Rosecrans. The idea that he was reacting to a fear of an imminent abandonment of Chattanooga is simply a pretext. Dana's telegram read in part, "If the effort which Rosecrans intends to make to open the river should be futile, the immediate retreat of this army will follow. It does not seem possible to hold out here another week without a new avenue of supplies," and ends, "If, on the other hand, we regain control of the river and keep it, subsistence and forage can be got here, and we may escape with no worse misfortune than the loss of 12,000 animals."

The "immediate retreat" would come only if Rosecrans' attempt to open the river supply route failed.[3]

After spending a day in Louisville with Stanton, Grant left for Nashville on the 20th; he continued on to Stevenson, Alabama, arriving on the 22nd. There he met Rosecrans who was headed north. Grant says in his *Memoirs*, "He came into my car and we held a brief interview, in which he described very clearly the situation at Chattanooga, and made some excellent suggestions as to what should be done. My only wonder was that he had not carried them out." On the evening of October 23, Grant, on crutches and having to be carried at some points along the route, arrived at Chattanooga. John Atkinson of the 3rd Michigan recalled,

> The Army of the Cumberland was not enthusiastic about General Grant. They had heard in a general way of his great victories, but knew less of him than those

who had been at home and who had an opportunity to read the papers. His appointment from another army seemed to be a reflection upon their own. When he came to Chattanooga, he was crippled. His leg had been hurt by his horse falling. He had made the long distance from Bridgeport over the mountains in two days. He suffered so much from his injuries that he had to be carried over rough places, not being able to endure the movement of his horse. He was thin and wore a look of intense anxiety upon his face. He was, at that time, but forty-one years of age, but looked much older. He was very far from being an ideal soldier.

James Harrison Wilson described the first Thomas-Grant meeting: "I found Grant on one side of the fireplace, steaming from the heat over a small puddle which had run from his sodden clothing. Thomas was on the other side, neither saying a word but both looking glum and ill at ease." Wilson continued:

> Learning ... that nothing had yet been offered for their comfort, and knowing that General Grant would not condescend to ask for an act of hospitality, I took the liberty of saying "General Thomas, General Grant is wet and tired and ought to have some dry clothes.... He is hungry ... and needs something to eat. Can't your officers attend to these matters for him?" This broke the silence and set the machinery of hospitality in motion.... What could have offended Thomas remained always a matter of conjecture, but it cannot be doubted that he felt justified in the reserve he showed to Grant, not only then but always afterwards.[4]

Evidently Thomas didn't see Grant as the savior of the army.

After supper, General "Baldy" Smith presented a plan for opening the supply line, the "cracker line," to Grant. Grant approved the plan which called for a force under Hooker to enter and seize Lookout Valley. This force was to meet up with two columns from Chattanooga under Generals Turchin and Hazen at Brown's Ferry.

One of the columns embarked by water under cover of darkness on October 27 at 3 a.m.; the other crossed the neck of Moccasin Bend. At daybreak the south bank of the river at Brown's Ferry was seized; Hooker's column, after defeating the Confederates at Wauhatchee, linked at Brown's ferry at 5 p.m. The now opened route from Bridgeport to Kelly's Ferry to Brown's Ferry to Chattanooga and the arrival of the steamer *Chattanooga* ended the partial siege of Chattanooga.

Usually in histories of the relief of Chattanooga, this plan is credited to General Smith. However General Rosecrans claimed and testified under oath before the Joint Committee of the War in 1865 that the plan was essentially his. The order from Thomas to Hooker at Bridgeport read, "You will use all possible dispatch in concentrating your command and preparing to move in accordance with the instructions of General Rosecrans."

A controversy began that was finally investigated by a Military Court of Inquiry in 1901. That inquiry concluded,

After a diligent search of the Official Records the board fails to find any evidence that Gen. W.F. Smith was the originator of the plan for the relief of Chattanooga, Tenn., by military operations to be conducted in Lookout Valley, October, 1863. On the contrary, there is abundant evidence in the Official Records to show that the plan, which contemplated crossings of the Tennessee River at Bridgeport and at the northern end of Lookout Valley, and which was successfully executed by General Thomas October 26 to 28, 1863, was devised and prepared for by General Rosecrans before relinquishing command, and that its execution was begun, under orders issued by General Thomas, the very night (October 19) that General Rosecrans was relieved from command of the Department of the Cumberland and without consultation with General Smith.

Herein lies an answer to Grant's wonderment that Rosecrans' plans weren't carried out.

Much of the dispute stems from what is meant by "mouth of Lookout Creek." Smith claimed that Rosecrans was unaware of Brown's Ferry and that it was Smith who discovered the site and conceived the plan for seizing it. Several persons who were present at Chattanooga including J.J. Reynolds, Frank Bond, and John Wilder attested that Rosecrans was aware of, visited and selected Brown's Ferry as the site for a pontoon bridge.

Some of the confusion comes from a map made in August prior to the army's entry into Chattanooga that misplaced Brown's Ferry near the tip of Lookout Mountain and Lookout Creek. Smith maintained that Rosecrans intended to place a pontoon crossing at this point which was directly in the Confederate line of fire from atop the mountain. The Court of Inquiry concluded that,

> to assume that an officer of General Rosecrans's attainments would have attempted to throw a bridge at the mouth of Lookout Creek, when the long-established road from Chattanooga into Lookout Valley crossed at Browns Ferry, much nearer Chattanooga and quite beyond the reach of the enemy's guns, is too preposterous for serious consideration. Undoubtedly the terms "mouth of Lookout Creek" were used as equivalent to the mouth of Lookout Valley.[5]

When Quartermaster William Le Duc was singled out in the memoirs of General Richard Johnson as the originator of the idea of building steamboats for the relief of Chattanooga, he sent a letter of correction to Johnson, which said,

> Please accept my thanks for your kindly mention, but you give me credit overmuch. If not beyond your control, could you not have your text changed, so as to express the exact truth, which is that I found a scow in process of construction on the banks of the Tennessee River, when I arrived there with General Hooker's command.... Rosecrans with prudent foresight had ordered the construction of five steamers on the Tennessee, and the repair of the railroad, two very important bridges of which had been destroyed by the rebels...
>
> General Rosecrans has not received the credit due him for his skillful conduct

of the campaign. He foresaw the probable need of river transportation, and, so far as giving orders provided for the emergency. Had those entrusted with the execution of these orders pushed through their work more energetically, and had the boats ready for use when needed, great loss of animals and distress of men would have been saved, and Rosecrans would have retained his position as commander of the Army of the Cumberland. The unfriendliness of Assistant Secretary Dana and the impatience of Secretary Stanton secured his downfall."[6]

If it is assumed that Rosecrans did in fact have a plan for opening the river and was on the verge of implementing that plan, why wasn't he allowed to carry it out?

The answer most often given is that Rosecrans was about to retreat from Chattanooga; however, the only source for this is Grant's interpretation of Dana's telegram. Hardly anyone then or now contends that Rosecrans was about to leave Chattanooga. Dana claimed to have sent a telegraph to that effect, but no record of such a telegram is in the Official Records.

The other justification for Rosecrans' removal is that after Chickamauga he had become incapable of action, "confused and stunned like a duck, hit on the head," in Lincoln's often-quoted phrase. If actions speak louder than words, what Rosecrans did from September 21 to October 19, 1863—fortifying Chattanooga, ordering bridges, pontoons, steamboats and sawmills built, defending against and pursuing Wheeler and planning a military action to reopen the river to Chattanooga—should rebut what Dana said about him.

At any rate the "stunned duck" quote has an interesting history. It was made on October 24 after Rosecrans had been removed. Of course what Lincoln knew about Rosecrans' state of mind was coming from third parties— mostly Dana. Perhaps Lincoln was justifying an action he didn't really want to take. Lincoln later said, "I find it is scarcely less than indispensable for me to do something for Gen. Rosecrans," and in time he did.[7]

Rosecrans always considered Chickamauga the battle for Chattanooga. In that sense it was not a loss, as the city remained in Union control for the duration of the war. Most of the Cumberlanders agreed. Emerson Opdycke, who was not an admirer of Rosecrans, wrote his wife, "Although we have been chastised a little, yet the *campaign* is a success. Rosecrans was to clear Tennessee of rebels troops, and occupy Chattanooga, which was done in a brilliant manner; but he was tempted to do more, and but for the cowardice of some of his officers, he would have put a period to the war in the West." Lyman G. Bennett of the 36th Illinois made this assessment thirteen years after the battle:

> But the verdict of time is not very different from that which our army gave as they entrenched themselves at the foot of Lookout, that provided we held Chattanooga it was for our army a great triumph. For, if to attain and hold the objective point of the campaign, to throw ourselves across such a river, and by wise and vigorous

marching day and night over mountains and through mountain gaps, threaten communications and then elude attack in detail, gather up our widely scattered forces and concentrate in the face of an outnumbering enemy, foil his plans to throw himself on our flanks, and then in a great battle not only hold him at bay, but inflict upon his overwhelming force such terrible losses that he was incapable of any but the most cautious following when we fell back to occupy the place for which we had been contending—if all this was not success, what was it?

John Turchin, whose brigade took part in the plan to open the "Cracker Line" wrote, "The battle of Chickamauga, instead of demoralizing our men, served as a fiery furnace, in which their bravery was steeled and hardened so as to be proof against any danger and undaunted under any reverse, however appalling."[8]

Some Southerners also questioned their victory on the banks of the "River of Death." Elise Bragg wrote to her husband,

I fear our victory is like all we ever are permitted to gain *undecisive* & with a fearful loss of men. We have the glory of some prisoners & cannon—Rosecrans still holds the points *he* aimed at, Chattanooga, East Tennessee, Cumberland Gap. When we succeed in retaking what we have just lost, I shall then believe some substantial good is obtained.

In 1865 William Loring said to journalist W.S. Furay,

Our cause is probably lost, but your temporary victories up to the latter part of 1863, had little to do with it. Not a man in the Southern Confederacy felt that you had really accomplished anything until Chattanooga fell.... As long as we held it, it was the closed doorway to the interior of our country. When it came into your hands the door stood open, and however rough your progress in the interior might be, it still left you free to march inside. I tell you, that when your Dutch General Rosecrans commenced his forward movement for the capture of Chattanooga, we laughed him to scorn; we believed that the black brow of Lookout Mountain would frown him out of existence; that he would dash himself to pieces against the many and vast natural barriers that rise all around Chattanooga; and that then the Northern people and the government at Washington would perceive how hopeless were their efforts when they came to attack the *real* South.

Furay asked Loring, "But the capture of Chattanooga convinced you that even the real South was vulnerable, did it?" who replied, "Yes, it was then only a question as to whether we could beat back your armies by sheer force of desperate fighting, and as you largely outnumbered us, and our resources were every day diminishing, the prospects to the thinking part of our people looked gloomy indeed." "But, general," Furay said, "there are people in the North who regard the Chickamauga campaign as a failure for the Union arms." "Ah!" Loring replied, "we would gladly have exchanged a dozen of our previous victories for that one failure."

General D.H. Hill wrote in 1886,

> There was no more splendid fighting in '61, when the flower of the Southern youth was in the field, than was displayed in those bloody days of September '63. But it seems to me that the *élan* of the Southern soldier was never seen after Chickamauga—that brilliant dash which had distinguished him on a hundred fields was gone forever....He was too intelligent not to know that ... the failure to strike after the success was crushing to all his longings for an independent South.... He fought stoutly to the last, but after Chickamauga, with the sullenness of despair and without the enthusiasm of hope. That "barren victory" sealed the fate of the Southern Confederacy.[9]

Before leaving Tennessee it is important to summarize briefly what happened in the weeks after Grant's arrival in Chattanooga and the opening of the river. On November 7, Grant ordered Thomas to make an "attack on the northern end of Missionary ridge, with all the force you can bear to bring against it, and, when that is carried to threaten and even attack, if possible, the enemy's line of communications between Dalton and Cleveland." Grant closed his orders, "Immediate preparations should be made to carry these directions into execution. The movement should not be made one moment later than to-morrow morning. You having been over this country, and having had a better opportunity of studying it than myself, the details are left to you."

This order was made less than two weeks after the supply line had been opened and before Sherman's arrival. The Army of the Cumberland was in no shape to launch a major offensive. Thomas and Baldy Smith were shocked. According to Smith, Thomas said to him, "You must get that order for an advance countermanded, I shall lose my army." Smith felt that "the whole idea seems to have crudeness entirely out of place in the mind of a general commanding an army." Thomas and Smith went to Grant on the night of November 7 and convinced him to wait until Sherman's arrival before attacking.

Grant eventually settled on a plan which called for Sherman to lead the assault on the north end of Missionary Ridge. The result of the fight on November 25 was that Sherman, with three army corps plus an extra division could not drive Cleburne's lone division plus two brigades and two divisions, off the ridge. It has been called by historian Peter Cozzens "one of the sorriest episodes of this or any battle of the war. Sherman's failure to turn Cleburne's line defies explanation."[10]

But there was still fighting to be done on the day. Grant ordered Thomas to attack the Confederate rifle pits at the base of the Ridge. Thomas reluctantly gave the order, which resulted in the Union troops being right in the line of Rebel fire from the top of the ridge. Then in one of the great moments of the war, the soldiers of the Army of the Cumberland, without orders, charged up Missionary Ridge and cleared the Rebels from it.

November 25 and the taking of Missionary Ridge was one the pivotal days in the entire Civil War. However the Union victory was not the result of any master plan engineered by Grant. Instead it was the unintended, unforeseen actions of the Army of the Cumberland, the army Rosecrans had built, which won the day. Grant would later claim that his plan all along was for Thomas to lead the main thrust and Sherman's attack was just a diversion. Hardly anyone accepts that.

It should be noted for the record that if John Rawlins is to be believed, Grant had resumed his use of intoxicating beverages while in Chattanooga.[11]

What the Army of the Cumberland accomplished from late June to late September in 1863 should be compared with subsequent, more famous movements of the war. Historian Edward Hagerman says of the Tullahoma Campaign,

> Rosecrans's speed of movement was remarkable.... He moved approximately eighty miles in only nine days, for an average of nine miles per day. Subtracting thirty-six hours that he halted at Hoover's Gap and sixty hours in front of Winchester, he averaged over sixteen miles a day. This rate exceeds Sherman's averages of around nine miles a day through the Carolinas.

Hagerman continues:

> Rosecrans's penchant for thorough organization again came into play as he paused for six weeks to await railroad repairs necessary for resupply.... When Rosecrans began his maneuver on August 16, the [wagon] train of the Army of the Cumberland was in excellent shape. ...So prepared, Rosecrans made his long trek across the mountains with, as [Montgomery] Meigs observed, "very little loss or injury."... Rosecrans moved approximately 130 or 140 miles in thirty days, for an average of just over 4 miles per day.... Even then, he moved faster than Sherman would subsequently move on his march with a mobile railroad that followed him from Chattanooga to Atlanta.[12]

Nearly every American who knows anything of his country's history has heard of Sherman and his campaigns. In contrast few know of Rosecrans, and even less what he did.

On the night of September 12, 1863, atop Lookout Mountain, Staff Officer Horace Newton Fisher shared a tent with Philip Sheridan. Fisher remembered, "We lay awake discussing every movement thus far made. Gen Sheridan then said to me: 'No matter in what campaigns either of us may participate hereafter, we shall never find another so worthy of study as a masterpiece of strategic genius. I consider it fully equal to Napoleon's famous campaign of 1796 in North Italy.'"[13]

The central fact of the William Rosecrans story is not that Sheridan's statement is debated but that it is unknown.

To conclude this discussion of Chickamauga and its aftermath, it is interesting to ponder the questions asked by Confederate General John B. Gordon:

From the standpoint of unbiased criticism the future historian will probably have some trouble in finding sufficient reasons for this removal. It is not my province to participate in the discussion of this interesting question. As a soldier, however, who fought on the Southern side, and who has studied with much interest this campaign of General Rosecrans, I wish to leave upon record two or three inquiries which it seems to me history must necessarily make.

First, how was it possible for the transfer of Longstreet's troops from Lee to Bragg to have escaped the attention of Secretary Stanton or General Halleck? This movement was reported to General Rosecrans by General Peck of the Union army stationed in North Carolina. It was suggested as probable by the Hon. Murat Halstead in the columns of his paper. General H. V. Boynton states in the most positive terms that Colonel Jacques, of the Seventy-third Illinois, tried in vain for ten days to gain admittance in Washington to communicate the fact of Longstreet's movements to Halleck and Stanton, and then, without accomplishing it, returned in time to fight with his regiment at Chickamauga.

Another question which history will probably ask is why no reenforcements were sent to the Union army while Rosecrans was in command and when Longstreet was moving to strengthen General Bragg, and yet after Rosecrans's removal immense reenforcements were sent, although both Longstreet and Buckner had then been detached from that immediate vicinity.

The heavy concentration of Union forces at Chattanooga, and the consequent defeat of Bragg's army at Missionary Ridge, was a master stroke; but justice to General Rosecrans seems to demand the above reflections. In the light of his previous strategic campaign and of his fight at Chickamauga, where, without reenforcements, he so stubbornly resisted Bragg's assaults while both Longstreet and Buckner were present, history will surely ask: "What would General Rosecrans probably have accomplished with his own army heavily reenforced, while Bragg's was reduced by the absence of both Longstreet's and Buckner's commands?"[14]

To end this brief summary it is profitable to read the words of Peter Cozzens regarding Grant:

> That he had made several questionable tactical decisions during these battles went unnoticed in the adulation that followed the lifting of the sieges of Chattanooga and Knoxville. He never satisfactorily explained his foolish order to seize only the rifle pits at the base of Missionary Ridge. *Instead, Grant chose to lie.* In both his report of the battle and his memoirs, he insisted that he had given Thomas express authority to carry the ridge itself and implied that he fully expected that to be done. General Thomas died just four years after the war, and in any case was not the sort to engage in egotistical bickering. Few chose to dispute Grant's version of events while Grant lived. [Emphasis added]

> Likewise in Grant's explanation of Sherman's role, Cozzens says, "In his report of the campaign and his memoirs, Grant puffed this praise *almost to outright mendacity*, implying that Sherman's attack had been a mere feint to draw troops away from Thomas's front, where the real effort to crush Bragg was to have been made all along." [Emphasis added][15]

Slowly word of Rosecrans' departure made its way to the soldiers of the Army of the Cumberland. Of the tens of thousands of men who were in the Army of the Cumberland at the time of Rosecrans' departure, only a small percentage left some type of testimony. Most were disappointed, others were shocked, some even angry. Some felt that Rosecrans was being promoted, perhaps going east to the Army of the Potomac. Some suspected political intrigue emanating from Washington. Here are but a few of their voices.

Harvey Reid of the 22nd Wisconsin wrote to his sister,

> You have heard of changes in military commanders here this week. The news has been received by the soldiers with great dissatisfaction. General Rosecrans has had the utmost confidence and affection of every soldier in his army and the news he was going to leave us was received with the greatest regret and even rage, since his being assigned no particular command left it to be inferred that he was removed for misconduct, which none of his soldiers is willing to admit "Old Rosey" can be guilty of.

James A. Connolly of the 123rd Illinois to his wife:

> Rosecrans relieved! Then comes the starveling of home politicians to defame his character, to defame a name that should stand bright on the pages of history, to steal away laurels such as they can never win. If such men and such reports are to mould public opinion, God help the republic! ...General Rosecrans was my *beau ideal* of a leader; I would follow him with the devotion of the Crusaders for "Peter the Hermit." This entire army was an army of Crusaders under his leadership. He was the light and life of this army. When the order for removal was made public this army said nothing, it was dumb, the blow too sudden and too severe for speech; we all now pursue our way of life quietly, as soldiers bound to obey the orders of our superiors; we used to obey because we loved our leader, but let it be announced tomorrow that Rosecrans was in command again, and every silent tongue in this quiet army would find a voice, whose loud acclaim would almost wake again to the deadly shock our sleeping comrades on Chickamauga's banks. But enough; we'll triumph under Grant just as well as Rosecrans, and perhaps it is right that generals should be dealt with unjustly sometimes as well as privates.

Henry Harrison Cummings of the 105th Ohio wrote,

> I have seen today, Monday, November 2, 1863, Northern papers printed since Rosecrans' removal became known.... It would seem that a set of enemies, such as any man in Rosecrans' position and of Rosecrans' will, spirit and determination will have, have had their hounds in training and now on the announcement of his removal they are all unloosed. Certain papers are teeming with rumors, charges, statements, petty, ridiculous, malignant, false, unjust, ungenerous, everything in short that weak, petty unscrupulous enmity and malignity can devise. The Army of the Cumberland admire, revere and love their great leader. They parted with him sorrowfully, but true to the instincts of military subordination and prompt acquiescence in orders that he had taught them, they made no complaint, questioned not the motives that prompted the change. Such weak partisan attacks upon

him, whose name alone has been a tower of strength, look badly for the cause of his opponents. The army of the Cumberland will be satisfied with no equivocal reasons for the sacrifice of their leader.

Horace Porter, who won a Medal of Honor at Chickamauga and later became an aide to Grant, upon hearing he was being ordered to Washington, wrote his mother, "I do not leave the department [Cumberland] with much regret now that our old hero General Rosecrans has gone."[16]

Of course an army is not a democracy, and a soldier is by definition someone who follows orders. Still there is no doubt that what Phil Sheridan wrote years after the events of 1863 when William Rosecrans' star was in descent if not eclipse is true:

> When his departure became known deep and almost universal regret was expressed, for he was enthusiastically esteemed and loved by the Army of the Cumberland, from the day he assumed command of it until he left it, notwithstanding the censure poured upon him after the battle of Chickamauga.

Rosecrans was not forgotten by the Army of the Cumberland even as it would march to victory under another commander. Colonel Frank Sherman wrote his wife in 1864,

> Everything is done so differently from what Rosecrans did. No one seems to look after the details as he did and know if the men are properly equipped and supplied. All the attention to the condition of the Army has passed away, and we are ordered here and there, and have to go with such as we have. This way of doing weakens the efficiency of the army and takes from it that esprit de corps which was so prominent under Rosecrans.

George Squire wrote in April 1865,

> I have had men get mad when I told them that Genl. Rosecrans had given better evidence of superior Generalship than the much lauded Sherman....[At Chickamauga] the field was lost, but Chattanooga was taken *and held*, and for *this* he was relieved from the command of the army of the Cumberland.... [Rosecrans] was relieved with disgrace and assigned a command which should have been given to some second class colonel. And for this gross injustice he is indebted to the unprincipled but once popular Genl. Halleck.

A soldier of the German 9th Ohio deemed it an honor to serve under Rosecrans, writing,

> Many a commander owed victories principally to the wholesale slaughter of America's sons on the battlefield. Rosecrans, innocent of that widespread defect, never won a battle for that reason ... he was a master at maneuvering, he knew how to use terrain....Rosecrans rightfully earned fame as a circumspect officer and battlefield commander; and he deserved his popularity as a humane and an amiable leader... we still remember him most kindly.[17]

The news of Rosecrans' removal was accompanied in some newspapers by stories purporting to explain the "real" reasons for the action. Reports originating with the *Washington Chronicle* and republished in the *New York Times* listed a cattle call of reasons:

First that Generals McCook and Crittenden had preferred charges against Rosecrans for "un-officer like conduct on the battlefield" and of "unsoldierly and mischievous conduct" in publicly reporting to both officers and men that the day was lost.

There was "governmental resentment of his disobedience of positive orders not to risk a general engagement by not advancing beyond Chattanooga before he was reinforced."

Going beyond just military reasons for the removal, the reports referred to an epilepsy attack suffered by Rosecrans during the battle. This was judged untrue, but the idea that he was "constitutionally and by education subject to fits of religious depression of the profoundest character, is correct, though he was an austere Roman Catholic, as is well known. In connection with this it may not be unsuitable to add that it is understood that the fourth specification of the preferred charged is an excessive use of opium."

The article concluded with reports of conflict between Rosecrans and Halleck before and after Chickamauga. It concluded that Rosecrans' removal "has been in contemplation for some time."[18]

The reaction in the press to Rosecrans' removal fell broadly into three categories. One saw the removal as unwarranted, politically motivated, and worthy of contempt. The following from the *Cincinnati Times* best exemplifies this point of view:

> There is wailing and weeping in the Army of the Cumberland to-day; there is the compressed lip and the dark scowl, and the cheeks of men that never blanched in the storm of battle are white. Indignation and sorrow strive for supremacy, and the stifled curse heaves from camp to camp, for the heroic Rosecrans has become another victim to the hate and policy of the President makers.

From the *Brooklyn Daily Eagle*:

> The Administration journals seem to have reasons plenty as blackberries to account for the removal of General Rosecrans.... The zeal displayed in justifying the administration in advance would seem to indicate that the Washington authorities are not entirely satisfied of the fact that their conduct in this instance will bear investigation....Surely the bitterest rebel journal never said as much against any of our generals as is made public by newspapers supposed to speak for the administration. The truth seems to be that Rosecrans' crime is that he was determined while at the head of his army to be its real and not nominal commander.[19]

The opposite view accepted most of the charges made against Rosecrans and happily welcomed the change of commanders. *Harper's Weekly* of October 31 typifies this view:

> General Rosecrans has been removed from the command of the Army of the Cumberland, and General Thomas, the hero of Chickamauga, appointed in his place—General Grant taking the supreme command of all the armies on the Mississippi and in East and Southern Tennessee. The announcement has taken everyone by surprise. But whereas, some months ago, the removal of a popular general from his command would have been a signal for a popular uproar, now even the Copperheads can barely get up a feeble hiss at the change; and the public at large, fully satisfied that the President knows what is required by the emergency, and is doing his duty faithfully, accept the event without murmur.
>
> Whatever may have been the faults of General Rosecrans, it is encouraging to see that the President, when satisfied that he ought to be removed, had the courage to remove him, without hesitation or explanation to the public.... Up to the hour of Rosecrans's removal he was believed to be nearly perfection. He was called prudent, daring, invincible, loyal to the back-bone, dexterous as a strategist, and always obedient to his superiors.
>
> He was contrasted with other generals, to their invariable disparagement. When he failed at Chickamauga, the Copperheads—whose implacable foe he had proved himself—threw the whole blame on Government, and entirely exonerated him. At one time loyal men clamored for his appointment to the command of the Army of the Potomac, and were only silenced when they were assured that the Army of the Cumberland had the more important duty of the two. Well, what if it should prove, when the truth comes to be known, that this paragon was prudent when he should have been daring, and rash when he should have been cautious; that the battle of Murfreesborough was lost by him, and afterward—when he had given it up—won by his subordinates; that he should have taken Chattanooga weeks before he approached it, and should never have advanced a step beyond; that, by his advance, he disarranged the general plan of campaign determined at Washington, which had been prepared with his aid and approval—and this seemingly from no other motive than a vain wish to win greater victories than Grant; that, so far from obeying orders promptly and cheerfully, he frequently disregarded the commands of the President; and that, so far from being the chivalric soldier we pictured him, he left the battle-field at Chicamauga in the middle of the fight, and was in bed at Chattanooga, snug and safe, when the gallant Thomas, with his handful of heroes, was stemming the furious onset of the rebel army.[20]

A middle opinion rejected the opium, cowardice and despair allegations, doubted that the military situation called for Rosecrans' removal but trusted in the judgment of the Washington authorities. The *Chicago Tribune* wrote on October 29,

> Gen. Rosecrans, either by his own volition, or by the threat of removal, has resigned the command of the Army of the Cumberland. A soldier of acknowledged ability, courage and devotion has been named for the place he lately filled. [This refers to Grant.] The public, shocked and astonished by the sudden downfall of one of its

idols, indignantly inquires why this has been done; but we, as ignorant as men can be of the causes that have produced this result, cannot answer the questions nor parry the complaints that come to us from all quarters. We can only say that we have confidence in what the President does, and that, within a few days at the utmost, we expect to be able to state the exact and we hope sufficient reasons for the action that has been had. In the meantime, we know that the army is in good hands; that all that old Rosey could or would have done will be done, and that until a new advance is necessary, his absence from the chief command will not be felt. With that we are at present content.[21]

An opinion from the *Richmond Examiner* gives a Southern perspective:

Meanwhile Lincoln is helping us. He has removed from command the most dangerous man in his army, and put two fools in his place. A variety of mean and damaging pretexts for Rosecrans' removal have been published by the Yankee press....Rosecrans, thus retired, is unquestionably the greatest Captain the Yankee nation has yet produced. His performances in the field are too fresh in the memory of every reader to necessitate recapitulation.[22]

Of course all of these were just newspaper opinions, ultimately powerless to decide who would command and who would not. Those decisions would be made by men influenced by events military and political. Late in 1863, Rosecrans would be the beneficiary of a political dispute in Missouri.

13. Missouri

Missouri was a slave state that remained in the Union. This naturally caused the state to be divided between Union and Confederate sympathizers. But there was a further division between radical, sometimes called Charcoals, and conservative, or Claybanks, loyalists. The governor of Missouri, Hamilton Gamble, was a conservative, while the department commander General Samuel Curtis tended to be more radical.

Disputes over issues such as assessments and confiscations, banishments, and the role of local militias versus Federal troops resulted in a call from conservatives to remove Curtis from power. Lincoln replaced Curtis with General John Schofield in May 1863. Lincoln was quite frank in a letter to Schofield revealing the reasons for the change in command:

> MY DEAR SIR: Having relieved Gen. Curtis and assigned you to the command of the Department of the Missouri—I think it may be of some advantage for me to state to you why I did it. I did not relieve Gen. Curtis because of any full conviction that he had done wrong by commission or omission. I did it because of a conviction in my mind that the Union men of Missouri, constituting, when united, a vast majority of the whole people, have entered into a pestilent factional quarrel among themselves, Gen. Curtis, perhaps not of choice, being the head of one faction, and Gov. Gamble that of the other. After months of labor to reconcile the difficulty, it seemed to grow worse and worse until I felt it my duty to break it up somehow; and as I could not remove Gov. Gamble, I had to remove Gen. Curtis. Now that you are in the position, I wish you to undo nothing merely because Gen. Curtis or Gov. Gamble did it; but to exercise your own judgment, and do *right* for the public interest. Let your military measures be strong enough to repel the invader and keep the peace, and not so strong as to unnecessarily harass and persecute the people. It is a difficult *role*, and so much greater will be the honor if you perform it well. If both factions, and neither, shall abuse you, you will probably be about right. Beware of being assailed by one, and praised by the other.[1]

It would not be long before Schofield would run afoul of the Charcoals. The sharpest area of contention was over slavery. The Emancipation Proclamation did not apply in Missouri since it was a loyal state. Questions arose over when and how emancipation should occur in Missouri, and whether the slaves of Unionist slaveholders should be recruited into military service.

Schofield tried to bridge the split between the two factions and temporarily suspended the recruitment of black soldiers. Schofield was also faulted by the radicals for William Quantrill's deadly August attack at Lawrence, Kansas, which at that time was in the Missouri Department. In September two delegations of Missouri and Kansas radicals met with Lincoln in Washington and demanded that Schofield be replaced by General Benjamin Butler. Lincoln refused and defended Schofield, but the problem would not go away.

In November the state legislature met to address the election of U.S. senators and a state convention to deal with emancipation. Complaints by the radicals that Schofield was interfering in these matters reached Lincoln who summoned him to Washington. The result of all these machinations was the decision of Lincoln to remove Schofield. But this would not be so easy. Questions remained as to who would succeed him and where he would go.

A line from a letter Lincoln wrote to Stanton is particularly interesting to the Rosecrans story: "I find it is scarcely less than indispensable for me to do something for General Rosecrans; and I find Henderson and Brown [the Missouri senators] will agree to him for the commander of their department." But there still were objections to Lincoln's plans. The radicals opposed Schofield remaining in command anywhere. As for Rosecrans,

> Grant and Sherman, for reasons he [Lincoln] did not understand, disliked Rosecrans; but that, on the contrary, they had a high opinion of Schofield, and wished him to command a corps of their army. That also while Schofield displeased the radicals in Missouri they would be satisfied with Rosecrans and that the transfer would thus not only set matters at ease in both these places, but would gratify the friends of Schofield by his promotion and the friends of Rosecrans by the important command he would thus receive.

The matter was resolved by the Department of Missouri being divided into three parts: Samuel Curtis would command in Kansas; Frederick Steele in Arkansas; William Rosecrans in Missouri. Schofield would go to Tennessee to head the Army of the Ohio. On January 30, 1864, Rosecrans reported to department headquarters in St. Louis to serve in his fourth theater of the war.

Another powerful senator, Benjamin F. Wade of Ohio, expressed his thoughts on the matter in a letter to Rosecrans: "I rejoice in the fact that you are to go to Missouri, it is a shame that you were not permitted to complete what you had so gloriously begun in the Department of the Cumberland, and I have not failed to let the Administration know my views upon the subject."[2]

The Department of the Missouri had been reduced in troop strength to about 25,000 men and officers, with about 17,000 ready for duty to defend an area of nearly 70,000 square miles. Various types of militia had been created and utilized to make up for the loss of Federal troops. Four days after Rosecrans took command in Missouri, General Orders No. 4 placed all state, militia under his control. He later in the year ordered the formation of two Enrolled Missouri Militia companies of 100 men from each county in the state. Another source of troops was slaves and ex-slaves. This was complicated by the fact that Missouri being a loyal Union slave state was not legally affected by the Emancipation Proclamation. Initially only slaves of disloyal owners were subject to conscription. Eventually the question of recruitment of the slaves of loyal owners arose. Some loyal slaveholders not willing to see their slaves conscripted into the army sent them out of state. To counteract this, Rosecrans issued General Orders No. 35 prohibiting the exportation of slaves from Missouri. Rosecrans also expressed his concern for the slaves and their families with the following missive to Lincoln: "Will the law provide that the pay of colored troops shall be the same as for other? Will the families of these men be made free? It is important and just that they should be so. Will you give me Colonel Sanderson? I beg an early reply." The request for Colonel John Sanderson led to one of the most important and controversial episodes in Rosecrans' Missouri tenure.

Missouri was divided internally almost to the point of a state civil war. The question of who was and who wasn't loyal prodded Rosecrans to issue several tough orders. He revoked an order prohibiting the circulation of the anti-war *Chicago Times*, but still maintaining

> that the military power should never interfere with the full and free expressions of the press upon all subjects except as a military measure, [Rosecrans] believes it to be the first duty of a military commander to protect the integrity of his Government from all attacks; and anything written or spoken, calculated materially to impair that integrity by weakening its authority or that of its officers, it is his plain duty to take cognizance of it, and to act according to his best judgment.[3]

More controversial was Special Order No. 61 which required members of the larger church organizations to take an oath of allegiance.

The question of loyalty even extended to the state militia. In June and July of 1864 a Rebel force under Colonel John C. Calhoun Thornton entered northwest Missouri looking for recruits. When they arrived at Parkville on July 7, the militia unit that was supposed to defend the town offered no resistance and some joined the Rebels. Three days later at Platte City the Confederate flag was raised over the town, and five companies of Paw Paws, as militia units suspected of dubious loyalty were called, went over to the Rebel side. Because the Paw Paws in 1863 had done some good service, there was an initial hesitancy on the part of Rosecrans to take immediate harsh measures against them. After the events at Parkville and Platte City, however, Rosecrans took actions to create a combined force of Missouri and Kansas troops to search out and destroy Thornton. By the end of July, Thornton's force had disintegrated, he had escaped across the Missouri River and many Paw Paws, hoping for mercy, returned to the Union side.

On June 7, Rosecrans received a telegram from his old chief of staff James Garfield who was attending the Baltimore Convention of the Republican or, officially, National Union Party. The telegram read, "Shall I propose you for Vice President—Answer immediately."

Rosecrans, who the previous summer had rebuffed an attempt to make him a presidential candidate, responded in a very guarded manner:

> Nothing but the conviction that it was demanded by a great National duty could induce me to become a candidate. Having as yet no data for such a conviction I must leave you and the convention guided by your knowledge of our perils and an enlightened and self sacrificing patriotism to discharge your great and solemn duty according to your convictions reserving my decision of what my duty is until informed and called on to decide. If the Baltimore convention can give us a ticket and a policy which will command the confidence of the nation I shall be content.

This was evidently an affirmative answer, as Rosecrans was said to be "sorry that he was not nominated." Garfield wrote Rosecrans on June 15,

> I telegraphed you from there on the first morning of the Convention in reference to using your name for the Vice Presidency—but received no answer. I proposed the matter to several prominent members and it was received with enthusiasm. The Ky. and Mo. Delegations were unanimous.... I think it would have been an easy thing to do. Not hearing from you and not feeling sure that it would please you I did not push the matter but I did enough to find that your name carries enthusiasm and strength with it especially in the West—notwithstanding the slights and indignities which you have so frequently suffered from the War Dept.

A belief existed that Rosecrans' response to Garfield's offer was intercepted by someone, perhaps Edwin Stanton. In 1866, Garfield wrote Rosecrans, "I have not been able to forget the telegraphic correspondence between you and myself at the Baltimore Convention—so strangely interrupted and to wonder what could have been the purpose of Divine Providence in turning aside a movement which likely have made you president—and instead gave us such a scourge as Andrew Johnson." There exists the real possibility that William S. Rosecrans could have been the seventeenth president of the United States. However, in the summer of 1864, Rosecrans' main concerns were military not political.[4]

The major focus of disloyalty and treason in Missouri centered on a group known as the Organization of American Knights, or OAK, and particularly the possibility of General Sterling Price leading a raid into Missouri sometime in 1864. Rosecrans had asked for Colonel John Sanderson to be sent to him, and despite the reluctance of Dana and Stanton, Sanderson was sent to Missouri and made provost marshall. Beginning in March he began to investigate and collect information from a variety of sources about subversive activities by the OAK. Several suspected leaders were arrested. After interviewing var-

13. Missouri

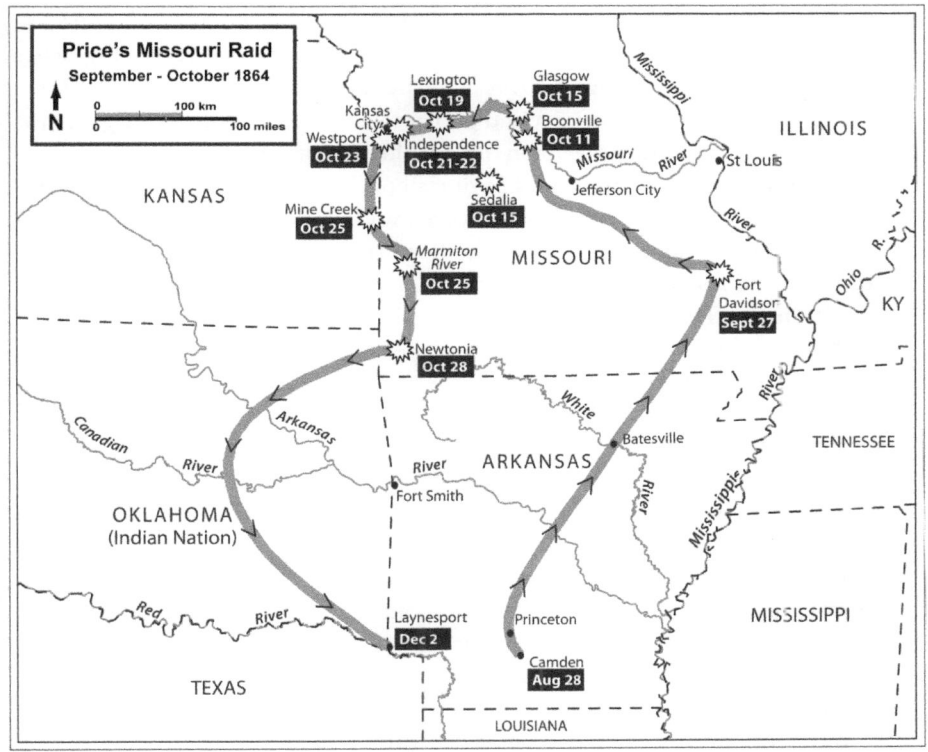

Price's Missouri Raid (Map by Phil Mobley).

ious persons he prepared a report over 1,000 pages long. Rosecrans wanted to send Sanderson to Washington with the report, but Lincoln demurred suggesting that the report "be sent by express." Rosecrans replied that the information was too grave to be sent by express and inveighed Governor Yates of Illinois to ask Lincoln to summon Rosecrans or Sanderson to Washington. Lincoln, sensing a political motivation behind Rosecrans' actions, told his secretary John Hay, "I am inclined to think that the object of the general is to force me into a conflict with the Secretary of War and to make me overrule him on this matter." Lincoln resolved the dispute by sending Hay to Missouri. Hay felt Lincoln underestimated the threat posed by the OAK, but it seems that Lincoln thought the threat of an uprising in the Northwest slight and downplayed Sanderson's report. Parts of the report were printed in newspapers, making the threat public. Rosecrans expected an invasion by Price and took steps to assemble a force to combat it.

In September that possible invasion became a reality. The idea for a raid into Missouri had been discussed and planned by Rebel military and political officials since June. The objectives were varied and included recruiting new troops in Missouri, seizing St. Louis and the supplies that were stored there, taking the capital Jefferson City and perhaps installing a Confederate government, creating a military diversion that would draw attention and troops from the Union forces in Georgia, and having all of this impact on the elections in November. The biggest problem, however, was a lack of manpower, so eventually a cavalry raid to be headed by Sterling Price was decided on. Price would lead a force made up of three divisions led by John Marmaduke, James Fagan, and Jo Shelby. This force would be at most 12,000 strong, but nearly a fourth of these would be unarmed.

Price headed north from Camden, Arkansas, on August 28. On September 13 he reached Pocahontas, Arkansas, near the Missouri border. Here he met up with Shelby. They spent several days there making preparations and then crossed into Missouri on September 19.

Rosecrans had been expecting some sort of invasion since June. His problem was that most of his troops had been sent east. Thirty-two Federal infantry regiments had been moved out of Missouri since May. General, and future Missouri governor, Thomas C. Fletcher, recalled how, while recuperating from a severe cold, "General Rosecrans sent for me and told me of the coming of Price's army towards Missouri, and explained in detail his situation and the extent to which his department was depleted of force and the terrible strait to which he was driven, and asked me to gather up and organize some force in southeast Missouri." On September 6 he asked Halleck for the troops of Major General A.J. Smith who were on route to Sherman. Halleck agreed, and Smith's force made its way to a point near St. Louis. He also called up several militia units so that by October he would have about 17,500 Federal troops and 15,000 Missouri militia to defend the entire state. Rosecrans was unsure what Price's chief objective was, therefore he decided not to send all of his troops to meet Price near the Arkansas border lest he be outflanked leaving no troops to put down any internal uprisings. Rosecrans concentrated his troops at Springfield, Jefferson City, Rolla and St. Louis. He also ordered General Thomas Ewing to patrol and garrison the Iron Mountain railroad that ran south of St. Louis and terminated at the town of Pilot Knob. Near Pilot Knob was the hexagonal earthen Fort Davidson. Ewing's force entered the fort on September 26.

On September 24, Rosecrans learned that Shelby was heading toward Pilot Knob southwest of St. Louis. He ordered General Thomas Ewing to scout out the area around Pilot Knob, sent two of Smith's brigades down the railroad, called out the St. Louis home guard, and even got help from 100 day regiments from Illinois to defend St. Louis.

On the Confederate side, Shelby was sent to destroy the railroad and Fagan to destroy the Union troops at Pilot Knob. On the evening of September 26 two companies of infantry sent by Ewing clashed with part of Fagan's forces at Ironton. Eventually the Confederates forced the Yankees back into Fort Davidson.

Price ordered artillery placed on Shepherd Mountain and Pilot Knob Mountain overlooking the fort and sent an emissary to demand its surrender. Ewing refused. Price decided against shelling Fort Davidson because he had been told that women and children were being held there. Instead he decided to launch a frontal assault against the fort. The attack began at 2 p.m. on September 27. Three assaults were made by the Confederates, and each time they were repulsed. By day's end, 1,500 of Price's men were dead or wounded; Ewing had lost 200 of his 900 troops. Still Ewing realized that it was unlikely he could survive another day's fighting. He decided to evacuate the fort at 3 a.m. A slow-burning fuse touched off an explosion in the fort that the Rebels interpreted as an accident that would hasten the fort's surrender. However the morning brought the discovery that the Yankees had escaped. A halfhearted attempt to pursue Ewing was soon called off.

The attack on Fort Davidson was not only an immediate disaster for the Rebels, but it destroyed any idea of attacking St. Louis. Instead Price turned his attention west to the Missouri capital of Jefferson City.

On October 1 the following was promulgated:

O.A.K.
HEADQUARTERS, Saint Louis, Mo., October 1, 1864
To THE MEMBERS OF THE ORDER OF
AMERICAN KNIGHTS OF THE STATE OF MISSOURI:

SIR KNIGHTS: Morning dawneth. General Price with at least 20,000 veteran soldiers is now within your State. Through your supreme commander (and with the approbation of the supreme council) you invited him to come to your aid. He was assured that if he came at this time with the requisite force you would co operate and add at least 20,000 true men to his army. He has hearkened to your prayer and is now battling for your deliverance. Sons of Liberty, will you falsify your plighted word? I know you will not. You are strong in numbers—full 30,000 strong—and your influence is potent. It requires but prompt action on the part of the members to insure the ultimate triumph of our cause. As you value your property, your liberties, your lives, and your sacred honor, fail not to give a helping hand in this crisis. Under and by virtue of the authority vested in me by section— of the code of the O.A.K.s, authorizing the appointment of a major-general to command the members called into the military service, I shall appoint that brave and true soldier, Missouri's favorite son, Maj. Gen. Sterling Price, military commander of the O.A.K.s of the State of Missouri.

All able-bodied men of the O.A.K.s are hereby called upon and required to render military service in behalf of our cause. All true knights will yield prompt obedience to the orders and commands of General Price. Meantime do all possible damage to the enemy. Seize all arms and munitions of war within your power. Take possession of and hold all important places you can, and recruit as rapidly as possible. If you cannot sustain yourselves fall back upon the army of occupation. In townships and counties where you cannot concentrate on account of the presence of the enemy repair singly or in squads without delay to the army, or to points where your brethren may be marshaling their forces, and in all cases be ready to obey the commands of your chieftain and unite with the forces when an opportune moment offers. Ye knights, who belong to the militia, a change of government is now impending and you possess peculiar advantages for doing good service, and it is believed you will not fail to act efficiently.

Rosecrans' and Sanderson's concerns about the OAKs had been proven right.[5]

Rosecrans determined to strengthen the Missouri capital. When Price reached Jefferson City on October 7 it was defended by 7,000 Union troops. Moreover an additional 9,000 under General Smith were on the way. Not wishing to repeat the disaster of Pilot Knob, Price decided not to attack Jefferson City and continued west. There would be no inauguration of a Confederate governor.

The Army of Missouri arrived at Boonville on October 10. This was the center of pro–Confederate sentiment in Missouri, and Price's army basked in the adulation of the citizens. More importantly, between 1,200 and 1,500 men joined Price's force at Boonville. Meanwhile Rosecrans had dispatched Major General Alfred Pleasonton to Jefferson City to take command of the Union forces there. Pleasonton sent 4,000 cavalry troops under John Sanborn to follow Price, but no general engagement was to be brought on until more troops arrived from St. Louis and Springfield. Rosecrans himself set out from St. Louis to confer with Pleasonton. On October 13, Price left Boonville and continued west toward Kansas City.

Rosecrans formulated a plan to trap Price. Pleasonton would pursue Price from the east, Prices's rear. Smith would come in from the south. To the west, Price's front, was Department of Kansas commander General Samuel Curtis with 15,000 troops, but the majority of them refused to cross the state line into Missouri. Eventually 2,000 of them agreed to cross the state line under Major General James Blunt. To the north was the Missouri River; Price would be boxed in.

Price continued his westward drift to Lexington, where he had won a battle in 1861. He encountered some of Blunt's troops on October 19 and pushed them back toward Independence. On October 21 the Rebels met a force of 2,000 Unionists under Blunt at the Little Blue River, thirteen miles east of Independence, where they pushed them across the river toward Independence. Although these were tactically Confederate victories, their greater impact was that they slowed Price's move west and allowed Pleasonton to close in from that direction. On the morning of October 22, Shelby outflanked Blunt at Bryam's Ford on the Big Blue River and forced him to retreat toward Westport.

On the night of October 22, Pleasonton wrote Rosecrans urging him to order General A.J. Smith to Independence. This would prove to be important, as Smith's departure would leave an escape route for Price.

General Curtis had concentrated his forces at Westport south of Kansas City and north of Brush Creek. Price, realizing his precarious position between Curtis and Pleasonton, decided to fight his way out of his predicament by fighting each northern general in detail. On October 23 he struck at Curtis first. The opposing armies crossed and recrossed Brush Creek. A flank attack on Price's left gave the Yankees the advantage. Meanwhile Pleasonton pushed Marmaduke across Bryam's Ford. Price was now threatened on three sides and decided to retreat southward. The absence of Smith's force allowed him to retreat into Kansas. Albert Castel noted, "Had Smith been [where] Rosecrans originally intended in all likelihood he would have been able to strike the Confederates as they retreated from Westport with the devastating power of his nine thousand veteran infantry and five batteries of artillery." He concludes that Rosecrans was "truly an ill-starred general, for with any luck he would have smashed Price's expedition and in part at least regained the reputation lost at Chickamauga."

On October 25, Price's army clashed three times, at Marais des Cygnes, Mine Creek and Marmiton River, and was forced south. Three days later at Newtonia, Missouri, he fought one last time while what was left of his army retreated into Indian territory (present-day Oklahoma). As one historian has put it, "Except for the operations, long past the end of the war, of guerillas, gangs, or individuals professing to be laboring for the Confederacy, the Civil War west of the Mississippi came effectively to an end when Price crossed the Arkansas River on November 7, 1864."

If Rosecrans hoped that the expulsion of Price from Missouri would improve his standing with Grant and the powers in Washington, he was mistaken. Indeed he was criticized for calling back Pleasonton from Kansas to Missouri. However, this ignores the fact that Pleasonton himself asked Rosecrans to call him back as his two brigades "were so broken down it would be impossible without fresh horses to strike the enemy another great blow." Rosecrans did, in accordance with Grant's orders, order Sanborn and McNeil to pursue what was left of Price's army into Arkansas. Sanborn felt that the pursuit of Price toward his supply bases only gave an incentive for Price's troops to stay together, whereas if the pursuit had stopped, "My own view is that all the efforts of General Curtis to drive the enemy—and they have been great and entitle him to credit—have been to our detriment and to our enemy's advantage for I believe one half of Price's army would have deserted north of the Arkansas [river] had it not been for fear of the pursuing foe."[6]

Halleck and Grant continued to criticize Rosecrans' conduct in Missouri. Grant wanted troops in Missouri sent to Thomas at Nashville. Grant suspected that Rosecrans was concealing troops and sent John Rawlins to investigate the situation and empowered him to give whatever orders to Rosecrans he deemed necessary. Rawlins concluded, "I will here state that General Rosecrans has shown since I met him here every disposition to hurry forward troops to General Thomas, and for that purpose to strip his command to the least possible number. He will be enabled to send more when the pursuit of Price ends."

But Rosecrans was a marked man. As far back as July, Grant complained that the most useful way to employ Rosecrans would be to station him at some convenient point on the northern frontier with the duty of detecting and exposing Rebel conspiracies in Canada. On October 11, while Price was plundering Booneville, Grant wrote Stanton, "A proper regard for the present and future interests of the service demands the removal of Rosecrans." Throughout the period of Price's raid, Grant continually spoke out against Rosecrans. On December 2, when he was asked by Stanton where Rosecrans should go after being replaced by Dodge, Grant replied, "Rosecrans will do less harm doing nothing than on duty. I know no department or army commander deserving such punishment as the infliction of Rosecrans on them." On December 9 the order came relieving him from command. He returned to Cincinnati awaiting orders—orders that never came. His role in the American Civil War was over.[7]

It is of value to review the actions of Ulysses S. Grant during the year 1864. On December 9, Grant also wrote, but never sent, an order directing General Thomas to turn over his command to General Schofield. A few days later he sent John A. Logan to relieve Thomas, but that move was canceled after Thomas' thorough victory at Nashville. Thomas' deficiency was an alleged slowness. In May 1864, Grant had started the Overland Campaign where he proposed "to fight it out along this line if it takes all summer." Now in midwinter Grant was bogged down in a siege at Petersburg. In July, Grant faced a threat to his rear when Jubal Early unexpectedly threatened Washington. The following from Dana to Rawlins on July 15, 1864, is illuminating:

> I have telegraphed you during the last week some things which might perhaps have been better said in a letter, but it seemed important that you should know the interior truth of some matters at once. I can only say that however severe some of my expressions may have seemed, they have been rather too weakly colored to do justice to the truth. You find that the responsibility for this whole disgraceful affair will be put upon the general's shoulders. You did know the truth, but there are not many who will ever know it as we do, and the inaction of the general toward

those who are really guilty will only confirm the opinion which will be made to prevail that it is his fault. In the first place, it will be said, he is the commander in chief, & is bound to provide for the whole field of operations. In the second place it was by his order & request that both Washington & Baltimore have been stripped of troops, so that when the enemy arrived there was no body but militia to defend either. In the third place, it was he who sent Hunter to Lynchburg leaving the valley open for Early. Fourthly, he does nothing to call Hunter to account for retreating to the Ohio river whence he could not possibly get his troops up to interfere with Early's movement. And fifthly he does not send troops enough to Washington til it is too late to do any thing more than begin a useless pursuit of an enemy whose escape with all his plunder we are impotent to prevent. These are some of the things which are already beginning to be said & which will be said more & more. I must also tell you that I hear from friends of the general & of the cause the decided opinion that the campaign is already a failure and that we are worse off, in a worse position & weaker, than we were the day you left Culpepper. Seventy thousand men have been killed & wounded, they say, to produce this net result. It is vain to suggest that the failure was caused by Butler's total incompetency to make the best use of the troops under his command which landed at City Point on May 5, or that at least 20.000 men have been slaughtered by Meade's blind, unconsidered, fragmentary assaults at Cold Harbor and Petersburg, assaults even more deficient in all the elements of generalship than Burnside's infamous massacre at Fredericksburg. I say it is vain to say these things, for the answer is instant,—"But Grant is the commander, and he neither removes Butler nor Meade,—he is satisfied with their conduct, and adopts it for his own.—"That is true & there is no answer to it. I suppose he will also adopt Halleck's conduct and give that the benefit of his prelating approval, and so on til the end. The black & revolting dishonor of this siege of Washington with all its circumstances of poltroonery & stupidity, is yet too fresh & its brand is too stinging for one to have a cool judgment regarding its probable consequences; but, as far as I can now see, they are very likely to be the defeat of Mr Lincoln & the election of Gen. McClellan to the Presidency, not to mention a thousand other things almost as fatal to the country, which will come in the same concatenation. Possibly Sherman may have the good fortune to end the war in Georgia. God grant it!—for otherwise I fear it will have to be ended by a younger, more earnest, more manly & less self complacent race of men than the mental dwarfs & moral cowards who have the control of it at present.[8]

Although William S. Rosecrans' role in the field was over, he was not quite finished with the war. On April 24, 1865, he testified before the Joint Committee on the Conduct of the War. When asked, "For what reason were you ultimately removed from that command?" Rosecrans responded:

No reason was ever assigned to me, nor have I ever, directly or indirectly, heard of any reason for it until within the last six weeks. I have lately heard, from three or four different sources, that I was removed at the personal request of General Grant, who was supposed, by the parties giving me that information, to be extremely hostile to me. As no occasion for any such hostility has ever been given by me, so far as I know, I am at a loss to understand it. General Grant's chief of staff, General

Rawlins, visited me after the close of the campaign of General Price. He mixed freely with the citizens, and took the pains to volunteer the statement, in my office, in the presence of various members of my staff, that he was satisfied that things had been managed wonderfully well during that campaign; that few could have done as well, and probably none better.

Rosecrans was next asked, "Has there been any misunderstanding between you and General Grant at any time?" He answered,

Never. On one occasion, when some of his staff told my staff that he was under the impression that the newspaper correspondents who, in 1862, attacked him in the *Chicago Tribune* and other papers, had received some countenance at my headquarters, I had a conversation with him upon the subject. He expressly stated that he did not suppose it came from me; and after conversation with him, in which I answered him that there was not the slightest foundation for such a feeling, he not only expressed himself satisfied, but we parted, promising continued friendly intercourse wherever duty might throw us.[9]

So the question is why was William S. Rosecrans relieved of command? If that question is not much asked today, it was in the years after the war. It deserves to be asked and attempted to be answered today.

14. A Spy in the Army

On March 30, 1867, John Russell Young, editor of the *New York Tribune*, sent a letter to Congressman James A. Garfield. It read,

> My dear General
>
> I see that Rosecrans' resignation has been accepted at last, and that he is to go out of the Army. I wish you would sit down before you leave Washington and give me a memorandum of his military career—how he was removed four times—each time at the end of a victory—as to enable me to write an editorial about him. Give me your ideas.... And I will try to do him justice.[1]

The next day Garfield sent the following reply:

> Yours of yesterday came to hand this morning and I have made a few notes of dates and events in the career of Gen. Rosecrans—which may aid you. I am glad it is in your heart to notice his exit from the army—in a way that will recognize the service he rendered to the nation when it needed friends—For nearly a year my relations with him were so intimate we scarcely had a separate thought on any question affecting the great contest. If the president makers had let him alone he might have been at the head of our armies today—but in the fatal summer of 1863 he was enveloped in clouds of incense and visions of the presidency were constantly thrust before him—I think that this made him a little over cautious and increased the delay in beginning the campaign of Middle Tennessee—which though brilliant and successful came so late as to be somewhat obscured by the achievement of Grant's army at Vicksburg and the army of the Potomac at Gettysburg—*I think also that the political leaders became alarmed at his increasing fame and were not unwilling to see evil befall him. Certain it is that the War Dept seemed very ready to find fault with him from that time forward.*
>
> I have never before put these thoughts on paper and have rarely spoken them to my dearest friends—The events are too recent to make it prudent but the time may come when they will be known [emphasis added].[2]

If one accepts what Garfield, a Washington insider, wrote—that political leaders were not unwilling to see evil befall Rosecrans—the question becomes, who were those leaders?

Ironically one of those suspected of being disloyal and responsible for Rosecrans' fall was Garfield himself. In the summer of 1863 while he was Rosecrans' chief of staff, Garfield wrote a series of letters to Salmon P. Chase expressing his disappointment in Rosecrans' failure to move sooner than Garfield desired.

After Chickamauga, while en route to Washington, Garfield crossed paths with Stanton in Louisville. Several accounts have Garfield making negative comments to Stanton about Rosecrans. Stanton wrote, "Generals Garfield and Steedman are here on their way home. Their representations of the incidents of the battle of Chickamauga more than confirm the worst that has reached us from other sources as to the conduct of the Commanding General and the great credit that is due to General Thomas."[3]

The rumor of Garfield's duplicity became public in 1874 when Charles A. Dana published in his *New York Sun* an item charging that the cause of Rosecrans' removal was a private letter from Garfield to Chase, the representations of which "were such as to convince Mr. Lincoln that Rosecrans must be removed without delay. It was upon this letter of Garfield's that the President acted."

Assistant Secretary of War Charles A. Dana. Widely regarded as a spy in the army his dispatches of dubious veracity provided the justification for the removal of Rosecrans from command of the Army of the Cumberland.

In 1879, Dana printed the allegations again in an article in which he denied he "ever had any quarrel with Gen. Rosecrans and never made any threats respecting him." Furthermore Dana said he "carefully informed the Administration of all that happened in Chattanooga without recommending any course of action." Rather it was a "private communication" from Garfield to Chase that caused "the Administration to act decisively upon the subject."

When Rosecrans, living in California, heard about these allegations, he wrote Garfield, "I wish you would write me what there was in your letter to Chase." Garfield answered "...that any charge, whether it comes from Dana, or any other liar to the effect that I was in any sense untrue to you has no particle of truth in it. I met Mr. Stanton in Louisville, and when he denounced you in vigorous language, I rebuked him and earnestly defended you. I fearlessly challenge all the rascals in the world to publish any such letters written by me."[4]

In 1880 both men were successful candidates for public office: Rosecrans, a Democrat, for Congress from California, and Garfield, a Republican, for president. When a newspaper in California taunted Rosecrans for criticizing Garfield after having praised him in 1863, Rosecrans replied with a "card" stating, "Seventeen years is a long period, and many a splendid young man, in less time, has descended from honor to infamy, and mortified admiring and devoted friends by being put in the penitentiary." This rather sharp comment was perhaps ignited by a campaign biography that elevated Garfield's military record at the expense of Rosecrans.' A somewhat remorseful Rosecrans wrote his onetime chief of staff, "Do we stand on the ground of cordial regard which existed between us before the election and which began in that fraternity of patriotism with which you were admitted to my military family, and even to my own quarters in the winter of 1862–3?"

Garfield replied that the card Rosecrans had written "with its wicked and unjust implication was widely circulated as your opinion of me, and is an insuperable barrier to the restoration of our old relations." Thus ended a friendship that had begun in 1863 and once stirred Garfield to say "he loved every bone" in Rosecrans' body. The breech was never healed as President Garfield died of the consequences of an assassin's bullet on September 19, 1881, the eighteenth anniversary of the first day of Chickamauga.[5]

In 1882, Dana revived the controversy by publishing the July 27, 1863, letter from Garfield to Chase that expressed Garfield's concern and unhappiness about Rosecrans' failure to advance at a pace to Garfield's liking. Dana wrote that Rosecrans' removal was brought about not by that letter but others written after Chickamauga. Rosecrans asked Dana about the newspaperman's own role in his removal. Dana replied in part that "no doubt there are passages... which you will regard as having been unjust to you; many concerning which you will tell me, probably with justice, I was entirely misinformed." Indeed Dana had so convincingly persuaded Rosecrans that Garfield was to blame that the general wrote Dana, "I now begin to think I have done you an injustice all these years."[6]

The purported post–Chickamauga Garfield-Chase letters were still unpublished, as was Dana's correspondence to Washington from 1863.

A number of stories involving a Garfield letter or statement being the cause of the removal of Rosecrans have circulated, but no letter written explicitly recommending that action has ever surfaced. Garfield was for the most part loyal to Rosecrans. He delivered a speech in the House of Representatives in February 1864 defending Rosecrans when the general was left out of a resolution thanking Thomas and the Army of the Cumberland, concluding, "Who commanded the *Army of the Cumberland*? Who organized, disciplined and led it? Who planned its campaigns? The General whose name is omitted in this resolution, Major-general W. S. Rosecrans." Furthermore in June of that year at the Baltimore Convention he sought out Rosecrans for the vice presidency. No doubt Garfield—a politician first, a soldier second—took his own interests into account when dealing with Rosecrans, and as a Garfield biographer has noted, "Garfield's friendship for Rosecrans was stained by a deception that no kind acts or words could wash away." However he regarded his old chief as someone worthy of being defended. Indeed when Garfield was asked why Rosecrans was removed, the answer he gave was because of political not military concerns.[7]

For Dana to blame Garfield for Rosecrans' removal goes beyond irony to the most brazen duplicity imaginable. Charles A. Dana was a strange character even by the standards of Civil War personages. Descended from an old but economically modest New England family, He was to a great extent self-educated but was able to study literature and philosophy at Harvard before declining eyesight forced him to end his studies. He was for a while a member of the Brook Farm Transcendentalist commune in Massachusetts. After the collapse of Brook Farm he dabbled in literary and journalistic endeavors before joining the *New York Tribune* in 1847. He freelanced in Europe for several American newspapers including the *Tribune* and reported on the revolutions in Europe in 1848. Among the people he met was Karl Marx, who later was a columnist for the *Tribune*. Dana became managing editor of that newspaper in 1849. In early 1862 he was fired by Horace Greeley over differences of opinion, including the fact that while Greeley "was for peace I [Dana] was for war, and that as long as I stayed on the *Tribune* there was a spirit there which was not his spirit—that he did not like."[8]

He eventually found his way to Washington where he was appointed to a special commission investigating corruption at the supply depot at Cairo,

Illinois. After becoming involved in cotton speculation, Dana became in the words of one historian "a convert to rectitude." He was appointed to another commission investigating the army pay service in the west, but it was universally believed that his role was to be a spy for the War Department. He was sent to Mississippi to gather information on Grant and his army. This visit encompassed the time period of a notorious drunken bender by Grant on the steamer *Diligent* in June 1863. John Rawlins wrote Grant, "The great solicitude I feel for the safety of this army leads me to mention what I had hoped never again to do the subject of your drinking.... To-night I find you where the wine bottle has just been emptied, in company with those who drink and urge you to do likewise, and the lack of your usual promptness of decision and clearness in expressing yourself in writing tended to confirm my suspicions."

James Harrison Wilson wrote in his diary, "General G. intoxicated." However, in a letter to Elihu Washburne, Dana wrote, "My impressions concerning Grant do not differ from yours. I tell everybody that he is the most modest, the most disinterested, and the most honest man I have ever known. I have met hundreds of prominent and influential men to whom I have said that and other things in the same directions. To the question they all ask, 'Doesn't he drink?' I have been able from my own knowledge, to give a decided negative."

Years later in 1887, Dana's *New York Sun* published an article entitled "General Grant's Occasional Intoxication," which said in part,

> General Grant's seasons of intoxication were not only infrequent, occurring once in three or four months, but he always chose a time when the gratification of his appetite for drink would not interfere with any important movement that had to be directed or attended by him. We were alone with General Grant when General Rawlins rode up and delivered that admirable communication [presumably the June letter]. After putting Rawlins' missive in his pocket Grant wound up going on board a steamer ... and getting as stupidly drunk as the immortal nature of man would allow; but the next day he came out fresh as a rose, without any trace of the spree he had just passed through. So it was on two or three other occasions of the sort and when it was all over, no outsider would have suspected such things had been.

Clearly Dana had lied in 1863. In the words of a Grant biographer, "The spy became one of Grant's biggest advocates."[9]

Why did he lie? Perhaps an answer lies in a letter Dana wrote in the summer of 1863 which refers to Grant's "very great chances" of becoming president and noted that the "elements of popularity of [Grant's] case are much like those of old Zack [Taylor] 16 years ago, and Grant is more of a man than that ancient hero."[10]

Later Dana, now officially assistant secretary of war, was sent to Tennessee to spy on Rosecrans. Dana's reports to Washington became a key reason Rosecrans was removed. The central question is how truthful was Dana and his reports? It has been shown that Rosecrans had no intention of evacuating Chattanooga and was not despondent and incapable of action. Dana himself conceded to Rosecrans that his reports were "unjust" to Rosecrans and on many subjects he was "misinformed."

Dana's own actions at Chickamauga were subject to criticism. According to John Wilder of the lightning brigade, Dana panicked at the time of the Confederate breakthrough and ordered Wilder to retreat to Chickamauga. Wilder felt he could have stayed on the battlefield and possibly stopped the Rebel onslaught. Not surprisingly Dana told a different version of this story. He lied about events in Mississippi; now it seemed he was lying in Tennessee. His zeal to make Garfield the key figure in Rosecrans' removal when Dana himself was much more central suggests a need to protect himself and pin the blame on someone else. His false claim that he possessed a letter from Garfield to Chase written after Chickamauga shows Dana was not unwilling to misrepresent the truth long after the events under discussion had occurred.

Dana's role in the Rosecrans story is crucial. If he deliberately lied in his reports, then Rosecrans' removal was for political rather than military reasons. In fact the decision to replace Rosecrans with Grant was probably made as early as October 3 when Grant was ordered to Cairo, Illinois. On October 10, Sherman wrote Grant, "I feel sure you will be ordered to Nashville to assume a general command over all the forces operating to the southeast, say, Rosecrans your center, Burnside left wing, and Sherman right."[11]

If in fact the decision had already been made, Dana's telegrams were really about justifying something already determined. But Dana was only assistant secretary of war. The actual decision to remove Rosecrans had to be made by someone in Washington.

The man to whom Dana reported was of course Secretary of War Stanton. Stanton's animosity to Rosecrans was no secret and dated back to 1861 when Rosecrans went to Washington with his plan to unify troops in Virginia and Stanton refused to receive him. As head of the War Department, it was Stanton who was one of the recipients of Rosecrans's many requests for more men, supplies and horses in the summer of 1863. John Sanderson, whom Rosecrans sent to Washington to ask for more assistance, wrote, "I frankly told him [Rosecrans] all that occurred at Washington, what Stanton's feelings towards him, and what he had said of him, and warned him of the doom, I was fully satisfied, would sooner or later await him." So certainly Edwin Stanton was one of those political leaders that Garfield referred to. But as powerful as Stanton was, he was not commander in chief. That man was Abraham Lincoln.[12]

Lincoln's relationship with Rosecrans was overall supportive and grateful. He said he could "never forget" the victory at Murfreesboro, and when Grant questioned Murfreesboro as a victory, Lincoln expressed his disagreement. After Rosecrans was relieved, Lincoln felt a "need to do something for General Rosecrans" and couldn't understand Stanton and Halleck's dislike for him. The point needs to be reemphasized that Lincoln did not make the decision to relieve Rosecrans. He drew up two orders, one keeping him in command and one relieving him. It was left to Grant to make the final decision regarding Rosecrans' fate. It was not the first time or the last that Grant would impact Rosecrans' future. Grant had worked for Rosecrans' transfer out of Mississippi in 1862 and would relieve him from command in 1864 in Missouri. Grant is one of the men most responsible for Rosecrans' fate. But to understand Grant and Grant's motivations, it is imperative to understand the man most responsible for Grant's Civil War career: Elihu B. Washburne.

15. Washburne

Washburne is the most important little-known figure of the Civil War. His importance stems from his relationships with Lincoln and especially Grant. A native of Maine, Washburne eventually settled in Galena, Illinois. His rise in local politics coincided at times with that of Lincoln. He, like Lincoln, made the jump from Whig to Republican. He was the only member of Congress to meet Lincoln at the train station upon his arrival in Washington in 1861.

His role in the rise of U.S. Grant is essential. When the war broke out, Grant had been out of the army since 1854. He, like Grant, made his way to Galena. It was Washburne who got Grant his commission as a colonel and later as a brigadier general. Grant was quite aware of Washburne's role in his ascent, writing in September 1861, "Mr. Washburne, allow me to thank you for the part you have taken in giving me my present position. I think I see your hand in it, and admit that I had no personal claims for your kind office in the matter. I can assure you, however, my whole heart is in the cause which we are fighting for, and I pledge myself that, if equal to the task before me, you shall never have cause to regret the part you have taken." Lincoln himself wrote, "Gen. Grant was appointed chiefly on the recommendation of Hon. E.B. Washburne."[1]

The role Washburne played in Grant's rise was not a secret and was not unique. There were many generals who owed their appointments to men in Washington. However, it is Washburne's actions when Grant came in for criticism that are of particular interest. After the battles of Forts Henry and Donelson, battles which brought Grant national acclaim, Grant came under scrutiny and criticism. This criticism centered on the charge that Grant had failed to send reports to Washington. Halleck wrote McClellan,

> I have had no communication with General Grant for more than a week. He left his command without my authority and went to Nashville. His army seems to be as much demoralized by the victory of Fort Donelson as was that of the Potomac by the defeat of Bull Run. It is hard to censure a successful general immediately after a victory, but I think he richly deserves it. I can get no returns, no reports, no information of any kind from him. Satisfied with his victory, he sits down and enjoys it without any regard to the future. I am worn-out and tired with this neglect and inefficiency. C. F. Smith is almost the only officer equal to the emergency.

Elihu B. Washburne. The most important unknown figure of the Civil War.

McClellan responded, "Your dispatch of last evening received. The future success of our cause demands that proceedings such as Grant's should at once be checked. Generals must observe discipline as well as private soldiers. Do not hesitate to arrest him at once if the good of the service requires it, and place C.F. Smith in command. You are at liberty to regard this as a positive order if it will smooth your way."[2]

General Cadwallader Washburn wrote his brother Elihu Washburne (who had added an *e* to his surname), who in turn talked to Lincoln. Halleck later said Grant was "indispensable." One observer concluded that Grant "would have been crushed had it not been for the powerful influence of E.B. Washburne." No doubt rivalries in Washington were one of the causes of this episode. It is an indication that military promotion and demotion was not necessarily tied to what happened on the battlefield.

After Shiloh, Grant came under even greater criticism for his conduct during that battle. As negative comments came in from many corners including the battlefield, Washburne took to the floor of the House of Representatives to defend Grant, saying at one point in the speech, "There is no more temperate man in the army than General Grant. He never indulges in the use of intoxicating liquors at all," a claim that he knew wasn't true as John Rawlins had informed him in a letter that "a gentleman made [Grant] a present of a box of Champagne wine, and on one or two occasions he drank a glass of this with his friends." Grant's wife and father both sent letters of thanks to Washburne. Julia wrote, "It is indeed gratifying to know that he finds in you so true a friend and one who manifests such a ready willingness to exonerate him from the malicious and unfounded slanders of the press."

Jesse Grant surmised, "I suppose it was through your influence that he was brought before the Jubilee. And I hope you may never have occasion to report the interest you have taken in his favor." Gustave Koerner, a general and Lincoln confidant, remembered, "Indeed, when the accounts of those who were present at Shiloh were heard, a deep feeling of indignation pervaded the nation. Had it not been for the most strenuous efforts of Washburne, who stood very high at Washington, and the fact that General C.J. Smith, the real hero of Donelson, was then about dying, there is no doubt but Grant would have been deprived of his command."[3]

Washburne's speech may have saved Grant after Shiloh, but the criticism continued.

Chicago Tribune editor Joseph Medill wrote to Wasburne in February 1863: "No man's career in the army is more open to destructive criticism than Grant's. We have kept off him on your account. We could have made him stink in the nostrils of the public like an old fish had we properly criticized his military blunders."[4]

In late March 1863, Washburne's brother, General Cadwallader C. Washburn, wrote to his brother:

> I regret today that our prospects are most decaying. There is no immediate prospect of taking Vicksburg. The matter on Yazoo Pass would have been a splendid success had Genl. Grant properly availed himself of it. I am thoroughly disgusted. The truth is, Grant has no plan for taking Vicksburg, and is frittering away time and strength to no purpose. The truth must be told even when it hurts. You cannot make a silk purse out of a sow's ear. The truth is the President and Sec'y of War know nothing of the conditions here. ...*The whole thing is too disgraceful to think of. My principal hope for taking Vicksburg now is from Rosecrans. The president would do a worse thing to order 50,000 men of the army before Vicksburg to travel militarily to Nashville & reinforce Rosecrans, & give battle there at once, & wipe out the [Rebel] army.* They have all the transports and could go there in six days, at no expense additional expense to gov't. I tell you if they do nothing where they are. [Emphasis added][5]

What is interesting about this letter, in addition to its despairing tone, is the suggestion that Rosecrans' army is the key to victory and should be reinforced.

On April 11, General Washburn wrote another letter to his brother:

> I was hoping you would come down here & go down to the fleet. The campaign is badly damaged. I am sure of it. I fear a calamity before Vicksburgh. All of Grant's schemes have failed. He knows that he has got to do something or off goes his head. My impression is that he intends to attack in front. If he does it may succeed but it is the act of a desperate man and nine chances out of ten are that our Army will be slaughtered. *The past six months has been worse than thrown away, as I could show you.... I say to you that I am distressed at our prospects and cannot sleep nights thinking of these things. Time seems to be no object here.* I have been here and yet

have not been able to get a list of troops to compose my command. You are responsible for Grant. You must go to see him and talk with him. He can do no less than tell you what his plans are. As one after another schemes fail, I hear that he says he has a plan of his own which is yet to be tried in which he has the greatest confidence [emphasis added].⁶

Noteworthy is General Washburn's dismay at the lack of action. It is usually Rosecrans who is criticized for inaction after Stones River, but here Grant is chided for "throwing away six months."

The essential question is why was Congressman Washburne so interested in having Grant succeed? The usual answer is that he had faith in Grant, that he was convinced that Grant was the man for the job. The curious fact is that Washburne really knew very little about Grant. He had never even met him prior to 1861. If both hadn't been living in Galena, Illinois, in 1861, it is unlikely Washburne would have had any interest in Grant or his military career. Until they met again in the fall of 1862, Washburne had to rely on others for information about Grant, and much of that information was negative. If Washburne's support wasn't based on a deep personal knowledge of Grant, what was the basis? One answer is that Washburne had hitched his political fortunes to Grant's military star. If Grant succeeded, Washburne would profit politically. And what higher political goal was there than the presidency?

The renomination, much less the reelection, of Abraham Lincoln was far from a sure thing. The names of Fremont, Chase, Banks and Butler among others were mentioned as possible candidates. Rosecrans himself had been sounded out by an emissary from Horace Greeley. One potential candidate, Butler, received the following letter from Chicago:

> Dear Sir: On looking about among the politicians here I find that there is more activity here than elsewhere in reference to Prospective Politics. Hon. E.B. Washburne is making the business already of committing men to Grant for the Presidency. He is wealthy, shrewd, and in earnest, determined that Grant is to be the man. I hear good men say he will go into a nominating convention stronger than Lincoln went.⁷

The conventional view is that Grant was not interested in the presidency. Indeed when the question was put to him, he responded with the following letter which Grant wrote to deny any presidential aspirations:

> Your letter of the 7th inst. asking if you will be at liberty to use my name before the convention of the "War Democracy," as candidate for the office of the Presidency is just received.—This question astonishes me. I do not know of anything I have ever done or said which would indicate that I could be a candidate for any office whatever within the gift of the people.
>
> I shall continue to do my duty, to the best of my ability, so long as permitted to remain in the Army, supporting whatever Administration may be in power, in their

endeavor to suppress the rebellion and maintain National unity, and never desert it because my vote, if I had one, might have been cast for different candidates. Nothing likely to happen would pain me so much as to see my name used in connection with a political office. I am not a candidate for any office nor for favors from any party. Let us succeed in crushing the rebellion, in the shortest possible time, and I will be content with whatever credit may then be given me.... I wish to avoid notoriety as far as possible, and above all things, desire to be spared the pain of seeing my name mixed with politics. Do not therefore publish this letter but wherever, and by whatever party, you hear my name mentioned in connection with the candidacy for any office, say that you know from me direct that I am not "in the field," and cannot allow my name to be used before any convention.[8]

It must be remembered that in the nineteenth century it was deemed unseemly for someone to openly seek the presidency. The office should seek the man, not the man the office. Even if Grant were interested in the presidential nomination, he would never publicly reveal that interest, particularly when he would be displacing a sitting president in the middle of a civil war. It is perhaps also important that the letter of denial was written to a Democrat, since the Republicans would seem to have first claim on him.

In any discussion of Grant's Civil War career, Elihu B. Washburne's presence must be taken into account. It is important to note that in the letter from J.K. Herbert to Butler cited above, it is Washburne who is "making the business" for Grant's nomination, not Grant himself. The essential question is not did Grant himself want the presidency, but did Washburne want the presidency for Grant? A look at Washburne's correspondence provides some clues. A letter from J.W. Sheehan, editor of the Democrat newspaper *Chicago Post*, began,

Do you intend to let Grant be the president or not? Or do you intend that the Democracy [Democratic Party] shall nominate some other man who hasn't the ghost of a chance. That Lt. generalship has been pretty adroitly managed by you. If the administration will only let Grant have his way and sweep the rebellion into the sea I who think such a result of even greater importance than the success of the Democracy will forgive your robbing us of our only available candidate.[9]

Another letter from O.B. Mattison of Utica, New York:

I think you must be about the happiest man on this continent or any other... [because of the success of Grant].... There is one other thing that you may rely on if he captures Richmond before the Baltimore Convention. No power on earth can prevent his being the next president whether he wishes it or not.[10]

A cautionary letter warned, "Keep him away from Washington, out of politics, and in the field for the next four years."[11]

These letters clearly show that Grant was talked about for the presidency and that Washburne was seen as the key figure in that discussion.

One person who was interested in Grant's possible presidential aspirations was Abraham Lincoln. The president, who had never met Grant, asked Washburne about Grant's ambitions. Washburne referred Lincoln to J. Russell Jones, who was summoned to Washington by the chief executive. Jones gave the letter cited above in which Grant disavowed an interest in the presidency to Lincoln, who after reading it said, "My son, you will never know how gratifying that is to me. No man knows, when that Presidential grub gets to gnawing at him, just how deep it will get until he has tried it; and I didn't know but what there was one gnawing at Grant."[12]

It was during the winter of 1863 that the idea of reviving the rank of lieutenant general and conferring it on Grant arose. The author of this proposal was Elihu Washburne. The common perception at the time was that the bill was a reward to Grant for staying out of politics, and in fact it was not signed by Lincoln until after his meeting with Jones. The House version was controversial because it specifically named Grant for the rank, whereas the Senate version made no specification. Grant's name was deleted by the Senate in the final version. On February 29, Lincoln signed the bill and that same day submitted a bill naming Grant as lieutenant general. It was not until March 1864, when Grant came to Washington, that he met Lincoln for the first time. Political talk and intrigue would continue up to the nominating conventions.[13]

The Republican, or National Union Party, Convention was scheduled for June 7 and 8 in Baltimore. Some radical Republicans, unhappy over the prospect of Lincoln's renomination, bolted from the party, met in Cleveland, and on May 31 nominated John C. Fremont. He had been the first Republican presidential candidate in 1856 and in 1861 in Missouri had issued a quickly overturned emancipation proclamation. Always a darling of the radicals, Fremont had replaced Rosecrans in West Virginia in 1862.

The Democrats were scheduled to meet in Chicago on August 29 to 31. Several variables came into play regarding Grant, Washburne and any other aspirants for the presidency. Even though Grant's promotion was seen as keeping him in the military field and out of politics, the reality was that Grant as a valuable commodity and success on the military front could translate into success on the political front. Rawlins wrote to General James Harrison Wilson,

> I cannot conceive how the use of General Grant's name in connection with the President can result in harm to him or our cause, for if there is a man in the United States who is unambitious of such honor, it is certainly he, yet the matter is not in such shape as to justify him in writing a letter declining to be a candidate for the Presidency. The nomination for the office has not been tendered him by the people; nor has it by either of the great political parties or any portion thereof. To write a letter of declination now, would place him in much the position of the old maid

who had never had an offer declaring she "would never marry"; besides it would be by many construed into a modest way of getting his name before the country in connection with the office, having, as he always has, avoided public notice or newspaper talk relating to him.

In regard to Washburne, Rawlins wrote,

> The Honorable E.B. Washburne I am sure is not in favor of Grant for the Presidency. He is for Mr. Lincoln, and if he has made use of the language imputed to him, it has been to further the passage of his Lieutenant-Generalcy bill; nothing more I am certain. This is my own opinion. That Washburne should seemingly arrogate to himself the exclusive championship of the General, is not at all strange when we reflect upon the fact that two years ago he was the only man in Congress who had a voice of condemnation for the General's maligners. His defence of Grant aided to keep him in his position and enabled him to achieve the successes that have placed him first in the World's History as a military man, and secured for him the gratitude of his countrymen. Grant cannot neglect writing to him, but of course should be guarded in what he writes him as well as in what he writes others. One in the General's position can scarcely write a private letter that in any manner touches upon passing events, because of the eagerness of every one to give to the public that which they so easily conceive to belong to it, coming as it does from one to whom all look to dispel the dark clouds of war that have drenched our land with blood, and reveal to their longing eyes the bright sky of peace beyond.[14]

What at first reading seems to be an unequivocal denial of Grant's political ambitions on a closer look raises lots of questions. Why speculate if the use of Grant's name can cause harm to him or "our cause?" Why shouldn't Grant write "a letter of declination" now? What is the "imputed" language that Washburne has used only to further the lieutenant generalcy bill and "nothing more?" How else could it be interpreted? Why should Grant "be guarded" in what he writes Washburne if Washburne is unequivocally for Lincoln?

A further look at Washburne's correspondence sheds some light. Joseph Medill wrote Washburne in May 1864 that he

> didn't care if the convention is put off till August. I oppose it in the paper [*Chicago Tribune*] moderately, but will not be distressed if the committee postpone it a couple of months. I was opposed to calling it so early. If it should happen that Lincoln loses the nomination he will have nobody but himself to blame for it.
>
> The great question is would Grant allow them [Democrats] to use him as their candidate? Would he accept the nomination at their hands under any condition?
>
> I suppose you know his secret mind as well as any living man and ought to have more influence with him than any man in the world. For you have been indispensable to him. You have been the ladder on which he climbed. The Atlas who held him up when he was sinking into oblivion. And he ought to listen to your advice.
>
> Now what is your opinion? Have you any positive knowledge? If Grant should accept the Copperhead nomination he might beat us and to bring that party into

power would be destructive of the best interests of the country and would make shipwreck of all that has been done. If Grant will content himself with a Lieut. Generalship and calmly apply himself to closing up the war and putting out the last embers of the rebellion, he will have all he can attend to for a couple of years [He will have] the Administration with him and the great party of freedom on his side and four years hence will be their candidate and president for *eight years*.

Now let me whisper a word in your private ear. How would you like a seat in Lincoln's cabinet. The postmaster general's place? There you could control an immense patronage.

Now sir if you keep Grant clear of copperhead temptation and out of their hands Lincoln must give you that seat in the cabinet if you want it he *dare* not refuse it. My confidential advice is to make the arrangement. It would give a satisfaction to the party. Once in the cabinet you would be the master spirit of the administration. I would have this arrangement take effect very soon after the Baltimore Convention and not later than the copperhead Chicago convention.

What I have written I have hinted to no living being. I would like to get at your confidential views of the matters I have touched upon.[15]

This is a remarkable letter that addresses many topics: the possibility that Grant would be nominated by the Democrats and might accept their nomination; that Washburne knew Grant's "secret mind" and had great influence over Grant; that the office of lieutenant general was something to occupy Grant until he would be elected and reelected president; that Washburne could name his price for his managing of Grant and that price could be the postmaster generalship with its "immense patronage"; and that all of this needed to be kept confidential. It clearly connects Grant and the presidency via the efforts of Elihu Washburne.

Even if one rejects the idea that Washburne was pushing Grant for the presidency in 1864, there can be no doubt that he wanted Grant to run in 1868. In order for that to happen he first had to make sure Grant would be the leading military figure to emerge on the Northern side during the war. So his motivation and actions would essentially be the same whether Grant ran in 1864 or four years later.

One might find the foregoing interesting discussion but still ask, "What does this have to do with William S. Rosecrans?" It is an important question.

An answer can be found in the second half of the partially cited letter from J.K. Herbert to Gen. Benjamin Butler.

Dear Sir: On looking about among the politicians here I find that there is more activity here than elsewhere in reference to prospective politics. Hon. E.B. Washburne is making a business already of committing men to Grant for the Presidency.

He is wealthy, shrewd, in earnest, determined that Grant shall be the man. I hear good men say he will go into a nominating convention stronger than Lincoln went.

They are trying to get Grant in command of Rosecrans' army & his own too, with perhaps additional reinforcements—send him across to the Atlantic and eastward on Richmond—hoping thereby to make him irresistible in a Nominating Convention. If the administration see the joke, they will see to it that he does not get an opportunity. But if Grant & his western friends can do this thing they will—I am not misinformed—*they are bending every energy for the enterprise* [emphasis added].[16]

This letter was written in August 1863—before Chickamauga. The recipient of the letter, General Benjamin Butler, was a political general who not only wanted the presidency but had support for his candidacy, particularly from the radicals in the Republican Party. The letter was accurate in predicting that Grant would get command of Rosecrans' army and would march on Richmond. The only part that did not come to pass was Grant's irresistibility to a nominating convention. But that was not without trying; had Grant taken Richmond in May 1864, he may very well have been irresistible. It is worth noting that the battle of Cold Harbor began on May 31, and the last assault, about which Grant said, "I have always regretted that the last assault at Cold Harbor was ever made," was on June 3. Emory Upton wrote about Cold Harbor in a letter to his sister, "I am disgusted with the generalship displayed. Our men have, in many instances, been foolishly and wantonly sacrificed. Assault after assault has been ordered upon the enemy's entrenchments, when they knew nothing about the strength or position of the enemy. Thousands of lives may have been spared by the exercise of a little skill; but, as it is, the courage of the poor men is expected to obviate all difficulties." In another letter written a day later he called Cold Harbor "murderous," writing that he had seen "but little of generalship during the campaign" but hoping that "mere numbers will yet enable us to enter Richmond." Perhaps the fact that the Baltimore Convention opened on June 7 explains what to Upton seemed a loss which was "very heavy, and to no purpose."[17]

So here is evidence of Garfield's answer that "political leaders" were responsible for Rosecrans' removal. There were several players backing various generals, but the ultimate beneficiary was Ulysses Grant. Garfield knew what he was talking about when he said political leaders were not unwilling to see evil befall Rosecrans.. He had played the game himself, even trying to make Rosecrans vice president in 1864.

To put it plainly, William Starke Rosecrans was removed from command of the Army of the Cumberland and eventually from any role in the Civil War because people with influence in Washington feared he might be too successful and either be a candidate for the presidency or prevent others, specifically Ulysses S. Grant, from becoming a present or future candidate.

To many this may seem a far-fetched conspiracy theory. However, the participants of the time had little doubt that their fate was being determined by non-military matters. In June 1864, Gordon Granger, a hero of Snodgrass

Hill and Missionary Ridge, sent the following letter to Rosecrans. Referring to the fact that it was Granger's troops who swept the Rebels off Missionary Ridge, he wrote

> This made poor Sherman and the miserable satellites which surround him and Grant including that loathsome pimp Dana fearful, jealous and nothing would satisfy them except my destruction which they have accomplished as you are aware. Baldy Smith was also in the clique and did his best to ruin me—he is a bad man, a hypocrite, beware of him.[18]

Horace Newton Fisher, who was a staff officer in the Army of the Cumberland, wrote to Congressman John D. Long in 1889,

> After his victory at Stone River there came a set of disgruntled politicians to Rosecrans to get him to run as opposition candidate to Prest. Lincoln.... I have always thought that the fact of the overture thus made became known in Washington... and that this created a determination to get rid of him and led to his removal from command.[19]

A contemporary observer made the following observations:

> Of all the generals who achieved notoriety during the civil war, he [Grant] is the one whose career as a soldier will bear the least scrutiny. Of a coarse fiber, no culture, and of limited intelligence, his memory serves to illustrate either that his fame rests on newspaper fiction, fostered by political partisanship, or that, to be a successful military man, a marked lack of intellectual qualities is a necessity. We have seen how at Shiloh he suffered a surprise and merciless slaughter in the enemy's country; how at Fort Henry he failed to have his forces on hand to reap the fruits of Commodore Foote's victory; how at Fort Donelson he absented himself mysteriously from the field at the critical moment when the Confederates, cutting their way out, could have been captured to a man. History now tells us that in the combined operation against Price and Van Dorn, he failed to co-operate and enabled Price to march off three miles and fall with his full weight of overwhelming numbers upon Rosecrans, who subsequently defeated Van Dorn at Corinth without Grant's aid, although the Confederates had double the force that our general of real military genius had under him. It is strange that so unsuccessful a general should be able to retain the confidence of the War Department at Washington, that must have known of his blunders and habits.
>
> There is a solution to this mystery found in the name and career of Elihu Benjamin Washburne, a remarkable man of Maine birth and parentage and New England training and culture, if that word can be applied to a coarse, strong man, who made up in cunning all that he lost in brain. From early life to the close of his public career, he was a most successful politician. To great strength of character he added a purity of motive as rare as it was admirable in the time when frauds in public office began to organize for plunder upon a helpless people, exhausted and dazed by one of the bloodiest wars that ever poor humanity suffered. A lawyer by profession, Washburne soon passed to the more congenial pursuit of politics, and in Illinois, where he opened a law office, soon grew to be a noted and influential

leader. He was returned to Congress so frequently that he came to be the father of the House, and was widely noted for his jealous guardianship of the public treasury.

The Hon. Elihu B. Washburne had little interest in and less knowledge of war. But, in common with many, he was well aware that out of that war, if successful, would come a military leader to claim the recognition of the people he had served, and Elihu resolved to be the patron and friend of that man. He selected Grant, and his choice was as strange as his faithful support was without parallel. Here was a man forced from the old army because of his habits, who had risen only to the rank of captain in the service, and an utter failure in all that he attempted as a means of subsistence in civil life. Through all his early military career, as a small farmer near St. Louis, as a clerk at Galena, he not only gave no evidence of ability of any sort, but no one of his associates or family ever suspected him of aught beyond the dullest common place; and yet, through good and evil report, the Hon. Elihu stood by his protege. It was a powerful support. Not only the President, but the Secretary of War, regarded Washburne as a man of sterling integrity, as well as a politician whose following among the people was so earnest that he was a power at Washington not to be neglected or slighted. Every promotion gained by Grant was really given by Washburne.[20]

These are powerful, some might say inflammatory, words. The man who wrote them was Donn Piatt. Forgotten today, Piatt was at various times a diplomat, journalist, newspaper publisher, soldier, and historian. He would have been in a position to know of what he was talking. The real wonder is not that someone made this accusation over 100 years ago but rather that no one today seems to be interested in the claims made or the questions raised. They are not refuted, just ignored.

The author believes the point that politics in Washington caused the downfall of William S. Rosecrans has been proved as conclusively as possible. However, three major objections will be looked at to further bolster this contention.

The first objection is that the idea that officials in Washington would ever allow politics, particularly presidential politics, to interfere with the prosecution of a war is not possible. The fact is that politics and personal ambition have played a part in all wars, indeed in every human endeavor. However, it is fruitful to look at the war immediately before the Civil War—the Mexican War. Anyone who looks at that conflict closely will discover that President James K. Polk, a Democrat, favored his fellow party members in the appointments he made. Moreover the two leading generals, Zachary Taylor and Winfield Scott, were both Whigs. Polk feared that one of them would become the hero of the war and as a result president. Polk, worried more about Taylor than Scott, replaced Taylor with Scott. Everyone involved, including Taylor and Scott, had no doubt that politics was the determining factor.

One veteran of the Mexican War wrote the following years after the war:

> The Mexican war was a political war, and the administration conducting it desired to make party capital out of it. General Scott was at the head of the army, and, being a soldier of acknowledged professional capacity, his claim to the command of the forces in the field was almost indisputable, and does not seem to have been denied by President Polk, or Marcy, his Secretary of War. Scott was a Whig and the administration was Democratic. General Scott was also known to have political aspirations, and nothing so popularizes a candidate for high civil positions as military victories. It would not do, therefore, to give him command of the "army of conquest." The plans submitted by Scott for a campaign in Mexico were disapproved by the administration, and he replied, in a tone possibly a little disrespectful, to the effect that if a soldier's plans were not to be supported by the administration, success could not be expected. This was on the 27th of May, 1846. Four days later General Scott was notified that he need not go to Mexico. General Gaines was next in rank, but he was too old and feeble to take the field. Colonel Zachary Taylor—a brigadier-general by brevet—was therefore left in command. He too was a Whig, but was not supposed to entertain any political ambitions; nor did he; but after the fall of Monterey—his third battle and third complete victory—the Whig papers at home began to speak of him as the candidate of their party for the Presidency. Something had to be done to neutralize his growing popularity. He could not be relieved from duty in the field, where all his battles had been victories; the design would have been too transparent. It was finally decided to send General Scott, and to authorize him to carry out his own original plan: that is, capture Vera Cruz and march upon the capital of the country. It was no doubt supposed that Scott's ambition would lead him to slaughter Taylor or destroy his chances for the Presidency, and yet it was hoped that he would not make sufficient capital himself to secure the prize. The administration had indeed a most embarrassing problem to solve. It was engaged in a war of conquest which must be carried to a successful issue, or the political object would be unattained. Yet all the capable officers of the requisite rank belonged to the opposition, and the man selected for his lack of political ambition had himself become a prominent candidate for the Presidency. It was necessary to destroy his chances promptly. The problem was to do this without the loss of conquest and without permitting another general of the same political party to acquire like popularity. The fact is, the administration of Mr. Polk made every preparation to disgrace Scott, or, to speak more correctly, to drive him to such desperation that he would disgrace himself.[21]

The author of that clear, cold analysis was Ulysses S. Grant.

So it can be concluded that there was a precedent for presidential politics to influence military policy. Still some would say that that was the Mexican War, a controversial and to some an unnecessary war, but the Civil War was different. It was, to both sides, a holy war, a war whose most famous anthem was the "Battle Hymn of the Republic" and whose Southern motto was *Deo Vindice*, which can be translated various ways but always with the word God. Surely Abraham Lincoln and the single-minded radical Republicans would never allow personal political ambition to interfere with the prosecution of such a holy and noble cause. The truth is more complicated.

During the Civil War the Republican Party controlled Congress and the presidency. However, the party was a new party, founded in 1854, and among Civil War generals it had relatively few members. The most prominent Republican general was John C. Fremont, who had been the party's first presidential nominee in 1856. He would also briefly be a presidential candidate opposing Lincoln in 1864. Most of the generals were either Democrats or had little interest in party politics. The most prominent and popular Democrat general during the early part of the war was George B. McClellan. He would be his party's presidential candidate in 1864. Many generals' political preferences were either indeterminate or non-existent. Ulysses Grant fell into this category. Therefore he was coveted by partisans of both parties. In general there was a belief among Democrat generals that they were hurt by their party ties. The fact that prominent Democrats like McClellan, Buell, McClernand, and Rosecrans were either removed or not in command when the war ended strengthened that idea. Some might say that those generals deserved their fate, but it is interesting to observe that generals who were or would become Republican such as John A. Logan, John Fremont, John Pope, Nathaniel Banks, John Schofield, and most strikingly Ambrose Burnside, survived despite their military blunders.

Gideon Welles wrote in his diary in 1862,

> The introduction of Pope here, followed by Halleck, is an intrigue of Stanton's and Chase's to get rid of McClellan. A part of this intrigue has been the withdrawal of McClellan and the Army of the Potomac from before Richmond and turning it into the Army of Washington under Pope.
> The defeat of Pope and placing McC. in command of the retreating and disorganized forces after the second disaster at Bull Run interrupted the intrigue which had been planned for the dismissal of McClellan, and was not only a triumph for him but a severe mortification and disappointment for both Stanton and Chase.[22]

A particularly relevant case to the Rosecrans story is the man who is considered to be the quintessential political general, John McClernand. He was a Democrat and protégé of Stephen A. Douglas. He had also been a political and professional colleague of Lincoln in Illinois. The two maintained a cordial relationship, and the president named McClernand a general in part to satisfy Illinois Democrats. McClernand is usually portrayed as an unsuccessful general who took his complaints directly to Lincoln, bypassing his military commander, Grant. However, in one of the most recent and comprehensive biographies of McClernand, his biographer wrote,

> From November 1861 until 19 May 1863, McClernand had been part of victory after victory. He had made mistakes, but so had Grant, who had been severely criticized for his absence at Fort Donelson and at Shiloh at the moment of Confederate

attack. Sherman had been inexcusably unprepared at Shiloh and defeated at Chickasaw Bayou. Sherman's and McPherson's assaults on 19 May, assaults directed by Grant, had also failed, as did their attacks on 22 May. John McClernand's record thus compares quite favorably with those of the luminaries of the western theater—luminaries whose stars would continue "ever in the ascendant."[23]

He concluded, "McClernand's combat record of courage and success afforded no grounds for relief from command." So why was McClernand removed from his command? Officially he was removed for the publication in the newspapers of a congratulatory letter he wrote to his troops, which was in violation of orders. But some have surmised that other factors, especially jealousy between West Point and non–West Point generals, resulted in McClernand's removal. Robert McCormick, a Grant idolizer and grandson of Joseph Medill, concluded that a "conspiracy" brought down McClernand.

What makes McClernand's story relevant to Rosecrans' story is that it involves a familiar cast of characters: Grant, Sherman, Rawlins and Charles A. Dana. Indeed Dana wrote a telegram to Washington, saying, "McClernand has not the qualities necessary of a good commander even of a regiment." The important point is not that McClernand was totally blameless for his fate but that his downfall was not the result of his military actions. The answer to the question as to whether cliques, jealousies, and partisan politics played a determining role in the careers of Civil War generals is a definite yes.[24]

The third question is to what extent did political or non-military factors effect Ulysses Grant's decisions. Grant played a major part in the McClernand story. Another general whose fate was controlled by Grant was Benjamin Butler. Butler was a political as well as military rival to Grant. In July of 1864, Grant made the decision to replace Grant with General W.F. Smith. When Butler learned about his imminent removal, he went to Grant's headquarters and personally confronted the only general who outranked him. Grant rescinded the order relieving Butler. Smith in 1864 wrote the following in a letter:

> Since I have been in New York, I have heard from two different sources (one being from General Grant's headquarters and one a staff officer of a general on intimate official relations with General Butler) that General Butler went to General Grant and threatened to expose his intoxication if the order was not revoked. I also learned that General Butler had threatened to make public something that would prevent the President's re-election. General Grant told me (when I asked him about General Butler's threat crushing me) that he had heard that General Butler had made some threat with reference to the Chicago convention, which he (Butler) said "he had in his breeches pocket," but General Grant was not clear in expressing what the threat was. I refer to this simply because I feel convinced that the change was not made for any of the reasons that have been assigned, and whether General Butler has threatened General Grant with his opposition to Mr. Lincoln at the coming

election, or has appealed to any political aspirations which General Grant may entertain, I do not know, but one thing is certain, I was not guilty of any acts of insubordination between my appointment and my suspension, for I was absent all those days on leave of absence from General Grant.[25]

Grant never attempted to explain this reversal or even mentioned it in his *Memoirs*. Most historians come to the conclusion that politics explains Grant's action. The assumption is that Butler was too politically powerful to be removed. Some speculate that Lincoln himself ordered the reversal of the dismissal order. Here is a clear example of Ulysses Grant using non-military reasons to determine a general's fate. Grant ultimately did relieve Butler in January 1865.

To some, the firings of McClernand and Butler were warranted no matter the motivation. They were political generals who interfered with Grant's efforts to win the war. But Grant's treatment of another general, George H. Thomas, is not so easily explained away.

Thomas is, like Rosecrans, a successful general who has fallen into obscurity. He is best known for being the "Rock of Chickamauga." Less well known is his decisive victory at Nashville in December 1864. Rarely discussed is the fact that Grant planned to relieve Thomas before the battle. Grant, accusing Thomas of being slow, composed a telegram removing Thomas. Grant, whose own army was immobile before Petersburg, seemed unaware that an ice storm forced Thomas to delay the start of the battle. Grant decided to go to Nashville himself to remove Thomas. He made it as far as Washington when word came of Thomas' decisive victory. Luckily for Grant's subsequent reputation the second telegram relieving Thomas was never sent. Grant would have replaced Thomas with either John M. Schofield or John A. Logan, both "political generals." Grant was about to do to Thomas what he had done to Rosecrans. Although Thomas was not relieved after Nashville, his army was dismembered and Thomas had no further active command role in the war.

Despite his relative obscurity, there have been a number of biographies written about Thomas. Many of them make the claim that Thomas is the great figure of the war. A few, mostly older works, maintain that Rosecrans' successes were really due to Thomas. There is no evidence that there was ever a rift or even a rivalry between Thomas and Rosecrans. A friend of both men said that he once asked Thomas if he blamed Rosecrans for what happened at Chattanooga. "No farther than this," was the reply: "Rosecrans, after getting Chattanooga, should have acted as I did [at Nashville in 1864]—he should have paid no attention to Halleck or Stanton, or the pressure from Washington. The 'Army of the Cumberland' had done a good nine months' work in driving the Rebels out of Tennessee, and getting a foot-hold south of the river. Rosecrans should have waited to get another 'good ready' before he pushed forward again. I would have asked to be relieved."

In 1866 Thomas was quoted as saying, "Chickamauga! A battle in which I received great credit at the expense of a better soldier. General Rosecrans." Even allowing for General Thomas' well-known modesty, that quote shows he did not have a low opinion of his old commander. When in that same year Rosecrans was considering retiring from the army, Thomas wrote him, "Whether you remain in the army or not you may be assured of one thing: my unceasing friendship and esteem."[26]

The following citation, from Gideon Welles' diary, is famous for the reference to Lincoln's prophetic dream on the night before he was assassinated, but Lincoln's opinion of the Battle of Stones River and Grant's reaction to that opinion is also interesting. Welles' footnote is also noteworthy:

> April 14, Friday. Last night there was a general illumination in Washington, fireworks, etc. To-day is the anniversary of the surrender of Sumter, and the flag is to be raised by General Anderson.
> General Grant was present at the meeting of the Cabinet to-day, and remained during the session....
> ...Inquiry had been made as to army news on the first meeting of the Cabinet, and especially if any information had been received from Sherman. None of the members had heard anything, and Stanton, who makes it a point to be late, and who has the telegraph in his Department, had not arrived. General Grant, who was present, said he was hourly expecting word. The President remarked it would, he had no doubt, come soon, and come favorable, for he had last night the usual dream which he had preceding nearly every great and important event of the War. Generally the news had been favorable which succeeded this dream, and the dream itself was always the same. I inquired what this remarkable dream could be. He said it related to your (my) element, the water; that he seemed to be in some singular, indescribable vessel, and that he was moving with great rapidity towards an indefinite shore; that he had this dream preceding Sumter, Bull Run, Antietam, Gettysburg, Stone River, Vicksburg, Wilmington, etc.—General Grant said Stone River was certainly no victory, and he knew of no great results which followed from it. The President said however that might be, his dream preceded that fight.

Welles added the following footnote:

> *General Grant interrupted to say Stone River was no victory,—that a few such fights would have ruined us. The President looked at Grant curiously and inquiringly; said they might differ on that point, and at all events his dream preceded it. This was the first occasion I had to notice Grant's jealous nature. In turning it over in my mind at a later period, I remembered that Rawlins had been sent to Washington to procure action against General McClernand at Vicksburg. Later there was jealousy manifested towards General Thomas and others who were not satellites. —G.W.* [Emphasis added][27]

The cold, cruel fact is that William S. Rosecrans is forgotten today because of Ulysses S. Grant. It is not just a matter of Grant's fame obscuring

Rosecrans, but something more serious. Grant's version of the truth is not only at odds with Rosecrans' version but frequently with the historical record. Furthermore many historians have tended to protect Grant by ignoring the historical record. This has been at the expense of Thomas as well as Rosecrans. When reading a book touching on the Rosecrans-Grant conflict, it should be judged by how the author treats a number of key topics: Grant's absence at Iuka and Corinth; Grant calling Rosecrans back after Corinth; the roles of Charles Dana and Elihu Washburne; the government ordering Rosecrans to advance in Tennessee before he was ready; the failure of that same government to reinforce Rosecrans before Chickamauga; the credit for opening the supply line to Chattanooga; Grant and Sherman's Memoirs compared to the record; and Grant's treatment of other generals, particularly George Thomas.

A word must be said about the man who was the greatest defender of William S. Rosecrans, George H. Thomas, and the men who fought and died in the armies they led: Henry Van Ness Boynton. He is another important person from that time who is forgotten today. Boynton won the Medal of honor for his actions at Missionary Ridge, a battle in which he was severely wounded. After the war he became Washington correspondent for the *Cincinnati Gazette*. A contemporaneous biography said of him,

Henry van Ness Boynton. Wounded Medal of Honor winner. First Commissioner of the Chickamauga Battlefield Park. Staunch defender of George H. Thomas and William S. Rosecrans.

His keen, incisive efforts in that line [journalism] gave his journal a national reputation. He was soon put at the head of the Washington Bureau, in which a syndicate of several leading papers was formed, and to-day he is regarded as at the front in his profession; one of the most noted, loved, feared and respected of journalists. General Boynton's great quality in the army was his high courage that was animated by the purest and deepest patriotism. His distinguishing characteristic as a journalist is his sterling integrity, inspired by a sense of justice, that can be appealed to at all times. He is feared by knaves of all sorts, for his singularly incisive style, backed by his courage, makes him terrible in his assaults on wrong. He has driven some of the worst lobbyists from Washington, and is feared as no other man ever was by the entire lobby.[28]

He investigated and reported on the myriad scandals of the period after the Civil War. He wrote numerous articles and books defending Rosecrans, Thomas and the Army of the Cumberland, most famously *Sherman's Historical Raid*, which was a sharp critique and analysis of Sherman's *Memoirs*.

In addition to his writing, Boynton also found time to serve as president of the District of Columbia School Board, be a governing commissioner of the capital's Rock Creek Park and also be the prime force in the establishment of the Chickamauga and Chattanooga National Military Park, the first in the nation, which set precedents for the other military parks that followed. President Theodore Roosevelt attended his burial in Arlington in 1905. Boynton's writings should be read and their conclusions taken very seriously when studying the histories of Grant, Sherman, Rosecrans, Thomas and the claims of their supporters. Boynton was present at the events he wrote about, he feared no man, and he suffered a grievous wound fighting for his country. His opinions deserve to be treated with the greatest respect.

16. After the War

In July 1865, Rosecrans made his way to San Francisco where after a welcome of bands, parades and fireworks he addressed a crowd of 10,000 from the balcony of the Occidental Hotel. Apart from time in government service, the Golden State would be his home for the rest of his life. In his speech Rosecrans said, "I want to see one or more iron bands extending across this great metropolis of the Pacific with the distant shores of Maine. I want to hear the shrill whistle of the locomotive wake up the echoes of the Rocky Mountains and the solitudes of the great interior desert."[1]

In 1867 Rosecrans officially resigned from the army. The reason was a familiar one: Ulysses S. Grant. David Stanley told sculptor James Kelly, "I begged Rosecrans not to resign from the army. But he said he didn't propose to take orders from that ignorant, stupid Sam Grant.... But he resigned and has had to scramble for his bread ever since."

In notes for a biography of her father that was never published, the general's daughter Anita wrote,

> It may not be known why Rosecrans ... resigned. It occurred in this wise. Grant in the presence of a dozen officers at a social gathering said speaking of Rosecrans, "Gentlemen as long as I am at the head of the army that man shall not have a command." When Rosecrans heard this he resigned at once rather than lead a life of idleness under the [control] of such a man as Grant.[2]

With his military career over, Rosecrans would need to earn a living. He returned to his pre-war profession of mining and also became involved in railroad development. Rosecrans was one of the eleven incorporators of the Southern Pacific Railroad. However he eventually would lose control of his shares, and they would be auctioned off. His interest turned south to San Diego and the idea of building a transcontinental railroad that would terminate in that city.

An ancillary result was that Rosecrans became so enamored of Southern California that he purchased a city block in San Diego and 16,000 acres of the Rancho San Pedro, encompassing much of the area around present-day Gardena, California.

In the summer of 1868 Rosecrans was appointed by President Andrew Johnson as minister plenipotentiary to the government of Benito Juarez in

Mexico. He arrived at his post in December. Rosecrans became interested in promoting railway construction. He believed, "The United States should push our railroad and telegraph lines to the northern border of Mexico. At the same time, we ought to secure organization for the construction, by Americans, of one or two grand trunk lines of railways, penetrating the heart of the country."

After his diplomatic career, Rosecrans himself would lead a consortium wishing to build a transnational Mexican railroad.

Always a blunt man when it came to expressing his opinions, Rosecrans found the Juarez government guilty of having "no great measures for the relief of the country." He felt the government had lost the confidence of Mexican foreign investors; the army was demoralized and unhappy; public justice was "notoriously retarded or corrupted, the public highways infested with robbers and kidnappers"; "the country everywhere full of discontent and despair." He also felt that "as Mexico is our neighbor, its prosperity or adversity must affect us." In a private meeting with the Mexican cabinet he endeavored to "inspire them with a determination to take measures for the development of the natural resources of the country, the relief of industry from its onerous burdens of taxation; to support the construction of railroads and the opening of the country to immigration." He felt American capital, particularly railroads, was part of the solution for the country's ills.[3]

Rosecrans' tenure as minister would be short-lived. Ulysses Grant became president in March 1869, and Rosecrans' term was ended in June of that year. However, he would return to Mexico in a few years as a businessman.

Prior to going to Mexico, Rosecrans in 1868 became involved in a domestic political issue involving the defeated South and Robert E. Lee. That year was a presidential election year, and the candidates were Democrat Horatio Seymour and Republican Ulysses Grant. Rosecrans was a Democrat and naturally would support the party's nominee. The fact that the opposition was his bitter rival, Grant, surely added to Rosecrans' desire to defeat him.

An argument used by Republicans was that if a Democrat were elected the fruits of victory in the war, particularly in regard to the freed slaves, would be lost. Rosecrans knew that White Sulphur Springs in now West Virginia was where many prominent Southern leaders spent part of the summer. He resolved to reach out to them there and have them agree to accept the finality of the war and its results. The result was a letter, the so-called White Sulphur Springs Manifesto, that stated in part,

> Whatever opinions may have prevailed in the past with regard to African slavery or the right of a State to secede from the Union, we believe we express the almost unanimous judgment of the Southern people when we declare that they consider that these questions were decided by the war, and that it is their intention in good faith to abide by that decision.

It stopped short of full political rights for the freedmen, saying, "It is true that the people of the South, in common with a large majority of the people of the North and West, are, for obvious reasons, inflexibly opposed to any system of laws that would place the political power of the country in the hands of the negro race." It should be noted that only five states North or South had allowed free blacks to vote in 1860. The letter concluded:

> The great want of the South is peace. The people earnestly desire tranquility and restoration of the Union. They deplore disorder and excitement as the most serious obstacle to their prosperity. They ask a restoration of their rights under the Constitution. They desire relief from oppressive misrule. Above all, they would appeal to their countrymen for the re-establishment, in the Southern States, of that which has been justly regarded as the birth-right of every American, the right of self-government. Establish these on a firm basis, and we can safely promise, on behalf of the Southern people, that they will faithfully obey the Constitution and laws of the United States, treat the negro populations with kindness and humanity and fulfill every duty incumbent on peaceful citizens, loyal to the Constitution of their country.[4]

The "Manifesto" was signed by twenty-six prominent Southerners including Lee, Beauregard, Longstreet, and Alexander Stephens. Whatever effect it may have had on improving sectional differences, it had little benefit for the Democrats as Grant handily won the election.

Rosecrans himself had the opportunity to run for public office many times. He was offered the Democratic nomination for governor of Ohio and California; he also could have run for mayor of San Francisco and as a congressman from Nevada. He declined all those proffered nominations, gaining the sobriquet "the Great Decliner." He did however have a keen interest in public affairs, writing *Theory and Practical Workings of Our System of Government* and co-authoring a book *Popular Government* with newspaperman Josiah Riley. In 1880 he did finally run and was elected as a congressman from the First District of California. He was reelected in 1882.

During his time in Congress he served as head of the Democratic Caucus and also was chairman of the Military Affairs Committee. When a bill was introduced in 1885 to give President Grant a pension in those days before presidential and congressional pensions, Rosecrans voted against it, saying in a speech,

> It is my duty to say that in reality the bill is a plain proposition to reward Gen. Grant for his distinguished military services, and it is my duty to say that I can not vote for that bill. It is not my intention, sir, to recount any of the historical reasons why I think that military reputation has been exaggerated and misrepresented under the exigencies of party interest and power; and can only suggest that, when true history comes to be written, it will be pared down to very different dimensions. I do not propose to go into that subject, sir, although I am one of the four living

army commanders contemporary with him, and would feel quite qualified to express opinions of my own on that subject. But, Mr. Speaker, this House by the passage of this bill is called upon by solemn act to renew and reaffirm all the exaggerations and misstatements of fact which have been popularly impressed on the public mind under the circumstances to which I have alluded. It was the interest of a great political party of this country to make the services of Gen. Grant appear as large and important as possible, for he was their servant and tool to secure power. He himself kept an aide-de-camp in his back office, and there prepared the first two volumes of Badeau's "Life of Grant," upon which the students of history have put the stamp of unworthiness to be trusted.[5]

The distrust, animosity and bitterness that began in Mississippi in the fall of 1862 never healed. It never even tempered. The bill passed and was signed by President Arthur.

Rosecrans declined to run for a third term but in 1884 was named register of the treasury by Democrat president Grover Cleveland. He held the office until resigning due to health problems in 1893. Because of his office, Rosecrans' signature appears on a number of government notes issued during his tenure as register.

Death visited the Rosecrans family in 1876 when the General's oldest child, Father Adrian Rosecrans, died. Adrian had been ordained as a Paulist priest in 1872. He died in New York City, and his funeral Mass was said by his uncle, Bishop Sylvester Rosecrans. He is buried in St. Paul the Apostle Church in Manhattan.

Adrian's sister Mary Louise Rosecrans died the next year at the age of twenty-six of tuberculosis. She had become a Brown County, Ohio, Ursuline nun and took the name Sister St. Charles. Her sister Anne, also called Anita, entered the same convent but later left the religious life.

Bishop Rosecrans died at the age of fifty-one on October 21, 1878, a day after St. Joseph's Cathedral in Columbus was dedicated. He is buried in the crypt of the church he was largely responsible for building.

On Christmas Day, 1883, the general's wife died. She was buried in Mt. Olivet Cemetery in Washington, D.C., in the shadow of the monument marking the grave of Colonel Garesche who had been killed at Stones River. Surely Rosecrans intended to be buried with his beloved wife and near his beloved friend. That was not to happen, however.

There were of course happy times in his family life, especially when his son Carl married in 1882 and his daughter Lily was married to Joseph Toole, a future governor of Montana, in 1890. Grandchildren arrived, including a namesake grandson, Rosecrans Toole, in 1891.

Rosecrans was involved with the Society of the Army of the Cumberland, attending the third reunion and serving as president of the society. He was involved in the founding of the veteran's group the Grand Army of the Republic. He addressed the Fifteenth Annual Reunion of West Point graduates.

In May 1884 he made a return to his birthplace of Delaware County, Ohio, to participate in Decoration Day ceremonies. John Beatty, who had soldiered under the General, wrote, "The General is in splendid health, and was in the best of humor. He said he did not propose to make a speech at Delaware, but would simply give a free and easy talk to his old neighbors, and went on to say that he remembered the town very well."[6]

In 1889 the Chickamauga Battlefield Park was dedicated; Rosecrans was in attendance and addressed the assembled veterans from North and South, saying, "People shall come and visit with the interest due to the greatness of the events which occurred on this battleground. It took great men to win that battle, but it takes greater men to wipe away all the ill feeling which naturally flows out of such a contest."[7]

His last public appearance for veterans was in 1892 at a Grand Army reunion. When the electric lights failed, President Hayes lit a match and held it close to his onetime commander's face so that the veterans could see him. A great roar of applause came from the assembled crowd.

In its centennial year of 1889, Georgetown University bestowed an honorary doctor of laws degree on Rosecrans, and in 1896 Notre Dame bestowed the Laetare Medal on him.

In 1893 Rosecrans resigned as treasury register and retired to Los Angeles. He lived most of the time with his daughter Anita at the Hotel Redondo overlooking the Pacific Ocean. His son Carl lived nearby at the family homestead with his wife, Lilian, and their children, William Rosecrans III and Carmelita.

The general rarely left the vicinity of his ranch as he grew older and age began to take its toll on him. His daughter Lily wrote in 1894 that "this salubrious climate has done wonders for my father, who, though not strong enough to attend to business, is able to walk, drive himself, and enjoy a great many things."

In January 1898, Anita wrote, "My father is a very great invalid, and has been so for five years, but the genial climate of Southern California is prolonging his life." In February of that year Lily planned to visit her father. Her son Rosecrans Toole took ill in San Francisco and died of the croup. Lily described a consequence of the boy's death:

> We lost our oldest boy, Rosecrans, named for papa, on the 20th of February. He died from croup in San Francisco. My father was devoted to the child, and was expecting a visit from him. They told him the little fellow was ill and took three days to prepare him for the worst, but when the blow really came it was more than he could bear. He remained perfectly rigid for eleven minutes, and they thought

he was paralyzed. Then making apparently an heroic effort to control himself, he rallied and even spoke several times of the child. The next day, however, there was a complete physical, and for the first time, mental collapse. He did not appear to recognize any one and he remained in that condition about a fortnight, though he was entirely conscious before his death and his end was very peaceful.[8]

William Starke Rosecrans died March 11, 1898, at the age of seventy-nine. His funeral was one of the largest in the history of Los Angeles up to that time. He lay in state at city hall. Items of interest on display were the bullet-riddled flag he carried in battle at Carnifex Ferry and a sword given to him by the people of Cincinnati inscribed with the words Rosecrans spoke to the people of Western Virginia: "My mission among you is that of a fellow citizen charged with the duty by the Government of restoring law and order." On the general's breast were pinned medals of the Grand Army, the Loyal Legion and the Army of the Potomac as well as the Laetare Medal. His funeral mass was said by Bishop Montgomery at St. Vibian Cathedral on March 17. Federal, county and city offices as well as scores of businesses closed to show their respect. School sessions were suspended, and many children lined the streets along the route of the funeral procession. Eight active pallbearers, four Union veterans and four Confederate veterans, attended the casket. The burial was at Rosewood Cemetery. After Bishop Montgomery said the final prayers over the casket, the service was turned over to the military. Part of the last letter the General wrote, dated February 22, 1898, Washington's Birthday, was read to his comrades The letter said in part,

> to our Brothers of the South, my heart goes out in greeting and sympathy knowing well their dash and gallantry in the face of leaden hail, and their indomitable courage in the face of overwhelming obstacles. Happily recruited and bound to us in bonds of closest sympathy, would grim war ever again assail us, there will be none more ready "with arms to strike and souls to dare as quick as far" as those gray-clad heroes and their descendants of the land of waving cotton and the palm. May an all wise Providence keep you for many years to mingle thus happily together, and transmit to those who follow us the lessons of fraternity, charity and loyalty to the flag of our great republic.[9]

His grave was visited by thousands, and there was a movement to erect a monument to him in Los Angeles. Apparently the monument was never built. In 1902 his family decided to have the general buried in Arlington National Cemetery, and on May 8, accompanied by his son Carl, William Rosecrans took his last train ride to Washington, D.C., compliments of one-time railroad president and New York senator Chauncey DePew.

Attending his burial were president Theodore Roosevelt; Speaker of the House David Henderson, who had fought under Rosecrans; and General James Longstreet. The *Washington Evening Star* reported:

It was a gathering of men, many of them veterans of the Civil War, who shed tears at the grave of the man they loved as a soldier leader. The man who was such a conspicuous figure in the war for the preservation of the Union was consigned to the earth of the old home of the leader of the "lost cause," against whom he fought. It was an occasion replete with pathos.

The morning was misty, and from the lowering clouds there came at times spirts of rain. As the procession reached the historic place of the dead the sun burst through the clouds as if nature were anxious to participate in the exercises and had taken this means of expressing her feelings for the man whose memory was to be honored.

After the services, which included the addresses by the President and other distinguished personages, the body was lowered to the grave in a foremost place in the home of the Union dead. Throughout the services there was a feeling of awe and reverence on the part of the assemblage. Only once or twice did applause follow the words of the speakers, and then it was when a patriotic sentence or inspiration made it almost incumbent upon the listeners to attest their appreciation.[10]

In charge of the arrangements for the funeral was Henry Van Ness Boynton, Rosecrans' strongest defender against his post-war critics. Perhaps forgotten in all the ceremony were two of the people closest to the general in life who lay buried just across the Potomac: Annie Rosecrans and Julius Garesche.

In the years after his death, his comrades in the Society of the Army of the Cumberland proposed that a statue be erected to him on the streets of the capital, but that never happened.

A soldier who fought under Rosecrans predicted that "the patriotic visitor to the Arlington Cemetery in the future, if not now, will be pointed with the finger of pride to Rosecrans grave, accompanied with the words: 'There lies all that is mortal of the hero of Rich mountain, Corinth, Stone's River, and Chattanooga. Peace be to his ashes.'"[11]

However, the memory of the general faded as new wars created new heroes that dominated the consciousness of the nation. He began to disappear not just from American history but even from Civil War history.

There were many disappointments in Rosecrans' life: the early deaths of his wife, children and grandchild. His railroad and mining plans never achieved great success. His political career was modest. Yet he did produce and have a loving family. He was admired by both his military comrades and foes. His strong religious faith, which in many ways was the defining mark of his personality, provided him with comfort and meaning for the vicissitudes of life. And of course he played a key, if not the crucial, role in the war that preserved the United States of America as a unified country and emancipated a race. For that alone his name should be remembered.

Some readers may say this work is overly praising and insufficiently critical of its subject. To be sure, Rosecrans had flaws and contemporaneous critics.

16. After the War

George Henry Thomas statue at Thomas Circle Washington DC. The steeple is of the National City Christian Church the successor church to the one James Garfield attended.

He possessed a sharp tongue and was not reluctant to use it when angered. It is true that in the heat of battle he was observed at times to become nervous and over excited. But in a war where the words "incompetence," "imbecility," "cowardice," "drunkenness" and even "murderous" were used to describe some generals, "overexcited" seems rather small. The author was surprised, as many readers may be, that he reached the conclusion about William Starke Rosecrans that he did. It was comments like the following that convinced him:

John Palmer, who at times felt himself unfairly treated and was critical of Rosecrans, wrote in his *Recollections*, "I was indignant at the manner in which Rosecrans was treated; no braver man ever lived."

Lucius F. Hubbard, who was at Corinth, Vicksburg and Nashville, wrote, "General W.S. Rosecrans is one of the most soldiery characters in the military history of the country. A master of strategy, unfaltering in determination in pressing his combinations to an issue, he gave evidence on many fields of skill, sagacity and courage not excelled by any of his contemporaries of the Civil War."

Confederate Dabney Maury who fought against Rosecrans recalled, "He was one of the ablest of the Union Generals, and his moderation and humanity in the conduct of war kept pace with his courage and skill. Our dead received from him all of the care due brave men who fell in manly warfare, and our wounded and prisoners who fell into his hands attest his soldierly courtesy."

Methodist bishop David H. Moore (no relation to the author) who fought under Rosecrans wrote upon the general's death,

> There died last Friday, in Los Angeles, the ablest tactician among the great generals of the Civil War. An impartial study of the history of that immortal contest will show that in this respect no man, on either side, surpassed William Starke Rosecrans....Was there any other Union officer who outgeneraled Robert E. Lee?... If permitted to develop his own plans, Rosecrans, in our judgment, would have topped the immortals.... "Old Rosey," the boys called him; and they loved him for his cheer and care and kindness....A devouter Christian there was not. We have not escaped the clutches of prejudice; but all must admit that, though wholly a Romanist, he was Catholic in his charity to those from whom he differed. He believed in God with all his heart.[12]

William Lamers concluded his groundbreaking and indispensable biography of Rosecrans with the words, "He touched the edge of glory." Glory, however, can fade. Achievements are eternal. Some of Rosecrans' achievements:

He won the first battle of consequence of the war, Rich Mountain.

He outgeneraled Robert E. Lee in 1861, which resulted in the creation of a new state, West Virginia.

He won the battles of Iuka and Corinth, which repulsed a Confederate invasion in the west and made the Vicksburg campaign possible.

He won the battle of Stones River of which Abraham Lincoln said, "Had there been a defeat instead, the Nation could scarcely have lived over."

He conducted the Tullahoma Campaign, a brilliant, bloodless campaign that captured Middle Tennessee for the Union.

He fought, outnumbered and unreinforced, the battle of Chickamauga, which resulted in Chattanooga being permanently occupied by the Union.

He repulsed Sterling Price's invasion of Missouri, which effectively ended the war west of the Mississippi.

He instituted new and revolutionary ideas in mapmaking.

He created a Pioneer Brigade and engineer division.

He presided over the construction of Fortress Rosecrans, the largest earthen fort built during the war, which proved essential to the success of the Atlanta campaign.

He developed the "Rosecrans ambulance" and hospital trains to aid wounded soldiers.

He promoted the use of the Spencer repeating rifle, which was first used at Hoover's Gap.

This is a record matched by few, if any, generals in the war. This is not a controversial statement; his contemporaries on both sides knew that. However, his story has been told to a great extent by his political and personal adversaries. The responsibility falls to us the living to make certain that the achievement of William Starke Rosecrans, and the men who fought with him, is remembered forever.

During his lifetime, Rosecrans felt he had been wronged. To James Garfield, the general once wrote,

> I who began by drilling home guards of Cincinnati, teaching the first Ohio troops how to encamp at Dennison, who fought the first successful battle involving important results in the War; made the first successful campaign against *Lee*... who fought Stone's River; drove Bragg from Shelbyville, Tullahoma and Chattanooga... drove Price from Missouri; and did much to give that State... freedom; an officer of sobriety, morality, and industry, abstinence from all intrigues military and political, I find myself put into retirement and apparent disgrace... I want to tax your friendship, in which I confide, to find out and give me an explanation of how and why this is.... You know I consider my present situation an outrage on justice having few parallels in this or any other War.

William Starke Rosecrans, 1819–1898.

Rosecrans ended his letter to Garfield, "But I am a firm believer in the final downfall of iniquity."[13]

If part of that iniquity is Rosecrans' undeserved obscurity, it is hoped this book is a step toward its downfall.

17. A Final Note

In 1868, after a campaign marked by typical nineteenth-century personal attacks, Ulysses S. Grant was elected the eighteenth president of the United States. John A. Rawlins was named secretary of war, but he would serve in that role for a little over six months before dying at the age of thirty-eight. Rawlins, who did so much to protect and defend the reputation of Grant, is mentioned four times in Grant's *Memoirs*. James Harrison Wilson felt it was "wicked to have [Rawlins] effaced from history as Badeau and even Grant (in his own Memoirs) have tried to do with him." One historian has conjectured, "It might be that Grant did not wish to praise Rawlins too profusely because of the current reports picturing Rawlins as the protector of Grant from his own bad habits."

It had been widely expected that Charles A. Dana would get the desirable and lucrative position of collector of the Port of New York, but that position went to someone else. Within a year Dana began to oppose and criticize Grant and his policies and opposed his bid for reelection in 1872. (The man who ran against Grant in 1872 was Horace Greeley.) When the bill to place Grant on the retired list and award him a pension came up in 1885, Dana opposed it suggesting that private donations be raised for Grant instead. Ironically, in opposing the measure Dana was on the same side of the issue as William Rosecrans.

Edwin Stanton was named to the Supreme Court by Grant in 1869. The nomination was approved by the Senate, but Stanton died before he took the oath of office as a justice. Charles Sumner made a speech in the Senate in June 1872 in which he read a letter from journalist Horace White which said in part, "The late Secretary Stanton, not once merely but several times expressed to me substantially the same opinion ... that General Grant had been greatly overrated as a military commander. As to the latter point I recall a long conversation with him after the fighting at Spotsylvania Court-House, in which he (Stanton) expressed more apprehension about of the results of the campaign than I had ever known him to feel concerning any campaign."

In a letter written in August 1871, Sumner wrote,

> He [Stanton] said that he knew Grant better than any other man or the country could know him—that it was his duty to study him, and he did study him night

and day,—when he saw and when he did not see him he then declared his utter incapacity.

Sumner's own opinion of Grant was stated thus,

> The more I reflect on the question, the more I am distressed for my country and the republican party at the idea of Grant's re-nomination. We could better have lost one of his bloody victories. His rule for the second term would be the imperialism of selfishness and vindictiveness,—without moral sense, without ideas, without knowledge.
>
> I think you will admit that he is the lowest President, whether intellectually or morally, we have ever had. Undoubtedly he is the richest since Washington, although he was very poor at the beginning of the war.

Elihu B. Washburne was named secretary of state but served only eleven days before being named minister to France. It is that office for which Washburne is best known today, especially for his actions during the siege of Paris and the time of the Commune. He was the only foreign minister to stay in the French capital during that period, and the journal he kept gives an unparalleled view of that turbulent time. In 1880 presidential politics brought Grant and Washburne together again as both were candidates for the Republican nomination which went to dark-horse candidate James A. Garfield. Grant felt that Washburne's candidacy had damaged his own chances for a third term, and consequently after 1880 he never spoke to Washburne again. Elihu B. Washburne, without whose efforts the name of Ulysses S. Grant would probably be unknown today, is mentioned briefly five times in the thousand plus pages of Grant's *Memoirs*.[1]

Appendix A

No one knew William S. Rosecrans the general better than James A. Garfield. On February 17, 1864 when Rosecrans' standing and reputation were at a low point, Garfield made the following speech on the floor of the House of Representatives.

Mr. Speaker,—I regret that this resolution has come before the House of Representatives as it is now presented. I had hoped I should not be compelled to refer publicly to the matters involved in it, and before I speak to the merits of the resolution itself, I must be indulged in the expression of my opinion in regard to the custom which is growing up in this body in reference to this class of resolutions. The practice of this House, during the brief period in which I have been a member, has led me to fear that the thanks of the Congress of the United States are becoming too cheap an article in the eulogistic literature of the world. Time was when a man must stand grandly pre-eminent in the estimation and affection of the American people to receive in the solemn forms of law the thanks of the nation, through its representatives in Congress assembled. To merit that was worth a lifetime of sacrifice and heroism. We have changed this worthy custom. Since this session began, many resolutions of thanks have been passed without being referred to the appropriate committees, without remarks, and almost without notice. They have been passed tacitly by a kind of common consent. We have not only thanked officers who were chiefs of armies, but also those who held subordinate positions in the various armies of the republic. No question has been asked whether the officer was entitled to this distinction, or whether, by thanking one, another was not robbed of his merited honor. I repeat that I have seen these things with a feeling that we are cheapening the thanks of Congress by distributing them without discrimination and without question. I have been so willing to thank any man who has served the country in this war that I have not felt disposed to interpose objection.

In many of the instances referred to I have had no knowledge of the merits of the case. But when it comes so close to my own experience and knowledge of the history of the war, I cannot permit a resolution of this kind to pass without my protest against this hasty and thoughtless style of legislation. I have been surprised that the honorable members of this House should treat so lightly the matters involved in thanking the public servants of the nation. I now appeal to your sense of justice whether it be right to single out a subordinate officer, give him the thanks of Congress, and pass his chief in silence. On what grounds are you now ready to ignore the man who has won so many of the proudest victories? I do not believe that such is the purpose or wish of this House.

This resolution proposes to thank Major-General Thomas and the officers and men under his command for gallant services in the battle of Chickamauga. It meets my hearty approval for what it contains, but my protest for what it does not contain. I should be recreant to my own sense of justice did I allow this omission to pass without notice. No man here is ready to say—and if there be such a man I am ready to meet him—that the thanks of this Congress are not due to Major General W.S. Rosecrans for the campaign which culminated in the battle of Chickamauga. It is not uncommon throughout the press of the country, and among many people, to speak of that battle as a disaster to the army of the United States, and to treat of it as a defeat. If that battle was a defeat, we may welcome a hundred such defeats. I should be glad if each of our armies would repeat Chickamauga. Twenty such would destroy the Rebel army and the Confederacy utterly and forever.

What was that battle, terminating as it did a great campaign whose object was to drive the Rebel army beyond the Tennessee, and to obtain a foothold on the south bank of that river which should form the basis of future operations in the Gulf States? We had never yet crossed that river, except far below, in the neighborhood of Corinth. Chattanooga was the gateway of the Cumberland Mountains, and until we crossed the river and held the gateway we could not commence operations in Georgia. The army was ordered to cross the river, to grasp and hold the key of the Cumberland Mountains. It did cross, in the face of superior numbers; and after two days of fighting, more terrible, I believe, than any since this war began, the Army of the Cumberland hurled back, discomfited and repulsed, the combined power of three Rebel armies, gained the key to the Cumberland Mountains, gained Chattanooga, and held it against every assault. If there has been a more substantial success against overwhelming odds since this war began, I have not heard of it.

We have had victories—God be thanked!—all along the line; but in the history of this war I know of no such battle against such numbers,—40,000 against an army of not less by a man than 75,000. After the disaster to the right wing on the bloody afternoon of September 20th, 25,000 men of the Army of the Cumberland stood and met 75,000 hurled against them; and they stood in their bloody tracks immovable and victorious when night threw its mantle around them. They had repelled the last assault of the Rebel army.

Who commanded the Army of the Cumberland? Who organized, disciplined, and led it? Who planned its campaigns? The general whose name is omitted in this resolution,—Major-General W.S. Rosecrans.

And who is this General Rosecrans? The history of the country tells you, and your children know it by heart. It is he who fought battles and won victories in Western Virginia under the shadow of another's name. When the poetic pretender claimed the honor and received the reward as the author of Virgil's stanza in praise of Caesar, the great Mantuan wrote on the walls of the imperial palace, "Hos ego versiculos feci, tulit alter honores." So might the hero of Rich Mountain say, "I won this battle, but another has worn the laurels."

From Western Virginia he went to Mississippi, and there won the battles of Iuka and Corinth, which have aided materially to exalt the fame of that general upon whom this House has been in such haste to confer the proud rank of Lieutenant-General of the Army of the United States, but who was not upon either of those battle-fields.

Who took command of the Army of the Cumberland, found that army at Bowling Green, in November, 1862, as it lay disorganized, disheartened, driven back from Alabama and Tennessee, and led it to the Cumberland, planted it in Nashville, and thence, on the first day of the new year, planted his banners at Murfreesborough "in torrents of blood," and, in the moment of our extremest peril, throwing himself into the breach, saved by his personal valor the Army of the Cumberland and the hopes of the republic? It was General Rosecrans. From the day he assumed the command at Bowling Green the history of that army may be written in one sentence,—it advanced and maintained its advanced position, and its last campaign under the general it loved was the bloodiest and most brilliant. The fruits of Chickamauga were gathered in November on the heights of Mission Ridge and among the clouds of Lookout Mountain. That battle at Chickamauga was a glorious one, and every loyal heart responded to it. But, sir, it was won when we had nearly three times the number of the enemy. It ought to have been won. Thank God that it was won. I would take no laurel from the brow of the man who won it, but I would remind gentlemen here, that, while the battle of Chattanooga was fought with vastly superior numbers on our part, the battle of Chickamauga was fought with still vaster superiority against us.

If there is any man upon earth whom I honor, it is the man who is named in this resolution, General George H. Thomas. I had occasion in my remarks on the Conscription Bill, a few days ago, to refer to him in such terms as I delighted to use; and I say to gentlemen here, that, if there is any man whose heart would be hurt by the passage of this resolution as it now stands, that man is General George H. Thomas. I know, and all know, that he deserves well of his country, and his name ought to be recorded in letters of gold; but I know equally well that General Rosecrans deserves well of his country. I ask you, then, not to pain the heart of a noble man, who will be burdened with the weight of these thanks that wrong his brother officer and his superior in command. All I ask is that you will put both names into the resolution and let them stand side by side.

Appendix B

Transcript of the Reunion of the Army of the Cumberland in Chattanooga in 1905 concerning the building of a memorial statue to General William S. Rosecrans.

> The Chair: General Sheridan yesterday presented a most excellent report of the Sheridan Statue Committee, and it has been ordered that the four thousand dollars in that fund be added to the fund appropriated by Congress for the same purpose, to be dedicated under the auspices of this Society at Washington when completed; and this will probably be the only instance where a meeting of this Society will be held otherwise than as we have just decided.
>
> General Price: If it is in order, I wish to state that three years ago this Society at considerable expense and trouble removed the remains of our late Commander, Rosecrans, from California to the National Cemetery at Washington, and when they arrived there suitable and appropriate exercises were held. Now, the remains are there with simply a shingle with his name, Rosecrans, on it. If we do not do more than we have done, it were better that the remains had been allowed to rest where first interred. I talked with General Boynton frequently about it, and had he lived he intended to bring the matter before this meeting. But he has passed away, and I express to you his wishes in the matter.
>
> It occurred to me, if it is proper, we might reconsider the action of yesterday by which this four thousand dollars raised for the Sheridan statue was directed to be paid over to the Congressional Committee and added to that appropriated by Congress for an equestrian statue of Sheridan, and divert this fund to build a shaft to Rosecrans. Then, visitors to this bivouac of the dead could point with pride to the spot where lies all that is mortal of the hero of Corinth, Stone River, and Chattanooga!
>
> Lieutenant Thomas J. Cannon: I was at the burial of General Rosecrans, and it was the greatest gathering since the "Grand Review"; and I know there is not a congressman or a senator, let him come from the North, South, East or West, but would vote fifty thousand dollars or more for the erection of a monument to Rosecrans. If this Society will pass a resolution recommending such action, I will have it introduced by a Maryland representative in the House and a Maryland representative in the Senate! [Applause.]
>
> The Chair: This is a subject which certainly appeals to every heart. However, I think the subscriptions to the Sheridan monument were personal subscriptions—to the personality of Phil Sheridan, and should not be diverted. But I think there

are ways by which arrangements may be made for a suitable memorial to General Rosecrans. A resolution to refer the matter to the Executive Committee, or to a special committee, would be in order.

Lieutenant Cannon: I move that a committee be appointed from this Society to take this matter up. It should be at once, for there need be no delay. We all know how many years this matter of erecting the Sheridan statue has been standing and nothing yet done. Our Government is fully able to build it and it should be done by the Government, not by the Army of the Cumberland. His service was good. We all remember him at Stone River, and we remember him at Chickamauga. When he brought his army to Stone River he made as fine a movement with an army as ever has been made, or ever will be! [Applause.]

The Chair: Will the gentleman name the number of members the committee shall have?

Lieutenant Cannon: I would leave that with the chairman of the committee, but should think a committee of five or seven would be satisfactory.

General Parkhurst: I rise to suggest that in appointing that committee you make our Vice President from Maryland the chairman. He is very enthusiastic and if he maintains his enthusiasm and works with the congressmen, he will succeed in getting the appropriation. The trouble has been heretofore that we have put upon committees men who have failed to attend to their duties. They lose their enthusiasm. I believe this comrade is not so old but he can keep up his enthusiasm. Let him be made chairman and we will get the appropriation.

General Mizner: I have full confidence that the enthusiasm of this Marylander will never fail. My desire is that this action shall be national for grand old General Rosecrans, for I was with him at Murfreesboro, and Stone River. I would invest full authority in this committee for action during this session of Congress, and not wait an hour. I want to see action, not precipitate, but coming from the heart and soul of every member of the Army of the Cumberland. I worship the memory of General William S. Rosecrans! [Applause.] I hold for him a reverence in my heart never to be effaced! [Applause.]

The Chair: Are there any further remarks? The Chair will be glad to have suggestions as to members who will be most useful in this matter. The motion of the member from Maryland is that a committee shall be appointed which shall take this matter up and petition Congress for an appropriation with which to erect a suitable memorial over the remains of our beloved comrade, General Rosecrans.

Captain Bremner: I thought he said an equestrian statue.

Lieutenant Cannon: No; I suggested a memorial to our great commander.

Mr. Somers: We are erecting equestrian statues to other great generals of the war, and now the proposition is made to mark the resting place of General Rosecrans in a cemetery. I want to say that I believe the work of the Army of the Cumberland has not been properly completed until an equestrian statue of General Rosecrans finds its place in Washington. He is as prominent as any general who ever rode at the head of columns. No general in the war, in the most critical period of battle, ever rode down the lines looking grander than General Rosecrans! [Applause.] I make no exception of any whose statues appear on the streets of

Washington. The monument would be an improvement over the board or shingle now on his grave, but if he stand not equal to those others, there is discrimination, which I protest against.

Captain Bremner: I raised the question because I thought a statue should be erected. I see no reason why an equestrian statue to General Rosecrans should not be placed in one of the parks at Washington as well as others. He certainly was second to nobody in the army of the United States. There was no one superior to Rosecrans! [Applause.]

General Mizner: I like the sentiment that an equestrian statue should be erected in the perfect city of the Nation, Washington,—not a monument, merely, in the cemetery. I second the suggestion for an equestrian statue, instead of a monument, to be placed prominently in the national capital.

Lieutenant Cannon: Mr. President, I am perfectly willing to withdraw my motion, since the sentiment seems to be in favor of such a statue. I will move, then, that a statue be erected in Washington, in keeping with others there, instead of a monument at Arlington. But it looks to me like a grand mistake, and that it should be put in Arlington. There is where General Rosecrans lies to-day, and I think every member of the Army of the Cumberland, whether private or officer, should agree that that is where the marker should be placed. On the streets in Washington, it would be passed without attention, just as others are passed; but in that grand old cemetery of Arlington, as long as our country lives, as long as that flag with all its stars floats over us, Americans will visit the grave of Rosecrans, the hero of Stone River and of Chickamanga. two of the greatest battles of the Civil War, and the monument will he seen and appreciated. But I am willing to abide by the decision of the members of the Society here.

General Price: I do not agree with the last speaker. At first I suggested some mark to be placed on the grave itself, a monument for the grave. I was modest. I know the feelings there have been about the Battle of Chickamauga, but Chattanooga was our objective point, and we took and held the place. Therefore, I say he was the hero of Chickamauga, as well as of Corinth and Stone River. But now I am decidedly in favor of what seems to be the prevailing sentiment of the house, an equestrian statue to be erected in one of the parks of Washington. If it is not placed there, it will show discrimination. We already have one of Thomas and soon will have one of Sheridan, and unless we do erect one there for Rosecrans, it will be inquired why the discrimination. As far as the statement, that it will not be as prominent in the streets of Washington as at Arlington, is concerned, I think it is a mistake. Many people visit Washington who never go to the cemetery.

And I want to say that I think in strategy Rosecrans was not surpassed by anyone in that war or any previous one. He secured this city in the face of a strong and powerful enemy, overcoming almost insurmountable difficulties, but he had the nerve to undertake it and I think the success of General Grant was due to Rosecrans' matchless strategy! [Applause.] I am surprised that the matter of erecting to him a suitable statue has been so long delayed. I was on the committee for the Thomas monument, and I hope the same zeal will characterize this committee as characterized the committee that had in charge the erection of the monument to General Thomas.

Captain Chamberlain: I have no doubt that the President will appoint a suitable and competent committee to take charge of this work, and I move that all matters pertaining to the character and location of the statue of General Rosecrans be referred to this committee with full power.

Motion seconded.

Colonel Blakeley: I want to make one suggestion. My recollection is that General Rosecrans' grave is in a very prominent part of the Arlington cemetery. It is on a high knoll fronting on the Potomac River, is my recollection, though I have not been there since the burial. I remember at the time it was spoken of as a remarkably appropriate place. As it is a conspicuous place, I make the suggestion (of course, leaving the decision of the whole matter to the committee) that a statue of General Rosecrans erected there would be in full view across the Potomac and even in Washington. I am certain that upon investigation it will be found better to place the statue at his grave.

Sergeant Steward: I want to say a word. I know the comrades want to do just the right thing, and it occurs to me that we will make a mistake to erect a statue of any sort at Arlington, for this reason: thousands of visitors to the capital city never see Arlington. Most people who go to Washington never visit Arlington, and never will. I think I get there about as often as the average American citizen, and I want to say to you that during all my numerous visits to Washington since I was a boy, I never but once visited Arlington, and that was on the occasion of the burial of our comrade, General Boynton. Then I went on the order of our Chamber of Commerce. Now, then, why erect a statue to so great a man in an obscure place, seldom visited. The object of this statue, as I understand it, is to perpetuate the memory of one of the greatest generals of the Civil War. Anyone who studies the campaigns from Murfreesboro to this city, gained by his splendid strategy, cannot fail to accord to him the place of one of the greatest leaders of his age. And this statue should have a place in Washington where it will stand as long as this republic endures. If placed in Arlington very few persons will see it. It is a long distance from Washington and a man must take the greater part of a day to go there. It will certainly be a mistake to put it there. A respectable monument, marking the last resting place of General Rosecrans, will answer the purpose there; but an equestrian statue should be erected in Washington in one of the numerous circles or parks provided for that purpose. I hope the committee, when it makes up its memorial to Congress, will ask that the statue be placed in Washington.

The Chair: The question is now upon the amendment of Captain Chamberlain, providing that when this committee shall be appointed it be given full power and discretion to ask for such memorial as it may deem best.

Amendment unanimously adopted.

The Chair: I will now put the original motion of the gentleman from Maryland providing that a committee of five or seven be appointed to take this matter in charge.

Motion unanimously adopted

In the capital city of the United States there are statues to Lincoln, Grant, Sherman, Thomas, Garfield, and even John Rawlins. However there is no statue to the man that many who participated in the great battles of the Civil War believed was most responsible for the military victory which preserved that nation: William Starke Rosecrans.

Chapter Notes

Chapter 1

1. William M. Lamers, *The Edge of Glory: A Biography of General William S. Rosecrans, U.S.A.* (Baton Rouge: Louisiana State University Press, 1999), pg. 10.
2. Ibid., pg. 12.
3. Ibid., pg. 12.
4. Ibid., pg. 13.
5. James A. Garfield, *The Wild Life of the Army: Civil War Letters of James A. Garfield*, ed. Frederick D. Williams (East Lansing: Michigan State University Press, 1964), pg. 227–28.
6. Lamers, *Edge of Glory*, pg. 16.
7. Ibid., pg. 17.
8. Ibid., pg. 18.

Chapter 2

1. *Official Records*, Series I, Volume 5, Part I, pg. 10. Hereafter referenced as *OR*.
2. John Beatty and Harrison Carroll Hobart, *The Citizen-Soldier; or, Memoirs of a Volunteer* (Cincinnati, OH: Wilstach, Baldwin & Co., 1879), pg. 24–25.
3. Allan Nevins, *The War for the Union*, vol. 1 (New York: Scribner, 1960), pg. 225; Douglas Southall Freeman, *R.E. Lee, a Biography* (New York: C. Scribner's Sons, 1934), pg. 602; Festus P. Summers, *The Baltimore and Ohio in the Civil War* (New York: G.P. Putnam's Sons, 1939), pg. 89.; *OR* I, 2, pg. 753.
4. *OR* I, 5, pg. 576–77.
5. Henry Heth and James L. Morrison, *The Memoirs of Henry Heth* (Westport, CT: Greenwood Press, 1974), pg. 152.
6. *New York Times*, November 3, 1862.
7. *OR* I, 5, pg. 130.
8. Ibid., pg. 148–49.
9. Lamers, *Edge of Glory*, pg. 52.
10. Jacob Dolson Cox, *Military Reminiscences of the Civil War* (New York: C. Scribner's, 1900), pg. 123; Thomas J. Riddle, "Reminiscences of Floyd's Operations in West Virginia in 1861," *Southern Historical Society Papers* 11 (1883): pg. 95; Robert E. Lee and Robert E. Lee, *Recollections and Letters of General Robert E. Lee* (New York: Doubleday, Page, 1904), pg. 51.
11. Ella W. Tompkins, "The Colonel's Lady: Some Letters of Ellen Wilkins Tompkins, July–December 1861," *Virginia Magazine of History and Biography* 69 (1961): pg. 410–12.
12. *OR* I, 5, p. 259; Edward Alfred Pollard, *Southern History of the War: The First Year of the War* (New York: C.B. Richardson, 1863), pg. 175.
13. *OR* I, 12, Pt. 3, pg. 81, 89.
14. Lamers, *Edge of Glory*, p. 75; Margaret Leech, *Reveille in Washington, 1860–1865* (New York: Harper & Brothers, 1941), pg. 215.
15. Granville Davisson Hall, *Lee's Invasion of Northwest Virginia in 1861* (Chicago: Press of the Mayer & Miller Co., 1911), pg. 150.

Chapter 3

1. Whitelaw Reid, *Ohio in the War: Her Statesmen, Her Generals, and Soldiers* (Cincinnati, OH: Moore, Wilstach & Baldwin, 1868), pg. 321.
2. *Wisconsin State Journal*, July 27, 1862.
3. *OR* I, 17, Pt. 2, pg. 15–16, 115.
4. *OR* I, 17, Pt. 1, pg. 67.
5. *OR* I, 17, Pt. 2, pg. 690.
6. Ulysses S. Grant, *Personal Memoirs of US Grant*, vol. 1 (New York: Century, 1895), pg. 338.
7. *OR* I, 17, Pt. 1, pg. 66.
8. Grant, *Memoirs*, pg. 341; *OR* I, 17, Pt. 1, pg. 118.

9. *OR* I, 17, Pt. 2, pg. 230.
10. Ulysses S. Grant, John Y. Simon, and John F. Marszalek, *The Papers of Ulysses S. Grant*, vol. VI (Carbondale: Southern Illinois University Press, 1967), pg. 66. Hereafter referenced as *Grant Papers*.
11. *OR* I, 17, Pt. 1, pg. 69.
12. Lamers, *Edge of Glory*, pg. 109–10.
13. William E. Smith and Ophia D. Smith, *Colonel A.W. Gilbert: Citizen-Soldier of Cincinnati* (Whitefish, MT: Kessinger Publishing, 2008), pg. 111.
14. *OR* I, 17, Pt. I, pg. 67; *Grant Papers*, Vol. VI, pg. 69–70.
15. Lamers, *Edge of Glory*, pg. 114.
16. Lamers, *Edge of Glory*, pg. 119; J.V. Frederick, ed., "An Illinois Boy in North Mississippi: Diary of John Wilson, February 15–December 30, 1862," *Journal of Mississippi History* 1 (1939): pg. 189.
17. Thomas D. Christie letter manuscript, September 21, 1862, *Thomas and Carmelite Christie and Family Papers*, MS, Minnesota Historical Society.
18. *OR* I, 17, Pt. 1, pg. 119.
19. William S. Stewart, "William S. Stewart Letters," *Missouri Historical Review* 61, no. 4 (July 1967): pg. 472–73.
20. J.B. Rogers, *War Pictures: Experiences and Observations of a Chaplain* (Chicago: Church & Goodman), pg. 189.
21. Grant, *Memoirs*, pg. 343; *OR* I, 17, Pt. 1, pg. 68.
22. Grant, *Memoirs*, pg. 343; *OR* I, 17, Pt. 1, pg. 68; Stephen Z. Starr, *The Union Cavalry in the Civil War: The War in the West 1861–1865*, vol. 3 (Baton Rouge: Louisiana State University, 1985), pg. 105.
23. *OR* I, 17, Pt. 1, pg. 64, 68; Grant, *Memoirs*, pg. 342.
24. John B. Sanborn, "Battles and Campaigns of September, 1862," in *Glimpses of the Nation's Struggle: Papers Read before the Minnesota Commandery of the Military Order of the Loyal Legion of the United States*, vol. 5 (St. Paul, MN: Review Publishing, 1903), pg. 223.
25. Lamers, *Edge of Glory*, pg. 124–27.

Chapter 4

1. William S. Rosecrans, "The Battle of Corinth," in *Battles and Leaders of the Civil War*, vol. 2 (New York: Century, 1887), pg. 741.
2. *OR* I, 17, Pt. 2, pg. 250.
3. *OR* I, 17, Pt. 1, pg. 160–61; John B. Lomax, *Thomas Lomax and His Descendants* (Menlo Park, CA: J.B. Lomax, 1995), pg. 26; Rogers, *War Papers*, pg. 195.
4. Lurton Dunham Ingersoll, *Iowa and the Rebellion: A History of the Troops Furnished by the State of Iowa to the Volunteer Armies of the Union, Which Conquered the Great Southern Rebellion of 1861–5* (Philadelphia, PA: J.B. Lippincott & Co., 1866), pg. 293; *OR* I, 17, Pt. 1, pg. 396.
5. William C. Holden letter in private collection of Fred Ray; Wisconsin Historical Society, *Quiner Scrapbooks*, Vol. 6, pg. 35; *Burial of General Rosecrans*, pg. 33; Rogers, *War Pictures*, pg. 199.
6. Lamers, *Edge of Glory*, pg. 153.
7. Cyrus F. Boyd and Mildred Throne, *The Civil War Diary of Cyrus F. Boyd: Fifteenth Iowa Infantry, 1861–1863* (Iowa City: State Historical Society of Iowa, 1953), pg. 77.
8. B.C. Bryner, *Bugle Echoes; the Story of Illinois 47th* (Springfield, IL: Phillips Bros., 1905), pg. 65.
9. Boyd and Throne, *Diary*, pg. 77.
10. Edwin Hedge Fay, *This Infernal War; the Confederate Letters of Edwin H. Fay* (Austin: University of Texas Press, 1958), pg. 166.
11. *OR* I, 17, Pt. 1, pg. 163–64; 164.
12. Ibid., pg. 163; 156.
13. Ibid., pg. 165.
14. Stephen Z. Starr, *Jennison's Jayhawkers; a Civil War Cavalry Regiment and Its Commander* (Baton Rouge, LA: Louisiana State University Press, 1974), pg. 210.
15. Rosecrans, "Battle of Corinth," pg. 755–56; Charles H. Smith, *The History of Fuller's Ohio Brigade, 1861–1865: Its Great March, with Roster, Portraits, Battle Maps and Biographies* (Cleveland, OH: A.J. Watt, 1909), pg. 118.
16. *OR* I, 17, Pt. 2, pg. 900–901.
17. William T. Sherman and James Gillespie Blaine, *Memoirs of Gen. W.T. Sherman*, vol. 1 (New York: C.L. Webster & Co., 1891); Josiah Gorgas and Frank Everson Vandiver, *The Civil War Diary of General Josiah Gorgas* (University: University of Alabama Press, 1947), pg. 54.
18. Grant, *Memoirs*, pg. 417, 419; *OR* I, 17, Pt. 2, pg. 269.
19. David S. Stanley, "The Battle of Corinth," in *Personal Recollections of the War*

of the Rebellion: Addresses Delivered before the Commandery of the State of New York, Military Order of the Loyal Legion of the United States: Second Series (New York: G.P. Putnam's Sons, 1897), pg. 278.

20. S.H.M. Byers, *With Fire and Sword* (New York: Neale Publishing), pg. 37–38.

21. Arthur Ducat to Rosecrans, April 24, 1885, *William S. Rosecrans Papers*, MS, University of California, Los Angeles.

22. *OR* I, 17, Pt. 2, pg. 286–87.

23. Grant, *Memoirs*, Vol. I, pg. 420.

24. *Grant Papers*, Vol. VI, pg. 275.

25. *OR* I, 17, Pt. 2, pg. 296.

26. Byers, *With Fire and Sword*, pg. 41–42.

27. Dabney Maury, "Recollections of Campaign against Grant in North Mississippi 1862–1863," *Southern Historical Society Papers* 13 (1885): pg. 306.

28. Joseph Medill to Elihu Washburne, February 19, 1863, *Elihu B. Washburne Papers*, MS, Library of Congress, or *Grant Papers*, Vol. VII, pg. 318.

Chapter 5

1. John F. Marszalek, *Sherman's Other War: The General and the Civil War Press* (Memphis, TN: Memphis State University Press, 1981), pg. 63–107.

2. *OR* I, 16, Pt. 2, pg. 642, 653.

3. James Henry Haynie, *The Nineteenth Illinois; a Memoir of a Regiment of Volunteer Infantry Famous in the Civil War of Fifty Years Ago for Its Drill, Bravery, and Distinguished Services* (Chicago: M.A. Donohue & Co., 1912), pg. 179; Hans Christian Heg and Theodore Christian Blegen, *The Civil War Letters of Colonel Hans Christian Heg* (Northfield, MN: Norwegian-American Historical Association, 1936), pg. 152; S.F. Fleharty, Philip J. Reyburn, and Terry Wilson, *Jottings from Dixie: The Civil War Dispatches of Sergeant Major Stephen F. Fleharty, U.S.A.* (Baton Rouge: Louisiana State University Press, 1999), pg. 64–65; *Report of the Adjutant General of the State of Kansas, 1861–'65* (Topeka: Kansas State Printing, 1896), pg. 111.

4. *OR* I, 16, Pt. 2, pg. 640.

5. M. Louise Garesché, *Biography of Lieut. Col. Julius P. Garesché, Assistant Adjutant-General, U.S. Army* (Philadelphia, PA: J.B. Lippincott & Co., 1887), pg. 350–62.

6. *OR* I, 20, Pt. 2, pg. 117,118,123–24.

7. *London Times*, October 9, 1862.

8. *OR* I, 20, Pt. 2, pg. 264, 265.

9. W.J. Worsham and C.W. Heiskell, *Old Nineteenth Tennessee Regiment, C.S.A. June, 1861–April, 1865* (Knoxville, TN: Press of Paragon Printing Co., 1902), pg. 69.

Chapter 6

1. Gilbert C. Kniffen, "Army of the Cumberland and the Battle of Stone's River," in *District of Columbia Military Order of the Loyal Legion of the United States War Papers*, vol. 4 (Washington, DC), pg. 19; Thos Speed, Alfred Pirtle, and R.M. Kelly, *The Union Regiments of Kentucky* (Louisville, KY: Courier-Journal, 1897), pg. 491.

2. John Beatty and Harrison Carroll Hobart, *The Citizen-Soldier; or, Memoirs of a Volunteer* (Cincinnati: Wilstach, Baldwin & Co., 1879), pg. 202.

3. Mrs. C Moyer, *Journal and Letters Franklin F. Moyer* (Delta, OH: C. Moyers, 1865), pg. 68; Henry Briedenthal, *Ohio State Journal*, January 24, 1863; Heg and Blegen, *Civil War Letters*, pg. 186; *OR* I, Vol. 20, Pt. 1, pg. 219; John M. Palmer, *Personal Recollections of John M. Palmer the Story of an Earnest Life* (Cincinnati, OH: R. Clarke & Co., 1901), pg. 147.

4. Lamers, *Edge of Glory*, pg. 235; John Fitch, *Annals of the Army of the Cumberland: Comprising Biographies, Descriptions of Departments, Accounts of Expeditions, Skirmishes and Battles; Also Its Police Record of Spies, Smugglers and Prominent Rebel Emissaries; Together with Anecdotes, Incidents, Poetry, Reminiscences, Etc., and Official Reports of the Battle of Stone River and the Chickamauga Campaign* (Philadelphia, PA: J.B. Lippincott & Co., 1864), pg. 677; John L. Yaryan, "Stone River," in *War Papers: Read before the Indiana Commandery, Military Order of the Loyal Legion of the United States* (1898), pg. 174–75; Thomas L. Crittenden, "The Union Left at Stone's River," in *Battles and Leaders of the Civil War*, vol. 3 (New York: Century, 1888), pg. 633; Gilbert C. Kniffen, "The Third Day at Stone's River," in *War Papers: Read Before the Commandery of the District of Columbia, Military Order of the Loyal Legion of the United States*, vol. 3 (Washington, DC), pg. 453.

5. Gideon Welles and Howard K. Beale, *Diary of Gideon Welles; Ed. and with an Introd.*

by Howard K. Beale; with the Assistance of Alan W. Brownsword, vol. 2 (New York: Norton, 1960), pg. 282–83.

6. Alexander F. Stevenson, *The Battle of Stone's River near Murfreesboro, Tenn. December 30, 1862, to January 3, 1863* (Boston, MA: J.R. Osgood & Co., 1884), pg. 132.

7. Lot D. Young, *Reminiscences of a Soldier of the Orphan Brigade* (Louisville, KY: Courier-Journal, 1918), pg. 49.

8. Edwin Porter Thompson, *History of the Orphan Brigade* (Louisville, KY: L.N. Thompson, 1898), pg. 183.

9. Wilson J. Vance, *Stone's River, the Turning-Point of the Civil War* (New York: Neale Publishing, 1914), pg. 64–65; *Society of the Army of the Cumberland Twentieth Reunion Chattanooga, Tennessee 1889* (Cincinnati, OH: R. Clarke & Co., 1890), pg. 127–28.

10. James A. Garfield, B.A. Hinsdale, and Mary L. Hinsdale, *Garfield-Hinsdale Letters; Correspondence between James Abram Garfield and Burke Aaron Hinsdale* (Ann Arbor: University of Michigan Press, 1949), pg. 66.

Chapter 7

1. *OR* I, Vol. 20, Pt. 1, pg. 186; Vol. 20, Pt. 2, pg. 300; Vol. 20, Pt. 1, pg. 187.

2. Noah Brooks and Herbert Mitgang, *Washington, D.C., in Lincoln's Time. D., Introduction, by Herbert Mitgang* (New York: Collier, 1962), pg. 42–44.

3. Abraham Lincoln and Roy P. Basler, *The Collected Works of Abraham Lincoln*, vol. 6 (New Brunswick, NJ: Rutgers University Press, 1953), pg. 409; *OR* I, 52, Pt. 1, pg. 442.

4. *OR* I, 23, Pt. 2, pg. 67–68, 290–91; Robert J. Dalessandro, *Major General William S. Rosecrans and the Transformation of the Staff of The Army of the Cumberland* (diss., U.S. Army War College, 2002), pg. 15–16; Ralph C. Gordon, "Hospital Trains of the Army of the Cumberland," *Tennessee Historical Quarterly* 51, no. 3 (1992): pg. 186; David A. Rubenstein, *A Study of the Medical Support to the Union and Confederate Armies during the Battle of Chickamauga* (diss., U.S. Army Command and General Staff College, Fort Leavenworth, KS, 1990), pg. 24–25.

5. Philip L. Shiman, "Engineering and Command: The Case of General William S. Rosecrans, 1862–1863," in *The Art of Command in the Civil War* (Lincoln: University of Nebraska Press, 1998), pg. 105–6; *OR* I, 23, Pt. 2, pg. 38.

6. *OR* I, 23, Pt. 2, pg. 208; LeRoy P. Graf and Ralph W. Haskins, eds., *Papers of Andrew Johnson*, vol. 6, *1862–64* (Knoxville: University of Tennessee Press, 1983), pg. 211, 235.

7. Beatty, *The Citizen Soldier*, pg. 256–57, 260–63.

8. Lucretia Rudolph Garfield, James A. Garfield, and John Shaw, *Crete and James: Personal Letters of Lucretia and James Garfield* (East Lansing: Michigan State University Press, 1994), pg. 183; Theodore Clarke Smith, *The Life and Letters of James Abram Garfield, 1877–1882*, vol. 1 (New Haven, CT: Yale University Press, 1925), pg. 275.

9. Louis M. Starr, *Bohemian Brigade: Civil War Newsmen in Action* (New York: Knopf, 1954), pg. 183; Milo S. Hascall, *Personal Recollections and Experiences Concerning the Battle of Stone River* (Goshen, IN: Times Publishing, 1889), pg. 4–6; William Dennison Bickham, *Rosecrans' Campaign with the Fourteenth Army Corps, or the Army of the Cumberland* (Cincinnati, OH: Moore, Wilstach, Keys & Co., 1863), pg. 143; United States Military Academy, Association of Graduates, *Twenty-Seventh Annual Reunion* (Saginaw, 1896), pg. 66; James A. Garfield, *The Wild Life of the Army: Civil War Letters of James A. Garfield*, ed. Frederick D. Williams (East Lansing: Michigan State University Press, 1964), pg. 233, 250.

10. *OR* I, 23, Pt. 2, pg. 95, 111.

11. James R. Gilmore, *Personal Recollections of Abraham Lincoln and the Civil War, by James R. Gilmore* (Boston: L.C. Page, 1898), pg. 146.

12. *OR* I, Vol. 23, Pt. 2, pg. 163; *OR* I, Vol. 25, Pt. 2, pg. 450; William S. Rosecrans, "The Campaign for Chattanooga," *The Century* 34 (1887): pg. 130.

13. *OR* I, Vol. 23, Pt. 2, pg. 394–95; 376, 384.

14. *OR* I, Vol. 23, Pt. 1, pg. 8.

Chapter 8

1. *OR* I, Vol. 20, Pt. 1, pg. 699.

2. Ibid., pg. 698.

3. Thomas Lawrence Connelly, *Autumn of Glory; the Army of Tennessee, 1862–1865* (Baton Rouge: Louisiana State University Press, 1971), pg. 78.

4. Lamers, *Edge of Glory*, pg. 275; Victor

Hicken, *Illinois in the Civil War* (Urbana: University of Illinois Press, 1966), pg. 188.

5. John T. Wilder, "The Battle of Hoover's Gap," in *Sketches of War History, 1861–1865: Papers Read before the Ohio Commandery of the Military Order of the Loyal Legion of the United States*, vol. 6 (Cincinnati, OH: Monfort & Co., 1908), pg. 173, 172.

6. John T. Hubbell, *Battles Lost and Won: Essays from Civil War History* (Westport, CT: Greenwood Press, 1975), pg. 117.

7. C.T. Quintard and Arthur Howard Noll, *Doctor Quintard, Chaplain C.S.A. and Second Bishop of Tennessee Being His Story of the War (1861–1865)* (Sewanee, TN: University Press, 1905), pg. 87; *OR* I, 23, Pt. 2, pg. 518.

8. David M. Stanley, "The Tullahoma Campaign," in *Sketches of War History, 1861–1865: Papers Read before the Ohio Commandery of the Military Order of the Loyal Legion of the United States*, vol. 3 (Cincinnati, OH: R. Clarke & Co., 1890), pg. 179; *OR* I, 23, Pt. 1, pg. 489; *Burial of General Rosecrans, Arlington National Cemetery, May 17, 1902* (Cincinnati, OH: R. Clarke & Co., 1903), pg. 98.

9. Andrew N. Morris, *Forgotten Decisiveness: The Middle Tennessee Campaign of 1863* (diss., University of Kansas, 1996), pg. 373; Richard J. Brewer, *The Tullahoma Campaign: Operational Insights* (diss., U.S. Army Command and General Staff College, Fort Leavenworth, KS, 1991), pg. 1–2; Julian D. Alford, *The Tullahoma Campaign, The Beginning of the End for the Confederacy* (diss., United States Marine Corps Command and Staff College, 2002), pg. 36–38; Michael R. Bradley, *Tullahoma: The 1863 Campaign for the Control of Middle Tennessee* (Shippensburg, PA: Burd Street Press, 2000), pg. 94–95.

Chapter 9

1. Rosecrans, "Campaign for Chattanooga," pg. 130–31.
2. Ibid., pg. 132.
3. John Sanderson Letter Diary, August 16, 1863; October 20, 1863, *John R. Sanderson Papers*, Ohio Historical Society.
4. *OR* I, 23, Pt. 2, pg. 552.
5. Ibid pg. 555.
6. Ibid pg. 585.
7. Ibid pg. 592, 593.
8. Ibid pg. 594.
9. *OR* I, 52, Pt. 2, pg. 427–28, 434, 439.

10. James A. Garfield and B.A. Hinsdale, *The Works of James Abram Garfield*, vol. 1 and 2 (Boston: J.R. Osgood & Co., 1882), pg. 774.
11. Joseph E. Johnston, *Narrative of Military Operations, Directed, during the Late War between the States* (New York: D. Appleton & Co., 1874), pg. 211; *OR* I, Vol. 52, Pt. 2, pg. 514.
12. *OR* 30, Pt. 3, pg. 162.
13. *Grant Papers*, Vol. IX, pg. 475–76.

Chapter 10

1. William Babcock Hazen, *A Narrative of Military Service* (Boston, MA: Ticknor & Co., 1885), pg. 114–15; *OR* I, 30, Pt. 1, pg. 446; Dan Lee, *Thomas J. Wood: A Biography of the Union General in the Civil War* (Jefferson, NC: McFarland, 2012), pg. 123–25.
2. *OR* I, 30, Pt. 3, pg. 530.
3. *New York Herald*, September 9, 1863; *OR* I, 30, Pt. 3, pg. 339.
4. "The Battle of Chickamauga; Important and Interesting Statement by Col. Wilder," *New York Times*, October 4, 1863.
5. Richard A. Baumgartner, *Blue Lightning: Wilder's Mounted Infantry Brigade in the Battle of Chickamauga* (Huntington, WV: Blue Acorn Press, 1997), pg. 165.
6. Charles A. Dana, *Recollections of the Civil War: With the Leaders at Washington and in the Field in the Sixties* (New York: D. Appleton & Co., 1898), pg. 113; *OR* I, 30, Pt. 1, pg. 69.
7. Henry M. Cist, *The Army of the Cumberland, by Henry M. Cist* (New York: C. Scribner's Sons, 1882), pg. 220.
8. Stephen William Berry, *House of Abraham: Lincoln and the Todds, a Family Divided by War* (Boston: Houghton Mifflin, 2007), pg. 147.
9. *OR* I, 30, Pt. 1, pg. 70.
10. *OR* I, 30, Pt. 1, pg. 103, 983–84; Lamers, *Edge of Glory*, pg. 344.
11. Thomas J. Wood, "The Gaps at Chickamauga," *New York Times*, November 19, 1882; *OR* I, 30, Pt. 1, pg. 500, 580.
12. William Sumner Dodge, *History of the Old Second Division, Army of the Cumberland. Commanders: M'Cook, Sill, and Johnson* (Chicago: Church & Goodman, 1864), pg. 559; Austin Stebbins, "A Daring Movement," *National Tribune*, October 19, 1899; Dean R. Chester to A. Chester, November 13, 1863, available at *Abraham Lincoln Papers at the*

Library of Congress, Manuscript Division, http://memory.loc.gov/ammem/alhtml/alhome.html; Thomas J. Ford, *With the Rank and File Incidents and Anecdotes during the War of the Rebellion, as Remembered by One of the Non-commissioned Officers* (Milwaukee: Press of the Evening Wisconsin, 1898), pg. 23–24.

13. Peter Cozzens, *This Terrible Sound: The Battle of Chickamauga* (Urbana, IL: University of Illinois Press, 1992), pg. 403.

14. Rosecrans, "Campaign for Chattanooga," pg. 134; Cox, *Memoirs*, vol. 2, pg. 10.

15. *OR* I, 30, Pt. 3, pg. 741; Cozzens, *Terrible Sound*, pg. 440.

16. *OR* I, 30, Pt. 1, pg. 948.

17. Ibid., pg. 140, 142.

18. Ibid., pg. 142–43.

19. Ibid., pg. 192.

20. Ibid., pg. 141, 145.

21. James Longstreet, *From Manassas to Appomattox: Memoirs of the Civil War in America* (Philadelphia, PA: J.B. Lippincott & Co., 1896), pg. 445–56.

Chapter 11

1. *OR* 1, 30, Pt. 1, pg. 142–43.
2. Ibid., pg. 192–93.
3. Ibid., pg. 193–94.
4. Ibid., pg. 449.
5. Charles A. Dana, *Recollections of the Civil War: With the Leaders at Washington and in the Field in the Sixties* (New York: D. Appleton & Co., 1898), pg. 116–17.
6. John Thomas Wilder, "Preliminary Movements of the Army of the Cumberland Before the Battle of Chickamauga," in *Paper of John T. Wilder ... Read before the Ohio Commandery of the Loyal Legion, November 4, 1908* (1908), pg. 270.
7. Ninety-Second Illinois Infantry, 1862–1865, *Ninety-Second Illinois Volunteers* (Freeport, IL: Journal Steam Publishing, 1875), pg. 112; George S. Wilson, "Wilder's Brigade of Mounted Infantry," in *War Talks in Kansas* (Kansas City, MO: Franklin Hudson Publishing, 1906), pg. 67.
8. *OR* I, 30, Pt. 1 pg. 254, 255.
9. *OR* I, 30, Pt. 4, pg. 681; *OR* I, 52, Pt. 2, pg. 534.
10. *OR* I, 30, Pt. 1, pg. 197–98.
11. William G. Le Duc, "The Little Steamboat That Opened the 'Cracker Line,'" in *Battles and Leaders of the Civil War*, vol. 3 (New York: Century, 1884, 1888), pg. 676.
12. *OR* I, 30, Pt. 1, pg. 154–55, 146.
13. Ibid., pg. 199.
14. Ibid., pg. 202.
15. *OR* I, 30, Pt. 3, pg. 891.
16. William Passmore Carlin, Robert I. Girardi, and Nathaniel Cheairs Hughes, *The Memoirs of Brigadier General William Passmore Carlin, U.S.A.* (Lincoln: University of Nebraska Press, 1999), pg. 108.
17. James H. Montgomery, entry September 22, 23, 1863, *Montgomery Diary*, Library of Congress.
18. Lyman G. Bennett and Wm M. Haigh, *History of the Thirty-Sixth Regiment Illinois Volunteers during the War of the Rebellion* (Aurora, IL: Knickerbocker & Hodder, 1876), pg. 486; Harvey Reid and Frank L. Byrne, *The View from Headquarters; Civil War Letters of Harvey Reid* (Madison, WI: State Historical Society of Wisconsin, 1965), pg. 93–94.; Edna J. Hunter, John Daniel Shank, and Oscar Fitzalan Harmon, *One Flag, One Country, and Thirteen Greenbacks a Month: Letters from a Civil War Private and His Colonel* (San Diego, CA: Hunter Publications, 1980), pg. 30.
19. Judith Lee Hallock and Grady McWhiney, *Braxton Bragg and Confederate Defeat*, vol. 2 (Tuscaloosa, AL: University of Alabama Press, 1991), pg. 114; *OR* I, 31, Pt. 3, pg. 716.
20. *OR* I, 30, Pt. 3, pg. 821.
21. United States Congress, *Report on the Joint Committee on the Conduct of the War*, vol. 3 (Washington, DC: Government Printing Office, 1865), pg. 32–33.
22. Douglas R. Cubbison, "'That Awful Storm of Iron and Smoke': Union Artillery at Moccasin Bend, Chattanooga, September–November, 1863," *Tennessee Historical Quarterly* 58 (Winter 1999): pg. 281.
23. Charles Eugene Belknap, *History of the Michigan Organizations at Chickamauga, Chattanooga and Missionary Ridge, 1863* (Lansing, MI: R. Smith Printing, 1899), pg. 156, 158.
24. *OR* I, 30, Pt. 4, p 69.
25. *OR* I, 29, Pt. 1, p 151.
26. *OR* I, 30, Pt. 3, pg. 947–48; *OR* I, 30, Pt. 4 pg. 25.
27. *OR* I, 30, Pt. 1, pg. 201.
28. *OR* 1, 30, Pt. 4, pg. 90.
29. Ibid., pg. 322–23.
30. *OR* I, 30, Pt. 1, pg. 21.

31. *OR* I, 30, Pt. 4, pg. 404.
32. Lamers, *The Edge of Glory*, pg. 393–93; Society Army of the Cumberland, 1879 Reunion, pg. 176.
33. *OR* I, 30, Pt. 4, pg. 478.
34. Harvey Reid and Frank L. Byrne, *The View from Headquarters; Civil War Letters of Harvey Reid* (Madison: State Historical Society of Wisconsin, 1965), pg. 101.
35. Nevins, *The War for the Union*, vol. 3, pg. 203.

Chapter 12

1. Bruce Catton, *Grant Takes Command* (Boston: Little, Brown, 1969), pg. 26; Sylvanus Cadwallader and Benjamin Platt Thomas, *Three Years with Grant: As Recalled by War Correspondent Sylvanus Cadwallader* (New York: Knopf, 1955), pg. 117.
2. Grant, *Memoirs*, Vol. II, pg. 26; *OR* I, 30, Pt. 4, pg. 479; William S. Rosecrans, "Mistakes of Grant," *North American Review* 141 (July 1885): pg. 595.
3. *OR* I, 30, Pt. 1, pg. 221.
4. Grant, *Memoirs*, pg. 28; John Atkinson, "The Story of Lookout Mountain and Missionary Ridge," in *War Papers: Read Before the Commandery of the State of Michigan Military Order of the Loyal Legion of the United States*, vol. 2 (Detroit, MI: James H. Stone & Co., 1898), pg. 285; James Harrison Wilson, *Under the Old Flag; Recollections of Military Operations in the War for the Union, the Spanish War, the Boxer Rebellion, Etc.*, vol. 1 (New York: D. Appleton & Co., 1912), pg. 273–74.
5. *OR* I, 30, Pt. 4, pg. 485; *Report of a Board of Army Officers*, pg. 20–21, 31.
6. Richard W. Johnson, *A Soldier's Reminiscences in Peace and War* (Philadelphia, PA: J.B. Lippincott & Co., 1886), pg. 419–20.
7. John Hay and Tyler Dennett, *Lincoln and the Civil War in the Diaries and Letters of John Hay* (New York: Da Capo Press, 1988), pg. 106; Lincoln to Stanton, December 18, 1863, in Abraham Lincoln and Roy P. Basler, *The Collected Works of Abraham Lincoln*, vol. 7 (New Brunswick, NJ: Rutgers University Press, 1953), pg. 79.
8. Emerson Opdycke, Glenn Longacre, and John E. Haas, *To Battle for God and the Right: The Civil War Letterbooks of Emerson Opdycke* (Urbana: University of Illinois Press, 2003), pg. 101; Lyman G. Bennett and William M. Haigh, *History of the Thirty-Sixth Regiment Illinois Volunteers during the War of the Rebellion* (Aurora, IL: Knickerbocker & Hodder, 1876), pg. 478; John Basil Turchin, *Chickamauga* (Chicago, IL: Fergus Printing, 1888), pg. 163.
9. Judith Lee Hallock and Grady McWhiney, *Braxton Bragg and Confederate Defeat*, vol. 2 (Tuscaloosa: University of Alabama Press, 1991), pg. 85; W.S. Furay and G.C. Kniffin, *The Real Chickamauga* (n.p., 1888), pg. 2–3; Daniel H. Hill, "Chickamauga: The Great Battle of the West," *The Century* 33, no. 6 (April 1887): pg. 962.
10. *OR* I, Vol. 31, Pt. 3, pg. 3; William F. Smith, "An Historical Sketch of the Military Operations around Chattanooga, Tennessee, September 22 to November 27, 1863" pg. 192; Peter Cozzens, *The Shipwreck of Their Hopes: The Battles for Chattanooga* (Urbana: University of Illinois Press, 1994), pg. 241.
11. *Grant Papers*, Vol. IX, pg. 475.
12. Edward Hagerman, *The American Civil War and the Origins of Modern Warfare: Ideas, Organization, and Field Command* (Bloomington: Indiana University Press, 1938), pg. 212–13.
13. Horace Cecil Fisher, *The Personal Experiences of Colonel Horace Newton Fisher in the Civil War; a Staff Officer's Story* (Boston, MA, 1960), pg. 81.
14. John Brown Gordon, *Reminiscences of the Civil War* (New York: Charles Scribner's Sons, 1903), pg. 225–26.
15. Cozzens, *Shipwreck*, pg. 391, 392.
16. Harvey Reid, *The View from Headquarters* (Madison: State Historical Society of Wisconsin, 1965), pg. 100; James A. Connolly, *Three Years in the Army of the Cumberland* (Bloomington: Indiana University Press, 1959), pg. 134; Jason Nelson Fradenburgh, *In Memoriam Henry Harrison Cummings* (Oil City, PA: Derrick Publishing, 1913), pg. 79; Horace Porter to his mother October 26, 1863, *Horace Porter Papers*, Library of Congress.
17. Philip Henry Sheridan, *Personal Memoirs* (New York: Webster, 1888), pg. 300; Francis Trowbridge Sherman and C. Knight Aldrich, *Quest for a Star: The Civil War Letters and Diaries of Colonel Francis T. Sherman of the 88th Illinois* (Knoxville: University of Tennessee Press, 1999), pg. 105; George W. Squier et al., *This Wilderness of War: The Civil War Letters of George W. Squier, Hoosier Volunteer*

(Knoxville: University of Tennessee Press, 1998), pg. 107–8; Constantin Grebner and Frederic Trautmann, *"We Were the Ninth": A History of the Ninth Regiment, Ohio Volunteer Infantry, April 17, 1861, to June 7, 1864* (Kent, OH: Kent State University Press, 1987), pg. 22–23.
18. *New York Times*, October 22, 1863.
19. *Cincinnati Times*, October 27, 1863; *Brooklyn Daily Eagle*, November 7, 1863.
20. *Harper's Weekly*, October 31, 1863.
21. *Chicago Tribune*, October 29, 1863.
22. *Richmond Examiner*, October 26, 1863.

Chapter 13

1. Lincoln to Schofield, May 27, 1863, in Abraham Lincoln and Roy P. Basler, *The Collected Works of Abraham Lincoln*, vol. 6 (New Brunswick, NJ: Rutgers University Press, 1953), pg. 234.
2. Lincoln to Stanton, December 18, 1863, in Abraham Lincoln, John G. Nicolay, and John Hay, *Complete Works: Comprising His Speeches, Letters, State Papers, and Miscellaneous Writings*, vol. 2 (New York: Century, 1894), pg. 462.; John G. Nicolay and John Hay, *Abraham Lincoln: A History*, vol. 8 (New York: Century, 1890), pg. 474; Benjamin F. Wade to Rosecrans, December 24, 1863, *Rosecrans Papers*.
3. *OR* I, 34, Pt. 2, pg. 381, 363.
4. James A. Garfield to William S. Rosecrans, June 7, 1864; William S. Rosecrans to James A. Garfield, June 7, 1864, *Rosecrans Papers*, UCLA. Also on back of letter from R.S. Thoms to Garfield dated September 13, 1864, in *Garfield Papers*, Library of Congress. Another version in P.C. Headley, *Public Men of Today* (San Francisco: A. Bancroft & Co., 1882) has Rosecrans' reply being, "Nothing but the conviction that it was a high public duty could induce me to become a candidate for any political office. In this case I have no grounds upon which to base such a conviction. The Convention must therefore discharge its high and responsible duties, in view of the exigencies of the Nation, according to its judgment and conscience, leaving me to the exercise of mine until I shall know its decision"; Garfield to Rosecrans, November 17, 1866, *Rosecrans Papers*, UCLA.
5. John Hay and Tyler Dennett, *Lincoln and the Civil War in the Diaries and Letters of John Hay* (New York: Da Capo Press, 1988); Thomas C. Fletcher, "The Battle of Pilot Knob and the Retreat to Leasburg," in *War Papers and Personal Reminiscences, 1861–1865: Read before the Commandery of the State of Missouri, Military Order of the Loyal Legion of the United States*, vol. 1 (St. Louis, MO: Becktold, 1892), pg. 30, 187; *OR* I, 41, Pt. 3, pg. 975–76.
6. Albert E. Castel, *General Sterling Price and the Civil War in the West* (Baton Rouge: Louisiana State University Press, 1968), pg. 236–37; Starr, *The Union Cavalry in the Civil War*, vol. 3, pg. 526; *OR* I, 41, Pt. 1, pg. 314; *OR* I, 41, Pt. 4, pg. 545.
7. *OR* I, 41, Pt. 4, pg. 545; *OR* I, 41, Pt. 3, pg. 773; *OR* I, 41, Pt. 4, pg. 742–43.
8. Charles A. Dana to John A. Rawlins, July 15, 1864, *Grant Papers*, Vol. XI, pg. 252–53.
9. United States Congress, Joint Committee on the Conduct of the War, Report of the Joint Committee, vol. 3, pg. 55–56.

Chapter 14

1. John Russell Young to James A. Garfield, March 30, 1867, *Garfield Papers*.
2. Garfield to Young, March 31, 1867, *Garfield Papers*.
3. *OR* I, 31, Pt. 1, pg. 684.
4. Theodore Clarke Smith, *The Life and Letters of James Abram Garfield, 1877–1882*, vol. 2 (New Haven, CT: Yale University Press, 1925), pg. 865–66; Garfield to Rosecrans, February 3, 1880, *Garfield Papers*.
5. Smith, *Life and Letters of Garfield*, vol. 2, pg. 867–68.
6. Lamers, *Edge of Glory*, pg. 445; Rosecrans to Dana, March 17, 1882, *Charles A. Dana Papers*, Library of Congress.
7. Lamers, *Edge of Glory*, pg. 411–13; Garfield speech in the House of Representatives, February 17, 1879, also in James A. Garfield, B.A. Hinsdale, and Mary L. Hinsdale, *Garfield-Hinsdale Letters; Correspondence between James Abram Garfield and Burke Aaron Hinsdale* (Ann Arbor: University of Michigan Press, 1949), pg. 778; Margaret Leech and Harry James Brown, *The Garfield Orbit* (New York: Harper & Row, 1978), pg. 154.
8. Frank M. O'Brien, "The Story of the Sun," *Munsey's Magazine*, October 1917, pg. 129–36; Charles A. Dana, *Recollections of the Civil War: With the Leaders at Washington and

in the Field in the Sixties (New York: D. Appleton & Co., 1898), pg. 2.

9. William S. McFeely, *Grant: A Biography* (New York: Norton, 1981), pg. 123; *Grant Papers*, Vol. VIII, pg. 322–25; James Harrison Wilson, *Diary*, June 7, 1863; Dana to Washburne, August 29, 1863, *Washburne Papers*; *New York Sun*, June 28, 1887; McFeely, *Grant*, pg. 128.

10. Janet E. Steele, *The Sun Shines for All: Journalism and Ideology in the Life of Charles A. Dana* (Syracuse, NY: Syracuse University Press, 1993), pg. 54–55.

11. *OR* I, 30, Pt. 4, pg. 55, 236.

12. John B. Sanderson, *Diary*, October 20, 1863, *Sanderson Papers*.

Chapter 15

1. *Grant Papers*, Vol. II, pg. 183; Vol. IV, pg. 119.

2. *OR* I, 7, pg. 679–80.

3. S.W. McMaster, *60 Years on the Upper Mississippi: My Life and Experiences* (Rock Island, IL, 1893), pg. 200; Washburne speech in House of Representatives, *Congressional Globe*, May 2, 1862; *Grant Papers*, Vol. IV, pg. 116; Julia Grant to Washburne, May 16, 1862; Jesse R. Grant to Washburne, May 16, 1862; *Washburne Papers*. Library of Congress also in Mark Washburn, *Biography of Washburne*, vol. 2, pg. 146–47; Gustav Philipp Körner and Thomas J. McCormack, *Memoirs of Gustave Koerner, 1809–1896: Life-Sketches Written at the Suggestion of His Children*, vol. 2 (Cedar Rapids, IA: Torch Press, 1909), pg. 216.

4. Joseph Medill to Washburne, February 19, 1863, *Washburne Papers*, also in *Grant Papers*, Vol. VII, pg. 318.

5. Cadwallader Washburn to Elihu Washburne, March 28, 1863, *Washburne Papers*; Mark Washburn, *Biography of Washburne*, vol. 2, pg. 240.

6. Cadwallader Washburn to Elihu Washburne, April 11, 1863, *Washburne Papers*; Washburn, *Biography of Washburne*, vol. 2, pg. 242–43.

7. Benjamin F. Butler and Jessie Marshall, *Private and Official Correspondence of Gen. Benjamin F. Butler during the Period of the Civil War; Privately Issued*, vol. 3 (Norwood, MA: Plimpton Press, 1917), pg. 99.

8. Ulysses S. Grant to Barnabas Burns, December 17, 1863, *Grant Papers*, Vol. IX, pg. 541.

9. J.N. Sheehan to Washburne, March 17, 1864, *Washburne Papers*.

10. O.B. Mattison to Washburne, March 22, 1864, *Washburne Papers*.

11. Shaffer to Washburne, February 11, 1864, *Washburne Papers*.

12. Ida M. Tarbell, *Abraham Lincoln*, vol. 2 (New York: S.S. McClure, 1895), pg. 188.

13. James H. Wilson to U.S. Grant, *Grant Papers*, Vol. X, pg. 37.

14. James Harrison Wilson, *The Life of John A. Rawlins, Lawyer, Assistant Adjutant-General, Chief of Staff, Major General of Volunteers, and Secretary of War* (New York: Neale Publishing, 1916), pg. 184–85.

15. Joseph Medill to Washburne, May 30, 1864, *Washburne Papers*.

16. Butler and Marshall, *Private and Official Correspondence of Butler*, vol. 3, pg. 99.

17. Grant, *Memoirs*, Vol. II, pg. 276; Peter S. Michie, *The Life and Letters of Emory Upton, Colonel of the Fourth Regiment of Artillery, and Brevet Major-General, U.S. Army* (New York: D. Appleton & Co., 1895), pg. 108–9.

18. Gordon Granger to Rosecrans, June 6, 1864, *Rosecrans Papers*.

19. Horace Newton Fisher to John D. Long, January 14, 1889, *Horace N. Fisher Papers*.

20. Donn Piatt, Henry V. Boynton, and George H. Thomas, *General George H. Thomas: A Critical Biography by Donn Piatt, with Concluding Chapters by Henry V. Boynton* (Cincinnati, OH: R. Clarke & Co., 1893), pg. 233–234.

21. Grant, *Memoirs*, Vol. I, pg. 91.

22. Gideon Welles, *Diary*, vol. 1, pg. 108–9.

23. Richard L. Kiper, *Major General John Alexander McClernand: Politician in Uniform* (Kent, OH: Kent State University Press, 1999), pg. 545.

24. Richard L. Kiper, *Major General John Alexander McClernand: Politician in Uniform* (Kent, OH: Kent State University Press, 1999), pg. 311; Robert Rutherford McCormick, *Ulysses S. Grant, the Great Soldier of America* (New York: D. Appleton-Century, 1934), pg. 95; *OR* I, 24, Pt. 1. pg. 87.

25. William Farrar Smith, *From Chattanooga to Petersburg under Generals Grant and Butler: A Contribution to the History of the War, and a Personal Vindication* (Boston: Houghton Mifflin, 1893), pg. 178.

26. John Watts De Peyster, *Major-General George H. Thomas: The Annual Address Delivered before the New York Historical Society ... January 5, 1875* (New York: Atlantic Publishing, 1875), pg. 571; Gilbert C. Kniffin, "Major-General William Starke Rosecrans, U.S. Army," in *District of Columbia, Military Order of the Loyal Legion of the United States War Papers*, vol. 4 (Washington, DC, 1908), pg. 4; George H. Thomas to Rosecrans, January 16, 1866, *Rosecrans Papers*.

27. Gideon Welles, *Diary*, pg. 282–83.

28. Henry Howe, *Historical Collections of Ohio ... an Encyclopedia of the State: History Both General and Local, Geography ... Sketches of Eminent and Interesting Characters, Etc., with Notes of a Tour over It in 1886*, vol. 1 (Columbus, OH: H. Howe & Son, 1889), pg. 852.

Chapter 16

1. *New York Times*, August 27, 1865, from *San Francisco Bulletin*, July 31, 1865.

2. William B. Styple, *Generals in Bronze: Interviewing the Commanders of the Civil War* (Kearny, NJ: Belle Grove Publishing, 2005), pg. 191; Anita Rosecrans in notes and outline for a life of William S. Rosecrans, *Rosecrans Papers*.

3. Edward J. Berbusse, S.J., "General Rosecrans' Forthright Diplomacy with Juarez's Mexico, 1868–1869." *The Americas* 36, no. 4 (1980): pg. 511, 508, 507.

4. Douglas Southall Freeman, *R.E. Lee, a Biography*, vol. 4 (New York: C. Scribner's Sons, 1934), pg. 375.

5. *Appleton's Annual Cyclopedia* 10 (1886): pg. 226.

6. Harvey S. Ford, ed., "The Diary of John Beatty, January–June 1884, Part IV," *Ohio History* 59, no. 2 (October 1950): pg. 176.

7. Henry Van Ness Boynton, *The National Military Park, Chickamauga, Chattanooga, An Historical Guide, with Maps and Illustrations* (Cincinnati, OH: R. Clarke & Co., 1895), pg. 222.

8. Allen Rosenkrans, *The Rosenkrans Family in Europe and America* (Newton, NJ: New Jersey Herald Press, 1900), pg. 316–17.

9. *Los Angeles Times*, March 17, 1898.

10. *Burial of Rosecrans*, pg. 28–29.

11. Samuel W. Price, "The Cracker Line," in *War Papers: Read Before the Commandery of the District of Columbia, Military Order of the Loyal Legion of the United States*, vol. 3 (Washington, DC, 1907), pg. 17.

12. John Palmer, *Personal Recollections*, pg. 199; Lucius F. Hubbard, "Minnesota in the Battles of Corinth," in *Glimpses of the Nation's Struggle: Papers Read before the Minnesota Commandery of the Military Order of the Loyal Legion of the United States*, vol. 6 (St. Paul, MN: August Davis, 1909), pg. 496; Dabney Maury, *Campaign against Grant*, pg. 301; L.W. Mulhane, *Memorial of Major-General William Stark Rosecrans* (Columbus, OH: Columbian Printing, 1898), pg. 62–65.

13. Lamers, *Edge of Glory*, pg. 4–5.

Chapter 17

1. E.B. Long, "John A. Rawlins; Staff Officer Par Excellence," *Civil War Times Illustrated* 27 (January 1974): pg. 43; *Congressional Globe*, June 6, 1872; Octavius Brooks Frothingham, *Gerrit Smith, a Biography* (New York: G.P. Putnam's Sons, 1878), pg. 331.

Bibliography

Manuscripts

Thomas and Carmelite Christie and Family Papers. St. Paul. Minnesota Historical Society.
Charles A. Dana Papers. Washington. Library of Congress.
Horace Newton Fisher Papers. Boston. Massachusetts Historical Society.
Julius P. Garesche Collection. Washington. Georgetown University.
James A. Garfield Papers. Washington. Library of Congress.
William Holden Letter Collection of Fred Ray.
James H. Montgomery Diary. Washington. Library of Congress.
John Patton Memoir. Washington. Library of Congress.
Horace Porter Papers. Washington. Library of Congress.
William S. Rosecrans Papers. Los Angeles. University of California, Los Angeles.
John P. Sanderson Papers. Columbus. Ohio Historical Society.
Elihu B. Washburne Papers. Washington. Library of Congress.
James Harrison Wilson Diaries. Wilmington. Delaware Historical Society.

Books, Articles, Dissertations

Alexander, Augustus W. *Grant as a Soldier*. St. Louis, MO: Author, 1887.
Alford, Julian D. *The Tullahoma Campaign: The Beginning of the End for the Confederacy*. Diss., U.S. Marine Corps Command and Staff College, 2002.
Ambler, C.H. "General R.E. Lee's Northwest Virginia Campaign." *West Virginia History Magazine* 5, no. 2 (1944): 101–18.
Anders, Leslie. *The Eighteenth Missouri*. Indianapolis, IN: Bobbs-Merrill, 1968.
———. *The Twenty-First Missouri: From Home Guard to Union Regiment*. Westport, CT: Greenwood Press, 1975.
Andrew, A. Piatt. *Some Civil War Letters of A. Piatt Andrew, III*. Gloucester, MA, 1925.
Ankeny, Henry Giesey, and Horatia Faustina Newcomb Ankeny. *Kiss Josey for Me!* Santa Ana, CA: Friis-Pioneer Press. 1974.
Appletons' Annual Cyclopedia and Register of Important Events. Vol. 10. New York: D. Appleton & Co., 1886.
Atkinson, John. "The Story of Lookout Mountain and Missionary Ridge." In *War Papers: Read before the Commandery of the State of Michigan Military Order of the Loyal Legion of the United States*, vol. 2. Detroit, MI: James H. Stone & Co., 1898.
Bailes, Clarice L. "Jacob Dolson Cox in West Virginia." *West Virginia History* 6, no. 1 (October 1944): 5.
Banks, Robert W. "Civil War Letters of Robert W. Banks." *Journal of Mississippi History* 5 (July 1943).
Bates, David Homer. *Lincoln in the Telegraph Office: Recollections of the United States Military Telegraph Corps during the Civil War*. New York: Century, 1907.
Baumgartner, Richard A. *Blue Lightning: Wilder's Mounted Infantry Brigade in the Battle of Chickamauga*. Huntington, WV: Blue Acorn Press, 1997.
Bearss, Edwin C. *Decision in Mississippi: Mississippi's Important Role in the War Between the States*. Jackson: Mississippi Commission on the War Between the States, 1962.
Beatty, John, and Harrison C. Hobart. *The Citizen-Soldier; or, Memoirs of a Volunteer*. Cincinnati, OH: Wilstach, Baldwin & Co., 1879.
Beaudot, William J.K. *The 24th Wisconsin Infantry in the Civil War: The Biography of a Regiment*. Mechanicsburg, PA: Stackpole Books, 2003.

Belknap, Charles Eugene. *History of the Michigan Organizations at Chickamauga, Chattanooga and Missionary Ridge, 1863*. Lansing, MI: R. Smith Print Co.,1899.

Bennett, Lyman G., and William M. Haigh. *History of the Thirty-Sixth Regiment Illinois Volunteers during the War of the Rebellion*. Aurora, IL: Knickerbocker & Hodder, 1876.

Berbusse, Edward J. "General Rosecrans' Forthright Diplomacy with Juarez's Mexico, 1868–1869." *The Americas* 36, no. 4 (1980): 499–514.

Berry, Stephen William. *House of Abraham: Lincoln and the Todds, a Family Divided by War*. Boston: Houghton Mifflin, 2007.

Bickham, William Dennison. *Rosecrans' Campaign with the Fourteenth Army Corps, or the Army of the Cumberland*. Cincinnati, OH: Moore, Wilstach, Keys & Co., 1863.

Blassingame, John W. "The Recruitment of Negro Troops in Missouri." *Missouri Historical Review* 58 (April 1964): 326–38.

Bobrick, Benson. *Master of War: The Life of General George H. Thomas*. New York: Simon & Schuster, 2009.

Boehm, Robert B. "The Battle of Rich Mountain, July 11, 1861." *West Virginia History* 20, no. 1 (1958): 5–15.

Bowers, John. *Chickamauga and Chattanooga: The Battles That Doomed the Confederacy*. New York: HarperCollins, 1994.

Boyd, Cyrus F., and Mildred Throne. *The Civil War Diary of Cyrus F. Boyd: Fifteenth Iowa Infantry, 1861–1863*. Iowa City: State Historical Society of Iowa, 1953.

Boynton, Henry Van Ness. *Errors in School Histories Compared with the Official Record*. Washington, DC: Speech Publishing Co., 1903.

_____. *The National Military Park. Chickamauga. Chattanooga. An Historical Guide. With Maps and Illustrations*. Cincinnati, OH: R. Clarke & Co., 1895.

_____. *Sherman's Historical Raid: The Memoirs in the Light of the Record; a Review Based upon Compilations from the Files of the War Office*. Cincinnati, OH: Wilstach, Baldwin & Co., 1875.

_____. *Was General Thomas Slow at Nashville? With a Description of the Greatest Cavalry Operations in Tennessee, Alabama, and Georgia*. New York: F.P. Harper, 1896.

Bradley, Michael R. "Tullahoma." *Blue and Gray* 27, no. 1 (2010).

_____. *Tullahoma: The 1863 Campaign for the Control of Middle Tennessee*. Shippensburg, PA: Burd Street Press, 2000.

Brandt, Robert S. "Lightning and Rain in Middle Tennessee." *Tennessee Historical Quarterly* 52, no. 3 (1993): 158–69.

Brewer, Richard J. *The Tullahoma Campaign: Operational Insights*. Diss., U.S. Army Command and General Staff College, Fort Leavenworth, KS, 1991.

Broadwater, Robert P. *General George H. Thomas: A Biography of the Union's "Rock of Chickamauga."* Jefferson, NC: McFarland, 2009.

Brooks, Noah, and Herbert Mitgang. *Washington, D.C., in Lincoln's Time*. New York: Collier, 1962.

Broome, Doyle D. *Intelligence Operations of the Army of the Cumberland during the Tullahoma and Chickamauga Campaigns*. Diss., U.S. Army Command and General Staff College, Fort Leavenworth, KS, 1989.

Brown, Leonard E. "Fortress Rosecrans: A History 1865–1900." *Tennessee Historical Quarterly* 50, no. 3 (1991): 135–41.

Bryner, B.C. *Bugle Echoes; the Story of Illinois 47th*. Springfield, IL: Phillips Bros., 1905.

Burial of General Rosecrans, Arlington National Cemetery, May 17, 1902. Cincinnati, OH: Robert Clarke & Co., 1903.

Butler, Benjamin F., and Jessie Marshall. *Private and Official Correspondence of Gen. Benjamin F. Butler during the Period of the Civil War*. Norwood, MA: Plimpton Press, 1917.

Byers, S.H.M. *Iowa in War Times*. Des Moines, IA: W.D. Condit, 1888.

_____. *With Fire and Sword*. New York: Neale Publishing, 1911.

Cadwallader, Sylvanus, and Benjamin Platt Thomas. *Three Years with Grant: As Recalled by War Correspondent Sylvanus Cadwallader*. New York: Knopf, 1955.

Calkin, Homer L. "James H. Fauntleroy's Diary for the Year 1862." *Civil War History* 11 (1956).

Canan, Howard V. "The Missouri Paw Paw Militia of 1863–1864." *Missouri Historical Review* 62, no. 4 (July 1968): 431–48.

Canfield, S.S. *History of the 21st Regiment Ohio Volunteer Infantry in the War of the Rebellion*. Toledo, OH: Vrooman, Anderson & Bateman, 1893.

Capron, Thaddeus H. "War Diary of Thaddeus H. Capron, 1861–1865." *Journal of the*

Illinois State Historical Society 12, no. 3 (October 1919): 330–406.

Carlin, William Passmore, Robert I. Girardi, and Nathaniel Cheairs Hughes. *The Memoirs of Brigadier General William Passmore Carlin, U.S.A.* Lincoln: University of Nebraska Press, 1999.

Carnahan, James R. "Personal Recollection of Chickamauga." In *Sketches of War History, 1861–1865: Papers Read before the Ohio Commandery of the Military Order of the Loyal Legion of the United States*, vol. 1. Cincinnati, OH: R. Clark, 1888.

Carpenter, Arthur B. "Yankees in Arms: The Civil War as a Personal Experience." *Civil War History* 19 (September 1973).

Castel, Albert E. *Decision in the West: The Atlanta Campaign of 1864.* Lawrence: University Press of Kansas, 1992.

———. *General Sterling Price and the Civil War in the West.* Baton Rouge: Louisiana State University Press, 1968.

———. "Victorious Loser: William S. Rosecrans (Part I)." *Ohio History* 19, no. 4 (July/August 2002).

———. "Victorious Loser: William S. Rosecrans (Part II)." *Ohio History* 19, no. 5 (September/October 2002).

Castel, Albert E., and Brooks D. Simpson. *Victors in Blue: How Union Generals Fought the Confederates, Battled Each Other, and Won the Civil War.* Lawrence, KA: University Press of Kansas, 2011.

Catton, Bruce. *Grant Takes Command.* Boston: Little, Brown, 1969.

Chetlain, Augustus L. "The Battle of Corinth." In *Military Essays and Recollections: Papers Read before the Commandery of the State of Illinois, Military Order of the Loyal Legion of the United States*, vol. 2. Chicago: A.C. McClurg & Co., 1894.

———. *Recollections of Seventy Years.* Galena, IL: Gazette Publishing, 1899.

Cist, Henry M. *The Army of the Cumberland, by Henry M. Cist.* New York: C. Scribner's Sons, 1882.

Clark, Charles T. *Opdycke Tigers, 125th O.V.I., a History of the Regiment and of the Campaigns and Battles of the Army of the Cumberland.* Columbus, OH: Spahr & Glenn, 1895.

Connelly, Donald B. *John M. Schofield and the Politics of Generalship.* Chapel Hill: University of North Carolina Press, 2006.

Connelly, Thomas Lawrence. *Army of the Heartland; the Army of Tennessee, 1861–1862.* Baton Rouge: Louisiana State University Press, 1967.

———. *Autumn of Glory; the Army of Tennessee, 1862–1865.* Baton Rouge: Louisiana State University Press, 1971.

Connolly, James Austin. *Three Years in the Army of the Cumberland; the Letters and Diary of Major James A. Connolly.* Bloomington: Indiana University Press, 1959.

Cooper, Edward S. *William Babcock Hazen: The Best Hated Man.* Madison, NJ: Fairleigh Dickinson University Press, 2005.

Coppee, Henry. *General Thomas.* New York: D. Appleton & Co., 1893.

Cox, Jacob D. "McClellan in West Virginia." In *Battles and Leaders of the Civil War*, ed. Robert U. Johnson and Clarence C. Buel, vol. 1. New York: Century, 1887.

———. *Military Reminiscences of the Civil War.* New York: C. Scribner's, 1900.

Cozzens, Peter. *The Darkest Days of the War: The Battles of Iuka & Corinth.* Chapel Hill: University of North Carolina Press, 1997.

———. *No Better Place to Die: The Battle of Stones River.* Urbana: University of Illinois Press, 1990.

———. *The Shipwreck of Their Hopes: The Battles for Chattanooga.* Urbana: University of Illinois Press, 1994.

———. *This Terrible Sound: The Battle of Chickamauga.* Urbana: University of Illinois Press, 1992.

Crawford, James Garvin, Martha Elizabeth Wilson, and Elizabeth Ethel Parker Bascom. *Dear Lizzie: Letters Written by James Jimmy Garvin Crawford to His Sweetheart Martha Elizabeth Lizzi Wilson While He Was in the Federal Army during the War between the States, 1862–1865.* Ridgewood, NJ: Bascom, 1978.

Cresap, Bernarr. *Appomattox Commander: The Story of General E.O.C. Ord.* South Brunswick, NJ: A.S. Barnes, 1981.

Crittenden, Thomas L. "The Union Left at Stone's River." In *Battles and Leaders of the Civil War*, ed. Robert U. Johnson and Clarence C. Buel, vol. 3. New York: Century, 1888.

Cubbison, Douglas R. "'That Awful Storm of Iron and Smoke': Union Artillery at Moccasin Bend, Chattanooga, September–November, 1863." *Tennessee Historical Quarterly* 58 (Winter 1999): 268–83.

Dalessandro, Robert J. *Major General William S. Rosecrans and the Transformation of the Staff of the Army of the Cumberland: A Case Study.* Diss., U.S. Army War College, 2002.

_____. *Morale in the Army of the Cumberland during the Tullahoma and Chickamauga Campaigns.* Diss., U.S. Army Command and General Staff College, Fort Leavenworth, KS, 1995.

Daly, Maria Lydig, and Harold E. Hammond. *Diary of a Union Lady, 1861–1865.* New York: Funk & Wagnalls, 1962.

Dana, Charles A. *Recollections of the Civil War: With the Leaders at Washington and in the Field in the Sixties.* New York: D. Appleton & Co., 1898.

Daniel, Larry J. *Battle of Stones River: The Forgotten Conflict between the Confederate Army of Tennessee and the Union Army of the Cumberland.* Baton Rouge: Louisiana State University Press, 2012.

_____. *Days of Glory: The Army of the Cumberland, 1861–1865.* Baton Rouge: Louisiana State University Press, 2004.

Davis, William C. *The Orphan Brigade: The Kentucky Confederates Who Couldn't Go Home.* Garden City, NY: Doubleday, 1980.

De Peyster, John Watts. *Major-General George H. Thomas: The Annual Address Delivered before the New York Historical Society ... January 5, 1875.* New York: Atlantic Publishing, 1875.

Dell, Christopher. *Lincoln and the War Democrats: The Grand Erosion of Conservative Tradition.* Rutherford, NJ: Fairleigh Dickinson University Press, 1975.

Dietz, J. Stanley, and Henry McCann. *The Story of Old Abe, the War Eagle.* Madison, WI: Democrat Printing Co., 1946.

Dittenhoefer, Abram J. *How We Elected Lincoln; Personal Recollections of Lincoln and Men of His Time.* New York: Harper & Brothers, 1916.

Dodge, William Sumner. *History of the Old Second Division, Army of the Cumberland. Commanders: M'Cook, Sill, and Johnson.* Chicago: Church & Goodman, 1864.

_____. *A Waif of the War or, The History of the Seventy-Fifth Illinois Infantry, Embracing the Entire Campaigns of the Army of the Cumberland.* Chicago: Church & Goodman, 1866.

Downey, Fairfax. *Storming of the Gateway; Chattanooga, 1863.* New York: D. McKay, 1960.

Doyle, Peter, and Matthew Bennett. *Fields of Battle: Terrain in Military History.* Dordrecht: Kluwer Academic, 2002.

Drake, Edwin L. *The Annals of the Army of Tennessee and Early Western History, Including a Chronological Summary of Battles and Engagements in the Western Armies of the Confederacy.* Nashville, TN: Printed by A.D. Haynes, 1878.

Ducat, Arthur C. *Memoir of Gen. A.C. Ducat.* Chicago: Rand, McNally & Co., 1897.

Dudley, G.W., and Monroe F. Cockrell. *The Lost Account of the Battle of Corinth, and Court-Martial of Gen. Van Dorn.* Wilmington, NC: Broadfoot Publishing, 1991.

Dudley, Harold M. "The Election of 1864." *Mississippi Valley Historical Review* 18, no. 4 (1932): 500–18.

Dyer, John P. *From Shiloh to San Juan.* Baton Rouge: Louisiana State University Press, 1961.

Ella, Tompkins W. "The Colonel's Lady: Some Letters of Ellen Wilkins Tompkins, July–December 1861." *Virginia Magazine of History and Biography* 69 (1961): 387–419.

Fay, Edwin Hedge. *This Infernal War; the Confederate Letters of Edwin H. Fay.* Austin: University of Texas Press, 1958.

Fehrenbacher, Don E. "The Making of a Myth: Lincoln and the Vice-Presidential Nomination in 1864." *Civil War History* 41, no. 4 (1995): 273–90.

Fisher, Horace Cecil. *The Personal Experiences of Colonel Horace Newton Fisher in the Civil War; a Staff Officer's Story.* Boston, MA, 1960.

Fitch, John. *Annals of the Army of the Cumberland.* Philadelphia, PA: J.B. Lippincott & Co., 1864.

_____. *Chickamauga, the Price of Chattanooga: A Description of the Strategic Plans, Marches, and Battles of the Campaign of Chattanooga.* Philadelphia, PA: J.B. Lippincott & Co., 1864.

Fleharty, S.F., Philip J. Reyburn, and Terry Wilson. *Jottings from Dixie: The Civil War Dispatches of Sergeant Major Stephen F. Fleharty, U.S.A.* Baton Rouge: Louisiana State University Press, 1999.

Fletcher, Thomas C. "The Battle of Pilot Knob and the Retreat to Leasburg." In *War Papers and Personal Reminiscences. 1861–1865. Read before the Commandery of the State of Missouri, Military Order of the Loyal Legion* of the United States, vol. 1. St. Louis, MO: Becktold, 1892.

Floyd, David Bittle. *History of the Seventy-Fifth Regiment of Indiana Infantry Volunteers: Its Organization, Campaigns, and Battles (1862–65)*. Philadelphia, PA: Lutheran Publication Society, 1893.

Force, M.F. *From Fort Henry to Corinth*. New York: C. Scribner's Sons, 1881.

Ford, Harvey S., ed. "The Diary of John Beatty, January–June 1884, Part IV." *Ohio History* 59, no. 2 (April 1950).

Ford, Thomas J. *With the Rank and File Incidents and Anecdotes during the War of the Rebellion, as Remembered by One of the Noncommissioned Officers*. Milwaukee: Press of the Evening Wisconsin Co., 1898.

Fradenburgh, J.N., and Henry Harrison Cumings. *In Memoriam, Henry Harrison Cumings, Charlotte J. Cumings*. Oil City, PA: Derrick Publishing, 1913.

Frederick, J.V., ed. "An Illinois Boy in North Mississippi: Diary of John Wilson, February 15–December 30, 1862." *Journal of Mississippi History* 1 (1939): 182–94.

Freeman, Douglas Southall. *R.E. Lee, a Biography*. New York: C. Scribner's Sons, 1934.

Freeman, Henry V. "Some Battle Recollections of Stone's River." In *Military Essays and Recollections: Papers Read before the Commandery of the State of Illinois, Military Order of the Loyal Legion of the United States*, vol. 3. Chicago: Dial Press, 1899.

Frothingham, Octavius Brooks. *Gerrit Smith, a Biography*. New York: G.P. Putnam's Sons, 1878.

Furay, W.S., and G.C. Kniffin. *The Real Chickamauga*. N.p., 1888.

Garesché, M. Louise. *Biography of Lieut. Col. Julius P. Garesché, Assistant Adjutant-General, U.S. Army*. Philadelphia, PA: J.B. Lippincott & Co., 1887.

Garfield, James A. *The Wild Life of the Army: Civil War Letters of James A. Garfield*. Edited by Frederick D. Williams. East Lansing: Michigan State University Press, 1964.

Garfield, James A., and B.A. Hinsdale. *The Works of James Abram Garfield*. Vols. 1 and 2. Boston: J.R. Osgood & Co., 1882.

Garfield, James A., B.A. Hinsdale, and Mary L. Hinsdale. *Garfield-Hinsdale Letters; Correspondence between James Abram Garfield and Burke Aaron Hinsdale*. Ann Arbor: University of Michigan Press, 1949.

Garfield, Lucretia Rudolph, James A. Garfield, and John Shaw. *Crete and James: Personal Letters of Lucretia and James Garfield*. East Lansing: Michigan State University Press, 1994.

Geer, Allen Morgan. *The Civil War Diary of Allen Morgan Geer, Twentieth Regiment, Illinois Volunteers*. Denver, CO: R.C. Appleman, 1977.

Genco, James G., and Harold James Bartlett. *To the Sound of Musketry and Tap of the Drum: A History of Michigan's Battery D through the Letters of Artificer Harold J. Bartlett, 1861–1864*. Rochester, MI: R. Russell-Books, 1983.

Gerteis, Louis S. "'An Outrage on Humanity': Martial Law and Military Prisons in St. Louis During the Civil War." *Missouri Historical Review* 96, no. 4 (July 2002): 302–22.

Gilmore, James Roberts. *Down in Tennessee and Back by Way of Richmond*. New York: Carleton, 1864.

———. *Personal Recollections of Abraham Lincoln and the Civil War, by James R. Gilmore*. Boston: L.C. Page, 1898.

Gordon, John Brown. *Reminiscences of the Civil War*. New York: Charles Scribner's Sons, 1903.

Gordon, Ralph C. "Hospital Trains of the Army of the Cumberland." *Tennessee Historical Quarterly* 51, no. 3 (1992): 147–56.

Gorgas, Josiah, and Frank Everson Vandiver. *The Civil War Diary of General Josiah Gorgas*. University: University of Alabama Press, 1947.

Gracie, Archibald. *The Truth about Chickamauga*. Boston: Houghton Mifflin, 1911.

Graf, LeRoy P., and Ralph W. Haskins, eds. *Papers of Andrew Johnson*. Vol. 6, *1862–64*. Knoxville: University of Tennessee Press, 1983.

Grant, Ulysses S. *Personal Memoirs of US Grant*. Vols. 1 and 2. New York: Century, 1895.

Grant, Ulysses S., and John Y. Simon. *The Papers of Ulysses S. Grant*. Carbondale: Southern Illinois University Press, 1967.

Grant, Ulysses S., John Y. Simon, and John F. Marszalek. *The Papers of Ulysses S. Grant*. Carbondale: Southern Illinois University Press, 1967.

Grant, Ulysses S., James Grant Wilson, and E.B. Washburne. *General Grant's Letters to a Friend, 1861–1880*. New York: T.Y. Crowell & Co., 1897.

Grebner, Constantin, and Frederic Trautmann. *"We Were the Ninth": A History of the Ninth Regiment, Ohio Volunteer Infantry, April 17, 1861, to June 7, 1864*. Kent, OH: Kent State University Press, 1987.

Green, Johnny, and Albert Dennis Kirwan. *Johnny Green of the Orphan Brigade: The Journal of a Confederate Soldier*. Lexington: University of Kentucky Press, 1956.

Gunn, Jack W. "The Battle of Iuka." *Journal of Mississippi History* 24 (1962): 142–57.

Hagerman, Edward. *The American Civil War and the Origins of Modern Warfare: Ideas, Organization, and Field Command*. Bloomington, IN: Indiana University Press, 1988.

Hall, Granville Davisson. *Lee's Invasion of Northwest Virginia in 1861*. Chicago: Press of the Mayer & Miller Co., 1911.

Hallock, Judith Lee., and Grady McWhiney. *Braxton Bragg and Confederate Defeat*. Vol. 2. Tuscaloosa: University of Alabama Press, 1991.

Hamilton, Charles S. "The Battle of Iuka." In *Battles and Leaders of the Civil War*, ed. Robert U. Johnson and Clarence C. Buel, vol. 2, 734–35. New York: Century, 1887.

Hamilton, James A. "The Enrolled Missouri Militia: Its Creation and Controversial History." *Missouri Historical Review* 69, no. 4 (July 1975): 413–32.

Hannaford, Ebenezer. *The Story of a Regiment: A History of the Campaigns, and Associations in the Field, of the Sixth Regiment Ohio Volunteer Infantry*. Cincinnati, OH: Author, 1868.

Hartje, Robert George. *Van Dorn, the Life and Times of a Confederate General*. Nashville, TN: Vanderbilt University Press, 1967.

Hascall, Milo S. *Personal Recollections and Experiences Concerning the Battle of Stone River*. Goshen, IN: Times Publishing, 1889.

Haselberger, Fritz, and Mark Haselberger. *Yanks from the South! The First Land Campaign of the Civil War, Rich Mountain, West Virginia*. Baltimore, MD: Past Glories, 1987.

Hay, John, and Michael Burlingame. *At Lincoln's Side: John Hay's Civil War Correspondence and Selected Writings*. Carbondale, IL: Southern Illinois University Press, 2000.

Hay, John, Michael Burlingame, and John R.T. Ettlinger. *Inside Lincoln's White House: The Complete Civil War Diary of John Hay*. Carbondale, IL: Southern Illinois University Press, 1999.

Hay, John, and Tyler Dennett. *Lincoln and the Civil War in the Diaries and Letters of John Hay*. New York: Da Capo Press, 1988.

Hay, Thomas R. "The Campaign and Battle of Chickamauga." *Georgia Historical Quarterly* 7, no. 3 (September 1923): 213–50.

Haynie, James Henry. *The Nineteenth Illinois; a Memoir of a Regiment of Volunteer Infantry Famous in the Civil War of Fifty Years Ago for Its Drill, Bravery, and Distinguished Services*. Chicago: M.A. Donohue & Co., 1912.

Hazen, William Babcock. *A Narrative of Military Service*. Boston: Ticknor & Co., 1885.

Headley, Joel Tyler. *Grant and Sherman; Their Campaigns and Generals*. New York: E.B. Treat, 1865.

Heg, Hans Christian, and Theodore Christian Blegen. *The Civil War Letters of Colonel Hans Christian Heg*. Northfield, MN: Norwegian-American Historical Association, 1936.

Herr, George Washington. *Nine Campaigns of the Civil War*. San Francisco: Bancroft, 1890.

Hess, Earl J. *Banners to the Breeze: The Kentucky Campaign, Corinth, and Stones River*. Lincoln: University of Nebraska Press, 2000.

Heth, Henry, and James L. Morrison. *The Memoirs of Henry Heth*. Westport, CT: Greenwood Press, 1974.

Hicken, Victor. *Illinois in the Civil War*. Urbana: University of Illinois Press, 1966.

Hight, John J., and Gilbert R. Stormont. *History of the Fifty-Eighth Regiment of Indiana Volunteer Infantry: Its Organization, Campaigns and Battles from 1861 to 1865*. Princeton, IN: Press of the Clarion, 1895.

Hill, Daniel H. "Chickamauga: The Great Battle of the West." *The Century* 33, no. 6 (April 1887): 937–62.

Hoffman, Mark. *My Brave Mechanics: The First Michigan Engineers and Their Civil War*. Detroit, MI: Wayne State University Press, 2007.

Holmes, Mead. *A Soldier of the Cumberland: Memoir of Mead Holmes, Jr., Sergeant of Company K, 21st Regiment Wisconsin Volunteers*. Boston: American Tract Society, 1864.

Holmes, W.C. "The Battle of Corinth." *Confederate Veteran* 27, no. 8 (August 1919).

Holzman, Robert S. *Stormy Ben Butler*. New York: Macmillan, 1954.

Horn, Stanley Fitzgerald. *The Army of Tennessee; a Military History*. Indianapolis: Bobbs-Merrill, 1941.

Horton, J.H., and Solomon Teverbaugh. *A History of the Eleventh Regiment (Ohio Volunteer Infantry)*. Dayton, OH: W.J. Shuey, 1866.

Hough, Alfred Lacey. *Soldier in the West; the Civil War Letters of Alfred Lacey Hough*. Philadelphia, PA: University of Pennsylvania Press, 1957.

Howe, Henry. *Historical Collections of Ohio ... an Encyclopedia of the State: History Both General and Local, Geography ... Sketches of Eminent and Interesting Characters, Etc., with Notes of a Tour over It in 1886*. Vol. 1. Columbus, OH: H. Howe & Son, 1889.

Hubbard, Lucius F. "Minnesota in the Battle of Corinth." In *Glimpses of the Nation's Struggle: Papers Read before the Minnesota Commandery of the Military Order of the Loyal Legion of the United States*, vol. 6. St. Paul, MN: August Davis, 1909.

Hubbell, John T. *Battles Lost and Won: Essays from Civil War History*. Westport, CT: Greenwood Press, 1975.

Hughes, Michael A. *The Struggle for Chattanooga, 1862–1863*. Diss., University of Arkansas, Fayetteville, 1991.

Hunt, Gaillard. *Israel, Elihu and Cadwallader Washburn; a Chapter in American Biography*. New York: Macmillan, 1925.

Hunter, Edna J., John Daniel Shank, and Oscar Fitzalan Harmon. *One Flag, One Country, and Thirteen Greenbacks a Month: Letters from a Civil War Private and His Colonel*. San Diego, CA: Hunter Publications, 1980.

Ingersoll, Lurton Dunham. *Iowa and the Rebellion: A History of the Troops Furnished by the State of Iowa to the Volunteer Armies of the Union, Which Conquered the Great Southern Rebellion of 1861–5*. Philadelphia, PA: J.B. Lippincott & Co., 1866.

Jackman, John S., and William C. Davis. *Diary of a Confederate Soldier: John S. Jackman of the Orphan Brigade*. Columbia, SC: University of South Carolina Press, 1990.

Jackson, Oscar L., and David Prentice Jackson. *The Colonel's Diary: Journals Kept before and during the Civil War*. Sharon, PA, 1922.

Jenkins, Brian. *Britain & the War for the Union*. Montreal: McGill-Queen's University Press, 1974.

Jenkins, Paul Burrill. *The Battle of Westport*. Kansas City, MO: Franklin Hudson Publishing, 1906.

Joens, David. "Ulysses S. Grant, Illinois, and the Election of 1880." *Journal of the Illinois State Historical Society* 97, no. 4 (2004/2005): 310–30.

Johnson, Mark W. *That Body of Brave Men: The U.S. Regular Infantry and the Civil War in the West, 1861–1865*. Cambridge, MA: Da Capo Press, 2003.

Johnson, Richard W. *A Soldier's Reminiscences in Peace and War*. Philadelphia, PA: J.B. Lippincott & Co., 1886.

Johnston, Joseph E. *Narrative of Military Operations, Directed, during the Late War between the States*. New York: D. Appleton & Co., 1874.

Keifer, Joseph Warren. "The Battle of Rich Mountain and Some Incidents." In *Sketches of War History, 1861–1865: Ohio Commandery of the Military Order of the Loyal Legion of the United States*, vol. 7. Cincinnati, OH: 1911. Cincinnati: R. Clarke & Co., 1896.

Keil, F.W. *Thirty-Fifth Ohio: A Narrative of Service from August, 1861 to 1864*. Fort Wayne, IN: Archer, Roush & Co., 1894.

Kendall, Henry Myron. *The Battle of Stone River*. Washington, 1903.

Kerby, Robert L. *Kirby Smith's Confederacy; the Trans-Mississippi South, 1863–1865*. New York: Columbia University Press, 1972.

Kerwood, Asbury L. *Annals of the Fifty-Seventh Regiment Indiana Volunteers: Marches, Battles, and Incidents of Army Life*. Dayton, OH: O.W.J. Shuey, 1868.

Kinnear, John R. *History of the Eighty-Sixth Regiment, Illinois Volunteer Infantry, during Its Term of Service*. Chicago: Tribune, 1866.

Kinsley, Philip. *The Chicago Tribune, Its First Hundred Years*. New York: Knopf, 1943.

Kiper, Richard L. *Major General John Alexander McClernand: Politician in Uniform*. Kent, OH: Kent State University Press, 1999.

Kirkman, Paul. *The Battle of Westport: Missouri's Great Confederate Raid*. Charleston, SC: History Press, 2011.

Kitchens, Ben Earl. *Rosecrans Meets Price: The Battle of Iuka, Mississippi*. Florence, AL: Thornwood Book, 1987.

Klement, Frank L. *Dark Lanterns: Secret Polit. Societies, Conspiracies, and Treason Trials in the Civil War*. Baton Rouge: Louisiana State University Press, 1984.

———. "General John B. Floyd and the West Virginia Campaign of 1861." *West Virginia History* 8 (1947): 319–33.

Kniffen, Gilbert C. "Army of the Cumberland and the Battle of Stone's River." In *District of Columbia Military Order of the Loyal Legion of the United States War Papers*, vol. 4. Washington, DC.

———. "The East Tennessee Campaign." In *Campaigns in Kentucky and Tennessee Including the Battle of Chickamauga, 1862–1864*, vol. 7. Boston: Military Historical Society of Massachusetts, 1908.

———. "Major-General William Starke Rosecrans, U.S. Army." In *District of Columbia, Military Order of the Loyal Legion of the United States War Papers*, vol. 4. Washington, DC, 1908.

———. "The Third Day at Stone's River." In *District of Columbia, Military Order of the Loyal Legion of the United States War Papers*, vol. 3. Washington, DC.

Korn, Jerry. *The Fight for Chattanooga: Chickamauga to Missionary Ridge*. Alexandria, VA: Time-Life Books, 1985.

Körner, Gustav Philipp, and Thomas J. McCormack. *Memoirs of Gustave Koerner, 1809–1896: Life-Sketches Written at the Suggestion of His Children*, vol. 2. Cedar Rapids, IA: Torch Press, 1909.

Lamers, William M. *The Edge of Glory: A Biography of General William S. Rosecrans, U.S.A.* Baton Rouge, LA: Louisiana State University Press, 1999.

Langsdorf, Edgar. "Price's Raid and the Battle of Mine Creek." *Kansas Historical Quarterly* 30 (Autumn 1964): 281–306.

Le Duc, William G. "The Little Steamboat That Opened the 'Cracker Line.'" In *Battles and Leaders of the Civil War*, ed. Robert U. Johnson and Clarence C. Buel, vol. 3, 676–78. New York: Century, 1884, 1888.

Le Duc, William Gates, and Adam Scher. *This Business of War: The Recollections of a Civil War Quartermaster*. St. Paul: Minnesota Historical Society Press, 2004.

Lee, Dan. *Kentuckian in Blue: A Biography of Major General Lovell Harrison Rousseau*. Jefferson, NC: McFarland, 2010.

———. *Thomas J. Wood: A Biography of the Union General in the Civil War*. Jefferson, NC: McFarland, 2012.

Lee, Robert E., and Robert E. Lee. *Recollections and Letters of General Robert E. Lee*. New York: Doubleday, Page & Co., 1904.

Leech, Margaret. *Reveille in Washington, 1860–1865*. New York: Harper & Brothers, 1941.

Leech, Margaret, and Harry James Brown. *The Garfield Orbit*. New York: Harper & Row, 1978.

Lesser, W. Hunter. *Rebels at the Gate: Lee and McClellan on the Front Line of a Nation Divided*. Naperville, IL: Sourcebooks, 2004.

Lewis, Lloyd. *Sherman, Fighting Prophet*. New York: Harcourt, Brace & Co., 1932.

Lincoln, Abraham, and Roy P. Basler. *The Collected Works of Abraham Lincoln*. New Brunswick, NJ: Rutgers University Press, 1953.

Lincoln, Abraham, John G. Nicolay, and John Hay. *Complete Works: Comprising His Speeches, Letters, State Papers, and Miscellaneous Writings*. New York: Century, 1894.

Livermore, Thomas Leonard. *Numbers & Losses in the Civil War in America: 1861–65*. Bloomington: Indiana University Press, 1957.

Lomax, John B. *Thomas Lomax and His Descendants*. Menlo Park, CA: J.B. Lomax, 1995.

Long, E.B. "John A. Rawlins; Staff Officer Par Excellence." *Civil War Times Illustrated* 27 (January 1974).

Longstreet, James. *From Manassas to Appomattox: Memoirs of the Civil War in America*. Philadelphia, PA: J.B. Lippincott & Co., 1896.

Lowry, Terry. *September Blood: The Battle of Carnifex Ferry*. Charleston, WV: Pictorial Histories Publishing, 1985.

Maihafer, Harry J. *The General and the Journalists: Ulysses S. Grant, Horace Greeley, and Charles Dana*. Washington: Brassey's, 1998.

Mallam, William D. "The Grant-Butler Relationship." *Mississippi Valley Historical Review* 41, no. 2 (1954): 259–76.

Manville, Craig J. *Limits of Obedience: Brigadier General Thomas J. Wood's Performance during the Battle of Chickamauga*. Diss., Army Command and General Staff College Fort Leavenworth, KS, 2005.

Marks, Solon. "Experiences at the Battle of Stone River." In *War Papers Read before the Commandery of the State of Wisconsin*, vol.

2. Milwaukee, WI: Burdick, Armitage & Allen, 1903.

Marszalek, John F. *Sherman's Other War: The General and the Civil War Press*. Memphis, TN: Memphis State University Press, 1981.

Marvel, William. *Burnside*. Chapel Hill: University of North Carolina Press, 1991.

Maslowski, Peter. *Treason Must Be Made Odious: Military Occupation and Wartime Reconstruction in Nashville, Tennessee, 1862–65*. Millwood, NY: KTO Press, 1978.

Maury, Dabney. "Grant's Campaign in North Mississippi." *Southern Magazine* 13 (1873): 410–17.

_____. "Recollections of Campaign against Grant in North Mississippi 1862–1863." *Southern Historical Society Papers* 13 (1885): 285–310.

McClay, J.H. "Defense of Robinette." In *War Sketches and Incidents: Papers Read by Companions of the Commandery of the State of Nebraska, Military Order of the Loyal Legion of the United States*, vol. 1. Omaha, NE: Burkley Print, 1902.

McCord, William R. "Battle of Corinth; The Campaign Preceding and Leading up to This Battle and Its Results." In *Glimpses of the Nation's Struggle: Commandery of the Military Order of the Loyal Legion of the United States*, vol. 4. St. Paul, MN, 1887.

McCormick, Robert Rutherford. *Ulysses S. Grant, the Great Soldier of America*. New York: D. Appleton-Century, 1934.

McDonough, James L. *Chattanooga: A Death Grip on the Confederacy*. Knoxville, TN: University of Tennessee Press, 1984.

_____. *Stones River: Bloody Winter in Tennessee*. Knoxville: University of Tennessee Press, 1980.

McFeely, William S. *Grant: A Biography*. New York: Norton, 1981.

McKinney, Francis F. *Education in Violence*. Detroit, MI: Wayne State University Press, 1961.

McKinney, Tim. *Robert E. Lee and the 35th Star*. Charleston, WV: Pictorial Histories Publishing, 1993.

_____. *Robert E. Lee at Sewell Mountain: The West Virginia Campaign*. Charleston, WV: Pictorial Histories Publishing, 1990.

McMaster, S.W. *60 Years on the Upper Mississippi: My Life and Experiences*. Rock Island, IL, 1893.

McPherson, James M. *Battle Cry of Freedom: The Civil War Era*. New York: Oxford University Press, 1988.

McWhiney, Grady. *Braxton Bragg and Confederate Defeat*. New York, NY: Columbia University Press, 1969.

Merrill, Louis T. "General Benjamin F. Butler in the Presidential Campaign of 1864." *Mississippi Valley Historical Review* 33 (1947): 537–70.

Meyers, Christopher C. *Union General John A. McClernand and the Politics of Command*. Jefferson, NC: McFarland, 2010.

Michie, Peter S. *The Life and Letters of Emory Upton, Colonel of the Fourth Regiment of Artillery, and Brevet Major-General, U.S. Army*. New York: D. Appleton & Co., 1895.

Monnett, Howard N., and John H. Monnett. *Action before Westport, 1864* Niwot, CO: University Press of Colorado, 1995.

Morelock, Jerry D. "Ride to the River of Death: Cavalry Operations in the Chickamauga Campaign." *Military Review* 64, no. 10 (1984): 2–21.

Morgan, W.A. "Brown's Ferry." In *War Talks in Kansas: Kansas Commandery of the Military Order of the Loyal Legion of the United States*, vol. 1. Kansas City, MO: Franklin Hudson Publishing, 1906.

Morris, Andrew N. *Forgotten Decisiveness: The Middle Tennessee Campaign of 1863*. Diss., University of Kansas, 1996.

Moyer, Mrs. C. *Journal and Letters of Franklin F. Moyer*. Delta, OH: C. Moyers, 1865.

Mulhane, L.W. *Memorial of Major-General William Stark Rosecrans*. Columbus, OH: Columbian Printing, 1898.

Neil, Henry Moore. *A Battery at Close Quarters*. Columbus, OH, 1909.

Nelson, Larry E. "Black Leaders and the Presidential Election of 1864." *Journal of Negro History* 63, no. 1 (January 1978): 42–58.

Nelson, Russell K. *The Early Life and Congressional Career of Elihu B. Washburne*. Diss., University of North Dakota, 1953.

Nevins, Allan. *The War for the Union*. 4 vols. New York: Scribner, 1960.

Newell, Clayton R. *Lee vs. McClellan: The First Campaign*. Washington, DC: Regnery Publishing, 1996.

Newlin, W.H. *A History of the Seventy-Third Regiment of Illinois Infantry Volunteers: Its Services and Experiences in Camp, on the March, on the Picket and Skirmish Lines, and in Many Battles of the War, 1861–65*. [Illinois?]: Published by Authority of the Regimental Reunion Association of Survivors of the 73d Illinois Infantry Volunteers, 1890.

Nicolay, John G., and John Hay. *Abraham Lincoln: A History*. 10 vols. New York: Century, 1890.

Ninety-Second Illinois Volunteers. Freeport, IL: Journal Steam Publishing, 1875.

O'Brien, Frank M. "The Story of the Sun." *Munsey's Magazine*, October 1917, 129–41.

Opdycke, Emerson, Glenn Longacre, and John E. Haas. *To Battle for God and the Right: The Civil War Letterbooks of Emerson Opdycke*. Urbana: University of Illinois Press, 2003.

Palmer, John M. *Personal Recollections of John M. Palmer the Story of an Earnest Life*. Cincinnati, OH: R. Clarke & Co., 1901.

Parkhurst, J.G. "Recollections of Stone's River." In *War Papers: Read Before the Commandery of the State of Michigan Military Order of the Loyal Legion of the United States*, vol. 1. Detroit, MI: Winn & Hammond Press, 1893.

Parks, Joseph Howard. *General Leonidas Polk, C.S.A., the Fighting Bishop*. Baton Rouge: Louisiana State University Press, 1962.

Parrish, William E. *Turbulent Partnership: Missouri and the Union, 1861–1865*. Columbia: University of Missouri Press, 1963.

Patrick, Marsena Rudolph, and David S. Sparks. *Inside Lincoln's Army; the Diary of Marsena Rudolph Patrick, Provost Marshall General, Army of the Potomac*. New York: T. Yoseloff, 1964.

Payne, James E. "The Sixth Missouri at Corinth." *Confederate Veteran* 36, no. 12 (December 1928): 462–65.

Peskin, Allan. *Garfield: A Biography*. Kent, OH: Kent State University Press, 1999.

Peterson, Cyrus A., and Joseph Mills Hanson. *Pilot Knob: The Thermopylae of the West*. Independence, MO: Two Trails Publishing, 2000.

Piatt, Donn, Henry V. Boynton, and George H. Thomas. *General George H. Thomas: A Critical Biography by Donn Piatt, with Concluding Chapters by Henry V. Boynton*. Cincinnati, OH: R. Clarke & Co., 1893.

Pittman, Walter E. "Tullahoma: Terrain and Tactics in the American Civil War." In *Fields of Battle: Terrain in Military History*, ed. Peter Doyle and Matthew R. Bennett. Norwell, MA: Kluwer Academic, 2002.

Pletcher, David M. "General William S. Rosecrans and the Mexican Transcontinental Railroad Project." *Mississippi Valley Historical Review* 38, no. 4 (1952): 657–78.

———. *Rails, Mines, and Progress: Seven American Promoters in Mexico, 1867–1911*. Ithaca, NY: Cornell University Press, 1958.

Plummer, Mark. "Missouri and Kansas and the Capture of General Marmaduke." *Missouri Historical Review* 59, no. 1 (October 1964): 90–104.

Poland, Charles Preston. *The Glories of War*. Bloomington, IN: AuthorHouse, 2004.

Pollard, Edward Alfred. *Southern History of the War: The First Year of the War*. New York: C.B. Richardson, 1863.

Powell, David A. *Failure in the Saddle: Nathan Bedford Forrest, Joseph Wheeler, and the Confederate Cavalry in the Chickamauga Campaign*. New York: Savas Beatie, 2011.

Price, Samuel W. "The Cracker Line." In *War Papers: Commandery of the District of Columbia, Military Order of the Loyal Legion of the United States*, vol. 3. Washington, DC, 1907.

Quintard, C.T., and Arthur Howard Noll. *Doctor Quintard, Chaplain C.S.A. and Second Bishop of Tennessee, Being His Story of the War (1861–1865)*. Sewanee, TN: University Press, 1905.

Reed, Rowena. *Combined Operations in the Civil War*. Annapolis, MD: Naval Institute Press, 1978.

Reid, Harvey, and Frank L. Byrne. *The View from Headquarters; Civil War Letters of Harvey Reid*. Madison: State Historical Society of Wisconsin, 1965.

Reid, Harvey, Frank L. Byrne, and William H. McIntosh. *Uncommon Soldiers: Harvey Reid and the 22nd Wisconsin March with Sherman*. Knoxville: University of Tennessee Press, 2001.

Reid, Whitelaw. *Ohio in the War: Her Statesmen, Her Generals, and Soldiers*. Cincinnati, OH: Moore, Wilstach & Baldwin, 1868.

Report of the Adjutant General of the State of Kansas, 1861–'65. Topeka: Kansas State Printing, 1896.

Richards, William J. "Rosecrans and the Chickamauga Campaign." In *War Papers: Read before the Indiana Commandery, Military Order of the Loyal Legion of the United States*. Published by the Commandery, 1898.

Richardson, Robert D. *Rosecrans' Staff at Chickamauga: The Significance of Major General William S. Rosecrans' Staff on the*

Outcome of the Chickamauga Campaign. Diss., U.S. Army Command and General Staff College, Fort Leavenworth, KS.

Riddle, A.G. *Recollections of War Time: Reminiscences of Men and Events in Washington, 1860–1865.* New York: G.P. Putnam's Sons, 1895.

Riddle, Thomas J. "Reminiscences of Floyd's Operations in West Virginia in 1861." *Southern Historical Society Papers* 11 (1883).

Robertson, William G. "The Armies Collide." *Blue and Gray,* Fall 2007.

_____. "The Battle of Chickamauga Day 1." *Blue and Gray,* Spring 2008.

_____. "The Battle of Chickamauga Day 2." *Blue and Gray,* Summer 2008.

_____. "Bragg's Lost Opportunity." *Blue and Gray,* Spring 2007.

_____. "The Fall of Chattanooga." *Blue and Gray,* November/December 2006.

Rogers, J.B. *War Pictures: Experiences and Observations of a Chaplain.* Chicago: Church & Goodman, 1863.

Rosebault, Charles J. *When Dana Was the Sun: A Story of Personal Journalism.* New York: R.M. McBride, 1931.

Rosecrans, William S. "The Battle of Corinth." In *Battles and Leaders of the Civil War,* ed. Robert U. Johnson and Clarence C. Buel, vol. 2, 737–56. New York: Century, 1887.

_____. "The Campaign for Chattanooga." *The Century* 34 (1887): 129–35.

_____. "Mistakes of Grant." *North American Review* 141 (July 1885): 580–99.

Rosenkrans, Allen. *The Rosenkrans Family in Europe and America.* Newton, NJ: New Jersey Herald Press, 1900.

Rubenstein, David A. *A Study of the Medical Support to the Union and Confederate Armies during the Battle of Chickamauga.* Diss., U.S. Army Command and General Staff College, Fort Leavenworth, KS, 1990.

Sanborn, John B. "Battles and Campaigns of September, 1862." In *Glimpses of the Nation's Struggle: Minnesota Commandery of the Military Order of the Loyal Legion of the United States,* vol. 5. St. Paul, MN: Review Publishing, 1903.

Schalk, Emil. *Campaigns of 1862 and 1863, Illustrating the Principles of Strategy.* Philadelphia, PA: J.B. Lippincott & Co., 1863.

Scott, William F. "The Last Fight for Missouri." In *Personal Recollections of the War of the Rebellion: Commandery of the State of New York, Military Order of the Loyal Legion of the United States,* vol. 3. New York: J.J. Little & Co., 1907.

_____. *The Story of a Cavalry Regiment: The Career of the Fourth Iowa Veteran Volunteers from Kansas to Georgia, 1861–1865.* New York: G.P. Putnam's Sons, 1893.

Scribner, B.F. *How Soldiers Were Made; or, The War as I Saw It under Buell, Rosecrans, Thomas, Grant and Sherman.* New Albany, IN: Donohue & Henneberry, 1887.

Serratt, John H. "Some Corrections of Grant's Memoirs as Regards General George H. Thomas." In *Military Essays and Recollections: Commandery of the State of Illinois, Military Order of the Loyal Legion of the United States,* vol. 2. Chicago: A.C. McClurg & Co., 1894.

Shaffer, Dallas B. "Rich Mountain Revisited." *West Virginia History* 28, no. 1 (1966): 16–34.

Shalhope, Robert E. *Sterling Price: Portrait of a Southerner.* Columbia: University of Missouri Press, 1971.

Shanks, William Franklin Gore. *Personal Recollections of Distinguished Generals, by William F.G. Shanks.* New York: Harper, 1866.

Sheridan, Philip Henry. *Personal Memoirs.* New York: Webster, 1888.

Sherman, Francis Trowbridge, and C. Knight Aldrich. *Quest for a Star: The Civil War Letters and Diaries of Colonel Francis T. Sherman of the 88th Illinois.* Knoxville: University of Tennessee Press, 1999.

Sherman, William T. *Memoirs of General William T. Sherman.* New York: D. Appleton & Co., 1875.

Sherman, William T., and James Gillespie Blaine. *Memoirs of Gen. W.T. Sherman.* Vols. 1 and 2. New York: C.L. Webster & Co., 1891.

Shiman, Philip L. "Engineering and Command: The Case of General William S. Rosecrans, 1862–1863." In *The Art of Command in the Civil War,* 84–117. Lincoln: University of Nebraska Press, 1998.

Simmons, Louis A. *The History of the 84th Reg't Ill.* Macomb, IL: Hampton Bros., 1866.

Simon, John Y. "From Galena to Appomattox: Grant and Washburne." *Journal of the Illinois State Historical Society* 58, no. 2 (1965): 165–89.

Sligh, Charles R. *History of the Services of the First Regiment Michigan Engineers and Mechanics, during the Civil War, 1861–1865.* Grand Rapids, MI, 1921.

Smith, Albert E. "A Few Days with the Eighth Regiment Wisconsin Volunteers, at Iuka and Corinth." In *War Papers Read before the Commandery of the State of Wisconsin,* vol. 4. Milwaukee, WI: Burdick & Allen, 1914.

Smith, Charles H. *The History of Fuller's Ohio Brigade, 1861–1865: Its Great March, with Roster, Portraits, Battle Maps and Biographies.* Cleveland, OH: A.J. Watt, 1909.

Smith, Theodore Clarke. *The Life and Letters of James Abram Garfield, 1877–1882.* Vols. 1 and 2. New Haven, CT: Yale University Press, 1925.

Smith, Timothy B. *A Chickamauga Memorial: The Establishment of America's First Civil War National Military Park.* Knoxville: University of Tennessee Press, 2009.

_____. *Corinth 1862: Siege, Battle, Occupation.* Lawrence: University Press of Kansas, 2012.

_____. *The Golden Age of Battlefield Preservation: The Decade of the 1890s and the Establishment of America's First Five Military Parks.* Knoxville: University of Tennessee Press, 2008.xxx

_____. "Henry Van Ness Boynton and Chickamauga." In *The Chickamauga Campaign,* ed. Stephen E. Woodworth, 165–87. Carbondale: Southern Illinois University Press, 2010.

Smith, William E., and Ophia D. Smith. *Colonel A.W. Gilbert: Citizen-Soldier of Cincinnati.* Whitefish, MT: Kessinger Publishing, 2008.

Smith, William Farrar. *From Chattanooga to Petersburg under Generals Grant and Butler: A Contribution to the History of the War, and a Personal Vindication.* Boston: Houghton Mifflin, 1893.

Snead, Thomas L. "With Price East of the Mississippi." In *Battles and Leaders of the Civil War,* ed. Robert U. Johnson and Clarence C. Buel, vol. 2, 717–33. New York: Century, 1887.

Society of the Army of the Cumberland. *Reunion of the Army of the Cumberland.*

Speed, Thos, Alfred Pirtle, and R.M. Kelly. *The Union Regiments of Kentucky.* Louisville, KY: Courier-Journal, 1897.

Spruill, Matt, and Lee Spruill. *Winter Lightning: A Guide to the Battle of Stones River.* Knoxville: University of Tennessee Press, 2007.

Squier, George W., Julie A. Doyle, John David Smith, and Richard M. McMurry. *This Wilderness of War: The Civil War Letters of George W. Squier, Hoosier Volunteer.* Knoxville, TN: University of Tennessee Press, 1998.

Stanley, David S. "The Battle of Corinth." In *Personal Recollections of the War of the Rebellion: Commandery of the State of New York, Military Order of the Loyal Legion of the United States,* vol. 2. New York: G.P. Putnam's Sons, 1897.

_____. *Personal Memoirs of Major-General D.S. Stanley, U.S.A.* Cambridge, MA: Harvard University Press, 1917.

_____. "The Tullahoma Campaign." In *Sketches of War History, 1861–1865: Ohio Commandery of the Military Order of the Loyal Legion of the United States,* vol. 3. Cincinnati, OH: R. Clarke & Co., 1890.

Starr, Louis M. *Bohemian Brigade: Civil War Newsmen in Action.* New York: Knopf, 1954.

Starr, Stephen Z. *Jennison's Jayhawkers; a Civil War Cavalry Regiment and Its Commander.* Baton Rouge, LA: Louisiana State University Press, 1974.

_____. *The Union Cavalry in the Civil War: The War in the West, 1861–1865.* Vol. 3. Baton Rouge: Louisiana State University, 1985.

Stebbins, Austin. "A Daring Movement." *National Tribune,* October 19, 1899.

Steele, Janet E. *The Sun Shines for All: Journalism and Ideology in the Life of Charles A. Dana.* Syracuse, NY: Syracuse University Press, 1993.

Stevenson, Alexander F. *The Battle of Stone's River near Murfreesboro, Tenn., December 30, 1862, to January 3, 1863.* Boston: J.R. Osgood & Co., 1884.

Stevenson, Thomas M. *History of the 78th Regiment O.V.V.I.* Zanesville, OH: H. Dunne, 1865.

Stewart, William S. "William S. Stewart Letters." *Missouri Historical Review* 61, no. 4 (July 1967): 463–88.

Strayer, Larry M., and Richard A. Baumgartner. *Echoes of Battle: The Struggle for Chattanooga: An Illustrated Collection of Union and Confederate Narratives.* Huntington, WV: Blue Acorn Press, 1996.

Strevey, Tracy Elmer. *Joseph Medill and the Chicago Tribune during the Civil War Period.* Diss., University of Chicago, 1930.

Stuart, Addison A. *Iowa Colonels and Regi-*

ments: *Being a History of Iowa Regiments in the War of the Rebellion; and Containing a Description of the Battles in Which They Have Fought.* Des Moines, IA: Mills & Co., 1865.

Styple, William B. *Generals in Bronze: Interviewing the Commanders of the Civil War.* Kearny, NJ: Belle Grove Publishing, 2005.

Summers, Festus P. *The Baltimore and Ohio in the Civil War.* New York: G.P. Putnam's Sons, 1939.

Sunderland, Glenn W. *Lightning at Hoover's Gap; the Story of Wilder's Brigade.* New York, NY: T. Yoseloff, 1969.

Swinton, William. *The Twelve Decisive Battles of the War; a History of the Eastern and Western Campaigns, in Relation to the Actions That Decided Their Issue.* New York: Dick & Fitzgerald, 1867.

Sword, Wiley. *Mountains Touched with Fire: Chattanooga Besieged 1863.* New York: St. Martin's Press, 1995.

Tarbell, Ida M. *Abraham Lincoln.* Vols. 1 and 2. New York: S.S. McClure, 1895.

Thomas, Joseph W. "Campaigns of Generals McClellan and Rosecrans in Western Virginia, 1861–1862." *West Virginia History Magazine* 5, no. 4 (1944): 245–308.

Thomas, Wilbur D. *General George H. Thomas, the Indomitable Warrior, Supreme in Defense and in Counter-attack; a Biography.* New York: Exposition Press, 1964.

Thompson, Edwin Porter. *History of the Orphan Brigade.* Louisville, KY: L.N. Thompson, 1898.

Thurston, Gates P. "Personal Recollections of the Battle in the Rear at Stone's River, Tennessee." In *Sketches of War History: Ohio Commandery of the Military Order of the Loyal Legion of the United States*, vol. 6. Cincinnati: R. Clarke & Co., 1896.

Tompkins, Ella W. "The Colonel's Lady: Some Letters of Ellen Wilkins Tompkins, July–December 1861." *Virginia Magazine of History and Biography* 69 (1961): 387–419.

Tourgee, Albion Winegar. *The Story of a Thousand: Being a History of the Service of the 105th Ohio Volunteer Infantry, in the War for the Union from August 21, 1862 to June 6, 1865.* Buffalo, NY: S. McGerald & Son, 1896.

Tucker, Glen. *Chickamauga: Bloody Battle in the West.* Indianapolis, IN: Bobbs-Merrill, 1961.

Tucker, Phillip Thomas. *Westerners in Gray: The Men and Missions of the Elite Fifth Missouri Infantry Regiment.* Jefferson, NC: McFarland, 1994.

Turchin, John Basil. *Chickamauga.* Chicago, IL: Fergus Printing, 1888.

United States Congress, Joint Committee on the Conduct of the War. *Report of the Joint Committee on the Conduct of the War at the Second Session, Thirty-Eighth Congress*, vol. 3. Washington, DC: Government Printing Office, 1865.

United States Military Academy, Association of Graduates. *Twenty-Seventh Annual Reunion.* Saginaw, 1896.

U.S. War Department. *Report of a Board of Army Officers upon the Claim of Maj. Gen. William Farrar Smith U.S.V., That He and Not General Rosecrans, Originated the Plan for the Relief of Chattanooga in October, 1863.* Washington, DC: Government Printing Office, 1901.

_____. *The War of the Rebellion: A Compilation of the Official Records of the Union and Confederate Armies.* 128 vols. Washington, DC, 1880–1902.

Vale, Joseph G. *Minty and the Cavalry: A History of Cavalry Campaigns in the Western Armies.* Harrisburg, PA: E.K. Meyers, 1886.

Van, Horne Thomas B. *The Life of Major-General George H. Thomas.* New York: C. Scribner's Sons, 1882.

Vance, Wilson J. *Stone's River, the Turning-Point of the Civil War.* New York: Neale Publishing, 1914.

Villard, Henry. *Memoirs of Henry Villard, Journalist and Financier, 1835–1900.* Boston: Houghton, Mifflin & Co., 1904.

"Vivid War Experiences at Ripley, Miss." *Confederate Veteran* 13, no. 6 (June 1905): 262–65.

Washburne, E.B., and Michael Hill. *Elihu Washburne: The Diary and Letters of America's Minister to France during the Siege and Commune of Paris.* New York: Simon & Schuster, 2012.

Washburne, Mark. *A Biography of Elihu Benjamin Washburne: Congressman, Secretary of State, Envoy Extraordinary.* Philadelphia, PA: Xlibris, 2000.

Waterman, Arba N. "The Battle of Chickamauga." In *Military Essays and Recollections: Papers Read before the Commandery of the State of Illinois, Military Order of the Loyal Legion of the United States*, vol. 1. Chicago: A.C. McClurg & Co., 1891.

Welles, Gideon, and Howard K. Beale. *Diary of Gideon Welles; Ed. and with an Introd. by Howard K. Beale; with the Assistance of Alan W. Brownsword.* New York: Norton, 1960.

Welles, Gideon, and Edgar Thaddeus Welles. *Diary of Gideon Welles, Secretary of the Navy under Lincoln and Johnson.* Boston: Houghton Mifflin, 1911.

West, Grenville C. "Personal Recollections of the Chickamauga Campaign." In *War Papers: Commandery of the District of Columbia, Military Order of the Loyal Legion of the United States,* vol. 4. Washington, DC.

Wilder, John T. "The Battle of Hoover's Gap." In *Sketches of War History, 1861–1865 Ohio: Commandery of the Military Order of the Loyal Legion of the United States,* vol. 6. Cincinnati, OH: Monfort & Co., 1908.

_____. "Preliminary Movements of the Army of the Cumberland before the Battle of Chickamauga." In *Sketches of War History, 1861–1865: Ohio Commandery of the Military Order of the Loyal Legion of the United States,* vol. 7. Cincinnati, OH: R. Clark, 1888.

Williams, Kenneth P. *Lincoln Finds a General; a Military Study of the Civil War.* 5 vols. New York: Macmillan, 1949–1959.

Williams, Samuel Cole. *General John T. Wilder, Commander of the Lightning Brigade.* Bloomington: Indiana University Press, 1936.

Wilson, George S. "Wilder's Brigade of Mounted Infantry." In *War Talks in Kansas: Kansas Commandery of the Military Order of the Loyal Legion of the United States.* Kansas City, MO: Franklin Hudson Publishing, 1906.

Wilson, James Harrison. *The Life of John A. Rawlins, Lawyer, Assistant Adjutant-General, Chief of Staff, Major General of Volunteers, and Secretary of War.* New York: Neale Publishing, 1916.

_____. *Under the Old Flag; Recollections of Military Operations in the War for the Union, the Spanish War, the Boxer Rebellion, Etc.* Vols. 1 and 2. New York: D. Appleton & Co., 1912.

Winders, Richard Bruce. *Mr. Polk's Army: The American Military Experience in the Mexican War.* College Station: Texas A&M University Press, 1997.

Wood, Thomas J. "The Battle of Missionary Ridge." In *Sketches of War History, 1861–1865: The Ohio Commandery of the Military Order of the Loyal Legion of the United States,* vol. 4. Cincinnati, OH: R. Clarke & Co., 1896.

_____. "The Gaps at Chickamauga." *New York Times,* November 19, 1882.

Woodcock, Marcus, and Kenneth W. Noe. *A Southern Boy in Blue: The Memoir of Marcus Woodcock, 9th Kentucky Infantry (U.S.A.).* Knoxville: University of Tennessee Press, 1996.

Woodworth, Steven E. *Nothing but Victory: The Army of the Tennessee, 1861–1865.* New York: Knopf, 2005.

_____. *Six Armies in Tennessee: The Chickamauga and Chattanooga Campaigns.* Lincoln: University of Nebraska Press, 1998.

Worsham, W.J., and C.W. Heiskell. *Old Nineteenth Tennessee Regiment, C.S.A. June, 1861–April, L865.* Knoxville, TN: Press of Paragon Printing Co., 1902.

Yaryan, John L. "Stone River." In *War Papers: Read before the Indiana Commandery, Military Order of the Loyal Legion of the United States.* 1898.

Young, Lot D. *Reminiscences of a Soldier of the Orphan Brigade.* Louisville, KY: Courier-Journal, 1918.

Zinn, Jack. *The Battle of Rich Mountain.* Parsons, WV: McClain Printing Co., 1971.

_____. *R.E. Lee's Cheat Mountain Campaign.* Parsons, WV: McClain Printing Co., 1974.

Zornow, William Frank. *The Union Party Convention at Baltimore in 1864.* Baltimore, MD, 1950.

Newspapers

Brooklyn Eagle
Chicago Tribune
Cincinnati Times
Congressional Globe
Harper's Weekly
London Times
Los Angeles Times
National Anti-Slavery Standard (New York)
National Tribune (Washington, DC)
New York Herald
New York Times
New York Tribune
Ohio State Journal
Richmond Examiner

Index

African Americans 8, 25, 27, 38, 40, 41, 74, 81, 153, 189–190
Alexander's Bridge 106
Alford, Julian D. 90
Anderson, Robert 52, 53, 185
Andrew, John 92
Antietam 27, 30, 34, 52, 72, 82, 185
Atkins, Smith D. 122
Atlanta, Georgia 1, 76, 89, 90, 100, 103, 104, 144, 196

Baird, Absalom 106, 107, 109, 111, 112
Baltimore and Ohio Railroad 10, 11, 21, 22
Baltimore Convention 154, 166, 174, 175, 177, 178
Banks, Nathaniel 21, 99, 137, 173, 182
Beatty, John 13, 63, 65, 76, 77, 112, 192
Beatty, Sam 63, 65, 69
Beauregard, Pierre 23, 24, 40, 190
Benham, Henry 15, 16, 18, 20
Bennett, Lyman 129, 141
Beverly, West Virginia 11, 13
Bickham, William 79
Big Blue River 159
Blunt, James 158, 159
Bond, Frank 113, 114, 118, 134, 140
Boonville, Missouri 158
Boyd, Cyrus 42, 43
Boynton, Henry V. 3, 145, 186, 187, 194, 205, 208
Bradley, Michael 90
Bragg, Braxton 23, 24, 27, 37, 45, 46, 52, 56, 58, 59, 60, 61, 62, 63, 65, 66, 67, 68, 69, 70, 73, 82, 83, 84, 85, 86, 88, 89, 90, 91, 92, 93, 94, 95, 96, 97, 98, 100, 101, 103, 104, 105, 106, 107, 109, 110, 111, 112, 114, 122, 123, 124, 130, 131, 132, 145, 197
Bragg, Elise 142
Breckinridge, John C. 56, 60, 61, 62, 63, 65, 69, 70, 84, 85, 98, 112
Brewer, Richard 89
Bridgeport, Alabama 92, 96, 98, 101, 124, 125, 126, 127, 128, 129, 131, 132, 133, 134, 138, 139, 140
Briedenthal, Henry 66
British Parliament 57, 58
Brooklyn Eagle 148
Brooks, Noah 72

Brown's Ferry 134, 139, 140
Bryam's Ford 159
Bryner, John 43
Buckner, Simon B. 82, 98, 101, 103, 145
Buell, Don Carlos 6, 20, 23, 24, 27, 28, 29, 37, 49, 52, 53, 55, 56, 75, 77, 93, 182
Bull Run 14, 27, 81, 120, 121, 122, 170, 182, 185; *see also* Manassas
Burnside, Ambrose 58, 82, 83, 96, 98, 100, 101, 103, 104, 106, 107, 119, 120, 121, 126, 161, 168, 182
Butler, Benjamin 152, 161, 173, 174, 177, 178, 183, 184
Byers, S.M.H. 47, 48

Cairo, IL 137, 167, 168
California 13, 165, 188, 190, 192, 205
Camp Chase 10
Camp Dennison 10, 197
Carlin, William 61, 128
Carnifex Ferry 15, 22, 193
Castel, Albert 3, 159
Charcoals 151
Chase, Salmon P. 10, 77, 97, 125, 163, 164, 165, 166, 168, 173, 182
Chattanooga, Tennessee 1, 3, 24, 27, 52, 55, 56, 73, 75, 83, 88, 89, 91, 92, 94, 96–101, 103, 104, 105, 106, 109, 110, 111, 113, 118, 119, 121–135, 137–145, 147, 148, 149, 165, 168, 184, 186, 194, 196, 197, 202, 203, 205, 207
Cheat Mountain 14, 17
Cheatham, Benjamin 60, 61, 63, 98, 109, 110, 112
Chester, Dean 117
Chicago Convention 1864 175, 177
Chicago Times 153
Chicago Tribune 51, 149, 162, 172, 176
Chickamauga (Battle) 1, 2, 60, 102, 107, 108, 110, 111, 112, 114, 120, 122, 123, 124, 141, 142, 143, 144, 145; "Fatal Gap" 113–116
Chickamauga Battlefield Park 187, 192
Chickasaw Bayou 58, 72, 183
Christie, Thomas 34
Cincinnati, Ohio 9, 10, 16, 27, 49, 70, 96, 160, 193, 197
Cincinnati Commercial 35
Cincinnati Gazette 186
Cist, Henry 112

Claybanks 151
Cleburne, Patrick 60, 61, 63, 65, 85, 86, 88, 98, 105, 110, 112, 143
Cleveland, Grover 191
Cold Harbor 161, 178
Connolly, James 146
Copperheads 149
Corinth, Mississippi 2, 23, 24, 25, 27, 29, 34, 37, 38, 39, 40, 41, 42, 43, 44, 45, 46, 47, 48, 49, 50, 51, 52, 55, 99, 107, 179, 186, 194, 195, 196, 202, 203, 205, 207
Cotton Hill 20
Cox, Jacob D. 14, 15, 17, 18, 20, 118
Cozzens, Peter 143, 145
Cracker Line, opening of 139–142
Crawfish Springs, Georgia 109, 111
Crittenden, Thomas 53, 59, 60, 61, 62, 68, 69, 73, 86, 87, 88, 90, 100, 101, 103, 105, 106, 109, 111, 114, 119, 127, 148
Crook, George 132
Croxton, John 107
Cummings, Henry 146
Cummins, Edward 41
Curtin, Andrew 92
Curtis, Samuel 38, 151, 152, 158, 159
Cushman, Pauline 88

Davies, Thomas 39, 40, 41, 43
Davis, Jefferson (Confederate president) 9, 24, 46, 58, 68, 85, 98, 124
Davis, Jefferson C. (Union general) 60, 61, 110, 111, 116, 118, 121, 127
Davis Bridge 43, 47
Davis' Crossroads, Georgia 105
De Lagnel, Julius 12, 13
Delaware, Ohio 4, 5, 192
Democratic Party 9, 165, 174–177, 180–182, 189–191; *see also* Chicago Convention
Dennison, William 10
Depew, Chauncy 193
Dickey, Theophilus 31
Dodge, William 116
Doubleday, Abner 6
Dubois, John 34

Early, Jubal 160, 161
Ector, Matthew 65
Emancipation Proclamation 69, 151, 153
Ewing, Thomas 156, 157

Fagan, James 156, 157
Farmington, TN 132, 133
Fay, Edwin 44
Fisher, Horace N. 144, 179
Fitch, John 67
Fletcher, Thomas C. 156
Foote, Andrew H. 179
Ford, Thomas 117
Forrest, Nathan B. 56, 59, 60, 73, 82, 86, 88, 106, 107, 123, 124
Fort Davidson 156, 157

Fort Donelson 38, 48, 56, 82, 170, 172, 179, 182
Fort Henry 56, 170, 179
Fort Monroe 7, 104, 107
Fort Sumter 10, 52, 185
Fortress Rosecrans 75
Foster, John 104, 107
Fox, Perrin V. 131
Fredericksburg, Virginia 58, 72, 82, 126, 161
Freeman, Douglas S. 14
Frémont, John C. 21, 173, 175, 182
Furay, W.S. 142
Fyffe, James 63, 65, 69

Galena, IL 170, 173, 180
Gamble, Hamilton 151
Gardena, California 188
Garesche, Julius P. 56, 61, 66, 67, 78, 79, 80, 191, 194
Garfield, James 77, 78, 80, 82, 83, 97, 113, 114, 118, 119, 120, 128, 154, 163, 164, 165, 166, 168, 178, 197, 198, 200, 201, 209
Garnett, Robert 11, 12, 13
Gauley Bridge 14, 15, 18, 20
Gaw, William 38
General Orders No. 4 (Missouri) 152
General Orders No. 35 (Missouri) 153
Georgetown College (University) 56, 192
Gettysburg 72, 88, 89, 90, 114, 126, 163, 185
Gilbert, A.W. 33
Gilmore, James 81
Gladstone, William 58
Gordon, John B. 144
Granger, Gordon 88, 106, 111, 119, 120, 121, 122, 127, 178, 179
Grant, Jesse 171
Grant, Julia (Mrs. U.S.) 36, 48, 171
Grant, Ulysses 1, 2, 3, 6, 9, 23, 24, 70, 82, 83, 88, 89, 90, 91, 94, 96, 97, 98, 99, 107, 125, 126, 127, 134, 137–141, 143, 144, 145, 146, 147, 149, 152, 159–162, 163, 167, 168, 169, 170–191, 207, 209; at Corinth 39–51; drinking 35–36, 99, 137, 144, 167, 171, 180, 183; at Iuka 27–38; at Missionary Ridge 143, 145; as presidential candidate possibility 173–178, 182–183, 200; and Thomas, George H. 139, 184; Washburne role in career 49, 51, 170–180; *see also* Rosecrans, William S.
Greeley, Horace 81, 166, 173, 199
Green, Martin 41
Griest, Alva 110
Grose, William 69

Hagerman, Edward 144
Haley Trace 131
Halleck Henry 22, 23, 24, 25, 27, 37, 39, 45, 46, 48, 49, 52, 53, 55, 56, 57, 58, 72, 76, 80, 83, 84, 93, 94, 95, 96, 97, 99, 104, 107, 119, 120, 125, 126, 130, 132, 137, 145, 148, 156, 160, 161, 169, 170, 171, 182, 184
Hamilton, Charles 29, 31, 32, 33, 36, 37, 39, 40, 41, 43, 49

Index

Hanson, Roger 69, 70
Hardee, William 56, 59, 60, 63, 70, 85, 86, 88, 98
Harmon, Oscar 129
Harper's Weekly 149
Hart, David 12
Hartsuff, Lucas 21, 82
Hascall, Milo 63, 79
Hay, John 155
Hayes, Rutherford B. 16, 192
Haynie, James 55
Hazen, William 66, 100, 101, 139
Healey, George P.A. 7, 8, 21
Heg, Hans 55, 66, 101, 110
Hebert, Louis 32, 40, 41
Helm, Benjamin 112
Helm, Emilie 112
Henderson, David 41, 193
Herbert, J.K. 174, 177
Heth, Henry 15
Highland Rim 86
Hill, D.H. 98, 105, 143
Hindman, Thomas 98, 105, 116
Hodges, Henry 133
Holden, William 41
Holly Springs, Mississippi 44, 45, 47, 50, 51, 58
Hooker, Joseph 30, 82, 95, 125, 126, 133, 134, 139, 140, 182
Hoover's Gap 86, 87, 88, 106, 144, 197
Horseshoe Ridge 118, 119
Hotel Redondo 192
Hubbard, Lucius 195
Hurlbut, Stephen 38, 43, 44, 46, 47, 48, 49, 126

Imitation of Christ 56
Iuka 2, 28-38, 38, 48, 49, 50, 99, 107, 186, 196, 203

Jackson, H.R. 20
Jackson, John 66
Jackson, Thomas J. (Stonewall) 8, 21, 22,
Jackson, Mississippi 38, 82, 99
Jackson, Tennessee 38, 40, 46
Jacques, James 145
Jay's Mill 107
Jefferson City, Missouri 156, 157, 158
Johnson, Andrew 76, 154, 188
Johnson, Bushrod 65, 106, 107, 109, 116
Johnson, Richard 60, 61, 109, 140
Joint Committee on the Conduct of the War 21, 130, 139, 161
Jones, J. Russell 175
Juarez, Benito 188, 189

Kanawha River (Valley) 14, 15, 17, 18, 20, 22
Kansas City, Missouri 158, 159
Kellogg, Sanford 113
Kelly, James 188
Kirk, Edward 61
Kniffen, Gilbert 68

Knoxville, Tennessee 56, 58, 96, 98, 100, 101, 145
Koerner, Gustave 172

Lagow, Clark 31
Laibold, Bernard 116
Lamers, William 2, 37, 196
Laurel Mountain (Hill) 11, 12, 13
Laws, Evander 109
Le Duc, William 125, 126, 140
Lee, Robert E. 2, 10, 15, 17, 18, 20, 22, 27, 30, 31, 36, 73, 82, 88, 89, 90, 98, 104, 107, 145, 189, 190, 196, 197
Lee and Gordon's Mills 105, 106, 109
Leech, Margaret 22
Liddell, St. John 65, 107, 109
Lieutenant General Bill (1864) 175, 176, 177, 203
Lincoln, Abraham 2, 3, 21, 22, 53, 69, 72, 73, 81, 89, 90, 93, 96, 97, 112, 117, 125, 126, 141, 150, 151, 152, 152, 153, 155, 161, 164, 168, 169, 170, 171, 172, 173, 175, 176, 177, 179, 181, 182, 183, 184, 185, 196, 209
Lincoln, Mary Todd 112
Little Blue River 158
Logan, John A. 46, 160, 184
Lomax, John 40
Longstreet, James A. 6, 30, 98, 107, 111, 114, 116, 117, 118, 119, 120, 122, 123, 130, 145, 190, 193
Lookout Mountain 91, 100, 101, 103, 104, 105, 106, 122, 123, 129, 130, 131, 141, 142, 144, 203
Lookout Valley 106, 130, 131, 133, 134, 135, 139, 140
Loomis, John 61, 63
Loring, William W. 15, 17, 20, 142
Los Angeles, California 192, 193, 196
Louisville, Kentucky 27, 52, 59, 73, 75, 91, 95, 137, 138, 164, 165
Louisville and Nashville Railroad 59
Lovell, Mansfield 40

Mahan, Dennis 6
Manassas, VA 14, 21; *see also* Bull Run
Maney, George 61, 63
Manigault, Arthur 61, 63
Marks, Albert 71
Marmaduke, John 156, 159
Martin, John A. 55
Martin, John D. 32
Marx, Karl 166
Matthews, Stanley 16
Mattison, O.B. 174
Maury, Dabney 32, 40, 50, 196
McArthur, John 34
McCalmont, John 80
McClellan, George B. 10, 11, 12, 13, 14, 21, 22, 27, 31, 78, 161, 170, 171, 182
McClernand, John 50, 182, 183, 184, 185
McCook, Alexander 53, 56, 59, 60, 61, 67, 68,

73, 86, 88, 90, 101, 103, 105, 106, 107, 109, 111, 112, 113, 114, 118, 119, 127, 130, 148
McCook, Dan 107
McCook, Edward 132
McCook, Robert 16, 17, 18
McCormick, Robert 183
McCown, John 60, 61, 63, 65, 84
McKean, Thomas 39, 40, 41, 43
McKinley, William 16
McLemore's Cove 103, 105, 106
McPherson, James 43, 48, 183
Meade, George 90, 161
Medill, Joseph 51, 172, 176, 183
Meigs, Montgomery 127, 128, 144
Memphis and Charleston Railroad 28, 38
Mendenhall, John 69
Mexican War 8, 9, 180, 181
Mexico 53, 137, 181, 189
Milner, John 7
Milton, Tennessee 82
Minty, Robert 82, 100, 106
Missionary Ridge 123, 143, 145, 179, 186
Missouri 21, 151–160, 175
Mobile, Alabama 44, 45, 85, 99, 137
Mobile and Ohio Railroad 39, 42
Moccasin Bend 130, 131, 139
Montgomery, James H. 129
Moore, David H. 196
Morgan, John H. 56, 58, 59, 60, 73, 88
Morris, Andrew 89
Morton, James St. Clair 53, 131
Mt. Olivet Cemetery 2, 191
Moyer, Franklin 66
Murfreesboro, Tennessee 1, 2, 56, 58, 59, 62, 68, 70, 71, 72, 73, 85, 86, 90, 91, 92, 122, 132, 135, 149, 169, 203, 206, 208
Murphy, Robert 29

Napoleon 144
Nashville, Tennessee 29, 56, 57, 59, 67, 69, 70, 74, 75, 76, 79, 91, 95, 125, 126, 128, 133, 138, 160, 168, 170, 172, 184, 195, 203
Nashville and Chattanooga Railroad 86, 91, 100, 132
National Union Party Convention 154, 175; see also Baltimore Convention
Negley, James 59, 60, 63, 65, 87, 105, 109, 111, 112
Nevins, Allan 13, 136
New Orleans, Louisiana 99, 137
New York Herald 104
New York Sun 164, 167
New York Times 16, 116, 148
New York Tribune 163, 166, 167
Newport, Rhode Island 8, 79
Newtonia, Missouri 159
Notre Dame University 192

Ohio River 11, 14, 38, 161
Oliver, John 39
Opdycke, Emerson 141

Ord, Edward 29, 30, 33, 34, 35, 36, 48, 49
Organization of American Knights (OAKs) 154, 155, 157, 158
Orphan Brigade 70, 112

Palmer, John 59, 60, 63, 67, 100, 109, 195
Palmer, Joseph 66, 109
Paris Commune 200
Paw Paws 153
Pegram, John 12, 13
Perryville, Kentucky 27, 46, 52
Petersburg, Virginia 104, 160, 161, 184
Philippi, West Virginia 11
Piatt, Donn 3, 180
Pillow, Gideon 47, 66, 69
Pilot Knob 2, 156, 157, 158
Pioneer Brigade 53, 63, 65, 74, 101, 131, 196
Pleasonton, Alfred 158, 159
Poinsett, Joel 6
Polk, James A. 180, 181
Polk, Leonidas 56, 59, 60, 63, 69, 70, 85, 86, 88, 98, 105, 111, 112, 114, 123
Polk, Lucius 112
Pollard, Edward 20
Pope, John 6, 23, 24, 27, 107, 182
Popular Government 190
Porter, Fitz-John 21, 77
Porter, Horace 147
Porterfield, George 10, 11
Preston, William 69
Price, Samuel 62, 63, 69
Price, Sterling 24, 27, 28, 29, 30, 31, 32, 33, 34, 35, 37, 38, 40, 41, 42, 43, 44, 51, 154, 155, 156, 157, 158, 159, 160, 162, 179, 196, 197

Quantrill, William 152

Raines, James 65
Rancho San Pedro 188
Rawlins, John A. 36, 48, 98, 99, 144, 160, 162, 167, 171, 175, 176, 183, 185, 199, 209
Reed's Bridge 106
Reid, Harvey 129, 135, 146
Reid, Whitelaw 23
Republican Party 21, 57, 81, 154, 165, 170, 174, 175, 178, 181, 182, 189, 200
Reynolds, J.J. 17, 20, 87, 109, 113, 114, 116, 134, 140
Rich Mountain 2, 11–15, 17, 22, 29, 99, 107, 194, 196, 203
Richardson, Albert 79
Richmond, Virginia 15, 17, 18, 20, 21, 58, 85, 91, 174, 178, 182
Richmond Examiner 150
Riley, Josiah 190
Ripley, Mississippi 28, 38, 43
Roberts, George 63, 65
Robinett, Battery 27, 38, 39, 42
Rogers, J.B. 36, 41, 42
Rogers, William 42

Index

Roosevelt, Theodore 187, 193
Rosecrans, Adrian 191,
Rosecrans, Anita (daughter) 188, 191, 192
Rosecrans, Ann E. (Mrs. William S.) 2, 7, 8, 21, 191, 192, 194
Rosecrans, Carl 191, 192, 193
Rosecrans, Crandall 5
Rosecrans, Jemima Hopkins 5
Rosecrans, Lily (Toole) 191, 192
Rosecrans, Mary L. 191
Rosecrans, Sylvester (Bishop) 5, 7, 117, 191
Rosecrans, William Starke: accomplishments of 196–197; business pursuits 9, 188; Chickamauga 100–120; Corinth campaign and battle of 40–45; death and burial 193–194; family 5, 7, 191–192; Grant and 6, 29, 34–37, 47–49, 137, 138, 160, 161, 162, 188–191; Halleck and 48, 55–58, 72, 76, 80, 83, 84, 104, 93–97, 130, 156, 169; innovations of 21, 24–25, 73–76, 144; Iuka 29–34; Lincoln and 72, 73, 86, 96, 97, 141, 152, 155, 168, 169, 185; presidential possibility 81, 179; Price's invasion of Missouri 156–159; religious beliefs 7, 71, 78–80, 117; resigns from army 188; Stanton and 21, 22, 72, 82, 89, 93, 141, 164, 165, 168, 169; Stones River 61–70; Thomas, George and 134–135, 184–185; Tullahoma Campaign 86–88; vice presidency offer 154, 218n4; West Virginia Campaign 12–20
Rosenkrantz, Harmon S. 5
Ross, C.F. 29, 35
Rossville, Georgia 106, 111, 118, 119, 120, 122, 123, 124
Rousseau, Lovell 60, 63, 65, 87, 92, 93, 98

St. Louis, Missouri 38, 152, 156, 157, 158, 180
San Diego, California 188
San Francisco, California 13, 188, 190, 192
Sanborn, John 32, 37, 158, 159
Sanderson, John P. 92, 93, 98, 153, 154, 155, 158, 168
Scammen, Eliakim 16
Schaefer, Frederick 63, 65
Schofield, John 99, 151, 152, 160, 182, 184
Scott, Winfield 14, 180, 181
Scribner, Benjamin 63
Seddon, James 98
Sequatchie Valley 91, 100, 101, 131, 132
Sewell Mountain 17, 18, 20
Sheehan, Cornelius (Con) 3
Sheehan, J.W. 174
Shelbyville, Tennessee 86, 88, 132, 197
Shepherd, Oliver 63, 65
Sheridan, Philip 60, 61, 63, 65, 82, 88, 101, 110, 111, 113, 116, 117, 118, 121, 130, 144, 147, 205, 206, 207
Sherman, Frank 147
Sherman, William T. 3, 6, 24, 25, 38, 44, 46, 50, 51, 52, 58, 72, 76, 99, 107, 126, 143, 144, 145, 147, 152, 156, 161, 168, 179, 183, 185, 186, 187, 209

Sherman's Historical Raid 187
Shiloh 23, 24, 37, 48, 52, 70, 77, 171, 172, 182, 183
Sill, Joshua 61, 63, 65
Simon, John Y. 33
Sister St. Charles *see* Rosecrans, Mary L.
Smith, A.J. 156, 158, 159
Smith, C.F. 170, 171, 172
Smith, M.L. 46
Smith, W.F. (Baldy) 134, 139, 140, 143, 179, 183,
Society of the Army of the Cumberland 1, 191, 194, 205
Southern Pacific Railroad 188
Spears, James C. 130
Special Order 61 (Missouri) 153
Spencer Rifles 87, 106, 123, 197
Spotsylvania Court House 199
Squire, George 147
Stanley, David 29, 31, 33, 36, 39, 40, 41, 42, 43, 47, 53, 67, 68, 80, 85, 89, 112, 188
Stanton, Edwin 2, 21, 22, 72, 82, 89, 93, 107, 121, 125, 126, 127, 133, 137, 138, 141, 145, 152, 154, 160, 164, 165, 168, 169, 182, 184, 185, 199
Starling, Lyne 114
Starr, Stephen Z. 36
Staunton and Parkersburg Turnpike 11, 12
Stebbins, Austin 117
Steele, Frederick 152
Stevenson, Alabama 92, 100, 101, 132, 138
Stevenson, Carter 59
Stewart, William 35
Stones River (Stone, Stone's) 50, 59, 60, 59, 60, 63, 66, 68, 69, 70, 71, 72, 73, 74, 79, 81, 83, 88, 89, 98, 116, 173, 179, 185, 191, 194, 196, 197, 205, 206, 207
Streight, Abel 82
Stringers Ridge 101
Summers, Festus 14
Sumner, Charles 199, 200
Sunbury, Ohio 4

Taylor, Zachary 167, 180, 181
Tennessee River 29, 52, 56, 57, 91, 92, 95, 96, 98, 100, 101, 122, 124, 126, 129, 131, 133, 134, 140, 202
Theory and Practical Workings of Our System of Government 190
Thomas, George H. 6, 52, 53, 59, 60, 63, 67, 68, 73, 75, 86, 87, 88, 90, 101, 103, 104, 105, 106, 107, 109, 110, 111, 112, 113, 114, 118, 119, 120, 121, 122, 123, 124, 127, 128, 134, 135, 137, 138, 139, 140, 143, 144, 145, 149, 160, 164, 166, 184, 185, 186, 187, 195, 197, 202, 203, 207, 208, 209
Tompkins, Christopher 18, 19
Tompkins, Ellen 18, 19
Toole, Joseph 191
Toole, Lily Rosecrans 191, 192
Toole, Rosecrans 191, 192

Truesdale, William 75
Tullahoma 2, 70, 82, 85, 86, 88, 89, 90, 100, 105, 144, 196, 197
Turchin, John 139, 142

Van Cleve, Horatio 61, 63, 69, 109, 111, 118, 127
Van Dorn, Earl 6, 23, 24, 27, 28, 29, 37, 38, 39, 40, 41, 42, 43, 44, 46, 47, 50, 51, 58, 82, 179
Van Horne, Thomas 105
Vaughan, Alfred 61
Vicksburg 2, 6, 44, 45, 46, 48, 50, 51, 58, 59, 70, 82, 83, 88, 89, 90, 91, 94, 96, 97, 98, 99, 137, 163, 172, 185, 195, 196

Wade, Benjamin 152
Wagner, George 66, 100, 101
Walden's Ridge 91, 100, 131, 132
Washburn, Cadwallader 171, 172
Washburne, Elihu B. 49, 51, 167, 169, 170–180, 186, 200
Washington Chronicle 148
Washington Evening Star 193
Wauhatchee, Tennessee 133, 139
Welles, Gideon 182, 185
Westport, Missouri 159
Wharton, John 61, 132

Wheeler, Joseph 56, 60, 73, 82, 86, 131, 132, 133, 141
Wheeling, West Virginia 11, 20, 21
Wheeling Convention 10, 14, 15
Whig Party 170, 180, 181
White, Horace 199
White Sulphur Springs, West Virginia 14, 15
White Sulphur Springs Manifesto 189
Widow Glen Cabin 109, 110, 113
Wilder, John T. 87, 88, 100
Willich, August 61, 86, 89
Wilson, James Harrison 139, 167, 175, 199
Wilson, John 34
Wise, Henry 14, 15, 17
Withers, James 60, 61
Wood, Thomas 59, 60, 61, 63, 100, 103, 110, 111, 112, 113, 114, 115, 116, 118, 127
Wright, Horatio 82
Wright, Joseph 72
Wyeth, John 88

Yaryan, John 67
Yates, Richard 92, 155
Young, John Russell 163
Young, L.D. 69

Zahn, Lewis 61

www.ingramcontent.com/pod-product-compliance
Ingram Content Group UK Ltd.
Pitfield, Milton Keynes, MK11 3LW, UK
UKHW041939140426
5217IPUK00014B/569